Doctoral Education in Context

Perspectives from Africa

Edited by
Jan Botha, Liezel Frick, Nompilo Tshuma

AFRICAN MINDS

Published in 2024 by African Minds
4 Eccleston Place, Somerset West, 7130
Cape Town, South Africa
info@africanminds.org.za
www.africanminds.org.za

ISBNs:
978-1-0672535-3-0 Print
978-1-0672535-4-7 e-book
978-1-0672535-5-4 e-pub

Copies of this book are available for free download at www.africanminds.org.za

ORDERS
For orders from Africa:
African Minds
Email: info@africanminds.org.za

For orders from outside Africa:
African Books Collective
PO Box 721, Oxford OX1 9EN, UK
Email: orders@africanbookscollective.com

This book is dedicated to Michael Hörig,
an innovative leader in international higher education

Contents

Section B PEDAGOGY

Section C SUPERVISOR–DOCTORAL CANDIDATE RELATIONSHIP

CONCLUDING REMARKS

Introduction

Jan Botha, Liezel Frick, Nompilo Tshuma

Doctoral education has evolved substantially over the past three decades within the broader context of global and local higher education and societal shifts (Taylor, 2023). These shifts have increasingly put research supervision in the spotlight, with the consequence that it is no longer considered a private space. This development was observed by Manathunga (2005:17) two decades ago when she described educational development for research supervisors as a 'recent phenomenon'. Since then, it has developed into a vibrant and well-established field of scholarship (e.g. see Ali et al., 2016; Bastalich, 2017; Haven et al., 2022; Kiley, 2011; Lee, 2018; McCallin & Nayar, 2012; McCulloch & Loeser, 2016). Evident from this growing body of literature are the advantages that educational development for research supervisors holds for improving professional student–supervisor relationships, pedagogical practices at the doctoral level, and ultimately, doctoral outcomes.

While similar trends – emphasising the importance of doctoral education and the growth in doctoral programmes and doctoral enrolments across the world – have been noticeable across the African continent too, these trends are often not well documented or well supported by supervisor development initiatives in Africa. In the context of the rapid growth in student enrolments at universities in Africa (Mohamedbhai, 2014), including a rapid increase of enrolments at doctoral level, the strategic plans and science policies adopted by various African countries and universities underscored and added to the importance of supervisor training. To mention three examples: since the beginning of the new millennium Ethiopia has established a number of new universities and instituted many new doctoral programmes; in 2012 South Africa's National Development Plan envisioned that the number of doctoral graduates should more than double during a relatively short period (from the base line of 1 876 in 2012 to 5 000 by 2030); in 2014 the Commission for University Education (CUE) in Kenya announced an intention to phase out the position of Assistant Lecturer and a five-year period was given to individuals in those positions to obtain doctoral degrees or risk losing their jobs at public universities. In many countries across Africa, there are similar developments (see ANIE, 2018). More recently, the African Research Universities Alliance (ARUA) in collaboration with the Mastercard Foundation launched sixteen collaborative PhD programmes that will commence in 2026. These four-year programmes are aimed at addressing the shortage of research capacity on the continent and will draw on supervisory and infrastructural capacity from across the continent and from the Guild of European Research-Intensive Universities. It is envisioned that there will be 1 000 PhDs graduating annually in 7 cohorts over a ten-year period (ARUA, 2014).

Such initiatives show that there is a realisation and broad consensus that Africa needs many more doctoral graduates to renew an ageing professoriate, to staff the rapidly expanding higher education field, to boost research, and to generate the high-level skills needed by growing economies to facilitate Africa's participation in the global knowledge economy (as also highlighted by Beaudry et al., 2018). African countries are confronted with the conundrum: to produce many more doctoral graduates, many more PhD supervisors are needed; but to have more supervisors, more PhDs are needed (MacGregor, 2013). Studies on the impact of massification in higher education, including a rapid growth in doctoral enrolments, have highlighted concerns about the quality and effectiveness of the provision (Altbach et al., 2010; ANIE, 2018). That these concerns are not unfounded has been evidenced by ongoing studies and investigations in various countries. To refer to two examples: a report of the CUE (2019) in Kenya questioned the exceptionally high number of doctoral degrees that were awarded by a university, and a report of the Council on Higher Education (CHE) (2022) in South Africa, following a national review of doctoral qualifications, highlighted many pertinent challenges related to the quality of doctoral candidates at entry level as well as the quality of the graduates at exit level.

Interventions (and the documentation thereof) have often focused on the doctoral programmes and the development of the students enrolled in these programmes, without giving much systematic thought to developing supervisory capabilities. This may be considered as putting the proverbial cart before the horse. There are, of course exceptions, for example, the health- focused programme of the Consortium for Advanced Research Training in Africa (CARTA) (see Fonn et al., 2016; Igumbor et al., 2022). In addition, evidence of supervisor development programmes across disciplines often has a national focus (e.g. see Bitzer et al., 2013; Keane, 2016). So, the playing field for providing such support across the continent and across disciplines remains uneven. Many doctoral supervisors based at universities across the African continent work in relative isolation, given the lack of qualified research and research supervision capacity and the lack of access to supervision development support (see Van't Land, 2011; Cloete et al., 2015, for examples from across Africa documenting these and other challenges related to researcher education). While evidence from a continent-wide study suggests that informal collegial support is positively related with supervisory competencies (Pyhältö et al., 2024), until recently there has been a lack of a coordinated effort to meet the need for inter-continental research into supervisor capacity development and building communities of practice across disciplines, institutions, and national boundaries.

In recent years, the German Academic Exchange Agency (DAAD) embarked on an initiative addressing this need for supervisor capacity development at African universities. The DAAD has a long history of supporting the science enterprise in Africa, *inter alia*, through scholarships, funding schemes for research projects, policy development initiatives, leadership development opportunities, and networking activities. In September 2016, the Dialogue on Innovative Higher Education Strategies (DIES) programme, a joint venture of the German Rectors' Conference and the DAAD, organised a seminar on the quality of doctoral education in Africa in collaboration with the Inter-University Council for East Africa and Kenya's Commission for University Education (Kuria & Ndivo, 2017). Experts and interested parties from across the continent participated in this seminar which was held in Nairobi, Kenya, including representatives from universities in Ghana, Kenya, Rwanda, South Africa, and Germany, and African collaborative ventures such as the CARTA, the African Network for Internationalization of Education (ANIE), and the International Centre for Insect Physiology and Ecology (ICIPE), a unit of the World Bank-affiliated Partnership for Skills in Applied Sciences, Engineering and Technology (PASET) in Africa. During that seminar, the need for opportunities for the training of the supervisors of doctoral candidates at universities in Africa was identified as one of the most urgent and important concerns. The DAAD subsequently issued a call for submissions to providers interested in developing and offering a course with financial support from the DAAD, and eventually the submission of the Centre for Research on Evaluation, Science and Technology (CREST) at Stellenbosch University in South Africa was accepted.

Since 2018, CREST has been offering the DIES/CREST Training Course for Supervisors of Doctoral Candidates at African Universities, in collaboration with the Centre for Higher Education Research, Teaching and Learning (CHERTL) at Rhodes University in South Africa, and the Centre for Higher and Adult Education (CHAE) at Stellenbosch University (Botha et al., 2019). The flexible, part-time, fully online nature of the course is unique for several reasons. First, it has enabled the collaboration of leading researchers in the field of doctoral education and supervision as facilitators on the course. This has allowed the participants to tap into both the latest research on these topics in the field, as well as engaging with leading scholars with a deep understanding and experience in doctoral education in different African contexts. Second, the course was envisioned for universities across the African continent, rather than the in-house offerings of most doctoral supervisor development courses of this nature. As such, the content and practices shared on the course are responsive to this diverse context. Third, the course was designed as a fully online course, with specific consideration of the technological and access challenges unique to various contexts across the African continent. Therefore, the logic of the design and timing of each module's resources, activities and live sessions with facilitators were cognisant of these challenges. Lastly, the facilitators were supported by a learning and graphics design team to develop a professional site, as well as initial support to address any challenges experienced by both facilitators and participants. This allowed the facilitators to focus on sharing their expertise and engaging effectively with participants, while the design team took care of the technical aspects. Unlike most supervisor development courses that were traditionally offered face-to-face and had to be adapted for the online environment during the pandemic (Vaughan et al., 2021), this course had already been running fully online for two years prior. By the end of 2023, more than 800 doctoral supervisors, affiliated with universities across 34 African countries, had participated in the course, and more than 500 had successfully completed the course.

The course was designed to provide participants with opportunities to achieve the following learning outcomes: (1) to be familiar with "doctoral supervisor" as a professional identity and "doctoral supervision" as a field of scholarship (including having a clear understanding of their role(s) and responsibilities as supervisor, mentor and counsellor; and to be knowledgeable about models and practices of doctoral supervision); (2) to be knowledgeable about institutional rules, regulations and resources; (3) to be able to contextualize the provision of doctoral education and the changing nature of research in a global and African context; (4) to be able to manage different types of relations in the context of being a supervisor (conflict resolution, intercultural understanding, etc.), (5) to be knowledgeable about the responsible conduct of research and ethics, (6) to have the capability to guide doctoral research processes from proposal development to completion and (7) to have strategies for effective supervision (e.g. communication, monitoring).

The achievement of these learning outcomes is enhanced by an approach that captures all the inputs, interactions and activities of the course participants through an online Learning Management System (LMS), including the capstone assignments submitted to meet the requirements of the course (De Klerk, 2024). Consequently, a unique and valuable source of information on doctoral supervision at universities in Africa has become available. The chapters published in this book were originally submitted as capstone assignments. The contributions were selected by the editors, considering the quality of the assignments but also with a view to ensure a diversity of countries and regions, languages, gender, fields of study, topics and approaches. Under the guidance of the editors, the contributors refined and developed their essays further and prepared the chapters for publication in this book. Given that there is a paucity of such specific literature that captures both the idiosyncrasies and diversity of doctoral education across the continent (as is evident in the work of Taylor et al., 2021; and Taylor, 2023), this book makes a noteworthy contribution to a continentally specific *and* continentally diverse understanding of the doctoral qualification in Africa, pedagogical approaches that capture a more indigenous understanding thereof, and a relational understanding of knowledge creation.

Since the study of the International Association of Universities (Van't Land, 2011) on doctoral education in selected universities in a number of African countries in West and East Africa, other similar studies were published, mostly on doctoral studies in general but sometimes also with specific attention to doctoral supervision. There has been an increase in the number of journal articles on doctoral education in Africa (Frick & Mouton, 2021; Hopwood & Frick, 2023). However, many of these studies focus only on South Africa (e.g. Cloete et al., 2015; Taylor et al., 2021), or on a small number of African countries (e.g. ANIE, 2018). Publications based on empirical research conducted in a broader range of African countries remain limited. Hence the need remains for more scholarly contributions on doctoral education from the Global South in ways that feed into global debates in both meaningful and challenging ways (Taylor et al., 2021; Hopwood & Frick, 2023). Such debates not only highlight the dominance of the Global North in debates on doctoral education, but emphasise the need for a more contextually rich and diverse understanding of what doctoral education can be – a view mirrored by the Hannover Recommendations (2019:2) that called for "an ecology of knowledges which recognizes and seeks to overcome existing inequalities in the access to doctoral education and the provision of knowledge" and which embraces a diversity of cultures, people and universities across the globe.

This book contributes to the (continental) contextual nature of doctoral education. As editors we do not believe that all chapters need to explicitly reflect African realities and experiences to justify the title of the book. This book contributes to filling this gap with chapters written by practising doctoral supervisors from 16 African countries, namely, Angola, Benin, Burkina Faso, Cameroon, Egypt, Guinea, Kenya, Mauritius, Namibia, Nigeria, Rwanda, South Africa, Sudan, Tunisia, Uganda, Zambia. Doctoral education is, after all, a global phenomenon. Being written by individuals based at African universities the book reflects (albeit in a loose sense) how an author (based at an African university) views a particular aspect of doctoral education. The topical essays included here relate to doctoral education globally, while the situatedness and positionality of the contributing authors as working at universities in Africa reflect links to African realities and experiences. The diversity of contributions demands that we also re-imagine doctoral pedagogies in ways that may disrupt our existing assumptions about doctoral forms and processes (as suggested by Akala, 2021; Gravett, 2021; and Okolie et al., 2020). Globally, there is an acknowledgement that regardless of the pedagogical approach, the relationship that supervisors and doctoral candidates build during the doctorate plays a key role in doctoral success (Corcelles-Seuba et al., 2023; Janssen et al., 2021; Kaur et al., 2022), but Buirski (2022) argues that an ontological understanding of these relationships is still lacking. The chapters selected for this book were therefore grouped into three themes: doctoral research and the doctoral qualification in Africa, doctoral pedagogy, and the supervisor–candidate relationship to address these issues and contribute a contextually rich and diverse understanding of current doctoral education practices from diverse African perspectives.

Section A: The doctoral qualification in Africa

This section on doctoral research and the doctoral qualification in Africa provides insights into how doctoral research and the doctoral qualification are viewed in diverse African contexts. It serves as an entry point into this book and provides a platform from which to explore the diversity associated with the doctorate across disciplines and countries. International discourses on the doctorate as an internationally recognised and comparable qualification often belie the contextual nuances and challenges associated with our understanding of what 'doctorateness' means (Rabe et al., 2021; Trafford & Leshem, 2009) and how its development is facilitated through supervision. The contributors to this section highlight the need for contextual understanding and sensitivity towards doctoral education.

Oosthuizen (Chapter 1) presents the results of an analysis of bibliometric data on research published on doctoral supervision. Oosthuizen extracted, identified, and discussed the main research topics in literature on doctoral supervision published between 1975 and 2018, with a more in-depth analysis of the period 1992-2018. He used Natural Language Processing (NLP) to perform a topic extraction, using an automated machine learning-based topic modelling approach to process the titles and abstracts of 949 publications. Based on probability, he identified the following five topics: research process and methods, student–supervisor relationship, research education, professional training programmes, and theses and research management.

Khalil (Chapter 2) gives an overview of the state of academic freedom in Africa, noting that many African countries score lower than most of the high-income countries in the Academic Freedom Index (AFI). Building on his conviction that academic freedom in postgraduate studies is an important condition for reliable research outcomes, he provides a critical analysis of four sets of constraints on academic freedom at African universities: institutional and bureaucratic constraints; funding and autonomy constraints; ethical, social, cultural, and religious constraints; and political constraints. He argues that doctoral supervisors have a role to play regarding academic freedom. Although supervisors do not 'own' academic freedom 'to give' it, they have a measure of authority over the work of doctoral students which means that they can facilitate, or restrict, a doctoral candidate's academic freedom.

Mutarindwa (Chapter 3) discusses the factors that have an impact on doctoral completion rates and time-to-degree. Taking his cue from the findings of studies in other parts of the world which showed that, compared to domestic programmes, students enrolled in foreign countries are more likely to complete their doctoral studies successfully and that they do so in a shorter duration, he surmises that the situation may be the same for African doctoral students studying abroad. Having reviewed the limited number of studies currently available on completion rates and on the trends in the duration of doctoral studies at African universities, he calls for more empirical research on these topics, and, given the challenge of 'brain drain', he also calls for tracer studies of the careers of African students who have graduated abroad.

Using the ten Salzburg Principles as a lens, Nwosu (Chapter 4) conducted a critical analysis of the state of doctoral education at the University of Nigeria, Nsukka. He considers issues related to education policy, expertise, funding, renumeration of university staff, and institutional network building within and beyond Nigeria. He found that the conditions that could be conducive to the application of the Salzburg Principles towards the improvement of doctoral education in Nigeria still seem to be largely absent. Nwosu identifies in Nigeria a hostility in government circles towards the support of high-quality research, as is evident in the poor funding allocated to universities and complacent attitudes towards the fulfilment of agreements with university staff on how to improve teaching and research conditions in the country's universities.

Bancole-Minaflinou (Chapter 5) did a case study of the doctoral qualification at the University of Abomey-Calavi, the leading university of Benin. She investigated the perceptions of doctoral students and supervisors on the quality of the current doctoral programmes and, due to the reported perception of a mismatch between their graduate attributes and the needs of the job market, she then considers proposals to make doctoral education more responsive to labour and educational market demands. She is cautious to note that not all research findings can be commercialised and not all PhDs can be translated into 'jobs'. She points out that the educational authorities in Benin are attuned to these and other challenges. The Agence Béninoise de l'Assurance Qualité de l'Enseignement Supérieur (ABAQES) and the Agence Béninoise de Valorisation de la Recherche et de l'Innovation Technologique (ABeVRIT) were recently rejuvenated and given the mandate to uphold and enhance standards and best practices in research in higher education in Benin.

Based on an analysis of the doctoral programmes offered by the four public universities in Mauritius as well as detailed statistical information on doctoral enrolment and graduation at the University of Mauritius, Manraj (Chapter 6) found that the low number of doctoral graduates is not due to high dropout rates but rather to the low enrolment rates. She maintains that this can be explained by the lack of research funds, lack of equipment, scarcity of potential supervisors, delays in the registration processes, but also the perception that the current MPhil/PhD is a lengthy and difficult journey. She argues that moving to a 1+3 structured format would make it more attractive to enroll in doctoral studies. Through course work students would be able to acquire the generic skills and tools to develop and defend a research proposal in the first year, and then to complete the programmes during a period of three years of full-time studies.

In his contribution, Faria (Chapter 7) provides a critical appraisal of the processes of the doctoral programmes offered at the University Agostinho Neto in Angola against the background of the broader political and higher education context in Angola. Three faculties started offering doctoral training from 2011, 2012 and 2015 and over this time these faculties have enrolled 259 PhD candidates, of whom only ten had graduated by 2021. Gathering reliable and up to date information (on doctoral enrolments, the number of candidates allocated per supervisor, and graduations) proved to be a major challenge and, according to Faria, it illustrates that, in a broader sense, research process and structures at UAN are inefficient. He ascribes it largely to the fact that the University

Agostinho Neto "cannot be completely dissociated from Angola's past and recent political trajectory". This context is described in the chapter.

N'Tsoukpoe (Chapter 8) writes about predatory publishing in francophone sub-Saharan Africa, particularly how it affects doctoral candidates. The African and Malagasy Council for Higher Education (CAMES) is mandated by its 19 member states to assure the quality of the evaluation and the promotion processes for academic staff. In terms of the CAMES system, decisions on promotions are currently largely based on the number of publications, making publication in predatory journals attractive for scholars, including the PhD candidates who are aiming at academic careers. He argues that doctoral supervisors can play an important role in addressing the problem of predatory publishing in francophone sub-Saharan Africa, not only through a guidance and monitoring role, but also to set an example through their own publication behaviour and more broadly, their behaviour as scientists in general. In addition to this role for supervisors, he also recommends several formal measures that can be taken to prevent publication in questionable journals.

Section B: Doctoral pedagogy

The second section of this book, on doctoral pedagogy, delves deeper into how doctoral education is enacted in different contexts across the continent in a variety of disciplinary and institutional settings. Doctoral pedagogy – referring to the relationship between the doctoral student, the supervisor(s), and the knowledge created within this relationship (Frick, 2022) – forms the basis for exploring how supervisors across the African continent engage and continuously redefine the complexities and contradictions inherent to knowledge creation at the doctoral level.

Drawing on her expertise in modelling, researching, and analysing complex business and organisational systems and processes, Meyer (Chapter 9) asserts that, by incorporating rigorous project management approaches in the PhD journey, the doctoral candidate will not only complete the PhD within reasonable time but will also develop valuable skills for the delivery of high-quality research that adds value in academic and/or industry contexts. She provides an overview of current perspectives on project management as an enabler of PhD completion and reflects on the potential value of facilitating the doctoral journey through project management, if it is positioned relative to and customised for the broader supervisory context. She presents four possible models of supervision that integrate elements of project management.

Williams (Chapter 10) explores doctoral supervision as it relates to the doctoral research of physician scientists (i.e. medical doctors who receive training in research and spend a substantial proportion of their time on research while also doing clinical work). In many African countries only a few clinically trained medical doctors are pursuing research careers. This situation threatens scientific advances in healthcare. The task of supervising a physician scientist on their doctoral research journey has unique issues. Clinical research is expensive. Physicians are often discouraged from research-oriented careers because research is remunerated poorly in comparison with clinical work. Clinical practice is demanding work and time intensive, and research competes with clinical demands. Because so few physicians are also active researchers, the physician scientist's journey is often a lonely one. Supervisors must understand this context very well and develop their supervisory, mentoring and research skills accordingly, to enable them to provide training for the next generation of physician scientists.

Nchito (Chapter 11) reviews the benefits and pitfalls of the current supervision practices in the School of Natural Sciences at the University of Zambia, including issues related to admission and funding, the current practices of allocating supervisors to doctoral students, the development of discipline-specific and structured PhD programmes, the need for supervisor training, and the provision of training and support for writing, lack of clarity and agreement on the purpose of doctoral programmes and graduate attributes. Against this description and assessment, Nchito concludes that many aspects of the PhD process need serious rethinking if the school wants to attract, retain and graduate doctorates who will be able to contribute positively to society and the economy.

Elsayed (Chapter 12) reports the results of a survey of the views of the doctoral students in the PhD programme in science offered by Alzaiem Alazhari University in Sudan. Amongst the findings: there is a need to clarify and explain roles and responsibilities because the students evidently did not understand what their or their supervisors' roles and responsibilities were. Notwithstanding the uncertainty about roles, 78% of the respondents were positive about their supervision even though 27.4% indicated that they did not choose their supervisors themselves. Despite the favourable rating, 15.6% of respondents had thought of changing their supervisors at some stage, and 31.2% would not or may not recommend their supervisor(s) to other students. This discrepancy could be explained by the fact that students culturally tend not to criticize those in authority. Dissatisfaction mostly revolves around organisational aspects (e.g. availability of supervisors and timely feedback) and personal relations between supervisor and candidate (e.g. understanding the challenges experienced by students and motivating students).

Orchard's study (Chapter 13) of supervisory practices in the School of Therapeutic Sciences at the of the University of the Witwatersrand in South Africa was prompted by her own initial uncertainty about her ability to supervise postgraduate candidates and her observation that many fellow researchers/supervisors appeared so capable and so confident. She wondered: 'When and how did they become so confident? What influences supervision knowledge and practice at the School of Therapeutic Sciences?' She did a survey to explore supervision styles, readiness and confidence and compare them to experience in supervision. She learned that confidence is something that comes with years of experience and from supervising more candidates. She writes an engaging narrative on how comforting it was to learn that no one supervisor knows everything, that we do sometimes go beyond our own realm of expertise. Supervising with co-supervisors or as a team appears to have many benefits and participation in courses on supervision can positively influence confidence levels. She argues that there is no gold standard for a supervision model, but that most supervisory styles are developed based on social learning and supervisors adopt their own preferences.

Wandera (Chapter 14) writes about his experience in a programme of the Consortium for Advanced Research Training in Africa (CARTA), using a cohort approach working towards a thesis in the thesis-by-publication format. Ten universities in Africa and ten universities elsewhere in the world (Europe and North America), including Makerere University in Uganda, are members of CARTA. Fellows in the programme participate in four advanced seminars that are offered during the four years of the programme. Doctoral committees guide and advise students from the beginning to the end of the process. The CARTA cohort supervision network of facilitators and supervisors guides and trains participants on how to identify reputable journals in which to publish. The thesis-by-publication format requires several rounds of peer review of the manuscripts submitted to journal articles during which the network members support the doctoral candidates. Wandera found that there are various practices in CARTA that could be followed to positive effect in all the doctoral programmes of Makerere University.

Balde (Chapter 15) reports the results of an evaluation of the doctoral programme of the Research and Valorization Center on Medicinal Plants in Guinea, offered in collaboration with Gamal Abdel Nasser University of Conakry in Guinea. The evaluation was done in terms of Cross and Backhouse's model for the evaluation of doctoral programmes in Africa. Recommendations made to enhance the quality of the programme include the standardisation of the ways in which the required credits can be obtained; making achieving an intermediate-level certificate in English compulsory; appointment of doctoral research committees for every candidate; compulsory workshops on various aspects of research methodology, grant writing, and scholarly publication; presentation of credit-bearing papers or progress reports during the course of the study; publication of a minimum of two peer reviewed publications as a requirement for graduation; and strengthening institutional partnerships.

Oketch (Chapter 16) investigated supervisors' perspectives on the development of their supervision skills, based on data gathered from supervisors in five disciplines affiliated to six different universities in Kenya. All the respondents indicated that they had learnt how to supervise primarily from their own experiences as postgraduate students when they were engaged in their own master's and doctoral studies. Only one respondent stated that he attained supervision skills from a doctoral supervision course offered to supervisors across Africa, while two others highlighted self-learning through practice, reading manuals on requirements for supervision as well as consultations. It transpired that the respondents were conscious that doctoral study in itself does not train one to become a supervisor and there is a need for specialized training in doctoral supervision.

Noting the extensive research across the world into technology-mediated supervision, Guidi (Chapter 17) investigated the modalities that low-tech, low-cost, readily available forms of technology might contribute to doctoral supervision in challenging contexts, focusing on the experience of supervisors and students relating to the use of WhatsApp for in the context of doctoral supervision in Benin. Data ware gathered through a survey of 22 participants in science-related disciplines (17 supervisors and five doctoral candidates). The mobile phone was the most accessible and frequently used technology and mobile data represented the most frequent way of connecting to the internet. Connecting via wi-fi at home was the least common method. Internet connection was deemed reliable by fifty-two per cent (52%) and unreliable by (31%). Nevertheless, WhatsApp proved to be effective and appreciated, with respondents noting effective information sharing but particularly the opportunities for collaboration and psychological support. Challenges mentioned included issues related to connectivity, reliable technology, technological skills, and data protection.

Section C: The supervisor–student relationship

The third section, on the supervisor–student relationship, provides readers of this book with an intimate view on the *who* dimension of doctoral education on the continent. Literature on the importance of doctoral student–supervisor relationships abound (see for example Al Makhamreh & Kutsyuruba, 2021; Liang et al., 2021; Mkhabela & Frick, 2016), while Cornér et al. (2017) highlight the importance of this relationship to both doctoral student wellbeing and completion. This section offers more than a mere stakeholder analysis of doctoral education as it takes us on a contextually complex journey on how supervisors (and their students) negotiate the tensions and fragilities of student–supervisor relationships.

Kimathi (Chapter 18) observes that doctoral supervisors in Kenya often have to supervise while they still have little or no previous experience, without mentors or formal training programmes. This is the case despite international trends showing increases in formal training, monitoring and accountability of doctoral supervisors in other parts of the world. She reports the results of her study, how novice supervisors learn to supervise and the challenges they face at the beginning of their careers as supervisors. Using the competing values framework proposed by Robert Quin and adapted by Tricia Vilinas as theoretical framework, and drawing on interviews with eight novice supervisors at six universities in Kenya, Kimathi reflects on the consequences of the predominantly 'trial and error' approach to supervision and prevailing conditions in Kenyan higher education on the quality of doctoral supervision and doctoral outputs. She maintains that much more weight must be given in Kenyan universities to the transition from being a doctoral candidate to becoming a doctoral supervisor.

Chemak (Chapter 19) argues that the quality of feedback to doctoral candidates is a particularly important issue within the context of African universities where the funds set aside for research and the development of supervisory skills are limited. He provides a reflective account of a suitable gateway to sustain clear and effective supervisory processes towards developing good and trusting relationships between the supervisor and the doctoral candidate, focusing on the potential value of the Feedback Expectation Tool (FET) proposed by Elke Stracke and Vijay Kumar. He found that FET was rated very positively by his colleagues as well as by early-career researchers at the National Institute for Agricultural Research of Tunisia. It is seen as a novel and interesting approach to investigate the supervisor–student relationship. Focusing on feedback constitutes a relevant approach to bringing students, supervisors and the institution together around suitable strategies to improve the supervisory process.

Informed by the views of selected graduate students in the Environmental Economics programme at the University of Pretoria, Karuaihe (Chapter 20) writes about the critical importance of feedback in doctoral supervision and thesis writing. The views of many of the respondents converged on issues related to the content of feedback, the type of feedback, the frequency and the providers of feedback. However, opinions were more divergent on issues related to the role of feedback in building and managing the relationships between supervisors and students and how feedback on emotional and cultural issues should be attended to. A particular thorny issue is how conflicting feedback is to be handled by students, and the role of the main supervisor in this regard.

Etomes (Chapter 21) maintains that more information on supervisor–student relationships is important against the background of the high dropout rate of doctoral candidates, the long duration of study of those who do graduate, and the (sometimes) low quality of doctoral theses in Cameroon. She collected data from 56 participants (32 PhD students and 24 PhD supervisors) across different disciplines at the University of Buea. She focused on the respondents' views of issues related to the allocation of supervisors, expectations and practices related to the contact time between supervisors and students, and the impact of feedback on the quality of the thesis. While there is a policy at the University of Buea regulating the allocation of supervisors and this policy is in general abided by, mismatches sometimes occur, which have an impact on various aspects of the doctoral programmes of the university. There is wide agreement that type of feedback, honouring scheduled times for feedback and the frequency of feedback improve the quality of the thesis.

Kwanya (Chapter 22) writes about the phenomenon of 'liminality' as an umbrella term for the many hurdles faced by doctoral candidates, referred in scholarly literature as the wavering between two worlds experienced after separation from a previous life but before getting incorporated into a new one. Doctoral candidates in liminal periods oscillate between learner and academic identities in their journeys to scholarly expertise. Kwanya observed that all fourteen doctoral students in information and knowledge management in Kenya who participated in the focus group discussions for this study indicated that they were stuck in a period of extended doctoral liminality. He identified three main categories of causes for periods of liminality among doctoral students in Kenya: (1) inadequacies in supervision and mentoring; (2) disengaged students, mostly due to the fact that they are doing their PhD studies on a part-time basis while they have to meet the responsibilities of their employment in the world of work; and (3) the availability and adequacy of institutional support and resources as well as clarity about expectations. Various interventions are recommended at individual, relational, and institutional/departmental levels to support doctoral candidates to get through liminal periods.

Kellermann (Chapter 23) draws on global research on the challenges and opportunities in aligning doctoral studies with employment opportunities in academia and industry as background for her investigation of the career guidance and development opportunities for biomedical PhD students at Stellenbosch University. Information was gathered from Stellenbosch University Career Services and the Doctoral Office of the Faculty of Medicine and Health Sciences. Both these units indicated that they do not provide career counselling to doctoral students and were not aware of any group that offers this on a formal basis within the faculty and university. These findings are concurrent with literature findings on a lack of formal career guidance for doctoral graduates, particularly for non-academic career trajectories. Among several strategies to improve employment outcomes for PhD graduates, Kellermann acknowledges the role of doctoral supervisors as often being the primary source of career guidance for doctoral students (although mostly on an informal basis and often with a bias to academic career paths) so she suggests that a more systemic approach be developed, involving a range of role players.

In conclusion

The variation across the different contributions, as is common in a compilation of this nature, reflects the diversity and uniqueness of doctoral education across the continent. We do not want to lose this multiplicity of voices. We did include an overarching question guiding the compilation. We asked: 'What can a multi-voiced anthology tell us about the state of doctoral education across the African continent?' Together this collection of chapters provides readers with a glimpse into how doctoral education is conceptualised and enacted within a variety of contexts on the African continent. While there may be similarities evident across these contributions, they also show the diversity in systems, policies and practices. Indeed, Africa is a continent with many countries, it is not only one country.

References

African Network for Internationalization of Education (ANIE). (2018). *Building PhD capacity in Sub-Saharan Africa*. British Council.

African Research Universities Alliance (ARUA). (2024, July 25). *ARUA ushers in new collaborative PhD programmes*. https://arua.org/arua-ushers-in-new-collaborative-phd-programmes/

Akala, B. U. (2021). Challenges in doctoral supervision in South African universities. *Open Science Journal, 6*(2), 1–24.

Al Makhamreh, M., & Kutsyuruba, B. (2021). The role of trust in doctoral student–supervisor relationships in Canadian universities: The students' lived experiences and perspectives. *Journal of Higher Education Theory and Practice, 21*(2), 124–128.

Ali, P., Watson, P., & Dhingra, K. (2016). Postgraduate research students' and their supervisors' attitudes towards supervision. *International Journal of Doctoral Studies, 11*, 227–241.

Altbach, P., Reisberg, L., & Rumbley, L. E. (2010). Tracking a global academic revolution. *Change, 42*(2), 30–39.

Bastalich, W. (2017). Content and context in knowledge production: A critical review of doctoral supervision literature. *Studies in Higher Education, 42*(7), 1145–1157.

Beaudry, C., Mouton, J., & Prozesky, H. E. (2018). *The next generation of scientists in Africa*. CREST, Stellenbosch University.

Bitzer, E. M., Trafford, V. N., & Leshem, S. (2013). 'Love it when you speak foreign': A transnational perspective on the professional development of doctoral supervisors in South Africa. *South African Journal of Higher Education, 27*(4), 781–796.

Botha, J., De Klerk M., & Vilyte, G. (2019, November 14). Digital training can help supervisors lift PhD output. *The Conversation*. https://theconversation.com/digital-training-can-help-supervisors-lift-phd-output-126391

Buirski, N. (2022). 'Ways of being': A model for supportive doctoral supervisory relationships and supervision. *Higher Education Research & Development, 41*(5), 1387–1401.

Cloete, N., Mouton, J., & Sheppard, C. (2015). *Doctoral education in South Africa – Policy, discourse and data*. African Minds.

Commission for University Education (CUE). (2019). *Inquiry on Kenyatta University of Agriculture and Technology PhDs*.

Corcelles-Seuba, M., Suñe-Soler, N., Sala-Bubaré, A., & Castelló, M. (2023). Doctoral student perceptions of supervisory and research community support: Their relationships with doctoral conditions and experiences. *Journal of Further and Higher Education, 47*(4), 481–491.

Cornér, S., Löfström, E., & Pyhältö, K. (2017). The relationship between doctoral students' perceptions of supervision and burnout. *International Journal of Doctoral Studies, 12*, 91–106.

Council on Higher Education (CHE). (2022). *Doctoral degrees national report*. CHE.

De Klerk, M. (2024). *The design and facilitation of an online short course at a residential university: A complex systems perspective* [Unpublished doctoral dissertation]. Stellenbosch University.

Fonn, S., Egesah, O., Cole, D., Griffiths, F., Manderson, L., Kabiru, C., Ezeh, A., Thorogood, M., & Izugbara, C. (2016). Building the capacity to solve complex health challenges in sub-Saharan Africa: CARTA's multidisciplinary PhD training. *Canadian Journal of Public Health, 107*, e381–e386.

Frick, L. (2022). In pursuit of doctoral pedagogy in the South: The role of global citizenship education in moving beyond narratives of doctoral production for the knowledge economy. In *Global Citizenship Education in the Global South* (pp. 63–85). Brill.

Frick, B. L., & Mouton, J. (2021). Doctoral education as a field of global scholarship: An analysis of Anglophone published research (2005-2018). In P. Riley, E. Bitzer, & L. Frick (Eds.), *The global scholar: Implications for postgraduate studies and supervision* (pp.43-62). SUNMEDIA.

Gebresenbet, F. (2020). 'Birth defect' in Ethiopia's expansion of doctoral studies: A student-centered analysis of a PhD program at Addis Ababa University [Unpublished capstone assignment].

Hannover Recommendations (2019). Forces and Forms of Doctoral Education. [Accessed 14 November 2024. https://www.doctoral-education.info/documents.php].

Gravett, K. (2021). Disrupting the doctoral journey: Re-imagining doctoral pedagogies and temporal practices in higher education. *Teaching in Higher Education, 26*(3), 293–305.

Haven, T., Bouter, L., Mennen, L., & Tijdink, J. (2022). Superb supervision: A pilot study on training supervisors to convey responsible research practices onto their PhD candidates. *Accountability in Research*, 1–18.

Hopwood, N., & Frick, B. L. (2023). Research supervision as praxis: A need to speak back in dangerous ways? *Journal of Praxis in Higher Education, 5*(2), 140–166. https://doi.org/10.47989/kpdc411

Igumbor, J. O., Bosire, E. N., Karimi, F., Katahoire, A., Allison, J., Muula, A. S., Peixoto, A., Otwombe, K., Gitau, E., Bonjers, G., Fonn, S., & Ajuwon, A. (2022). Effective supervision of doctoral students in public and population health in Africa: CARTA supervisors' experiences, challenges and perceived opportunities. *Global Public Health: An International Journal for Research, Policy and Practice, 17*(4), 496–511.

Janssen, S., van Vuuren, M., & de Jong, M. D. (2021). Sensemaking in supervisor-doctoral student relationships: Revealing schemas on the fulfillment of basic psychological needs. *Studies in Higher Education, 46*(12), 2738–2750.

Kaur, A., Kumar, V., & Noman, M. (2022). Partnering with doctoral students in research supervision: Opportunities and challenges. *Higher Education Research & Development, 41*(3), 789–803.

Keane, M. (2016). Coaching interventions for postgraduate supervision courses: Promoting equity and understanding in the supervisor–student relationship. *South African Journal of Higher Education, 30*(6), 94–111.

Kiley, M. (2011). Developments in research supervisor training: Causes and responses. *Studies in Higher Education, 36*(5), 585–599.

Kuria, M., & Ndivo, L. (2017). *Rapporteurs' report on the DIES seminar: Quality of doctoral education – A prerequisite for strong universities in Africa*. DAAD.

Lee, A. (2018). How can we develop supervisors for the modern doctorate? *Studies in Higher Education, 43*(5), 878–890.

Liang, W., Liu, S., & Zhao, C. (2021). Impact of student-supervisor relationship on postgraduate students' subjective well-being: A study based on longitudinal data in China. *Higher Education*, 1–33.

Manathunga, C. (2005). The development of research supervision: "Turning the light on a private space". *International Journal for Academic Development, 10*(1), 17–30.

McCallin, A., & Nayar, S. (2012). Postgraduate research supervision: A critical review of current practice. *Teaching in Higher Education, 17*(1), 63–74.

McCulloch, A., & Loeser, C. (2016). Does research degree supervisor training work? The impact of a professional development induction workshop on supervision practice. *Higher Education Research & Development, 35*(5), 968–982.

MacGregor, K. (2013, November 2). Where to from here for the African PhD? *University World News*. https://www.universityworldnews.com/post.php?story=20131102155412705

Mkhabela, Z., & Frick, B. L. (2016). Student-supervisor relationships in a complex society: A dual narrative of scholarly becoming. In L. Frick, P. Motshoane, C. McMaster & C. Murphy (Eds.), *Postgraduate study in South Africa: Surviving and succeeding* (pp. 13–24). SUN MeDIA.

Mohamedbhai, G. (2014). Massification in higher education institutions in Africa: Causes, consequences, and responses. *International Journal of African Higher Education, 1*(1), 60–83.

National Planning Commission. (2012). *National development plan 2030: Our future - Make it work*. The Presidency, South Africa. https://www.nationalplanningcommission.org.za/assets/Documents/NDP_Chapters/NDP 2030-Prelims.pdf

Nerad, M., Bogle, D., Kohl, U., O'Carroll, C., Peters, C., & Scholz, B. (2022). *Towards a global core value system in doctoral education*. UCL Press.

Okolie, U. C., Igwe, P. A., Nwajiuba, C. A., Mlanga, S., Binuomote, M. O., Nwosu, H. E., & Ogbaekirigwe, C. O. (2020). Does PhD qualification improve pedagogical competence? A study on teaching and training in higher education. *Journal of Applied Research in Higher Education, 12*(5), 1233–1250.

Pyhältö, K. M., Tikkanen, L., Van Lill, M., & Frick, B. L. (2024). Does professional support from colleagues influence supervisory competencies and experienced burnout among doctoral supervisors? *African Education Review, 20*(1-2), 92–112. https://doi.org/10.1080/18146627.2024.2351001

Rabe, M., Agboola, C., Kumswa, S., Linonge-Fontebo, H., & Mathe, L. (2021). Like a bridge over troubled landscapes: African pathways to doctorateness. *Teaching in Higher Education, 26*(3), 306–320.

Taylor, S. (2023). The changing landscape of doctoral education: A framework for analysis and introduction to the special issue. *Innovations in Education and Teaching International, 60*(5), 606–622. https://doi.org/10.1080/14703297.2023.2237962

Taylor, S., Kiley, M., & Holley, K. A. (2021). *The making of doctoral supervisors: International case studies of practice.* Routledge.

Trafford, V., & Leshem, S. (2009). Doctorateness as a threshold concept. *Innovations in Education and Teaching International, 46*(3), 305–316.

Van't Land, H. (2011). *The changing nature of doctoral studies in sub-Saharan Africa: Challenges and policy development opportunities at six universities in sub-Saharan Africa.* IAU. http://www.iau-aiu.net/sites/all/files/IAUFinal%20Report_Doctoral%20Programmes.pdf

Vaughan, S., Blackburn, C., & Curzon, R. (2021). Continuing conversations: Moving support for doctoral supervisors' professional development online. *Innovations in Education and Teaching International, 58*(6), 716–726. https://doi.org/10.1080/14703297.2021.1991423

Bibliometric analysis of doctoral supervision literature using topic modelling

Rudolph Oosthuizen

South Africa has a population of 62 million. The country has 26 public universities with a total enrolment of 1,1 million students. Doctoral enrolments in South Africa have increased from 9 994 in 2008 to 23 588 in 2020 (CHE Vitalstats). Between 2000 and 2018, a total of 32 025 doctoral students graduated at South African universities. Doctoral graduates increased from 972 in 2000 to 3 339 in 2019 (SciSTIP Tracer Study).

The **University of Pretoria** (UP) became an independent university in 1930, tracing its origins to the Normal College (est. 1902) and the Transvaal Technical Institute (est. 1904) which merged to form the Transvaal University College (1908). UP has 2 217 academic staff members working in nine faculties and a business school, with a total student enrolment of 53 900, which makes it one of the largest contact-education universities in Africa. In 2021 UP had 2 537 doctoral candidates.

1. Introduction

The doctorate's importance, worldwide and in Africa, has increased over the past few decades. Generally, the aim is to provide researchers with high-level skills required by the knowledge economy, placing a renewed focus on the doctoral supervisor's contribution and role (Cyranoski et al., 2011).

The South African Qualification Standard for Doctoral Degrees defines the purpose of a doctoral degree as to "develop the highest level of holistic and systematic understanding of scholarship in, and stewardship of, a field of study through an original contribution that advances the frontiers of knowledge" (CHE, 2018, p. 11). Doctoral studies need to display mastery in and develop appropriate research methods and skills to pursue knowledge in an inter-disciplinary and professional manner. Doctoral supervision plays a significant role in achieving these aims. Adequate doctoral supervision relies on the supervisor's and the student's skills, characteristics, and traits (CHE, 2018).

Strengthening the practice and knowledge of doctoral supervision requires research reported in scholarly articles. This chapter aims to extract and analyse the research topics in peer-reviewed articles on doctorate supervision. These topics were examined for structure and trend aspects to understand the current state of research in this field and to identify future opportunities and needs. The first step is to discuss using bibliometrics to support the planning and conduct of the research. Natural Language Processing (NLP), supported by data mining and topic modelling, is presented as a method that can be used to analyse bibliometric data. The next section explains the process of executing doctoral supervision literature topic modelling. Processing and analysing the captured data will provide insight into doctoral supervision research by discussing the topics' relative importance and temporal trends. This chapter concludes by discussing the topic modelling results to highlight the key findings.

2. Bibliometrics and Natural Language Processing

Scientists and researchers codify their findings in articles for journals, conferences or scholarly books. Because these articles are peer-reviewed with expert-based judgment, these building blocks of science and knowledge are validated (Hood & Wilson, 2001; Keathley-Herring et al., 2015). Bibliometric analysis is a systematic analysis method to analyse published research. Visualisation of the bibliometric outputs helps identify publication patterns and trends in a research field (Jie et al. 2014, Jiang et al., 2016). Publication and citation history trends may help researchers evaluate a field's prominent authors, growth, performance, and maturity (Aria & Cuccurullo, 2017; Kalantari et al., 2017). The most popular bibliometric indicators include citations, number of articles published, author statistics, keyword trend analysis, relational indicators (co-words, co-publication and co-citations), or research topics (Jia et al., 2018). Topic modelling can extract the core topics (concepts or themes) from a body of literature and calculate the trends (Lamba & Madhusudhan, 2019).

Traditionally, the manual bibliometric analysis process assigned articles to a predetermined topic list proposed by experts in the field. The number of articles available from journals and published conference proceedings has increased exponentially in most fields. Reading and sorting all of these articles into topics is time-consuming, challenging, and risks being biased. The manual analysis may also miss the hidden, latent, or emerging topics in a large text corpus. Automated topic modelling, implemented through machine-learning-based methods, will improve this process and eliminate or reduce these risks (Lee & Kang, 2018). This chapter focuses on automated topic modelling to identify the research trends in doctoral supervision literature.

Software analytics tend to struggle with processing unstructured text and free-format text. NLP converts unstructured text into numerical values possible for machine-learning algorithms to process, among other uses. NLP can extract relationships, key phrases, and patterns in a text corpus. Therefore, NLP is mainly applied to categorise and cluster text for document classification and summarisation to enable information extraction. Other uses include speech recognition and language translation (Banu & Chitra, 2015; Agrawal et al., 2018).

Machine-learning text-mining approaches have become more usable in recent times as the software, information, and computing power become increasingly accessible for researchers. Topic modelling provides an unsupervised text classification tool with quantitative statistical algorithms to extract semantic information from text. The computational algorithms automatically process a large text corpus to discover latent topics. Topic modelling assumes that words in a document constitute a set of intentional and latent topics. Topic modelling is independent of prior knowledge of the corpus (Jiang et al., 2016; Agrawal et al., 2018).

Latent Dirichlet allocation (LDA) is a popular topic modelling implementation algorithm. LDA identifies major thematic clusters from an extensive corpus of text documents to allocate each topic to each document. However, LDA requires input from the researcher on the number of issues for extraction. The algorithm extracts a distribution of keywords to define the topics. Despite being an unsupervised method, expert and domain knowledge are still required to name and describe the extracted topics (Tong & Zhang, 2016; Suominen & Toivanen, 2016; Hecking & Leydesdorff, 2019; Maier et al., 2018).

Despite some challenges, such as being non-deterministic and dependent on input parameters, topic modelling is more comprehensive and faster than manual methods. Topic modelling outputs enable researchers to quickly process a large corpus of articles for a more in-depth analysis of key elements within the literature. The automated process also provides information already in digital format for easier and more effective post-processing and reporting (Maier et al., 2018; Asmussen & Møller, 2019).

3. Method

The author applied the method discussed in this chapter in other fields, such as Systems Engineering, Technology Management and Sustainable Development (Oosthuizen & Pretorius, 2020).

3.1 Data capture

The research process used to process and analyse the titles and abstracts from articles on doctoral supervision is depicted in Figure 1. This research process uses Python-based algorithms and functions with the support of Microsoft Excel. A prerequisite for an automated topic modelling process is that the bibliometric data on the relevant published research is accessible in digital format. The articles for this analysis were extracted from the Scopus abstract and citation database using the search terms "**(doctoral OR doctorate OR PhD OR Ph.D) AND supervision**" over the period 1975-2018. The data captured in each article included the following:

1. Year of publication.
2. Authors.
3. Title.
4. Abstract.

3.2 Pre-processing

The SpaCy library in Python implemented the NLP algorithms. The raw captured text required pre-processing to prepare it for analysis. The first step removed articles not relevant to the field of doctoral supervision or not containing all the required information (e.g. authors, title, or abstract). Next, the titles and abstracts were combined to increase the text data's size to be processed. Titles of articles contain the most relevant words for the article, while the abstract summarises the problem and the research results.

Data cleaning also included the removal of publisher-related text (e.g. "Wiley & Sons", "Elsevier", "all rights reserved", etc.) and fixing spelling errors. Next, the process removed punctuation (i.e. periods, commas, exclamation points, ampersands, etc.), whitespaces, letters, numbers, and special characters that could affect the NLP algorithms. Although punctuation adds meaning to the text for a human reader, it is undesirable and uninformative for the NLP algorithm.

Figure 1: Bibliometric analysis process

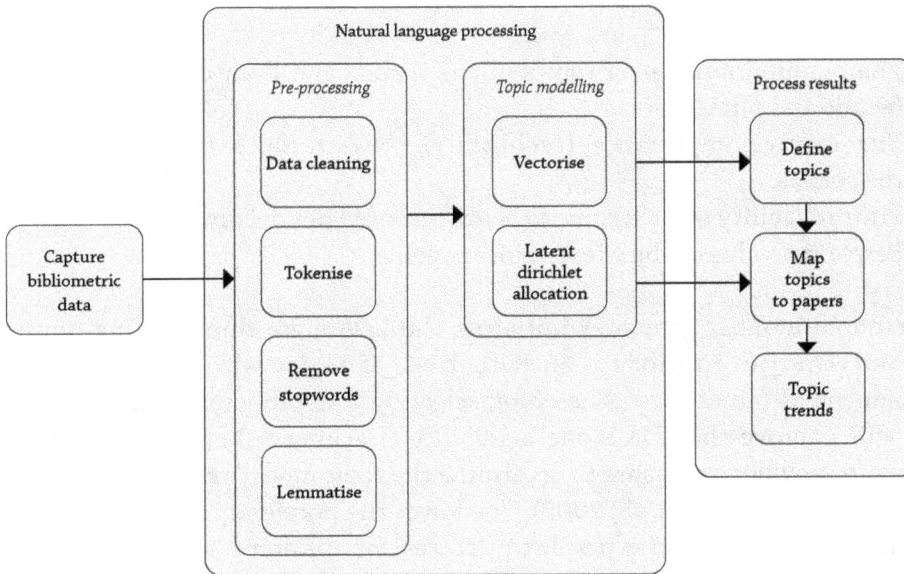

Tokenisation uses the spaces in the text to extract the linguistic units that represent the building blocks for sentences or paragraphs (Patel & Soni, 2012; Lin et al., 2016). Next, stop words (common words in a language that do not add real meaning to the text, such as "and", "the", "if", "a", etc.) are removed to reduce the dimensionality of the text (Maier et al., 2018). Lemmatisation also reduces the text corpus's dimensionality by deriving the base word by calculating each term's lemma. Python's SpaCy library was used to implement these steps.

Finally, generic words not contributing to identifying topics were also removed. The output of several test runs of the topic modelling software were manually investigated to identify words not contributing to the identification of the topics. These include common words due to the academic nature of the published articles, such as "represent", "aim", "paper", "example", and "define". Cleaning and preparing the text data for topic modelling is one of the most important steps to ensure quality topics are extracted.

3.3 Topic modelling

In this research, topic modelling is the key step in the process of bibliographic analysis. The Scikit-learn library in Python is used to vectorise the text and perform topic modelling with an LDA algorithm. The outputs of the LDA application provide the following:

1. The required number of topics in the corpus and their describing terms (words and phrases).
2. The relative importance (probability) of each term for the topic in the corpus.
3. The probability of each topic to be represented per document.
4. Perplexity value of the whole topic model.

The random number generator initiating the LDA algorithm training causes each software run to produce an output set of topics with some variation between the different runs. Therefore, selecting a suitable set of LDA parameters will improve the LDA model's stability (Hecking & Leydesdorff, 2019). Perplexity provides a measure to determine the topic model's statistical quality or goodness of fit (Blei et al., 2003). The lower the perplexity score, the better the model. Calculating the perplexity scores for different combination sets of parameter values for the model determines an optimum set of parameters (Hagen, 2018). The selected parameters must consider interpretability, replicability, external validity, and internal coherence between documents and topics (Isoaho et al., 2019).

3.4 Process results

Since the LDA algorithm only clusters documents by their topics, a manual analysis is still required to interpret and name each topic without indicating it. One way to assist interpretation is by using word clouds. The list of weighted terms is presented in a word cloud to assess the most important terms at a glance (Bashri & Kusumaningrum, 2017). Usually, a group of experts will be consulted, but the author performed it himself in the case of this chapter.

Calculating the topic popularity and trends utilises the probability of topic allocation per article. Multiple topics may be allocated per article since there is an overlap between topics. Therefore, using the most probable topic assigned per article is not the best solution. Also, because the total number of articles published per year is not constant, the data were transformed by dividing the total articles per topic by the total number of published documents. This provides the relative importance of topics in the published research on doctoral supervision.

4. Results

4.1 Pre-processing and parameter selection

At the start of the process, 1 467 journal articles, book chapters, and published conference proceedings were captured from the Scopus database with a Python algorithm using the search terms discussed above. Although the Scopus database may be limited regarding publications of doctoral supervision research conducted in Africa, it still provides a starting point for investigating the research topics in the field. The first cleaning exercise reduced the number of articles to 949 by manually removing articles not relevant to the field of doctoral supervision, as judged by the author. Only English articles were included in the sample to facilitate the NLP algorithms. Other articles removed include errata, corrections, editorials, and articles with incomplete data. Figure 2 shows a noticeable increase in articles published on doctoral supervision since the early 2000s, peaking around 2017. The graph in Figure 2 seems to agree with the findings of Cyranoski et al., (2011).

In addition to the pre-processing steps presented in section 3.2, the terms "doctoral", "supervision", "phd", and "supervise" were also removed before extracting the topics. Since these were the document search terms, they tend to be some of the most numerous words in the data sample. This project aims to find research topics published in the field of doctoral supervision. An extracted topic named "Doctoral Supervision" will add no value to the objective of this

Figure 2: History of articles on doctoral supervision

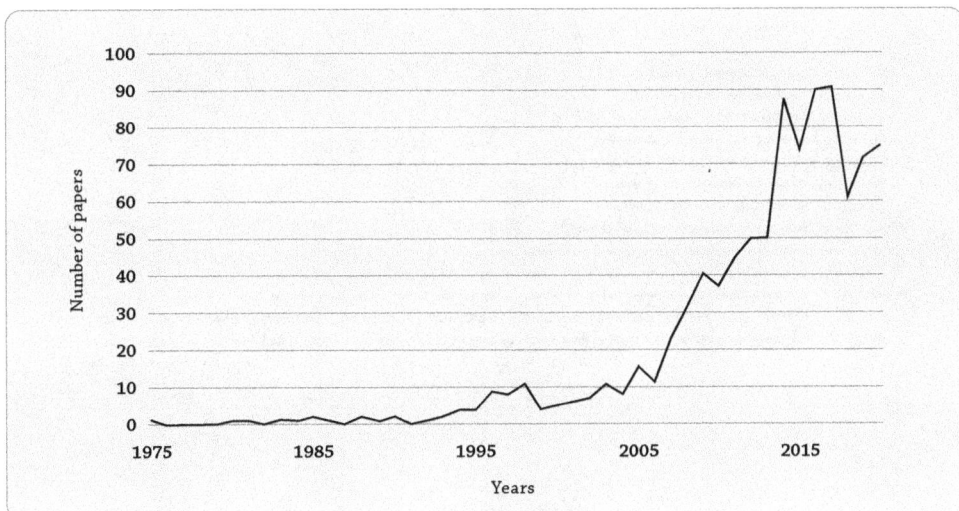

analysis. Therefore, removing these terms will ensure that the extracted topics are "within" the field of doctoral supervision. Figure 3 shows the word counts of the top 25 terms remaining for topic modelling processing.

The three main parameters that affect the topic extraction process are the minimum and maximum document frequency of the words in the processed text and the number of required topics for extraction. The minimum and maximum document frequency ensures that terms that occur in too few or too many documents are ignored. These terms affect the size of the data available for processing and the number of topics that can be extracted. The number of documents and their size affect the selection of values for these parameters.

After comparing the perplexity scores, a minimum document frequency of 0.13 and a maximum document frequency of 0.95 were selected. Therefore, the terms have to occur in more than 13% and less than 95% of the text corpus articles. The number of topics was chosen as five (5) as it was assumed that research into "Doctoral Supervision" should not result in too many straightforward and easy-to-name topics.

Figure 3: Word counts of the top 25 terms to be processed

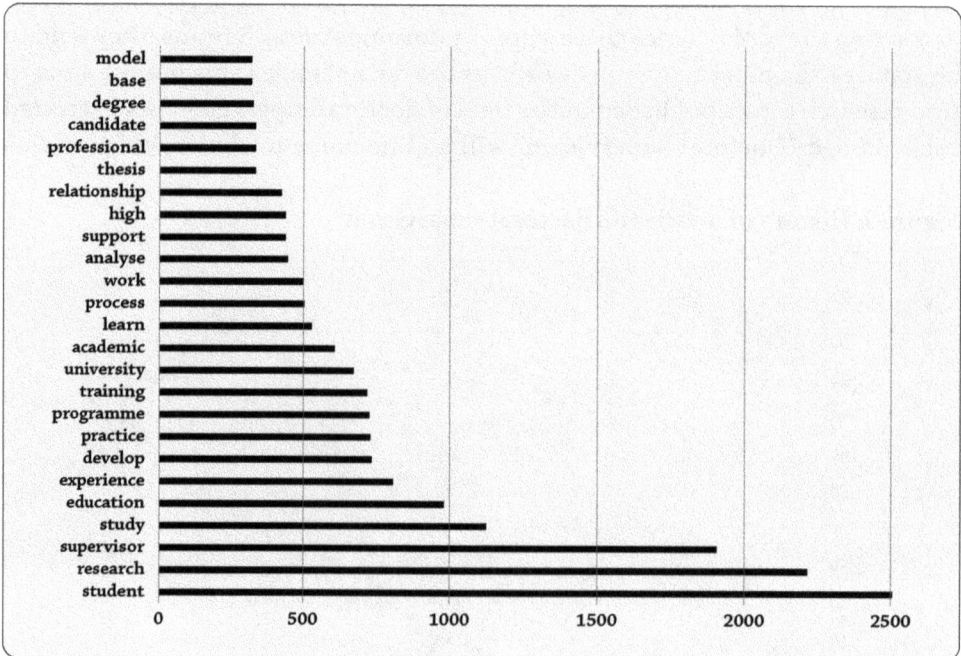

4.2 Doctoral supervision research topics

The topics extracted from the captured articles on doctoral supervision are listed, named and described in Table 1. The table presents the derived name and word cloud of each topic extracted from the extracted article's title and abstract.

The topic modelling process also provides the probability of each of the five topics allocated to each article in the text corpus. Summing up these ratios per article indicates the popularity of each topic over the publication history to provide a topic frequency, as seen in Figure 4. The "Research Process and Methods" topic is most prevalent in the processed articles. Another popular topic is about the relationship between supervisors and their doctoral students. The third and fourth most popular topics are about the students' research and professional skills training to equip doctoral students. Lastly, the least popular topic covers research and study process management.

Table 1: Topics with word clouds

Number	1	2	3
Name	Research process and methods	Supervisor–student relationship	Research education
Wordcloud			

Number	4	5	
Name	Professional training programmes	Theses and research management	
Wordcloud			

Figure 4: Topic frequency

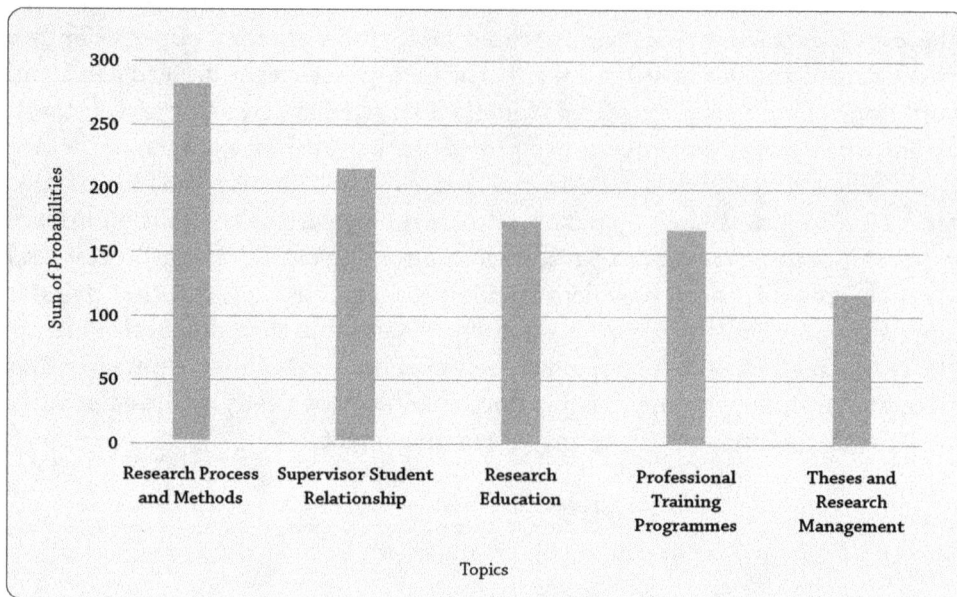

4.3 Research publication trends

The NLP and topic modelling process's data output provides a rich dataset for processing, depending on the focus question. This section generates trends for the extracted topics extracted from the articles on doctoral supervision to understand the current focus and identify future opportunities and needs for research. Figure 5 shows the trend per year of the five topics. The popularity is calculated by summing the allocation probability per article per topic per year. The data is only shown from 1992 to 2018 because the previous years contained only a few articles.

Since the graph in Figure 5 is not easy to interpret, smoothened trends are calculated using a fourth-order binomial regression due to the year-on-year variability. As seen in Figure 6, the trend lines for all the topics are on a steep, increasing trajectory. However, these trends are closely related to the annual increase in the total number of articles per year on doctoral students' supervision from Figure 2. This provides no information on the trends of the topics relative to each other.

Figure 5: Popularity per Topic

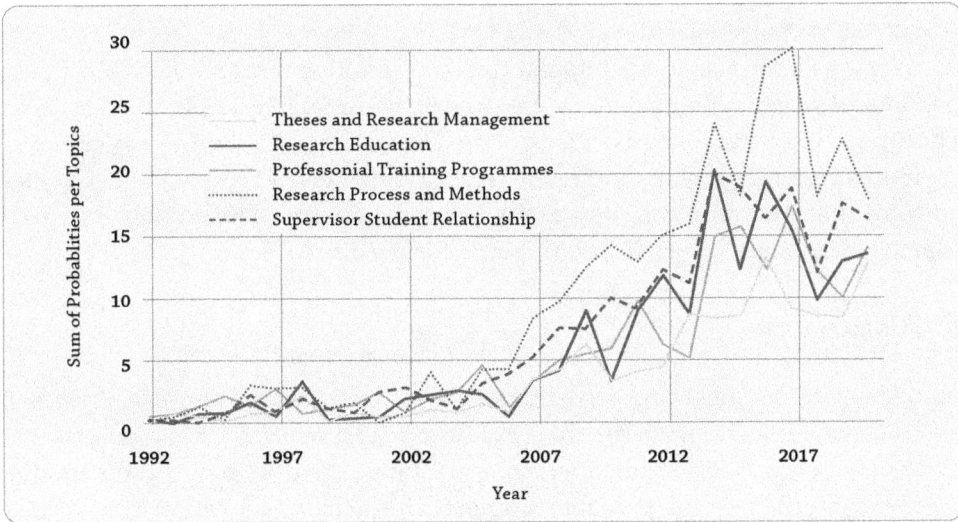

Since the number of articles per year is not constant, the data is transformed by dividing the topic allocation values per year by the number of articles for that year. This enables the calculation of the relative popularity between the topics per year. Figure 7 presents the transformed topic trends over the analysed publication years. However, the few articles during the early years resulted in

Figure 6: Smoothened topic trends

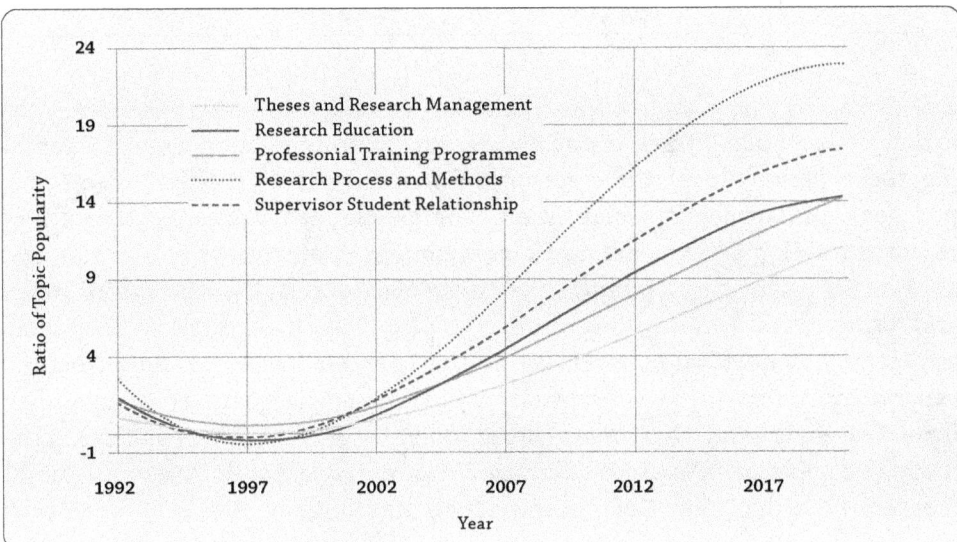

more widely disparate numbers. The later years, with a large number of articles, caused smoother graphs with subtle trends. However, this makes the identification of trends more difficult.

Despite being the most popular topic, "Research Process and Methods" has experienced a slight decline in the last decade. The topic of "Research Education" presents a similar trend. The "Professional Training Programmes" topic is experiencing a constant trend relative to the other topics. The two topics with an upward trend relative to the other topics are "Theses and Research Management" and "Supervisor–student Relationship".

5. Discussion

In this paper, the LDA process extracted a set of 5 topics from the titles and abstracts of 949 articles on the theme of doctoral supervision. Regardless of the limitations of automated unsupervised machine-learning- based topic modelling, it can still provide valuable support for doctoral education researchers when they do their literature studies. An in-depth analysis of the output topics could also support the development of a comprehensive list of research topics in the field. The five extracted topics can be grouped into two main themes, as seen in Table 2.

Table 2: Grouping of research topics

Educational or training topics	Supervisor roles
Research Education Professional Training Programmes Research Process and Methods	Supervisor–student Relationship Theses and Research Management

The extracted topics and the main themes from Table 2 also agree with the article by Bastalich (2017). In the article, she noted the importance of improving the supervision relationship within the context of political regulation, pedagogy and academic socialisation. The article also discusses the roles of research training and student and supervisor development.

Another interesting finding is the difference between "Research Education" and "Professional Training Programmes" topics. The data shows that both seem important for doctoral supervision as they exhibit similar trends. Doctoral supervision tends to be conceptual, a broad, knowledge-based educational, formative endeavour that requires the skills to perform the requisite activities. The topic of "Research Education" contains terms such as "research", "academic", "work", "quality", "knowledge", and "higher", while "Professional

Training Programmes" focus on "practice", "skill", "develop" and "experience." This shows that the two perspectives on doctoral supervision development can be treated equally and separately. "Education" seems to be more conceptual, comprehensive or formative (of the whole human being) in nature and "training" focuses on practical skills required during doctoral supervision (Bastalich, 2017).

Developing the required doctoral supervision skills requires a pedagogical approach. This is based on positive relationships supported by critical thinking skills. Students must also be exposed to scholarly research methods (Frick, 2019). These elements are present in the extracted topics. Botha and Mouton (2019) listed the primary task of the supervisor as the following:

1. Supervision of the research process through advice (relationship) and instruction (research education and training).
2. Coaching as part of the supervision relationship.
3. Project management.
4. Basic prerequisites for supervision (presence, commitment, and mutual conversation).

These tasks are compared to the extracted topics in Table 3. The table clearly shows that all the tasks can be related to one or more topics. This provides a form of validation for the extracted topics.

Table 3: Comparison of topics to supervisor tasks

No.	Topic	Supervision of the research process	Coaching	Project management	Basic prerequisites for supervision
1	Theses and Research Management			X	X
2	Research Education	X			
3	Professional Training Programmes	X			
4	Research Process and Methods	X			
5	Supervisor–student Relationship	X	X		X

6. Conclusion

NLP, implemented through unsupervised machine-learning methods, was applied to perform a bibliometric study on doctoral supervision research, published from 1975 to 2018. The analysis's output presents valuable biblio-metric information to support doctoral students' supervision and development research. It is important to note that the set of output topics resulted from unsupervised machine-learning, which may not be able to produce the perfect set of topics during each execution of the probabilistic algorithm. The selection of the parameters and the quality of the processed text data are significant factors in this process. However, the outputs are good enough to investigate the field of doctoral supervision and identify research opportunities within an extensive text dataset.

These topics can help researchers understand the current and historic research state and trends in doctoral supervision research. The output data provide rich information for further analyses to investigate specific questions about systems engineering. The topic model can be refined to give access to more, and detailed, topics in future work. These tools and methods may also be used to support literature reviews.

7. References

Agrawal, A., Fu, W., & Menzies, T. (2018). What is wrong with topic modeling? And how to fix it using search-based software engineering. *Information and Software Technology, 98*, 74–88.

Antons, D., Kleer, R., & Salge, T. O. (2016). Mapping the topic landscape of JPIM, 1984–2013: In search of hidden structures and development trajectories. *Journal of Product Innovation Management, 33*(6), 726–749.

Aria, M., & Cuccurullo, C. (2017). bibliometrix: An R-tool for comprehensive science mapping analysis. *Journal of Informetrics, 11*(4), 959–975.

Asmussen, C. B., & Møller, C. (2019). Smart literature review: A practical topic modelling approach to exploratory literature review. *Journal of Big Data, 6*(1), 93.

Banu, G. R., & Chitra, V. (2015). A survey of text mining concepts. *International Journal of Innovations in Engineering and Technology, 5*(2), 121–127.

Bashri, M. F., & Kusumaningrum, R. (2017). *Sentiment analysis using Latent Dirichlet Allocation and topic polarity wordcloud visualisation*. 5th International conference on information and communication technology (ICoIC7), Melaka, Malaysia 1–5. https://ieeexplore.ieee.org/document/8074651

Bastalich, W. (2017). Content and context in knowledge production: A critical review of doctoral supervision literature. *Studies in Higher Education, 42*(7), 1145–1157.

Blei, D. M., Ng, A. Y., & Jordan, M. I. (2003). Latent Dirichlet allocation. *Journal of Machine Learning Research, 3*(January), 993–1022.

Botha, J. (2019). *The nature, purpose, standard and format of the doctoral degree*. Course material of module 2 of the DIES/CREST training course for supervisors of doctoral candidates at African universities. Stellenbosch University.

Botha, J., & Mouton, J. (2019). *The preparation phase: Selection, supervisor allocation, and supervising the doctoral proposal*. Course material of module 5 of the DIES/CREST Training course for supervisors of doctoral candidates at African universities. Stellenbosch University.

Council on Higher Education (CHE). (2018). *Qualification standard for doctoral degrees*. CHE.

Cyranoski, D., Gilbert, N., Ledford, H., Nayar, A., & Yahia, M. (2011). The PhD factory: The world is producing more PhDs than ever before. Is it time to stop? *Nature, 472*(7343), 276–279.

Eker, S., Rovenskaya, E., Langan, S., & Obersteiner, M. (2019). Model validation: A bibliometric analysis of the literature. *Environmental Modelling & Software, 117*, 43–54.

Frick, L. (2019). *Supervisory models and styles.* Course material of module 4 of the DIES/CREST Training course for Supervisors of doctoral candidates at African universities. Stellenbosch University.

Hagen, L. (2018). Content analysis of e-petitions with topic modeling: How to train and evaluate LDA models? *Information Processing & Management, 54*(6), 1292–1307.

Hecking, T., & Leydesdorff, L. (2019). Can topic models be used in research evaluations? Reproducibility, validity, and reliability when compared with semantic maps. *Research Evaluation, 28*(3), 263–272.

Hood, W. W., & Wilson, C. S. (2001). The literature of bibliometrics, scientometrics, and informetrics. *Scientometrics, 52*(2), 291–314.

Isoaho, K., Gritsenko, D., & Mäkelä, E. (2019). Topic modeling and text analysis for qualitative policy research. *Policy Studies Journal, 49*(1), 300–324.

Jia, Y., Wang, W., Liang, J., Liu, L., Chen, Z., Zhang, J., Chen, T., & Lei, J. (2018). Trends and characteristics of global medical informatics conferences from 2007 to 2017: A bibliometric comparison of conference publications from Chinese, American, European and the Global Conferences. *Computer Methods and Programs in Biomedicine, 166*, 19–32.

Jiang, H., Qiang, M., & Lin, P. (2016). A topic modeling based bibliometric exploration of hydropower research. *Renewable and Sustainable Energy Reviews, 57*, 226–237.

Jie, L., Xiaohong, G., Shifei, S., & Jovanovic, A. (2014). Bibliometric mapping of "International symposium on safety science and technology (1998-2012)". *Procedia Engineering, 84*, 70–79.

Kalantari, A., Kamsin, A., Kamaruddin, H. S., Ebrahim, N. A., Gani, A., Ebrahimi, A., & Shamshirband, S. (2017). A bibliometric approach to tracking big data research trends. *Journal of Big Data, 4*(1), 30.

Keathley, H., Bean, A., Chen, T., Vila, K., Ye, K., & Gonzalez-Aleu, F. (2015). Bibliometric analysis of author collaboration in engineering management research. In E.-H. Ng, S. Long & A. Squires (Eds.), *Proceedings of the international annual conference of the American society for engineering management* (pp. 679–689). American Society for Engineering Management.

Lamba, M., & Madhusudhan, M. 2019. Mapping of topics in DESIDOC Journal of Library and Information Technology, India: a study. Scientometrics 120 (2), 477-505.

Lee, H., & Kang, P. (2018). Identifying core topics in technology and innovation management studies: A topic model approach. *The Journal of Technology Transfer, 43*(5), 1291–1317.

Lin, J. R., Hu, Z. Z., Zhang, J. P., & Yu, F. Q. (2016). A natural-language-based approach to intelligent data retrieval and representation for cloud BIM. *Computer-Aided Civil and Infrastructure Engineering, 31*(1), 18–33.

Maier, D., Waldherr, A., Miltner, P., Wiedemann, G., Niekler, A., Keinert, A., Pfetsch, B., Heyer, G., Reber, U., Häussler, T., & Schmid-Petri, H. (2018). Applying LDA topic modeling in communication research: Toward a valid and reliable methodology. *Communication Methods and Measures, 12*(2-3), 93–118.

Oosthuizen, R., & Pretorius, L. (2020, July 18–23). *A bibliometric method for analysis of systems engineering research* [Paper presentation]. 30th annual INCOSE international symposium, Cape Town, South Africa.

Patel, F. N., & Soni, N. R. (2012). Text mining: A brief survey. *International Journal of Advanced Computer Research, 2*(6), 243.

Suominen, A., & Toivanen, H. (2016). Map of science with topic modeling: Comparison of unsupervised learning and human-assigned subject classification. *Journal of the Association for Information Science and Technology, 67*(10), 2464–2476.

Tong, Z., & Zhang, H. 2016. A Text Mining Research Based on LDA Topic Modelling. Proceedings of the Sixth International Conference on Computer Science, Engineering and Information Technology (CCSEIT 2016), Vienna, Austria, May 21-22, 2016, pp.201-210.

CHAPTER 2

Academic freedom in doctoral studies in Africa

Mohamed A. M. Khalil

The **Arab Republic of Egypt** is in the northeastern corner of Africa and southwestern Asia, with a population of 112.7 million (UNFPA). Egypt has 27 state universities, 20 national universities, and 3 technological universities (MOHESR). Egypt has a long history in doctoral studies, with the first doctoral degree awarded in 1914. In 2003 there were 22 248 PhD students enrolled at Egyptian universities, reaching 35 000 in 2009. During 2011-2016 a total of 37 519 doctoral candidates graduated at Egyptian universities (Cantini, 2020).

Mansoura University (MU) is the sixth Egyptian university, founded in 1972 under the name East Delta University, later changed to Mansoura University. Its campus occupies an area of approximately 300 acres southwest of Mansoura City. The university has 18 colleges, a total of 7 315 faculty members, 25 659 employees, and 181 963 students, among them 32 864 postgraduate students (MANS).

1. Introduction

The United Nations Educational, Scientific and Cultural Organization, UNESCO, defines academic freedom as "the right to teach, discuss, carry out research, publication, express scientific opinion freely and participate in academic bodies without any external constraints from the authorities" (UNESCO, 2017; UNESCO, 2008). When Albert Einstein was asked about the essential nature of academic freedom, his answer was quoted by the AAUP-UC as having been:

[B]y academic freedom, I understand the right to search for truth and to publish and teach what one holds to be true. This right also implies a duty: one must not conceal any part of what one has recognized to be true. It is evident that any restriction of academic freedom acts in such a way as to hamper the dissemination of knowledge among people and thereby impedes rational judgment and action. (AAUP-UC, 2017)

2. Understanding academic freedom

The debate about academic freedom and rights in academic research has been discussed by many scholars like (Anderson, 1934; Emerson & Haber, 1963; Neave, 1998; Aarrevaara, 2010). They mostly agreed to define academic freedom as the ability of students, supervisors and institutions to express their academic opinions freely. Academic freedom is a driver of innovation, as it gives scholars and students the capacity to generate, debate and acquire knowledge, and thereby reflects societal conditions (Scholars at Risk, 2020). It is internationally accepted that academic freedom is the right to learn, teach, and express opinion freely from restrictions. According to Grimm and Saliba (2017, p. 47), academic freedom can be defined in a negative way to be "the absence of legal, physical, or structural interference by the state or non- state actors in a researcher's personal autonomy, independence and integrity". However, this absence of interference does not imply that academic freedom exists, as academic freedom is not absolute. It is integrated with the social, cultural, economic, and political conditions of the society.

Academic freedom continuously elicits debate among academics. While many universities and states around the world have committed to maintaining a high level of academic freedom, it remains under attack and is poorly understood in many places (Doğan, 2016; Kinzelbach et al., 2021).

Academic freedom is an important condition for quality and academic dignity. There are different types of academic freedom (Doğan, 2016). The first is the freedom guaranteed by the state and institutions to academics to produce science. The other type is the civil rights and freedom of academics as individuals. Therefore, academic freedom is a mix between scientific vision and moral issues, which are protected and guaranteed by academic institutions.

Many universities and research institutions state their principles and guidelines for academic freedom in doctoral studies in their programme rules. However, the level of freedom differs from place to place due to cultural, religious, political, or economic variations. The freedom in doctoral studies can be viewed through the perspectives of three role players: the candidate, the supervisor, and the institution. The following aspects of academic freedom will be discussed in this chapter:

- Scientific freedom: this includes the freedom to teach, learn, discuss, research, and publish the results.
- Administrative freedom: this includes the freedom to engage in the activities of academic bodies and the freedom to express academic opinions without external constraints.
- Economic freedom: this includes, on one hand, having equal opportunities to access funding and other supporting sources with clear criteria, and, on the other hand, freedom to act without constraints set by the funding providers.
- Political and social freedom: this includes the freedom to express an opinion about topics that may be sensitive from a political, cultural, or religious points of view.

Academic freedom in postgraduate studies is an important condition to achieve reliable outcomes. However, the academic freedom guaranteed for academics by the state, or the institution should be balanced with the freedom of individuals or the society in general. With the multicultural nature of many doctoral research programmes, academic freedom needs more attention when considered in different contexts and places. This requires more effort from supervisors to ensure academic freedom within available limits and constraints.

Recently the academic world witnessed cases where doctoral students, supervisors, and even institutions experienced limitations on academic freedom (Scholars at Risk, 2020). There is a growing body of literature on academic freedom; the concept, the principles, and how it helps to protect the values and functions of higher education (Finkin & Post, 2009; Fish, 2014; Downs, 2015). However, most of these studies discuss academic freedom in the context of western countries, where academic freedom is mostly well developed and protected by institutional legislation and constitutional rights. Recently in many countries that are moving toward more democratic regimes, academic freedom has come under discussion (Appiagyei-Atua et al., 2016). However, there is a need for more studies on academic freedom in the African context.

Informed by published literature, this chapter is a conceptual study that aims to shed light on the challenges that face the implementation of academic freedom in doctoral studies in Africa. In so doing, it tries to link this subject with the role of doctoral supervisors in enhancing the level of academic freedom within doctoral studies.

3. Historic overview of academic freedom

We may date back the struggle for academic freedom to the ancient Greek period when Socrates was accused of corrupting the youth of Athens. However, the modern debate begins in the twelfth century with the advent of universities. Universities in the Middle Ages were powerful, and they set their own rules, however, there were severe limits on research established by religious authorities (Stone, 2015).

Although they allowed for a variety of scholarly approaches, some of the early universities founded in North Africa and the Middle East, such as the University of Al-Azhar (est. in 972), were bound by religious and political oversight which limited the freedom of these institutions. Various modern universities had been established in North Africa by the beginning of the twentieth century, for example, the Egyptian University,[1] established in 1908, and the University of Algiers in Algeria, established in 1909 (Sherman, 1990). However, the academic growth of these institutions was negatively affected by European colonization because colonial regimes often restricted academic freedom (Dea, 2018).

By the beginning of the nineteenth century, academic freedom was reformed by Wilhelm von Humboldt with his concepts of *Lernfreiheit, Lehrfreiheid* and *Freiheit der Wissenschaft* (the freedom to teach and learn, and academic self-governance) which he discussed under the title of academic freedom (Smith, 2002). The **freedom to teach** refers to the freedom of professors to do research and publish their results without any constraints from political and religious authorities as well as the societal tradition, along with the freedom to choose the contents of the lectures and courses they teach. The **freedom to learn** refers to the freedom of students to freely participate in their choice of courses and study topics. Von Humboldt's third key term, **academic self-governance**, refers to the freedom of universities and research institutions to manage and control their internal affairs (Nybom, 2003; Smith, 2002)

Even though the notion of academic freedom was first explicitly used in Germany and then expanded to the entire world, this was ended by the Nazi regime in the 1930s. By this time academic freedom had been well established in the United States of America by the American Association of University Professors (AAUP).[2] The *AAUP 1915 Declaration of Principles* confirmed Humboldtian concepts, adding three sub-concepts: freedom to inquire and

---

1 Currently Cairo University, from 1908 to 1940 was known as the Egyptian University, from 1940 to 1952 was known as King Fuad I 'Fu'ād al-Awwal' University (Cairo University, 2017).

2 The American Association of University Professors (AAUP) is a nonprofit membership association of faculty and other academic professionals, founded in 1915, aiming to advance academic freedom and shared governance (See: https://www.aaup.org/).

achieve human knowledge, freedom to deliver instruction to students, and freedom to practise as experts in public services (Wilson, 2016). The 1915 AAUP declaration was re-issued in a shorter form by the American Council on Education as the *1925 Conference Statement on Academic Freedom and Tenure*. In 1940 the *Statement of Principles on Academic Freedom and Tenure* (AAUP, n.d.) was issued by the AAUP as a revised version of the 1915 declaration. The current version was issued in 1970 with some additions, and it is still the AAUP's official academic freedom statement (AAUP, n.d.; Smith, 2002; Dea, 2018). It is widely accepted that formal protection of academic freedom came into being only by the mid-20th century in 1940 when the American Association of University Professors (AAUP) and the Association of American Colleges and Universities (AACU) set out the principles of academic freedom in teaching and scientific research (Noori, 2014).

The academic freedom debate was considered at international level in the General Conference of UNESCO in 1993 (UNESCO 1993, par 1.14) and again in 1997 through the UNESCO Recommendation concerning the Status of Higher-Education Teaching Personnel (UNESCO, 2008). The recommendations highlighted the importance of removing any political pressure that could limit academic freedom. In the United States, the document known as the *Chicago Principles,* which is widely advocated across the country, was developed by the Committee on Freedom of Expression at the University of Chicago in 2014 (Chicago Statement, 2014). This document was adopted by more than 70 institutions across the United States, including the Foundation for Individual Rights in Education (FIRE, 2021).

Currently, academic freedom is considered a basic right in research, education, and, of course, doctoral studies. However, freedom, in general, and academic freedom specifically, has boundaries and conditions that academics should take into consideration to avoid any conflict between individual rights and society's needs (Axelrod, 2018).

4. Academic Freedom Index (AFI)

The Academic Freedom Index (AFI) for the advancement of free universities is a joint project[3] launched in 2019 to monitor the level of academic freedom in 175 countries and territories around the world (Spannagel et al., 2020). It uses five expert-coded indicators to assess the academic freedom level. These

---

3 The Academic Freedom Index (AFI) was developed by researchers at the Friedrich-Alexander University Erlangen-Nurnberg, the V-Dem Institute of the University of Gothenburg, and the Global Public Policy Institute in Berlin in close cooperation with the Scholars at Risk (SAR) network (Spannagel et al., 2020).

indicators are the freedom to research and teach; freedom of academic exchange and dissemination; institutional autonomy; campus integrity; and freedom of academic and cultural expression (Kinzelbach et al., 2021; Spannagel et al., 2020). The AFI is not only a research tool, but also an indication for policymakers about the level of academic freedom. The AFI has five objectives: to inform stakeholders, provide monitoring yardsticks, alter incentive structures, challenge university rankings, and facilitate research (Kinzelbach et al., 2021). The AFI uses a scale (0-1) to indicate levels of academic freedom.

According to the 2020 AFI report, 80% of academics worldwide experience some restriction on academic freedom. Figure 1 shows the global AFI levels in 2020, where we notice that many African countries are in class C, with an AFI between 0.6 and 0.4, which is lower than that of most developed countries.

When analysing AFIs on the African continent, we notice the huge variation between countries, which may be the result of political changes and legislative reforms relating to academic freedom. The analysis of the AFI data can help higher education authorities to assess their performance. The data provide an international monitoring mechanism for academic freedom.

5. The freedom to research in doctoral studies

According to James Turk, Director of the Centre for Free Expression at the Faculty of Communication and Design, Ryerson University (Canada), academic freedom in research extends beyond the freedom to teach and research to include the "freedom of intramural expression and freedom of extramural expression" (UNESCO, 2017:1). Intramural means that academics are free to participate in the administration of their institutions, and extramural means that academics can share the outcomes of their research, access the required knowledge sources, secure adequate funding, and take part in political debates (UNESCO, 2017). The core of academic freedom is to minimize interference of politicians, administrators, and trustees on scholarship and teaching, leaving the evaluation of academic quality to peers within the relevant discipline (Finkin & Post, 2009).

When reviewing the literature concerning academic freedom at the international level, we find that there is a clear definition of limits that may be imposed on academic freedom to ensure an academic environment free from constraint. However, in African and Middle East universities this debate is quite recent and still needs more adaptation to fit into cultural, economic, and political conditions (Noori, 2014). When considering academic freedom for doctoral studies we will find differences between higher educational institutions (HEI)

Figure 1: Global levels of Academic Freedom Index (AFI) in 2020 (Kinzelbach et al., 2021)

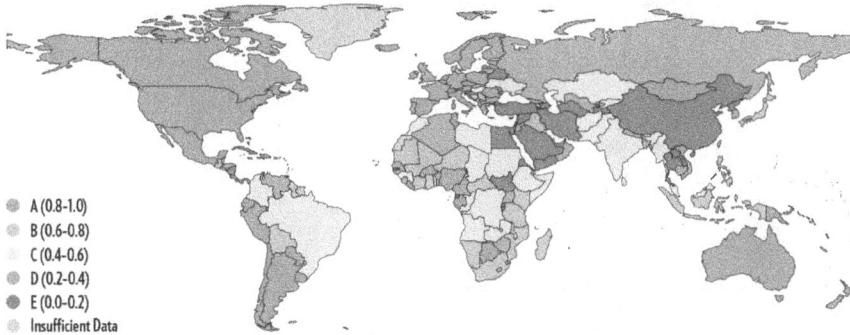

- A (0.8-1.0)
- B (0.6-0.8)
- C (0.4-0.6)
- D (0.2-0.4)
- E (0.0-0.2)
- Insufficient Data

in African countries compared to (HEI) in other parts of the world, as in most cases doctoral research may exceed the geographic region to include places with different political, cultural, and/or religious points of view. This adds to the complexity of academic freedom for collaborative doctoral studies between African countries and the many other countries in the world.

6. Academic freedom in African universities

The debate about academic freedom in the African context is fairly young, however, its actual achievement is still far behind to varying degrees from one country to another. From Figure 1 we can recognise the huge variation between African countries; we find a few countries in west and south Africa experience higher levels of academic freedom (AFi 0.8- 1.0), similar to the western world (Europe, UK, USA and Australia). On the other hand, 11 African countries[4] score the second-lowest level of academic freedom (AFi 0.6-0.8), like some countries in Asia (e.g. India and Pakistan); and five African countries have the lowest level of academic freedom in the world (AFi 0.0-0.2), comparable to China and some countries in the Middle East and South-East Asia. Despite the variety in the levels of academic freedom within Africa itself, as a region overall, the continent scores the lowest of all the regions in the world.

---

4 According to the United Nations Department for General Assembly and Conference Management, there are 54 countries in Africa, which are members of the United Nations (United Nations, n.d.).

Figure 2: Levels of Academic Freedom in Africa (years 2000, 2010 and 2020).

Source: extracted from AFI maps, based on V-Dem data (v11)[5]

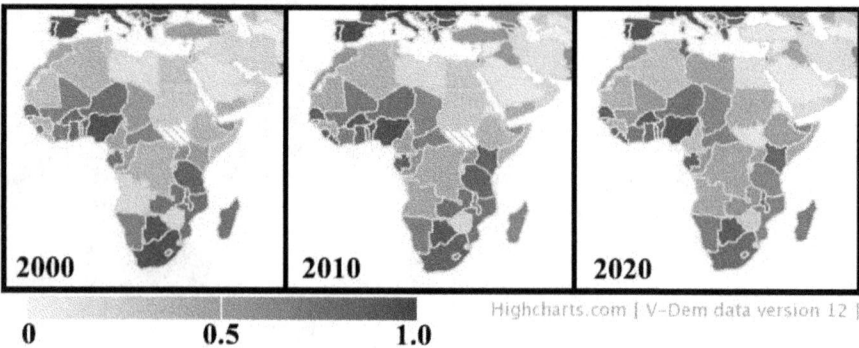

Figure 2 shows the changes in the AFI of African countries from 2000 to 2020, where we notice a slight increase in the AFI in a few west-African countries and a decrease in AFI in some north-African countries mostly because of political unrest.

African universities – like other African institutions and systems – were affected for long periods of the nineteenth and twentieth centuries by colonization and then the absence of democratic regimes. The debate about academic freedom rose in prominence with the democratic movements in many North African countries traced to the Arab Spring in the early 2010s. In a review of academic freedom in African universities, in line with the 1997 UNESCO recommendation, Appiagyei-Atua assessed levels of academic freedom, using four indicators: personal freedom, institutional freedom, institutional governance, and tenure (Appiagyei-Atua et al., 2016). They concluded that academic freedom had started to find its way back to African universities after a complete absence; however, the development of academic freedom in African universities has been slow compared with other academic developments during recent years.

One of the main movements by African scholars towards academic freedom was the *Dar es Salaam Declaration on Academic Freedom and Social Responsibility*[6] adopted in Tanzania in 1990 by six academic staff associations.

---

5 https://www.v-dem.net/data_analysis/MapGraph/

6 The Dar es Salaam Declaration on Academic Freedom and Social Responsibility of Academics was adopted by delegates from six academic staff associations at the end of the Inaugural Workshop held at Silversands Hotel on 19th April 1990. The six associations participated in Dar es Salaam Declaration are: Ardhi Institute Staff Assembly (ARISA) - Cooperative College Staff Association (COCOSA) - Institute of Development Management Staff Association (IDMASA) - Institute of Finance Management Staff Assembly (IFMASA) - Sokoine University of Agriculture Staff Association (SUASA) - University of Dar es Salaam Academic Staff Assembly (UDASA), (http://hrlibrary.umn.edu/africa/DARDOK.htm)

This declaration, along with the *Kampala Declaration on Intellectual Freedom and Social Responsibility*,[7] also adopted in 1990, paved the way for establishing the basics of academic freedom in African universities. The Dar es Salaam declaration argued for academic freedom through two main issues, academic rights and the autonomy of academic organisations, along with the security of tenure.

At the governmental level, Africa is taking positive steps towards improving people's and human rights. The most promising action is the *African Charter on Human and People's Rights* which came into effect on 25 January 2005 (ACHPR, 2005). However, the charter does not directly mention academic freedom. Adding to this movement, a series of conferences were held in Africa (July 2005 in Dakar, Senegal, then in May 2006 in El Jadida, Morocco, and July 2007 in the Democratic Republic of Congo), with the aim of learning from the European model known as the Bologna process. This series of conferences led some North African countries – such as former French colonies, Morocco, Algeria, and Tunisia – to adopt a model similar to the Bologna model, and re-align their higher education systems, "undergraduate, master, and doctorate", with the French higher-education system (EDSLR, 2008). The adoption of the Bologna model helps HEI in these countries to build more cooperative international relationships, which in turn helps with the adoption of clearer principles of academic freedom.

Currently, most African countries include academic freedom in their constitutions, however in different ways. In some cases, it is done indirectly as part of the freedom of expression, for example, article 16(1) of the South African Constitution states that "everyone has the right to freedom of expression ...". Other countries have a direct recognition of scientific or academic freedom, for example in article 49 of the Republic of Cape Verde Constitution "[E]veryone shall have the freedom to learn, educate, and teach" (Appiagyei-Atua et al., 2016). However, although academics are officially protected in many African countries, the actual achievement of academic freedom in research and doctoral studies still needs more development to be realised, given existing constraints (Scholars at Risk, 2020).

---

7 The Kampala Declaration on Intellectual Freedom and Social Responsibility (1990), adopted at a Symposium on Academic Freedom and Social Responsibility of Intellectuals held in Kampala, 29 Nov. 1990. (http://hrlibrary.umn.edu/africa/KAMDOK.htm)

7. Limits and constraints on academic freedom in doctoral studies

According to a 2012 report by the International Association of Universities and the Catalan Association of Public Universities (IAU-ACUP), the challenges facing doctoral studies, in general, could be summarised as: funding shortage (for both institutions and students); institutional capacity; supervision quality; inadequate responsiveness to national, social and economic needs; weak links to industry; lack of international information-sharing and lack of academic freedom (IAU-ACUP, 2012; Cloete et al., 2015).

According to Fish (2014), we may categorise academic supervisors into five 'schools' in terms of their justifications for academic freedom. Fish named the first school 'It's Just a Job' based on 'professionalism, pure and simple'. He named the second group the 'For the Common Good' school, which stresses the positive impact of academic freedom as 'shared governance and democracy'. The third type is the 'Academic Exceptionalism or Uncommon Beings' school, which claims the superiority of the moral and intellectual virtue of academics over other callings. The fourth is the 'Academic Freedom as Critique' school, which presents more critiques of society, politics, and academic norms. The fifth school, 'Academic Freedom as Revolution', goes deeper and advocates the revolutionary role of academic freedom (Downs, 2015; Fish, 2014). Fish argues that some academics are fulfilling only their jobs of teaching and research, avoiding moral guidance and political persuasion (Fish, 2014).

In the countries where academic freedom is fully protected by the constitution and realised, the debate moves to a focus on creating a balance between the freedom to research and other basic civil rights, public safety, and ethics (Santosuosso et al., 2007). Almost all the issues that affect higher education studies also affect academic freedom and limit its healthy application in doctoral studies (Scholars at Risk, 2020).

Levels of achievement of academic freedom are subject to many constraints. These may include, but are not limited to the following four, whose identification is based on the current author's observations of conditions affecting academic freedom in Africa. Gathering empirical data to test these observations is a project for further research.

7.1 Institutional and bureaucratic constraints

Institutional regulations could affect academic freedom in many ways, such as the selection procedures of doctoral candidates, the allocation of supervisors to students and limitations on research topics. It has become common in most research centres – especially in the sciences, where expensive laboratory equipment is required – to define research programmes and themes where prospective doctoral students must find a topic within that programme in one of the themes. This practice developed because of funding requirements and had a quality dimension, however, to avoid its limitation on academic freedom, it needs to be clearly communicated to both supervisor and candidate before starting the doctorate study, and any changes could be applied only on new candidates. The research programmes need to be flexible to fit a wide range of research themes within the discipline and the implementation should be equal for everyone.

The freedom to select a research topic, along with the freedom of the doctoral student to choose their supervisor, in addition to the freedom of the supervisor to select students, will create a healthy environment for academic freedom. Moreover, supervisors have an increasing role in the management of doctoral studies. The supervisor as a project manager (Grant & Manathunga, 2011; Pyhältö et al., 2015) is required to help students starting from registration and administration to funding support, not only the main role of scientific support (Waghid, 2006). Additionally, the supervisor has to manage academic freedom within the existing limits and constraints.

7.2 Funding constraints and autonomy

Funding is one of the main constraints on academics, especially with the limited resources in most public universities (Neave, 1998), and more so in African universities (Van't Land, 2011). The increasing number of doctoral students has a negative effect on supervisors. On one hand, it puts more academic pressure on them (Cloete et al., 2015), and on another hand, it could affect the supervisor's freedom to choose doctoral candidates which reflects on academic freedom. The supervisor should manage within the institutional constraints to achieve an acceptable level of academic freedom.

Currently, due to the globalization of technological exchange and financial sources, many research institutions encourage supervisors and students to find funding from industry, sponsors, or scholarships (Van't Land, 2011). In most universities and institutions, any external funding should be through an official academic authority that monitors the flow of funds and ensures that the money is allocated to the designated purpose. However, monitoring the financial flow should not interfere with the research itself, even by the funding sources or official authorities, to avoid compromising academic freedom.

The international funding of doctoral research is one of the main supports for developing doctorate programmes. Moreover, the financial support and scholarships offered for doctorate students from governments and organisations in some developed countries help to overcome cultural differences and enhance political relations (Axelrod, 2022). However, they could have a negative effect on academic freedom, as the students, supervisors, and even the institutions are threatened by rejection or withdrawal of financial support when discussing sensitive topics.

7.3   Ethical, social, cultural, and religious constraints

Academic freedom is not only practised in the academic community, but it reflects the degree of freedom in society and can be seen as an extension of it. Thus, academic freedom is embedded in the conditions and circumstances of the society in which it is practised (Axelrod, 2022). In other words, academic freedom can be seen as a reflection of public freedom and vice versa (Axelrod, 2018; Axelrod, 2022; Neave, 1998). However, doctoral research cannot be detached from intercultural relations, in some cases between student and supervisor, and in other cases between the location of the research institution and the location where the research is conducted (Lee, 2008; Martin & Price, 2021; Manathunga, 2014).

However, although doctoral students and supervisors are free to do research, in many cases it is complicated in certain cultures to deal with certain sensitive issues or topics. Many of the societies in Africa, and almost all the Middle East, are conservative societies where there are some inherited social habits that no one can speak about, and some religious boundaries that cannot be crossed. Even if doctoral students and supervisors wanted to research these topics, it would be very difficult to collect data or publish the results. Supervisors play a major role in guiding and adjusting students' freedom to research, respect and fit within the ethical, social, cultural and religious limits based on location, topic, and persons involved in the research.

7.4   Political constraints

The political situation in a country is the most obvious constraint on academic freedom in doctoral studies. Political conditions may limit research related to certain countries or places, prevent research into certain topics or encourage avoidance of some people or national figures in the research. In some cases, even with the full political freedom and ethical permissions to do research in one location or country, a problem may appear when the research is done in another location with less political freedom. There are some cases of researchers who are registered as doctoral students in institutions located in countries with high levels of academic freedom, and they do the research in another country with limited academic freedom. One such a case was the British PhD student, Matthew Hedges. His research focused on authoritarian regimes with an emphasis on the Arabian Peninsula. He was arrested in 2018 for about six months while conducting fieldwork research in the United Arab Emirates and considered a spy. He was later freed after a pardon (BBC News, 2018). Another case is the Italian PhD student, Giulio Regeni, who was brutally murdered in 2016 while doing research in Egypt. His case is still under investigation by Italian and Egyptian authorities (Walsh, 2017). In its report, Scholars at Risk highlighted many other examples around the world (Scholars at Risk, 2020).

8. Academic freedom and doctoral supervision in Africa

Insufficient or lacking academic freedom in certain disciplines, especially when it comes to sensitive topics, is one of the obstacles to doctoral studies in African universities. The supervisor needs to guide students throughout the research process to deal with all the constraints while maintaining an acceptable level of academic freedom, keeping in mind student safety and research quality. The supervisors may fulfil this role by *claiming, enhancing, managing,* and *limiting (as appropriate)* academic freedom throughout the research process.

Claiming academic freedom is the responsibility of all academics in general, and specifically also the responsibility of supervisors of doctoral candidates. Supervisors should implement the required academic rules while communicating the main principles of academic freedom within their field and in their institution. Full academic freedom in doctoral studies in African universities will never be achieved without supervisors' efforts to claim academic freedom, demanding more academic freedom for the doctoral candidates, the supervisor, and the institution.

Giving academic freedom is another role of supervisors. However, supervisors do not have ownership of academic freedom to give it; but they have a level of authority over doctoral students that, in some cases, can deny students' rights to academic freedom. Academic freedom is a basic right of everyone. Hence, supervisors are required to enhance the freedom of doctoral students, where applicable, to identify the topic within the available research themes; participate in the selection of the supervisor while considering specialization and availability; choose cases and locations which are suitable to their conditions and abilities while maintaining the quality and added value of the research; and discuss and publish their opinions freely which is the core of academic freedom. Academic freedom is indivisible; it must be guaranteed equally to all academics at all levels without any exceptions.

Creating and enhancing the optimal conditions for academic freedom is an essential role of the supervisor. The supervisor needs to support the doctoral candidate by helping them find sustainable funding sources and securing accurate and reliable data sources. In addition, the supervisor needs to manage any possible risks that may affect the research or the student's safety by informing the doctoral student about any ethical, cultural and political risks they may face during research.

Finally, limitations to academic freedom within the research environment. The supervisor as project manager of the doctoral research has the responsibility of setting the frames that define the research boundaries such as time, budget and research domain. However, the supervisor also needs to clarify the ethical constraints, societal cultural limits, and the limits of freedom. This does not mean minimizing the student's freedom or compromising the research quality but keeping the student aware of all circumstances and thus ensuring that the student is free to make informed decisions.

9. Conclusion

Academic freedom is a pre-condition for academic integrity and research quality; it is the right to learn, teach, and express opinions free from external constraints. Academic freedom in modern universities was first expressed explicitly in Germany at the beginning of the 19th century and then in other regions in the world. However, in Africa, academic freedom started to receive attention after the end of colonialism.

Academic freedom is not absolute; it needs to be protected and enhanced while taking cognisance of the social, cultural, economic, and political values and practices of society. Academic freedom in doctoral research must be practised at different levels, beginning with the institution, then the supervisor and the student. It is an important factor to achieve reliable results.

Academic freedom in doctoral studies entails everything throughout the research journey starting from supervisor–student allocation, topic and domain selection, constraint-free funding, and most importantly, the freedom to express opinions and publish results. All of this must be practised by everyone at all levels without exception and with no external constraints other than the research constraints themselves. Noting that academic freedom given to academics by the state or the institution should not interfere with the freedom of individuals or society.

With the multicultural nature of doctoral research, academic freedom needs more attention when implemented in different contexts and places. This requires more effort from the supervisor, as the project manager, to facilitate academic freedom within prevailing limits and constraints.

The author is conducting further study based on an analysis of the AFI data in the African context using semi-structured interviews and questionnaires to acquire solid results related to the role of supervisors in enhancing the level of academic freedom.

References

Aarrevaara, T. (2010). Academic freedom in a changing academic world. *European Review, 18*(1), S55–S69. https://doi.org/10.1017/S1062798709990317

American Association of University Professors (AAUP). (n.d.). *1940 Statement of principles on academic freedom and tenure*. https://www.aaup.org/report/1940-statement-principles-academic-freedom-and-tenure

American Association of University Professors–Utica College (AAUP-UC). (2017, September 27). Wednesday wisdom: Albert Einstein on academic freedom. https://aauputicacollege.org/2017/09/27/wednesday-wisdom-albert-einstein-on-academic-freedom/

African Commission on Human and Peoples' Rights (ACHPR). (2005). *African charter on human and people's rights*. African Union.

Anderson, W. M. A. (1934). Academic freedom. *Australasian Journal of Psychology and Philosophy, 12*(2), 138–142. https://doi.org/10.1080/00048403408541034

Appiagyei-Atua, K., Beiter, K. D., & Karran, T. (2016). A review of academic freedom in African universities through the prism of the 1997 ILO/UNESCO recommendation. *AAUP Journal of Academic Freedom, 7*. https://www.aaup.org/sites/default/files/Appiagyei-Atua.pdf

Axelrod, P. (2018, January 24). Academic freedom: Can history be our guide? *University Affairs*. https://www.universityaffairs.ca/features/feature-article/academic-freedom-can-history-guide/

Axelrod, P. (2022). Academic freedom and its constraints: A complex history. *The Canadian Journal of Higher Education, 52*(1), 51–66. https://doi.org/10.47678/cjhe.vi0.189143

BBC News. (2018, November 26). Matthew Hedges: Who is the man at the centre of the spy row? https://www.bbc.com/news/uk-england-tyne-46318655

Cairo University. (2017). *CU History*. https://cu.edu.eg/History

Chicago Statement. 2014. "Report of the Committee on Freedom of Expression" at the University of Chicago. https://freeexpression.uchicago.edu/

Cloete, N., Mouton, J., & Sheppard, C. (2015). *Doctoral education in South Africa: Policy, discourse, and data*. African Minds.

Dea, S. (2018, October 9). A brief history of academic freedom. *University Affairs*. https://www.universityaffairs.ca/opinion/dispatches-academic-freedom/a-brief-history-of-academic-freedom/

Doğan, D. (2016). Academic freedom from the perspectives of academics and students: A qualitative study. *Education and Science, 41*(184), 311–331. https://doi.org/10.15390/EB.2016.6135

Downs, D. A. (2015). Just a job [Review of the book *Versions of academic freedom: From professionalism to revolution*, by Stanley Fish]. *Academic Questions, 28*(2), 244–249. https://www.nas.org/academic-questions/28/2/just_a_job

EDSLR. (2008, May 25). The Bologna Process in Africa: A case of aspiration, inspiration, or both? *Global Higher Ed WordPress.* https://globalhighered.wordpress.com/2008/05/25/the-bologna-process-a-case-of-aspiration-and-inspiration-in-africa/

Emerson, T. I., & Haber, D. (1963). Academic freedom of the faculty member as citizen. *Law and Contemporary Problems, 28,* 525–572. https://scholarship.law.duke.edu/cgi/viewcontent.cgi?article=2967&context=lcp

Finkin, M. W., & Post, R. C. (2009). *For the common good: Principles of American academic freedom.* Yale University Press.

Foundation for Individual Rights in Education (FIRE). 2021. https://www.thefire.org/about-us/mission

Fish, S. (2014). *Versions of academic freedom: From professionalism to revolution.* University of Chicago Press.

Grant, B., & Manathunga, C. (2011). Supervision and cultural difference: Rethinking institutional pedagogies. *Innovations in Education and Teaching International, 48*(4), 351–354. https://doi.org/10.1080/14703297.2011.617084

Grimm, J., & Saliba, I. (2017). Free research in fearful times: Conceptualizing an index to monitor academic freedom. *Interdisciplinary Political Studies, 3*(1), 41–75.

International Association of Universities and Catalan Association of Public Universities (IAU-ACUP). (2012). *IAU-ACUP International seminar on innovative approaches to doctoral education and research training in sub-Saharan Africa.* http://www.acup.cat/sites/default/files/final-report-iau-acup-seminar-innovative-approaches-doctoral-education_1.pdf

Kinzelbach, K., Saliba, I., Spannagel, J., & Quinn, R. (2021). *Free universities: Putting the academic freedom index into action.* The Global Public Policy Institute. https://www.gppi.net/med

Lee, A. (2008). How are doctoral students supervised? Concepts of doctoral research supervision. *Studies in Higher Education, 33*(3), 267–281. https://doi.org/10.1080/03075070802049202

Manathunga, C. (2014). *Intercultural postgraduate supervision: Reimagining time, place, and knowledge.* Routledge.

Martin, R., & Price, M. (2021). Co-constructed transnational learning in postgraduate research supervision: Exploring issues of power and trust. *African Perspectives of Research in Teaching & Learning, 5*(1), 158–165. https://research.stmarys.ac.uk/id/eprint/5289/

Neave, G. R. (1998). Autonomy, social responsibility, and academic freedom: Thematic debate. UNESCO. https://unesdoc.unesco.org/ark:/48223/pf0000113549

Noori, N. (2014). Does academic freedom globalize? The diffusion of the American model of education to the Middle East and academic freedom. *PS: Political Science & Politics, 47*(3), 608–611. https://doi.org/10.1017/S1049096514000717

Nybom, T. (2003). The Humboldt legacy: Reflections on the past, present, and future of the European university. *Higher Education Policy, 16*(2), 141–159. https://doi.org/10.1057/palgrave.hep.8300013

Pyhältö, K., Vekkaila, J., & Keskinen, J. (2015). Fit matters in the supervisory relationship: Doctoral students and supervisors' perceptions about the supervisory activities. *Innovations in Education and Teaching International, 52*(1), 4–16. https://doi.org/10.1080/14703297.2014.981836

Saliba, I. (2018, January 25). Academic freedom in the MENA region: Universities under siege. *Youth, Society, Media & Culture, IEMed Mediterranean Yearbook: Strategics Sectors-Culture & Society,* 313–316. https://www.iemed.org/wp-content/uploads/2021/01/Academic-Freedom-in-the-MENA-Region-Universities-under-Siege.pdf

Santosuosso, A., Sellaroli, V., & Fabio, E. (2007). What constitutional protection for freedom of scientific research? *Journal of Medical Ethics, 33*(6), 342–344. https://doi.org/10.1136/jme.2007.020594

Scholars at Risk. (2020, November 18). *Free to think 2020: Report of the Scholars at Risk academic freedom monitoring project.* Scholars at Risk Network, New York University. https://www.scholarsatrisk.org/resources/free-to-think-2020/

Sherman, M. A. B. (1990). The university in modern Africa: Toward the twenty-first century. *The Journal of Higher Education, 61*(4), 363–385. https://doi.org/10.2307/1982076

Smith, S. E. (2002). Who owns academic freedom? The standard for academic free speech at public universities. *Washington and Lee Law Review, 59*(1), 299–360. https://scholarlycommons.law.wlu.edu/wlulr/
vol59/iss1/9/

Spannagel, J., Kinzelbach, K., & Saliba, I. (2020). *The Academic Freedom Index and other new indicators relating
to academic space: An introduction.* Varieties of Democracy (V-Dem) Institute, Department of Political
Science University of Gothenburg. https://v-dem.net/media/publications/users_working_paper_26.pdf

Stone, G. R. (2015). A brief history of academic freedom. In A. Bilgrami & J. Cole (Eds.), *Who's afraid of academic freedom?* (pp. 1–9). Columbia University Press.

UNESCO, (1993). Records of the General Conference. Twenty-seventh Session. Paris, 25 October to 16
November 1993. https://unesdoc.unesco.org/ark:/48223/pf0000095621.locale=en

UNESCO. (2008). *The ILO/UNESCO recommendation concerning the status of teacher (1966) and the status of
higher-education teaching personnel (1997) with a user's guide.* UNESCO. http://unesdoc.unesco.org/imag-
es/0016/001604/160495e.pdf

UNESCO. (2017, October 18). Protecting academic freedom is as relevant as ever. *UNESCO.* https://www.
unesco.org/en/articles/protecting-academic-freedom-relevant-ever

United Nations. (n.d.). Regional groups of member states. https://www.un.org/dgacm/en/content/
regional-groups

University of Chicago. (2021). *A history of commitment to free expression.* https://freeexpression.uchicago.edu/
history/

Van't Land, H. (2011). *The changing nature of doctoral studies in sub-Saharan Africa: Challenges and policy development opportunities at six universities in sub-Saharan Africa.* International Association of Universities
(IAU). https://doi.org/10.13140/RG.2.1.3560.2407

Waghid, Y. (2006). Reclaiming freedom and friendship through postgraduate student supervision. *Teaching in
Higher Education, 11*(4), 427–439. https://doi.org/10.1080/13562510600874185

Walsh, D. (2017, August 15). Why was an Italian graduate student tortured and murdered in Egypt? *The New
York Times.* https://www.nytimes.com/2017/08/15/magazine/giulio-regeni-italian-graduate-stu-
dent-tortured-murdered-egypt.html

Wilson, J. K. (2016). AAUP's 1915 Declaration of Principles: Conservative and radical, visionary and myopic.
Journal of Academic Freedom, 7. https://www.aaup.org/sites/default/files/Wilson_1.pdf

CHAPTER 3

Overseas education and degree completion: Evidence from African PhD students

Samuel Mutarindwa

Rwanda is a country located in East Africa, with a population of 13.2 million. It has 3 public universities with a total enrollment of 53 110 students (Ministry of Education Statistics). Doctoral enrollments in Rwanda have increased from 2 in 2013/14 to 280 in 2022. Between 2013 and 2022, a total of 25 doctoral students graduated at Rwandan universities (University of Rwanda). Doctoral graduates increased from 9 in 2020 to 25 in 2022 (UR statistics).

The University of Rwanda (UR) became an independent university in 2013 through a merger of 7 former public higher learning institutions, namely National University of Rwanda, Kigali Institute of Science and Technology, Kigali Institute of Education, Higher Institute of Agriculture and Animal Husbandry, School of Finance and Banking, Kigali Health Institute, and Umutara Polytechnic. UR has 1 256 academic staff members working in six colleges, with a total student enrollment of 26 894, which makes it one of the largest public universities in Rwanda. In 2022, UR had 280 doctoral candidates enrolled and awarded 25 doctoral degrees (UR statistics, 2022).

---

1. Introduction

This chapter – a conceptual paper – discusses the factors that support or constrain PhD completion rates and time-to-degree. The aim of the chapter is to show the extent to which overseas doctoral education has contributed to doctoral completion of African doctoral students.

With the increasing role of knowledge in development, through their universities, many countries have embarked on doctoral education to develop research capacities, particularly doctoral training, in sufficient number and quality. Van Schalkwyk et al. (2021) note that doctoral education has grown in both developed and developing countries and they attribute this development to two main issues, namely the need for universities (called 'academy' in their paper) to reproduce and grow themselves and the importance of doctorates in the production and transfer of knowledge for socio-economic development.

One of the indicators of the performance/efficiency of doctoral programmes is completion (time-to-degree and completion rate) (Mouton, 2011). Abedi and Benkin (1987) maintain that the main indicator of the quality of doctoral education is the ratio of students admitted to the doctoral programme and students who complete the programme. They also noted that the time taken to complete the PhD is another important measure of doctoral education quality. Groenvyncket et al. (2013) suggest that lower completion rates, longer time to completion, and doctoral dropouts adversely affect the return on investment on PhD programmes. Spronken-Smith et al. (2018) mention that different stake-holders, particularly governments, have vested interest in doctoral completion times. Information of doctoral throughput is used to strengthen doctoral education policies.

Torka (2020) highlights various concerns about doctoral throughput. At the student level, longer/non- completion of doctoral degree may affect a student's self-esteem, may reduce their chances of employability and career progression. Longer completion time can also affect supervisory capacities in terms of over-load. At the institutional level, longer completion times affect institutional reputation (e.g. failure to attract good students and funding support). Longer completion is also considered resource wastage by funding agencies.

As part of higher education studies today, doctoral education completion has been examined in several studies, specifically on the African continent (Academy of Science of South Africa, 2010; Cloete et al., 2015), with a focus on completion rates and times for different universities and programmes. The literature on doctoral completion can be divided into two strands. One strand of the literature focuses on the determinants of doctoral completion and the second focuses on stocktaking doctoral completion. Studies focusing on the determinants of doctoral completion show that candidate characteristics, doctoral supervision, and institutional factors are the main determinants of doctoral completion.

Studies examining the effects of candidate characteristics on doctoral completion specifically mainly look at mental, psychological and social experiences of students (Sverdlik et al., 2018), over-commitment and delays (Kearns et al., 2008), nature of study (part-time versus full-time) and doctoral completion (Neumann & Rodwell, 2009), and whether employment and labour demands affect their completion times and attrition rates (Bekova, 2021).

Another strand of literature examines the effects of supervision on completion of doctoral studies. In a meta-analytical review, Bair and Haworth (2005) show that among other factors, supervisory support, particularly supervisory availability and positive relationship between supervisor and student, contribute to student satisfaction and, ultimately, timely doctoral completion. Van Rooij et al. (2019) recently assessed the effects of several supervisory factors (supervision, doctoral project features and psychological factors) that affect the success (progress, satisfaction, and quitting) of doctoral students in the Netherlands. Taking a sample of 839 doctoral students, they found that students' experiences of workload adversely affected their progress and led to dropout intentions. They also find that good supervisory relationships positively affect student success. Supervisory selection and expertise (Ives & Rowley, 2005) as well as supervisory support in the form of early detection of difficulties that students may be experiencing, and pedagogical approaches of supervisors (Manathunga, 2005) are also instrumental in increasing student progress and completion.

Some studies have zoned in on how institutional factors affect doctoral completion. Institutional factors such as the financial capacities of universities (Ehrenberg & Mavros, 1992); model of doctoral education (Maloshonok & Terentev, 2019); research codes of best practice (Humphrey et al., 2012); clarifying of deadlines in programme structures (Skopek et al., 2020); academic disciplines with STEM disciplines having higher doctoral completion times and rates (Abedi & Benkin, 1987; Groenvynck et al., 2013; Horta et al., 2018; Van Ours & Ridder, 2003; Wright & Cochrane, 2000) were found to be some of the main predictive variables on timely completion of doctoral studies in different countries.

Other studies combine student characteristics, supervision, and institutional factors (Seagram et al., 1998; Spronken-Smith et al., 2018; Van de Schoot et al., 2013) in explaining the rate and time of doctoral completion across different contexts. Kyvik and Olsen (2014) note from the literature that the training system of the doctorate, the doctoral programme itself, the research environment, doctoral candidate characteristics, cultural and social contexts, and differences between fields account for differences in completion rates of doctoral students. Pitchforth et al. (2012) studied the effect of supervisory support management of the research centres and programmes. A South African report on PhDs (ASSAf, 2010) shows that student characteristics (such as age at time of enrolment, family and other commitments, socialisation experiences), poor supervisor relationships and funding problems lead to higher attrition rates among doctoral students in South African universities.

What remains unaddressed in empirical literature on doctoral completion is the extent to which country of study contributes to time-to-degree and completion/attrition rates. Studies focusing on the completion rates of African students pursuing doctoral studies in foreign countries are limited, and the only available studies focus on foreign students pursuing their PhD studies in South Africa. Understanding this phenomenon for Africa is important for several reasons. Müller et al. (2018) highlight that local universities in developing countries lack the capacities to provide sufficient and quality PhD training. Torka (2020), citing prior international literature, shows that, compared to domestic PhD students, international students are likely to complete their PhDs in shorter times.

Except for South Africa, very few other African countries have doctoral programmes and doctoral completion on the continent is the lowest in the world. Reporting results from British Council and DAAD (2018), Darley (2021) shows that most African countries have lower completion rates although the average years to completion (for those who complete) is not different from those in developed countries. He shows that completion rates in Kenya are at 11% and 10.7% in Ethiopia. South African PhD completion rates vary from 25% at UNISA to 60% at UWC.

Mouton (2016) notes that only South Africa boasts the highest number of international doctoral students from Africa compared to other African countries. He attributes this to improvement in supervisory quality, funding, and programme quality.

Van Schalkwyk et al. (2021) report that 1 out 3 doctoral students enrolled at South African universities were from the rest of Africa by 2019 and that the number of doctoral students from the rest of Africa graduating at South African universities grew from 7% in 2000 to 39% in 2019. Friesenhahn (2014) highlights that with few universities offering doctoral education in Africa, most African students pursue their PhD education overseas in the developed countries of Europe, the US and most recently, Asia. Van de Laar et al. (2016) note that many sub-Saharan PhD students do not get the necessary financial support and face institutional challenges such as heavy workloads, balancing work and family and getting little institutional support from the universities to pursue their doctoral studies. Stackhouse and Harle (2014) add that given the size of funding support from universities in high income countries, bilateral agencies or other research organisations attract African students to overseas universities. For instance, the UK alone hosts about 50 to 70 doctoral students under the Commonwealth Scholarship and Fellowship Plan every year (ACU, 2024). Seventy-one per cent of them were from sub-Saharan African countries in 2014 (Stackhouse & Harle, 2014). Other African doctoral students attend universities in the US, Canada, and some other European countries.

However, there is scant evidence on the efficiency of studying in overseas countries for African students. This is an empirical gap worth pursuing for scholars. The only evidence on overseas education relates to motives for pursuing studies overseas. For example, Kim (2011) focuses on the overseas education of Korean students and argues that students attend US universities to boost their employability; improve English language communication, and to connect with the rest of the professional globe. Van de Laar et al. (2016) argue that the quality of degree and employability issues have pushed doctoral students to migrate internationally to reputable universities worldwide.

So far, no empirical research exists that attempts to establish the time-to-degree of overseas African doctoral students. The current study contributes to this rare literature by descriptively reviewing the literature on the effects of overseas education on doctoral completion (rates, time, and attrition) with specific focus on African students pursuing doctoral education in countries overseas. At the end of each section, some testable propositions are suggested. This study contributes to literature in two ways. First, it adds to the debate linking overseas education to doctoral completion. Second, it adds to the literature on internationalization by specifically focusing on African students pursuing doctoral studies in overseas countries.

This chapter proceeds as follows: section 2 reviews the state of doctoral education in Africa and overseas doctoral education. Section 3 discusses the literature on overseas doctoral education of African students and implications for doctoral completion. Section 4 concludes and provides avenues for future research.

2. Literature review

2.1 African doctoral education

Several studies have provided excellent statistical evidence on the state of doctoral education in Africa (Bunting et al., 2014; Cloete et al., 2015) and more specifically, on South African PhD education (Cloete & Mouton, 2015; Herman, 2017; Mouton, 2007, 2011, 2016). Thus, this section focuses on providing, descriptively and summarily, evidence on the state of doctoral education and completion and the challenges thereof.

Cloete, Baily and Pillay (2011, pp.4–7) provide a detailed historical account of tertiary education in Africa. They note that most universities on the continent were originally founded to produce graduates to serve the human resource demands of countries, especially in public service, following the departure of colonialists. In later years, universities were considered as engines of development; therefore, countries had to invest in these institutions for them to realise this mandate. Later years were associated with internal wars, conflicts in most African countries and shifts in the focus of governments from support to interference in university affairs. Universities suffered cuts in government funding which affected their capacities to serve as development enablers. The authors note that university education was considered a luxury around this time, coinciding with reports from the World Bank on the lower return on investment of tertiary education compared to that of primary and secondary education in Africa.

Over time, the World Bank advised African governments to focus on primary and secondary education to achieve their economic development goals. Bloom et al. (2006) note that, for many years, most African countries and donor agencies paid little attention to tertiary education.

The 1990s saw a shift in thinking on the role of tertiary education. Cloete et al. (2011) shows that Castells's (1994) work on the role of tertiary education in development led donor agencies, particularly the World Bank, to refocus on tertiary education in Africa.

Since then, African states, with the support of the World Bank, have affirmed their commitment to increasing PhD programmes and PhD production in Africa. Universities are tasked with producing PhDs for the knowledge economy to foster growth through innovation (Molla & Cuthbert, 2016). Many African countries have set up (or are currently setting up) universities to establish PhD programmes, with South African universities leading in the offer of PhD degrees in different academic disciplines (Scherer & Sooryamoorthy, 2022).

Cross and Backhouse (2014) show that many countries in Africa have embarked on PhD education to improve their higher education systems, whose goal is understood as providing knowledge useful in solving local problems that countries face. However, they note that the effective delivery of PhD programmes in African countries is still hindered by inadequate funding and supervisory quality.

A report on African flagship universities (Cloete et al, 2018:41) shows that, except for the University of Cape Town, University of Botswana, and University of Ghana, less than 50% of academics in other flagship universities in Africa have PhDs. In the 8 flagship universities profiled, the proportion of staff with doctoral PhDs hardly grew during the period 2001 to 2014. Only 43% of total academic staff possessed PhDs in 2011, compared to the 42% figure in 2007. A British Council and DAAD study (2018)[1] on the state of doctoral training in six African countries shows that staff with PhDs in Ethiopia were 8%; 31% in Ghana; 34% in Kenya, 43% in Nigeria, and 43% in South Africa.

Citing an earlier study (Szanton & Manyika, 2002), Molla and Cuthbert (2016) summarised problems and challenges that face doctoral education in Africa. They mention that the supportive intellectual environment, scholarly engagement of students, modes of doctoral education delivery can address the needs of novice doctoral students.

Individual country studies on the state of doctoral training in Africa reveal alarming results for doctoral training completion. For instance, Nega and Kassaye (2018) present findings for Ethiopian doctoral capacities in their British Council and DAAD report (2018). They show that, in all Ethiopian universities, there were 3 135 doctoral students enrolled from 2006-2015. Doctoral student graduates grew from 7 graduates in 2005-2006 to 335 in 2014-2015. Addis Ababa University, the largest university, contributed 66% of total graduates (221 graduates). Another British Council–DAAD report for Ghana (Alabi & Mohammed, 2017) shows that there were 963 doctoral students enrolled in Ghanaian universities in 2012-2013. However, doctoral graduates were as few as 65 in 2012-2015, with the University of Ghana (UG) contributing to the highest number of graduates (34), followed by Kwame Nkrumah University of Science and Technology (KNUST) with 7 graduates. Moreover, another British Council–DAAD report (Dimé, 2018) on research and PhD capacities in Senegal shows that of the 2 059 doctoral students enrolled at Senegalese universities in the same year, only 256 doctoral students graduated.

Among the countries covered by the report, South Africa showed promising figures for doctoral graduation. The report shows that in 2005, 1 188 doctoral students graduated from South African universities (traditional, comprehensive and universities of technology). In 2014, the report shows that there was a tremendous increase of doctoral graduation (2 258), which showed 90% growth from the 2005 figures.

Summarising evidence from the British Council & DAAD report (2018), Darley (2021) shows that it takes on average ten years for a doctoral student to complete in Senegal. Moreover, completion rates for doctoral students are 11%, with higher dropout rates of between 20 to 50%. Completion rates for

---

1 Cited in Darley (2021).

Ethiopian PhD students is 10.7%, with completion times of six years. South African universities have relatively higher completion rates, ranging from 25% (University of South Africa) to 60% (University of the Western Cape). In a report on doctoral training in African countries, Scherer and Sooryamoorthy (2022) show that African doctoral training is characterized by high and alarming dropout rates, prolonged time to completion, and low government funding.

In consideration of this statistical evidence, I propose that:

> Proposition 1: *Studies are needed to establish the number of African students pursuing PhD studies abroad and the extent to which studying abroad contributes to higher completion rates/time.*

2.2 Overseas PhD education

There are two strands of literature that examine why doctoral students enroll in foreign and/or overseas universities, and these have been categorised into push and pull factors. According to Kim (2011), push factors include the characteristics of the student, significant related factors such as family, students' home country characteristics such as academic factors, economic factors, and political factors that inhibit their academic aspirations. Pull factors include the quality of host countries' universities including their reputation, the financial support provided to students, migration policies of host countries, economic and political support, and nearness to students' home countries (Kim, 2011, p.111). Van de Laar et al. (2016) argue that the quality of the degree and employability issues have pulled doctoral students to migrate internationally to resource-rich universities worldwide. An earlier study by Altbach (1986) highlighted that with strong research and knowledge systems, western countries' universities have always acted as training centres for their own doctoral students as well as those from developing countries, whose universities are considered peripheral. While this trend has changed over time, many universities in the west still attract and train many doctoral students from developing countries.

Some empirical studies focusing specifically on Asian countries have analysed this trend of doctoral education. Jung (2018) in South Korea finds that doctoral students attending overseas universities were likely to get good academic jobs in research-intensive universities after completion of their PhDs. Shin et al. (2014) assessed the productivity of scholars who attained their degrees in foreign universities as compared to their counterparts who studied in South Korean universities and found that they were likely to be more research productive after their graduation in some disciplines but were less productive in arts and humanities unless they furthered their research training through postdocs.

Sehoole (2011) analysed the role of the state in attracting international doctoral students in South African universities and found that state support in granting study permits, host country recruitment of students, pushes more international students to apply to South African institutions of higher learning. Another strand of empirical literature focuses on the non-return of foreign higher degree students after their overseas studies. Using data of students from 69 source countries, Bratsberg (1995) assessed the factors that contribute to non-return of foreign students who attended US universities. Results from this study show that political and economic differences in source countries discourage graduating students from returning to their countries.

Several theoretical studies have posited that overseas studies improve the chances of students and graduates getting career opportunities in developed countries, and their likelihood of being hired quickly on return to their home countries. Focusing on trained academics specifically, Ackers (2008) noted that graduates educated in top universities in the UK and US acquire reputational capital which raises their chances of getting hired in top universities.

From these studies, I posit:

Proposition 2: *While studies show returns to PhD education abroad after graduation, tracer studies on the efficiency of such education in terms of faster completion would be very important empirical contributions to this strand of literature on overseas education.*

3. Discussion

3.1 African students and overseas PhD education

In the decades after independence, most African countries were occupied with primary and secondary enrolment as tertiary education was deemed a luxury by the World Bank (Cloete et al., 2011). Thus, with exception of South African and a few East African universities which offer doctoral education, African scholars who embark on their PhD studies have had to move to the west (Europe and North America) and some to Asian countries, since most African countries and universities thereof lack capacities to produce doctoral graduates at home.

Western countries, which originally dominated knowledge production, are still major players today in international knowledge production and dissemination.

Van de Laar et al. (2016) note that some of the doctoral students from sub-Saharan Africa have been able to get scholarships to study at universities of developed countries such as in US, Canada, Europe and in some Asian universities, where they get access to high quality education as these countries have well-established, world-class research universities

Providing extensive figures, Stackhouse and Harle (2014) note that a total of eleven European countries offer higher education support to international doctoral students, with the UK alone hosting about 50 to 70 doctoral students under the Commonwealth Scholarship and Fellowship Plan every year. According to the authors, the UK had 4 130 African students pursuing research degrees, 71% of whom were from sub–Saharan African countries. Van de Laar et al. (2016) also note that with little institutional and financial support, many students from sub-Saharan African countries find it convenient to pursue their doctoral education in the developed countries of North America, Europe and Asia that offer high quality education and offer institutional support to the student. Students can pursue their studies on a full-time basis, which often is not possible when they study in their home countries.

Nerad (2011) provides statistical evidence on the number of international doctoral students in European and US universities. German universities enrolled 3 556 international PhD students between the years 2003 and 2005; UK universities enrolled about 6 650 international doctoral students in those years, and in the same period, US universities enrolled the highest number of PhD students (about 14 424 doctoral students).

Some African universities, especially in South Africa, have also tried to increase doctoral production over time. Mouton (2016) notes that South African universities increased their PhD production because of national policies, labour market demand for doctorates, demand from international students from the rest of Africa, improvement in supervisory quality, and funding. With these factors, South Africa comes out on top as a destination for postgraduate training in Africa.

Cloete et al. (2015) show that of the total graduates in South African universities in 2012, about 27% (521) were from other African countries (14% SADC, and 13% from the rest of Africa). South Africa produced the highest number of graduates (1 249). Van Schalkwyk et al. (2021) show that 4 out of 10 doctoral students enrolled in South African universities were international students. This shows that the figures of doctoral students from the rest of Africa grew from 9% in 2000 to 34% in 2019. Scherer and Sooryamoorthy (2022) highlight that, compared to other parts of Africa, South Africa has a good and strong education system, strong framework for doctoral training and is considered world class. The government has put in place programmes and policies for strengthening doctoral training and research. This makes South Africa a doctoral training destination for the rest of African students after Europe and North America (particularly US).

3.2 Overseas education and doctoral completion

Comparative literature on doctoral completion globally remains a challenge particularly on international doctoral students. Although some statistical evidence exists on doctoral enrolment in European and US contexts, it is a big challenge to establish numbers of international doctoral student completion rates and times. Literature is limited as well on the comparisons among countries as far as doctoral completion is concerned. A few studies make such attempts as discussed below.

In an extensive review of completion rates of doctoral students, Cloete, and Mouton (2015) make an international comparison of doctoral completion rates in Norway, UK, Canada, US, and South Africa. Across countries, doctoral completion rates vary by disciplines and the model of study (full-time vs part-time). They show among other things that international students complete their PhDs faster than domestic ones specifically in the UK and US. Van de Laar et al. (2017) note that on average 20% of (full-time) doctoral students enrolled at universities in the developed world complete their degrees and argue that this might be different in contexts where students do not have access to quality libraries, internet and supervisors who are well trained in doctoral supervision. They also note that whereas about 2% of the population in developed countries graduated with a PhD, the figure lies between 0 and 0.5% of the population south of the Sahara. They also warn that the rate of failures will be higher if conditions deteriorate on the candidates' side as this situation has pushed many students to seek admission in overseas countries, subsequently creating brain drain in their home countries. In developing countries, evidence shows that although doctoral enrolment has gradually increased, graduation rates remain low.

Cloete et al. (2015) show that of those enrolled at South African universities, less than 20% graduate and elsewhere in Africa, funding problems, supervisory deficiency led to lower completion rates. Mouton (2011) argues that although South African doctoral completion rates compare almost with the developed world, there are differences in the age of completion. With insufficient funding, most students study part time (almost 70%) in South Africa and most graduate at 42 years on average compared to US, Canada and UK doctoral graduates who complete at 33.3 years on average.

Cloete et al. (2015) compare doctoral completion rates and times for Norway (2001/2002 cohort), Canada (2001 cohort), UK (1996/97 cohort), US (1992/93/94 cohort), and South Africa (2006 cohort). Figures show that it took 8 years for doctoral students in Norway to complete their PhDs, 9 years for those studying in Canada, 7 for the UK students, 10 years for US, and 7 years for those studying in south Africa. However, there are big differences with completion rates among those countries. Norway had the highest doctoral completion rate (76%); followed by Canada (71%), UK (69%), US (57%), and South Africa with relatively lowest rate (46%).

4. Conclusion and future studies

The focus of this chapter was on investigating the extent to which overseas PhD education contributes to faster completion rates and shorter times. Although research evidence remains scant on this aspect, a few studies indeed show that African PhD scholars pursuing doctoral education in overseas countries complete faster than African doctoral scholars pursuing their education in African universities. This study adds to the debate on two strands of the literature. The first contribution is on establishing the literature linking overseas education to doctoral completion. The second contribution is on internationalization by specifically focusing on African students pursuing doctoral studies in overseas countries.

This study recommends that African universities and countries borrow experience from research universities in the North to strengthen their doctoral programmes to help doctoral students complete on time. Notably, among other issues, this would include substantial investment in PhD funding for students to enroll full time as most African students enroll on a part-time basis. Second, more training on doctoral supervision would help students acquire quality mentorship from their supervisors. The Centre for Evaluation on Research, Science and Technology (CREST) of Stellenbosch University has pioneered PhD supervisor training in Africa. Other universities from the African continent should borrow insights from CREST on such training. If this is not possible, they should encourage their staff to attend this kind of training at CREST.

Whereas attempts have been made to estimate and establish statistical evidence on doctoral completion and rates and times across different contexts, international comparative studies on doctoral completion remain very scarce.

Future studies could help provide international comparisons of doctoral completion, times, rates, as well as attrition rates.

References

Abedi, J., & Benkin, E. (1987). The effects of students' academic, financial, and demographic variables on time to the doctorate. *Research in Higher Education, 27,* 3–14.

Academy of Science of South Africa (ASSAf). (2010). *The PhD Study: An evidence-based study on how to meet the demands for high-level skills in an emerging economy.* ASSAf.

Ackers, L. (2008) Internationalisation, Mobility and Metrics: A New Form of Indirect Discrimination? *Minerva* 46, 411–435. https://doi.org/10.1007/s11024-008-9110-2

Alabi, G., & Mohammed, I. (2018). *Research and PhD capacities in sub-Saharan Africa: Ghana report.* British Council and DAAD.

Altbach, P. G. (1986). The foreign student dilemma. *Teachers College Record, 87*(4), 589–610.

Association of Commonwealth University. 2014. The Commonwealth Scholarship and Fellowship Plan (CSFP). https://www.acu.ac.uk/our-work/international-mobility/csfp/

Bair, C. R., & Haworth, J. G. (2005). Doctoral student attrition and persistence: A meta-synthesis of research. In J. C. Smart (Ed.). *Higher education: Handbook of theory and research* (pp. 481–534). Kluwer Academic Publishers.

Bekova, S. (2021). Does employment during doctoral training reduce the PhD completion rate? *Studies in Higher Education, 46*(6), 1068–1080.

Bloom, D. E., Canning, D., & Chan, K. (2006). *Higher education and economic development in Africa* (Vol. 102). World Bank.

Bratsberg, B. (1995). The incidence of non-return among foreign students in the United States. *Economics of Education Review, 14*(4), 373–384.

Castells, M. (1994). The university system: Engine of development in the new world economy. In J. Salmi & M. A. Verspoor (Eds.), *Revitalizing higher education: Issues in higher education* (pp. 14–40). Oxford, Pergamon)

Cloete, N., & Mouton, J. (2015). *Doctoral education in South Africa.* African Minds.

Cloete, N., Bailey, T., & Pillay, P. (2011). *Universities and economic development in Africa.* African Minds.

Cloete, N., Bunting, I. & Van Schalkwyk, F. 2018. *Research Universities in Africa.* African Minds.

Cloete, N., Maassen, P., & Bailey, T. (2015). *Knowledge production and contradictory functions in African higher education* (p. 310). African Minds.

Cloete, N., Mouton, J. M., & Sheppard, C. (2015). *The doctorate in South Africa: Discourse, data and policies.* African Minds.

Cross, M., & Backhouse, J. (2014). Evaluating doctoral programmes in Africa: Context and practices. *Higher Education Policy, 27,* 155–174.

Darley, W. K. (2021). Doctoral education in business and management in Africa: Challenges and imperatives in policies and strategies. *The International Journal of Management Education, 19*(2), 100504.

Dimé, M. (2018). *Research and PhD capacities in sub-Saharan Africa: Senegal report.* British Council and DAAD.

Ehrenberg, R. G., & Mavros, P. G. (1995). Do doctoral students' financial support patterns affect their times-to-degree and completion probabilities? *Journal of Human Resources, 30*(3), 581–609.

Friesenhahn, I. (2014, June 18). Making higher education work for Africa: Facts and figures. *SciDev.Net.* https://www.scidev.net/global/features/higher-education-africa-facts-figures/

Groenvynck, H., Vandevelde, K., & Van Rossem, R. (2013). The PhD track: Who succeeds, who drops out? *Research Evaluation, 22*(4), 199–209.

Herman, C. (2017). Looking back at doctoral education in South Africa. *Studies in Higher Education* 42(8), 1437-1454.

Horta, H., Cattaneo, M., & Meoli, M. (2018). PhD funding as a determinant of PhD and career research performance. *Studies in Higher Education, 43*(3), 542–570.

Humphrey, R., Marshall, N., & Leonardo, L. (2012). The impact of research training and research codes of practice on submission of doctoral degrees: An exploratory cohort study. *Higher Education Quarterly, 66*(1), 47–64.

Ives, G., & Rowley, G. (2005). Supervisor selection or allocation and continuity of supervision: PhD students' progress and outcomes. *Studies in Higher Education, 30*(5), 535–555.

Jung, J. (2018). Domestic and overseas doctorates and their academic entry-level jobs in South Korea. *Asian Education and Development Studies, 7*(2), 205–222.

Kearns, H., Gardiner, M., & Marshall, K. (2008). Innovation in PhD completion: The hardy shall succeed (and be happy!). *Higher Education Research & Development, 27*(1), 77–89.

Kim, J. (2011). Aspiration for global cultural capital in the stratified realm of global higher education: Why do Korean students go to US graduate schools? *British Journal of Sociology of Education, 32*(1), 109–126.

Kyvik, S., & Olsen, T. B. (2014). Increasing completion rates in Norwegian doctoral training: Multiple causes for efficiency improvements. *Studies in Higher Education, 39*(9), 1668–1682.

Maloshonok, N., & Terentev, E. (2019). National barriers to the completion of doctoral programs at Russian universities. *Higher Education, 77,* 195–211.

Manathunga, C. (2005). Early warning signs in postgraduate research education: A different approach to ensuring timely completions. *Teaching in Higher Education, 10*(2), 219–233.

Molla, T., & Cuthbert, D. (2016). In pursuit of the African PhD: A critical survey of emergent policy issues in select sub-Saharan African nations, Ethiopia, Ghana and South Africa. *Policy Futures in Education, 14*(6), 635–654.

Mouton, J. (2007). Post-graduate studies in South Africa: Myths, misconceptions and challenges. *South African Journal of Higher Education, 21*(8), 1078–1090.

Mouton, J. (2011). Doctoral production in South Africa: Statistics, challenges and responses. *Perspectives in Education, 29*(3), 13–29.

Mouton, J. (2016). The doctorate in South Africa: Trends, challenges and constraints. In M. Fourie-Malherbe, R. Albertyn, C. Aitchison & E. Bitzer (Eds.), *Postgraduate supervision: Future foci for the knowledge society* (pp.51–82). SUN PRESS.

Müller, M., Cowan, R & Barnard, H. (2018). On the value of foreign PhDs in the developing world: Training versus selection effects in the case of South Africa, *Research Policy, 47*(5), 886-900

Nega, M., & Kassaye, M. (2018). *Research and PhD capacities in Sub-Saharan Africa: Ethiopia report.* British Council and DAAD.

Nerad, M. (2011). What we know about the dramatic increase in PhD degrees and the reform of doctoral education worldwide: Implications for South Africa. *Perspectives in Education, 29*(1), 1–12.

Neumann, R., & Rodwell, J. (2009). The 'invisible' part-time research students: A case study of satisfaction and completion. *Studies in Higher Education, 34*(1), 55–68.

Pitchforth, J., Beames, S., Thomas, A., Falk, M., Farr, A., Gasson, S., Thamrin, T. & Mengersen, K. (2012) Factors affecting timely completion of a PhD: a complex systems approach. *Journal of the Scholarship of Teaching and Learning, 12*(4), 124-135.

Scherer, C., & Sooryamoorthy, R. (Eds.). (2022). *Doctoral training and higher education in Africa.* Routledge.

Seagram, B. C., Gould, J., & Pyke, S. W. (1998). An investigation of gender and other variables on time to completion of doctoral degrees. *Research in Higher Education, 39*(3), 319–335.

Sehoole, C. T. (2011). Student mobility and doctoral education in South Africa. *Perspectives in Education, 29*(3), 53–63.

Shin, J. C., Jung, J., Postiglione, G. A., & Azman, N. (2014). Research productivity of returnees from study abroad in Korea, Hong Kong, and Malaysia. *Minerva, 52,* 467–487.

Skopek, J., Triventi, M., & Blossfeld, H. P. (2022). How do institutional factors shape PhD completion rates? An analysis of long-term changes in a European doctoral program. *Studies in Higher Education, 47*(2), 318–337.

Spronken-Smith, R., Cameron, C., & Quigg, R. (2018). Factors contributing to high PhD completion rates: A case study in a research-intensive university in New Zealand. *Assessment & Evaluation in Higher Education, 43*(1), 94–109.

Stackhouse, J., & Harle, J. (2014). The experiences and needs of African doctoral students: Current conditions and future support. *Higher Education Policy, 27*, 175–194.

Sverdlik, A., Hall, N. C., McAlpine, L., & Hubbard, K. (2018). The PhD experience: A review of the factors influencing doctoral students' completion, achievement, and well-being. *International Journal of Doctoral Studies, 13*, 361–388.

Szanton DL & Manyika S 2002. "PhD programs in African universities: Current status and future prospects". The Institute of International Studies and Center for African Studies, University of California, Berkeley.

Torka, M. (2020). Change and continuity in Australian doctoral education: PhD completion rates and times (2005-2018). *The Australian Universities' Review, 62*(2), 69–82.

Van de Laar, M., Achrekar, S., Larbi, L., & Rühmann, F. (2016, June). Capacity building using PhD education in Africa. In *EdMedia + Innovate Learning* (pp. 512–528). Association for the Advancement of Computing in Education (AACE).

Van de Laar, M., Achrekar, S., & Rehm, M. (2017). 'Community of Learning' for African PhD students: Changing the scene of doctoral education? *Transformation in Higher Education, 2*(1), 1–9.

Van de Schoot, R., Yerkes, M. A., Mouw, J. M., & Sonneveld, H. (2013). What took them so long? Explaining PhD delays among doctoral candidates. *PLOS ONE, 8*(7), e68839.

Van Schalkwyk, F. B., Lill, M. H. V., & Cloete, N. (2021). Brain circuity: The case of South Africa as a hub for doctoral education. *South African Journal of Science, 117*(9-10), 1–9.

Van Ours, J. C., & Ridder, G. (2003). Fast track or failure: A study of the graduation and dropout rates of PhD students in economics. *Economics of Education Review, 22*(2), 157–166.

Van Rooij, E., Fokkens-Bruinsma, M., & Jansen, E. (2021). Factors that influence PhD candidates' success: The importance of PhD project characteristics. *Studies in Continuing Education, 43*(1), 48–67.

Wright, T., & Cochrane, R. (2000). Factors influencing successful submission of PhD theses. *Studies in Higher Education, 25*(2), 181–195.

CHAPTER 4

The feasibility of contextualizing Salzburg I and II Principles for improving Nigeria's doctoral education

Bernard Ugochukwu Nwosu

Nigeria is a West African country with an estimated population of about 200 million. It has 221 universities. Fifty (50) of the universities belong to the federal government, sixty (60) are owned by state governments, while one hundred and eleven (111) are private universities.

The **University of Nigeria, Nsukka** was established in 1960, making it the first indigenous university in Nigeria. At the time of its establishment, the University at Ibadan, Nigeria, was still a university college affiliated to the University of London. The faculty size of its combined campuses at Enugu and Nsukka is 3 130 with an undergraduate population of 46 401 and 7 320 postgraduate students (University of Nigeria, 2023). In 2018, the university awarded 480 doctoral degrees, the highest number of all Nigerian universities in that year.

1. Introduction

University education and research are considered an important part of development all over the world. Indeed, in high-income countries in Europe and North America, there is a general trend towards the knowledge economy hence, a significant emphasis is placed on research. Accordingly, a high premium is attached to high-level research which includes doctoral research in universities. Most countries regard their universities as centres where solutions can be devised to address development challenges through research and innovations (see Cyranoski et al, 2011). In fact, countries that spend a lot on research and development also rank among the top producers of PhDs in the world. Statistica (2018) reports that the top ten spenders on research and development in the world include the United States, China, Japan, Germany, South Korea, India, France, Russia, United Kingdom and Brazil. According to Cyranoski et al. (2011) the highest producers of PhDs in the world are China (which supplies 40% of the world's PhDs), India (8.5%), Korea (7.1%), Japan (6.2%), the United Kingdom (5.2%), and the United States of America (2.5%). It is therefore tempting to imagine a positive correlation between policy focus on research and development trends in doctoral education. However, Muller (2012) maintains that "there is no evidence to suggest a causal link between the number of doctorates and economic growth". Muller's observation notwithstanding, investment in R&D remains crucial for development and it is not easy to delink the contribution of investment to doctoral training to this outcome.

Doctoral research is given attention in national science and technology policies for several reasons. Essentially, policymakers hold that cutting edge findings in various fields emanate from the research efforts of doctoral researchers. Also, new leadership in scientific innovation draws from the content and quality of work done in the doctoral research environment. This crucial role of doctoral research defines its importance and relevance to the building of the knowledge economy, accumulation of expertise and advancement of science and technology. Accordingly, doctoral education circles are important knowledge hubs that governments nurture for growing the economy and other aspects of the society (see Cloete, 2015). It is the above idea and the desire to enhance research excellence that underpinned the gathering in Bologna on "doctoral programmes for the European knowledge society" held from 3 to 5 February 2005 and attended by European ministers of education (European University Association [EUA], 2005a). The seminar expressed awareness of the importance of the university as one of the pillars of a knowledge-based society. More specifically, it emphasised the necessity of going beyond the focus on higher education at the time to include doctoral level training as a third cycle, whereas the bachelors and master's degrees are the first and second cycles (EUA, 2005a).

Based on the conversations of the European ministers of education during the Bologna seminar, a consensus emerged on a set of ten basic principles upon which doctoral training in European universities could be grounded and these included

i)   The core component of doctoral training is the advancement of knowledge through original research.

ii) Embedding strategies and policies by universities to support them carry out doctoral training that meets new challenges and includes appropriate professional career building opportunities

iii) Emphasis on diversity that includes joint doctorates undergirded by sound practice

iv) Recognition of doctoral candidates as early-stage researchers who make key contributions to the creation of new knowledge, with corresponding rights.

v) Emphasis on the crucial role of supervision and assessment.

vi) Achievement of critical mass in doctoral production with the use of different innovative practices and openness to relevant diverse approaches that are useful for different contexts.

vii) Emphasis on the time limit of doctoral programmes which is recommended for a period of three to four years on full-time studies.

viii) Promotion of innovative structures to meet the challenge of interdisciplinary training.

ix) Increasing mobility of doctoral programmes in terms of geographical, interdisciplinary and international collaboration.

x) Ensuring appropriate funding for the development of quality doctoral programmes. (see Salzburg I, 2005)

The Salzburg I principles were enhanced by the Salzburg II principles which resulted in the *Seven Principles for Innovative Doctoral Training* (EUA). These seven principles address the following components of doctoral education: research excellence, an attractive institutional environment, interdisciplinary research options, exposure to industry and other relevant employment sectors, international networking, transferable skills and training, and quality assurance (EUA, 2005b). These principles have been domesticated to a good extent in many European countries such as the Netherlands (EUA-CDE, 2010), Spain (Muerza & Larrode, 2018) and France (Talby, n.d.) among others. It is worth noting that conditions for the advancement of doctoral education are not limited to Europe in spite of my focus on the European Salzburg principles. There are different nomenclatures and doctoral studies enhancement plans in other parts of the world. Japan for instance has what they refer to as Leading Programmes in doctoral education. The main goal of the programme is to foster PhDs with deep specialization and peer leadership who can compete well globally (Okamoto & Matsuzaka, 2015). The United Kingdom has a distinct organisation concerned with the promotion of high-quality graduate education. Indeed, between 2004 and 2009, a significant change in

UK graduate education was driven by international and national regulation and codification of what quality in doctoral education is (McGloin & Wynne, 2015). Australia has a Research Training Scheme (RTS) specifically for supporting research training for research master's and doctoral students. Among the major objectives of the RTS, it enhances the research training provision and ensures the relevance of research degrees to employment needs (McGloin & Wynne, 2015). However, the progress and quality of doctoral training in Europe draws majorly from the underpinning Salzburg principles and according to Salzburg II Recommendations (2010), doctoral education in Europe has been extremely impressive.

In Africa, however, the quantity and quality of doctoral graduates do not compare with those trained in high-income countries in Europe, America and Asia, essentially due to differences in the degree of internalization of the underpinning Salzburg principles or similar policies and other contingent factors. I am convinced that the Salzburg principles can be contextualized and adapted to speak to the realities, challenges and opportunities of doctoral education in African countries. Simply put, doctoral education in Africa could benefit greatly from the implementation of the Salzburg Principles or a set of principles, contextualized for the continent and its goals and needs, inspired by the Salzburg principles. In this chapter, I will illustrate how that could possibly be done using the University of Nigeria, Nsukka, as a case, whose existing practice could draw useful insight from the Salzburg Principles.

Subsequent sections of the chapter will include a comparative review of national experiences of doctoral education in relation to how the Salzburg I and II principles have impacted doctoral education in different countries. This is followed by a presentation of the Nigerian experience of doctoral education, especially the challenges. I further contextualize the work on the empirical case of the University of Nigeria, Nsukka, by examining the university's practices vis-à-vis the ten Salzburg Principles. Finally, I conclude the chapter by synthesizing the narratives.

2. Enhancing doctoral education with reference to the Salzburg I and II Principles: A review of national experiences

Salzburg I and II Principles are of European origin. It was founded on a process that began in Bologna in 1999 and was initially primarily concerned with the first two cycles, bachelor's and master's. But the Salzburg seminar of European ministers of education took place between 3 to 5 February 2005 and was concerned with the third cycle (doctorate). Thus, the historical transition from

Bologna to Salzburg goes back to the 1999 Bologna meeting whose chain of succeeding events, including Salzburg I and II, are referred to as the Bologna process. Overall, the Bologna process is a basis for the doctoral education reforms (see Witte, 2006).

I look at some national context in Europe vis a vis how they have been fairing in doctoral education in the light of the Bologna process. Thus, I consider the UK, selected European countries like the Netherlands, France and Denmark. I also broaden the review to look at the changing environment of doctoral education in non-European countries like Colombia, a few Asian and then Africa formations. The non-European nations provide context for comparative consideration with European states for which the Bologna process was designed.

According to Matas (2012), the UK was one of the countries to heed the call from the Bologna process that gave birth to the principles which made the UK commence training in transferable and generic skills for doctoral and postdoctoral researchers. This was aimed at improving employability through research excellence. The main policy report that created the conditions for the adoption and implementation of the Salzburg Principles in the UK was Roberts' report (2002). Roberts' report demonstrated an understanding of the importance of funding for the promotion of research excellence through transferable skills and prompted government support for doctoral research reforms with the sum of GBP 120 million (Research Councils UK, 2010). An eight-year impact evaluation of the response to Roberts' report carried out in 2010 by an independent review panel commissioned by Research Councils UK found impressive results not only in terms of the competitiveness of young researchers, but also in making British higher education more attractive to international students (Research Councils UK, 2010).

Similarly, the Netherlands, and France have effected reforms that focus doctoral skills development through emphasis on transferable skills (Matas, 2012). Talby (n.d.) attests in the case of France that doctoral education has evolved during the two decades until 2018 since adoption of the Salzburg Principles and recommendations for innovative doctoral training. The general point of widening the scope of doctoral training in these countries is the need to make the training and skills of PhD graduates relevant beyond the classroom and more useful to the wider research and development needs of industries and the market. In the cases of the UK and France, it is easy to observe a clear policy commitment to the growth of doctoral training. Not only does the state assume a central role in supporting knowledge production, but it is also an active part of international processes to set up benchmarks of excellence in that regard. These countries have been quick to contextualize and apply international policies that support knowledge production which is central to the transformation of their societies and maintenance of their economic progress.

In the experience of Spain, in evaluating Spanish PhD adaptation to the Bologna process, Muerza and Larrode (2018) discuss the contextual factors in the implementation mechanisms for quality assurance of their doctorates in mechanical engineering and identified five factors, namely: (1) the creation of doctoral schools, (2) competences (3), tutoring and supervision, (4) collaboration and internationalization, (5) doctoral programmes and (6) duration of studies. According to this study, specialized doctoral schools in Spain had risen from the first one created in 2006 to a phenomenal 42 in 2015. The reason for this was perhaps to eliminate the distractions of simultaneously managing first and second cycle education with the third cycle which is the PhD. Competences range from knowledge and technical skills of the doctoral candidates' academic training to their personal maturity. Tutoring and supervision focus on the progress of the students towards the completion of their studies. The authors highlighted the social setting, the personalities, relationships between the supervisor and student and the supervisor's expertise as important elements that condition the progress of doctoral education. Regarding internationalization, Spain is said to promote the mobility of students and teaching internationalization. Muerza and Larrode (2018) provide more details in this regard by arguing that international mobility experiences allow interchange of theoretical methods and techniques within a subject of study and give thrust to the growth of knowledge without borders. More specific measures include openness to students from other countries, promotion of short research visits to foreign universities, incorporation of teachers and foreign PhD candidates and engagement with thesis of the international student. According to Muerza and Larrode (2018), such engagement with the thesis implies

- a research visit of at least three months to other research centres and or foreign universities;
- presenting and defending part of the doctoral dissertation, featuring a summary and conclusion in English at the very least; and
- to have two reports from international PhD experts who may not be part of the thesis assessment board. This implies that the subject of the research covers aspects with international relevance (Muerza & Larrode, 2018).

There are seven criteria for the evaluation of research and development of plans for research project of international students:

i)   The proposal must establish the main novel aspects of the research to be developed and the primary expected result with a well-written and detailed structure,

ii) gather basic up-to-date references on which the research is going to be based,

iii) provide a relevant methodology with technical scientific details,

iv) establish a work plan for the entire research period which shows the phases of research development,

v)   demonstrate the possibility of establishing connections with other studies or research carried out in other institutions related to the current research,

vi) present a programme of planned publications on the expected results in high impact journals,

vii) establish the scope of the research and the technological scientific means required to perform it. (Muerza & Larrode, 2018)

Doctoral programme and duration relate to the content of the PhD training and the length of time by which they are expected to be completed. The doctoral programme refers to the scientific, general and professional contents of the training while the duration is managed by a regulation which requires a three-year completion period for a PhD programme with full-time dedication and five-year completion period for a part-time PhD. Based on the above factors, the authors reported a steady increase of doctoral student enrolments from the 2009/2010 school year to 2014/2015 especially in the field of engineering which was studied by Muerza and Larrode (2018). They ascribed this change to transformations in doctoral regulations in Spain which draws from efforts to adapt to the Salzburg Principles. The Spanish case study here draws attention to an institutional embedding of the elements of the Salzburg Principles. In fact, the five drivers of progress they discussed while evaluating the Spanish PhD adaptation to the Bologna process bear the essence of the Salzburg Principles. The authors equally appeared to take government support for doctoral education for granted. But it is doubtful that the five drivers of progress could have been possible without conscious state support in funding or facilitation of the same or without institutional support for doctoral candidates. Again, it remains to be seen whether equal attention is accorded to the science, technology, engineering and mathematics disciplines on the one hand and the arts and humanities disciplines on the other hand.

In a broader comparative study of six countries, including Canada, Colombia, Denmark, Finland, the UK and the USA, Andres et al. (2015)[1] considered three major factors which include massification, professionalization and the introduction of quality assurance in doctoral studies. Their work reveals a striking significance of the impact of the Salzburg Principles for the European countries in the study. Note that the emphasis of the discourse here is Salzburg which was made for European countries. The rationale is to extend the analysis to non-European contexts to identify comparable policies that may have emerged due to Salzburg. In Denmark, Finland and the UK, the Salzburg Principles are important in considerations of massification, professionalization and quality assurance. In terms of massification, the six countries that were studied experienced a major rise in the number of PhD graduates produced. Increasing the number of PhD graduates is one of the emphases of the Salzburg Principles. In the area of professionalization, countries in the European Higher Education Area – in the case of this study Denmark, Finland and UK – shared very important characteristics in terms of emphasising generic skills and interdisciplinarity, harmonization of PhDs based on European standards and the growth in the number of graduate schools.

Despite these shared characteristics, there are still national differences which condition the thrust of each country's policies around doctoral education. Important to note is how these European countries tend more towards internationalization of quality assurance along the lines of the European Higher Education Area.

A few issues stand out in the discussions above. First, the studies are centred around high-income countries, except Colombia which is an upper middle-income country. Second, the contextual differences in the six countries compared in the study of Andres et al. (2015) are still important determinants of their rates of progress in doctoral education. There is a move towards quality standardisation in Western Europe, although this does not imply an inferior status to other countries studied. However, Andres et al. (2015) noted that Canada needs more effort to achieve the goal of massification of doctorates to meet the needs of the knowledge economy.

Placing the progress of Western Europe in the broader European context, the story of the transition countries of Eastern and Central Europe, according to Kwiek (2004), indicates gaps in the capacity to match the progress of Western Europe. Further, Kwiek (2004, p. 759) holds that higher education in Central and Eastern Europe has been "in a state of permanent crisis since the fall of communism." Besides, there are contextual factors mostly grounded in

---

1 The UK was still a part of the European Union when this study was conducted.

funding which limit the implementation of the Salzburg Principles to legislation that is difficult to implement at institutional levels. In effect, the operative conditions, including the political economy of the transitional states of Central and Eastern Europe both in terms of educational funding and institutional processes, are insufficient for the actualization of the Salzburg Principles (see Kwiek, 2004).

Deem et al. (2008) maintains that the popularity of the Salzburg Principles in Western Europe and their impact on doctoral education in the region provides impetus for other parts of the world to cluster towards the principles and therefore organise their university systems around the essence of the process. Deem et al. (2008) argue that developments that emanated through the Bologna process are framing the direction of several universities in Asia. Centrally, the quest by universities to attain 'world-class' status, which is another way of referring to teaching and learning along the Salzburg Principles, has spread across Asian universities. The writers noted that universities in Hong Kong, China, Japan, Malaysia and Taiwan and other universities in East Asia are increasingly under pressure to compete internationally and are eager to achieve high rankings in the global universities league which are rated mostly on parameters that could be grounded on European standards.

Looking at the group of countries that rank quite high in PhD production in Asia, one observes how they tend to be high spenders on research and development in addition to funding of universities. Melin and Janson (2006) highlight how countries like South Korea, Taiwan, Singapore, China and others, that used to be small players in the production of doctorates, are growing. Looking at some of the transformations in some of these Asian countries, it is quite tempting to infer that even though their framework of progress may be differently labelled, they are, in essence, implementing the Salzburg Principles.

Bringing the implementation of quality assurance mechanisms in doctoral education closer to Africa, Charlier and Croche (2009) argued on a critical note that one of the tacit objectives

of the Bologna process which supports doctoral studies with Salzburg I and II, was to increase the flow of (good) non-European students into Europe and that while Africa was not the core target of this policy, the relationship between the continent's universities and those of their former colonizing powers made for easy transfer of the best African students to European universities. Continuing, they noted that African concerns were not considered in the Bologna process, hence reforms in African universities can only mimic the forms constructed in Europe. Such mimicry even lacks a guarantee of success because higher education systems in Africa are mostly in crises rooted in resource gaps and fast-growing student populations.

African conditions for doctoral education differ from their European counterparts. To sum it up, Charlier and Croche maintain that Africa's universities are hindered by many social, economic and political constraints in their environments. Consequently, African universities are not globally competitive. In the university rankings South Africa has most of the globally competitive universities in the continent, with the University of Cape Town as the best. Besides, among African universities, South Africa has for many years continued to produce more than half of the best and this includes the contemporary global rankings (see Times Higher Education [THE], 2019). This would suggest that South Africa harbours a more research-friendly environment than other states on the continent. Perhaps this is attested to by the fact that Africa's 1% contribution to global knowledge capital drops by a third if South African quota is eliminated (Teferra, 2014). Based on these figures, Teffera (2015) noted quite correctly that South Africa is the largest knowledge producer in the continent.

The country arguably has the most attractive funding for doctoral education on the continent. This again takes us to the importance of political will of national governments to grow knowledge for the purpose of development.

In a study of the Southern African region, Bitzer (2016) applied Trafford and Leshem's (2009) categorisation of the factors that influence provision of doctoral education which include contextual factors, administrative factors and academic factors. The contextual factors include international, national and market demands/influences on quality, the functions of doctoral education, career projections, employment opportunities, supervisors and students. The administrative factors refer to the framework in which the degree is constructed, offered and undertaken in addition to all the factors that apply in every stage of the study. Academic factors refer to the scholarly/research considerations that culminate in the quality of the doctorates that are awarded. Considering these factors, he concludes that institutional research (IR) in Southern Africa is still a long way from reaching maturity due to limited emphasis on IR on doctoral education, issues of availability of data from research as a basis of further action, gaps in tracking of candidates and information systems for comparative work with other higher institutions.

Bitzer's conceptual framework is interesting in its own right, but its explanatory power for the applicability of the Salzburg Principles in Africa is limited because, when the ten principles of Salzburg I are considered, it becomes difficult to draw a line between some academic, administrative and contextual factors. Some of the principles crisscross academic, administrative and contextual factors. For instance, the third principle[2] is both contextual and academic because it involves a synergy of universities, educational policies of governments and other contexts of practice that would support joint doctorates.

Also, the fourth principle[3] about the recognition of PhD candidates as early-stage researchers is one in which administrative factors play a major role. But besides that, it is equally contextual. At the University of Waikato, New Zealand, for instance, one of the important administrative considerations for the admission of a doctoral researcher is the availability of working space to assign to the candidate, with a functioning computer, telephone access, allocation of a sum of money for printing and photocopying, specific funding for the attendance of a maximum two university-funded conferences and the sharing of some facilities with university faculty.[4] So it becomes difficult to locate this principle in only one of the categories of Bitzer's (and Teferra's) framework. Equally, the fifth Salzburg Principle[5] is both academic and contextual. In some national experiences, international assessment is invited, while it is not in others. This cross-cutting character applies to a couple of other Salzburg Principles in terms of their location in the framework.

Research by Cross and Backhouse (2014) outlined a framework for the evaluation of doctoral education in Africa. The elements considered in this framework include the candidates' context, the curriculum of the training, institutional structure for the doctoral training, resources and funding and finally partnership opportunities which all together lead to the expected outcomes. The authors considered the expected outcomes with a view to the rationale for the PhD, namely whether it is for the training of a scholar or for knowledge production. However, in light of the Bologna process, it should be both because knowledge production in the process anticipates relevance for both academia

2 "The importance of diversity: the rich diversity of doctoral programmes in Europe – including joint doctorates – is a strength which has to be underpinned by quality and sound practice" (Salzburg 1, 2005, Principle 3).

3 "Doctoral candidates as early stage researchers: should be recognized as professionals – with commensurate rights – who make a key contribution to the creation of new knowledge" (Salzburg I, 2005, Principle 4).

4 The author is a PhD graduate of the University of Waikato and in the study period between 2010 and 2013 these facilities where available to him. It is also necessary to note that in some universities in New Zealand, academic departments print business cards for doctoral candidates as a subtle strategy to support their network building. In using personal experience which is also a valid source of research data supported by autoethnography (Adams et al., 2017), its limitations in this case can be controlled for by the verifiability of an author's claims from the group s/he writes about.

5 "The crucial role of supervision and assessment: in respect of individual doctoral candidates, arrangements for supervision and assessment should be based on a transparent contractual framework of shared responsibilities between doctoral candidates, supervisors and the institution (and where appropriate including other partners)" (Salzburg I, 2005, Principle 5).

and industry. Relevance to academia refers to the ability of the findings to increase understanding in their field of engagement, while industry relevance, which is similar to societal relevance, refers to their ability to serve the needs of society through application to relevant sectors of society (Shaw & Elgar, 2013). For the candidates in context, the framework seeks to answer the question of who is undertaking the doctoral training. The study observed that most doctoral candidates in Africa are already established professionals who do not have the time for full-time doctoral study. The curriculum addresses the model of training which on the continent is mostly based on the master-apprenticeship model which has become outdated. The structure involves integrating the doctoral candidate into an academic unit or department, where they collaborate with a supervisor or a supervisory team over a designated period to conduct new research. This structure is bound up with the environment of the research both in terms of research infrastructure, educational policies and quality of knowledge production. Here, Cross and Backhouse present one of the most decisive setbacks to doctoral education in Africa, namely, that academic departments in most universities lack a conducive environment for research indicated by paucity of active researchers, limited research seminars and developmental workshops, limited funding and time to attend conferences, mentorship and opportunities to gain external input for their research. PhD scholars find it difficult to travel. Poor funding affects the quality of library resources, poor internet connectivity associated with the high cost of internet and lack of technological support. Finally, African universities have limited partnership opportunities which they could utilise to exploit economies of scale, share experiences and best practices.

All these elements need to be considered side by side with the Nigerian context, but in an analytical approach that grounds each of the setbacks to doctoral education on the applicable Salzburg Principle. In providing an overview of the Nigerian context of doctoral studies in the next section, the ten elements of the Salzburg Principles are discussed in relation to how their realisation is impinged on by socio-economic and political conditions in the country. There are issues related to funding, university staff emolument issues, education policy issues, issues related to expertise, issues related to institutional network building with other institutions within and outside Nigeria.

3. Doctoral education in the Nigerian context

Various accounts of the Nigerian context of doctoral education present a gloomy picture of Nigeria. For example, according to Saint et al. (2003) much of the academic practice in Nigerian universities is based on traditional ways of teaching and research and falls short of the Nigerian government's own standards. Besides, the expansion of the higher education system during the last three decades (see Van't Land, 2011) has overwhelmed the government's funding ability. Saint et al. (2003) go on to discuss various challenges and problems facing higher education institutions in Nigeria: poor remuneration of university staff and constant disagreements between university staff and the government on wages result in constant industrial actions which have at times left universities closed for several months almost every year since the late 1980s. The Nigerian *Tribune* newspaper (cited by Ashiru, 2022) reports that between 1999 (when military rule ended) and 2020, the lecturers' union in Nigeria went on strike 17 times for a total 1 450 days. The strikes are usually related to issues of funding and emoluments. Due to the challenges of poor funding, research is not prioritized by government. The budget allocation fails to separate funding for tertiary institutions and special funds for doctoral education, as the focus on doctoral studies as a key driver of economic progress does not appear to be a priority for Nigerian policymakers. Further, the incidence of corruption and misuse of the little available funds are part of the local contextual issues that impede on the rise of conditions that could enhance doctoral research in Nigeria.

University education commenced in Nigeria through an affiliate campus of the University College London in 1948 and later metamorphosed into a full-fledged university in 1962, namely the University of Ibadan (University of Ibadan, n.d.). The University of Nigeria, Nsukka, was established on 7 October 1960 as the country's first indigenous university. These two universities were followed by the University of Lagos, the University of Ife (now Obafemi Awolowo University), and Ahmadu Bello University (Obafemi Awolowo University, 2021; The Higher Education Foundation, n.d.). These first five are known as the first-generation universities. They have varying histories in terms of doctoral education. The first ever PhD in Nigeria was awarded by the University of Ibadan in 1964 (Falola & Aderinto, 2011). The expanding population of Nigeria and growing need for higher education has led to the expansion of institutions of higher learning and the corresponding need for highly skilled staff to teach in them. The shortage of adequate academic staff to teach in the universities led to the recruitment of non-PhDs to fill those positions in many Nigerian universities A report in the University World News (Fatunde, 2008) recounts a scenario of a non-PhD, who was not a professor, supervising a PhD. In 2012, the National Universities Commission in Nigeria carried out a needs assessment of Nigerian public universities and found that only 43% of lecturers had PhDs and in only seven universities did up to 60% of the lecturers have doctorates (see *The Nation*, 2018). The National Universities Commission, which regulates universities in Nigeria, threatened that non-PhD lecturers should be sacked by 2009 (Fatunde, 2008). As a result, the drive for more PhDs has been more vigorous in Nigeria not only for public universities but also for the countries' rising number of private universities. Suleiman Bogoro (2021), head of the Tertiary Education Trust Fund (TET Fund), noted that 60% of Nigerian lecturers now have doctorates. This progress may be accounted for by a few factors including the need to secure teaching jobs and escape the threat of termination by the NUC; the funding support from the government especially for lecturers in federal universities who were still completing their doctoral studies. Through the TET Fund, some lecturers benefitted from funding including for overseas travel for doctoral training.

In November 2021, the National Universities Commission provided the list of 198 universities in Nigeria including 45 federal universities, 54 state universities and 99 private universities (Odunsi, 2021). Out of this number, 30 federal universities, 28 state universities and 28 private universities had accreditation to offer postgraduate courses at master's and PhD levels, while two private universities had approvals to provide master's level training (NUC, 2019). The application for postgraduate admission is increasing especially at the doctorate level and raises concerns about the quality of the qualifications resulting from the training. The degree to which these universities meet the attributes described by Trafford and Leshem (2009) under the rubric of 'doctorateness' needs to be investigated. The term refers to the extent of emphasis on research excellence, capacity to teach transferable skills, attractive institutional environment, interdisciplinary research options, exposure to industry and other relevant employment sectors, international networking, as well as quality assurance in doctoral education within these universities. In some sense, the term 'doctorateness' aligns well with the aims of the Bologna process. The question then is whether doctoral training in Nigeria commits to the principle of doctorateness at least or whether there are elements in Nigerian training practices that lend the systems to the Salzburg Principles.

The conditions in which doctoral training takes place in Nigerian universities are mirrored in the findings of a study of six pilot universities by the International Association of Universities (Van't Land, 2011) on the changing nature of doctoral studies in sub-Saharan Africa (SSA), namely Cameroon, Nigeria, Kenya, Benin, Senegal and Rwanda. In their study the IAU reported that doctoral education in these six countries is subject to the following circumstances:

a) At institutional level, there is a general lack of systematically disaggregated data on doctoral studies and doctoral programmes. There tends to be a lumping up of information on postgraduate studies in a manner that limits sufficient emphasis on the development of PhD studies; there is also a lack of synergies between students' doctoral research and institutional research focus. Indeed, in some instances there is a clear lack of institutional research strategies.

b) At the national levels, government research priorities (in instances where they exist) are not aligned with local development needs and such poor articulation of research priorities affects the developmental usefulness of doctoral research. Consequently, other sources of funding drive research directions in higher education rather than national priorities. More importantly, doctoral research is not shaped by a clear policy that factors in national collaboration and or regional networks in sub-Saharan Africa.

c) At regional SSA level, there is an absence of strategically coordinated collaboration and exchange of expertise to support and enrich research in the region. The IAU report equally stressed progressive decline in doctoral research as well as poor infrastructure/facilities of research. This is further disaggregated into the paucity or total absence of research databases; limited internet connectivity which hinders both national and regional networking; dated library holdings and facilities as well as ill-equipped science laboratories; and lack of dedicated seminar rooms.

In terms of supervision, the IAU reports a lack of transparency, clear information or tracking mechanisms about who is registered where, who supervises them and the progress of the students; absence of proper synergy between supervisors and their students which limits the introduction of such students to their supervisors' research networks or consideration of the doctoral candidates as early-stage researchers who deserve to be valued as such. Students are hardly availed of opportunities for internationalization by being exposed to international networks in order to link up with other experts in their fields of research both at the local, regional and international levels. Supervisors, on their part, are in many instances overloaded with teaching and supervisory tasks in a way that undermines efficiency. Besides, they seldom benefit from institutionally supported staff development opportunities for the enhancement of their own skills (Van't Land, 2011).

There is a disturbing absence of comprehensive centralized information and data collection and management systems on doctoral programmes that could be used for policymaking, planning and institution management in most

SSA universities. These elements are decisive for policy, governance, planning, implementation, monitoring and evaluation of doctoral programmes. Perhaps this gap may account for why institutional research strategies are not well connected with national research and innovation strategies (Van't Land, 2011).

In the area of internationalization of doctoral programmes, the IAU report revealed the absence of institution-wide internationalization strategies in the studied institutions. Doctoral students are not required to participate in international conferences even when there is funding for this purpose. Official international collaboration agreements are generally unknown to most universities. Where these agreements exist at all, they focus mostly on the northern hemisphere and almost completely ignore the need for South–South cooperation for the growth of knowledge.

A contrary point to this IAU finding is expressed in the work of Akudolu and Adeyemo (2018) which noted an increase in the last ten years in collaboration between Nigerian and overseas institutions. Moreover, a recent analysis of research output in the STEM disciplines in SSA reveals that West and Central Africa have higher degrees of collaboration than East and Central Africa. Six out of fifteen centres that are designated African Centres of Excellence are hosted by Nigeria. While the above developments indicate some progress in internationalization, it reports on only a few Nigerian experiences and is, therefore, insignificant in comparison to the number both of Nigerian and other African institutions that engage in knowledge production that would have benefitted more from a better coordinated and more systematic international cooperation. Again, IAU reported the absence of awareness raising campaigns at the national level to signal the importance of doctoral studies in regional development or even for the effective dissemination and use of research findings.

In summary, the IAU report suggests that in sub-Saharan Africa, there is a general absence of conditions that could make the Salzburg Principles applicable for the improvement of doctoral education in Nigeria. The two core contexts for stimulating such conditions are the political context of the government and the context of the universities. In the political context, a demonstration of commitment by governments to the improvement of doctoral education through policies and their effective implementation is fundamental. In the context of the universities, the structures and processes of doctoral education must be aligned to government policies aimed at a contextual reproduction of the kind of principles that were made in Salzburg. It is therefore not impossible to consciously create such principles which would be sustainable in the African situation to reorganise doctoral education in most of the continent and Nigeria.

In the next section, I consider a Nigerian institutional context where doctoral education takes place side by side with the Salzburg Principles.

4. Doctoral education at the University of Nigeria, Nsukka, through the lens of the Salzburg Principles

The University of Nigeria, Nsukka, is an institution operating within the Nigerian doctoral education milieu. Its research practices are affected by the larger systemic characteristics that are engendered by the overarching political economy of the national attitude on research and doctoral education. In this section we consider the ten Salzburg I Principles and relate the discussion with the seven principles of innovative research synthesized in Salzburg II. I shall relate these principles to practices in the University of Nigeria, and then consider the conditions that affect doctoral education at the university.

4.1 First Principle: Advancement of knowledge through original research

The present practice in doctoral education at the university is that students first have to complete course work and then qualify through a written examination to be admitted to the writing of their thesis. At the end of the process, the research reported in the thesis is examined for the purpose of the doctoral award. The University of Nigeria states in Section 39 (iii) of its Postgraduate Regulations (2018, p. 39) that

> *for a thesis to be approved for oral examination for the degree of Doctorate, it shall embody original research of the candidate, display critical judgement and contain materials publishable as definite contribution to knowledge. This must be demonstrated (except for professional doctorate) by at least an acceptance letter in any Impact Factor Indexed Journal approved by the university for promotion ...*

An initial guarantee of originality must be established as a matter of requirement of section 39 (i) of the regulation which provides for a plagiarism test and a plagiarism test certificate before the oral examination. This provision verges on both originality and research ethics.

'Originality' does not necessarily mean 'relevance' (BennichBjorkman, 1997, cited in Baptista et al. 2015). Additionally, creativity is essential in doctoral research, as innovation must be aligned with the significance and applicability of the knowledge produced. On the higher end of originality and creativity is innovation. All these elements could culminate in research excellence when new findings are not only creative but can solve societal and industry needs and drive national economic growth. The University of Nigeria has established structures that suggest its awareness of the connection between original, creative and innovative research and economic growth. The Research Policy of the University of Nigeria (University of Nigeria, 2013:17) mentions the office of Patents and Innovations as wells as strategies for commercialization and links to society and industry. Nonetheless, there is no systematic linking of the contents of the research policy and promotion of innovative doctoral research. Research within the university is hardly linked to the needs of relevant industry. Neither the university nor industry is moving towards mutual tapping of their respective and each other's potentials. This may be part of the overall poor collaboration between universities and industries in Nigeria and a definite setback to the growth of postgraduate research entirely. Such collaboration would have been an important exposure to the existing practice in industries and a basis for exploring new frontiers for improvement on observed practices. The point here is that university–industry collaboration is a support factor for innovation in research and that, despite its research policy, the university has not consciously pursued it as a strategy for growing doctoral research.

The most decisive factor about original and innovative research is funding. The university of Nigeria, Nsukka, is as poorly funded as other Nigerian universities. Nigeria's education budget has never gone above 12% since 1999, while the 2018 allocation to the sector was a paltry 7%. At the university of Nigeria, the quarterly (three-monthly) allocation by the university to its academic departments for expenditure on goods and services in 2018 was approximately NGN 300 000. This translates to about USD 722 to be used over a period of three months. More important about this is that these funds are often sent only in one or two out of the four quarters in a year or even not sent at all. Moreover, the funding is for goods and services used in running both undergraduate, master's and doctoral programmes. Evidently, there are no specially dedicated funds for doctoral studies. Three personal interviews with former heads of academic units and departments at the university (17 May 2022), corroborate the lack of specific funding for doctoral studies. The respondents separately explained that the funds for goods are services are not even sent to the departments. The university only asks departments to approve any of the university registered vendors to supply a few of the needs of the department. Consequently, some of the unmet needs that are part of students' research needs are procured as out of pocket expenditure for the students (Personal communication, May 17, 2022). Such needs, which students privately meet, are usually quite costly in the STEM disciplines.

4.2 Second Principle: Embedding institutional strategies and policies for PhDs that meet new challenges

The University of Nigeria has institutional strategies for doctoral education in place, some of which were discussed under the first principle. However, these strategies are limited by two major factors. First is the inadequacy of funding to support some of the plans on paper (as discussed in the previous paragraph). The second is the absence of political prioritization of knowledge production as a framework for economic growth and national development. This is evidenced by poor budgetary allocations to education and absence of policy support for doctoral education. In fact, low wages and poor funding of the universities are reasons why academic staff unions often go on strike. From 14 February to October, Nigerian federal university academic staff were on strike in 2022. Among their demands was the disbursement of the university revitalization fund (Olaniyi, 2022) which is to be used to provide essential infrastructure for research.

We can, however, refer to some of the university's efforts in improving the relevance of its postgraduate output for addressing the challenges facing the country. The curriculum of doctoral training has introduced new components with transferable broad skills, like grant-writing. But some of the new components are organised in the form of one-day seminars for students, which is hardly enough time for any meaningful training. Hence such changes in the PhD curriculum do not yet amount to any fundamental transformation in the content of the training.

4.3 Third principle: The importance of diversity

The university of Nigeria has minimal opportunity to integrate diversity into its doctoral education. It has few opportunities for split-site doctoral studies. Several such cases are internationally sponsored through direct application of the concerned student in competitive processes. The split-site doctorate allows the candidate to spend some time in a foreign university to carry out their research, usually under the supervision of an expert in their field of research. They normally return to their university to complete their studies. Ultimately, the PhD degree is awarded by the home university in Nigeria. However, the university does not have a properly structured diversity practice either in the form of joint doctorates that it co-supervises with other universities or doctoral training programmes in which the private sector participates. This problem impedes the development of industry-relevant knowledge that contributes to solving societal problems.

4.4 Fourth Principle: Recognition of doctoral candidates as early-stage researchers

This Salzburg principle would entail a couple of practices that give the doctoral candidates a sense of membership to a new community where they are expected to contribute to knowledge creation, rather than being trainees waiting for certification. Some of the conditions necessary to underscore such recognition include among others: (a) provision of a working space where the candidate would have a computer assigned to them or an opportunity to purchase a university-subsidized laptop; (b) university-provided internet connectivity with sufficient bandwidth to use the internet. Such connectivity would be useful for accessing library e-resources and other external research resources available on the internet; (c) provision of funding as incentive for students to participate in at least two conferences before the completion of their doctoral training; (d) support by the supervisors for joint publication with their candidates. In such publication, where the student has made a more significant contribution, they should receive lead author credit for the paper; (e) creation of a framework in which the student is accorded commensurate benefits if their work leads to the registration of a patent(s). The University of Nigeria currently does not have any of the above arrangements. In fact, some faculties do not have office space at all. So, it would be unthinkable to prioritize doctoral students in that regard when many newly hired faculties lack basic work facilities.

4.5 Fifth Principle: Crucial role of supervision and assessment

The relationships between supervisor and doctoral candidate at the University of Nigeria is still overwhelmingly defined by the master–apprentice approach. Although, the Postgraduate Regulations provide for the change of a supervisor when a candidate has well-founded reasons for that (University of Nigeria, 2018), in most cases complaints about poor supervisory behaviour end up with the doctoral candidate's work being frustrated. Many supervisors tend to struggle with state-of-the-art doctoral supervision knowledge, and this sometimes extends to the knowledge of their subject areas.

The university's School of Postgraduate Studies started organising annual compulsory training for postgraduate supervisors, which in most cases lasted for two days. This commenced in 2017 and continued in 2018. While it is commendable, the training courses are not deep and may not result in any major transformation in supervisory behaviour. This matters because the quality of supervision, together with the quality of a student's work, usually determines the success or otherwise of a doctoral candidate.

4.6 Sixth Principle: Achieving critical mass

The number of applications for PhDs in the University of Nigeria has grown significantly over the years. But this growth is mostly driven by the need for teaching staff in universities. As demonstrated by Akudolu and Adeyemo (2018), it was after the 2012 needs assessment of Nigerian universities and the discovery that only 43% of Nigerian university teachers had PhDs and subsequent recommendation that faculty obtain their doctorates that the drive for larger numbers of PhD graduates in Nigeria began. There is no evidence of industry needs being considered in this drive for more doctorates.

The massification drive is also reflected in the number of PhDs graduated by the University of Nigeria. For instance, at the 2018 convocation ceremony, 480 PhDs graduated from the university (Mbamalu, 2018). This number is the highest ever achieved in any Nigerian university. While this progress is being made in the direction of achieving critical mass, it is important to note that the industrial sector has not figured much in this production. So, the kind of innovative research that addresses social needs and drives the market is yet to gain attention. This is another pointer to limited university–industry cooperation in research. This kind of cooperation is expected to condition research directions and add to massification.

4.7 Seventh Principle: Duration

The Salzburg principle recommends a duration of 3 to 4 years for full-time continuous doctoral study. For the university of Nigeria, the duration specified in the university's policies are a minimum of eight semesters and a maximum of 12 semesters for full-time study. This translates to 4 and 6 years respectively. Part-time study is given a duration of a minimum of 10 semesters and a maximum of 14 semesters which translate to 5 and 7 years respectively (University of Nigeria, 2018).

The conditions that affect the possibility of meeting these specifications of the university's Postgraduate Regulation include many factors such as: high attrition rate of PhDs due to lack of finance to fund the studies and research; issues of supervision, lack of facilities to perform certain studies, especially in the STEM disciplines; poor funding of universities; and the lack of an organised monitoring system to follow through the progress of the candidates. But more importantly, the massification could easily reach a saturation point because there is little preparedness on the part of industries to find use for university research while at the same time, researchers in the universities do not target the possible needs of industry.

4.8 Eighth Principle: Promotion of innovative structures to meet the challenges of interdisciplinary training and the development of transferable skills

This principle tends to summarise what many other components of the Salzburg Principles set out to achieve and have been addressed in the foregoing discussions.

4.9 Ninth principle: Increasing mobility

This component is about interdisciplinary and intersectoral mobility of candidates during their doctoral training as well as internationalization. It is not cheering to point out that formalized inter-university collaboration for improved doctoral training in Nigeria is almost at zero. The University of Nigeria participates in this narrowly focused training of doctorates. Apart from the invitation of subject experts from other Nigerian universities to serve as external examiners, the sharing of expertise that requires candidates in training to spend some time in other universities within the country is absent. Also, such mobility at international levels, whether it is within Africa or beyond, is quite minimal. In the instances that they occur at all, it is through the efforts of students who win such opportunities through competitive applications. While students are in the most recent Postgraduate Regulations required to attend at least one international conference, there is no form of support from the university for that purpose. Consequently, those who manage to attend such conferences are few and they usually end up attending local Nigerian conferences that are labelled as international.

4.10 Tenth Principle: Ensuring appropriate funding

It would be obvious from the consideration of the entire points above, that poor funding is a recurrent decimal in the factors that challenge the feasibility of reproducing the essence of the Salzburg I and II Principles in doctoral training in Nigeria. There are at least 585 institutions of higher learning in the country including universities, polytechnics and colleges of education. These institutions together with primary and secondary levels of education combine to share the little annual budgetary allocation for the educational sector in the country. What each university receives from the federal government owned universities does not add up to a scratch in terms of the funding needs of a modern university. In Nigeria the federal university funding is allocated and distributed by the National University Commission, which applies the following parameters: enrolment specification, student academic ratios, academic staff structure (professoriate, senior lecturers and other lecturers), non-teaching support staff ratio to academic staff ratio, allowances for direct teaching and services based on facilities and other equipment required, line item funding (such as library costs, research development), administrative support cost and other services (such as university health services), non-academic expenditures (personal emoluments), retirement policy, local income or internally generated revenue and total salaries (Akinsolu, 1990, cited in Ahmad et al., 2016).

There is, however, a special Tertiary Education Trust Fund (TET Fund) that is dedicated to research, staff and the equipment of universities. The TET Fund had been applied to support the doctoral training of academic staff at universities (including overseas training) and upgrade some obsolete equipment and structures of research. In addition, the TET Fund also has a research funding component that includes doctoral research. Doctoral students' applications are submitted at the national level where all applications from public universities in the country are assessed for the grant. But the process of applying for the TET Fund is a bureaucratic nightmare beset by numerous delays, while winning the research grant is quite rare.

In addition to the paucity of research funding, access to basic infrastructure like electricity, presentation facilities for seminars, laboratory chemicals is still problematic. At the university of Nigeria, several aspects of operating costs that could not be met through official funding sources are complemented by students. Thus, despite this government funding, the cost of doctoral training on the part of students is quite high and the environment of such training is replete with funding and other gaps.

5. Synthesis

Considering the discussions above, we can synthesize the factors that affect doctoral studies and the feasibility of applying the Salzburg Principles in Nigeria into political economy factors. The roots of the relationship between market and research in Europe goes back to the industrial revolution where several scientific works were supported by business especially in Britain. Continuous growth of the market and progress of universities also led to the support and sponsorship of various forms of market-relevant research through the establishment of professorial chairs and scholarships in specific areas. The state's role in creating conditions for the growth of the market and research to address societal problems also increasingly moved towards the university in the search for solutions not just of matters of policy and governance but also for growing industries and market. Hence, supporting university research also became an important part of official policies. The decisiveness of doctoral research for this purpose culminated in the Bologna process which led to the articulation of the Salzburg Principles.

It is important to see the strong hand of European states in support of the Bologna process and the policies and actions that emerged in their ministers meeting in Berlin which named the European Higher Education Area (EHEA) and European Research Area (ERA) as the two pillars of a knowledge-based society (Witte, 2006). Based on the Bologna process, governments in Europe and other advanced countries have prioritized knowledge and devoted significant chunks of their annual budget to the support of doctoral studies with a clear expectation of the economic, technological and other benefits for their societies.

In contrast, Nigeria's ruling class demonstrate a hostile posture to the development of universities and qualitative research that grows a knowledge-based society. This is evidenced by the poor funding allocated to universities to complacent attitudes to the fulfilment of their agreements with university teachers on how to improve teaching and research conditions in the country's higher education. Besides, the linkage between universities, industry and state is quite tenuous, not based on formalized processes for the uptake of research findings from the universities, nor is university research demand driven. These factors account for the lack of political will to invest in research in Nigeria and the continuing poor environment of doctoral training. The weakness of this important linkage means that implementation of the Salzburg Principles in Nigeria would be a hard task.

References

Adams, T., Ellis, C., & Jones, S. H. (2017). Autoethnography. In J. Martins, C. S. Davis, & R. E. Potter (Eds.), *International Encyclopedia of Communication Research Methods* (pp.1-12). Wiley. https://onlinelibrary. wiley.com/doi/epdf/10.1002/9781118901731.iecrm0011

Ahmad, A., Garba, K., & Soon, N., Bappah, A. (2016). Higher education funding in Nigeria: Issues, trends, and opportunities. In K. S. Soliman (Eds.), *Proceedings of the 27th international business information management association conference, Milan, Italy* (pp. 2110–2118). IBIMA. https://www.researchgate.net/ publication/305789766_Higher_Education_Funding_in_Nigeria_-_Issues_Trends_and_Opportunities

Akudolu, L., & Adeyemo, K. (2018). *Research and PhD capacities in Sub-Saharan Africa: Nigeria report.* British Council and DAAD. https://www.daad.de/medien/der-daad/analysen-studien/research_and_phd_capac-ities_in_sub-saharan_africa_-_nigeria_report.pdf

Andres, L., Bengtsen, E., Castano, L. P. G., Crossouard, B., Keefer, J., & Pyhältö, K. (2015). Drivers and inter-pretations of doctoral education today: National comparisons. *Frontline Learning Research, 3*(3), 5–22.

Ashiru, D. (2022). 17 strikes in 23 years: a unionist explains why Nigeria's university lecturers won't back down. *The Conversation* September 8, 2022

Baptista, A., Frick, L., Holley, K., Remmik, M., Tesch, J., & Åkerlind, G. (2015). The doctorate as an original contribution to knowledge: Considering relationships between originality, creativity, and innovation. *Frontline Learning Research, 3*(3), 55–67. https://doi.org/10.14786/flr.v3i3.147

Bitzer, E. (2016). Research into doctoral education: A survey of institutional research projects in Southern Africa. In J. Botha & N. Muller (Eds.), *Institutional research in South African higher education* (pp. 121–140). SUN PRESS.

Bogoro (2021). "How TET Fund is changing the landscape of our tertiary institutions — Bogoro". *Vanguard* 20 June 2022.

Bologna Seminar on "Doctoral Programmes for the European Knowledge Society". (2005). *Conclusions and recommendations.* Bologna Seminar, February 3-5. https://www.eua.eu/publications/positions/salz-burg-2005-conclusions-and-recommendations.html

Charlier, J., & Croche, S. (2009). Can the Bologna Process make the move faster towards the development of an international space for higher education where Africa would find its place? *Journal of Higher Education in Africa, 7*(1-2), 39–59.

Cloete, N. (2015). Nurturing doctoral growth: Towards the NDP's 5000? [Commentary] *South African Journal of Science, 111*(11/12). http://www.scielo.org.za/pdf/sajs/v111n11-12/08.pdf

Cross, M., & Backhouse, J. (2014). Evaluating doctoral programmes in Africa: Context and practices. *Higher Education Policy, 27,* 155–174.

Cyranoski, D., Gilbert, N., Ledford, H., Nayar, A., & M Yahia M. (2011). Education: The PhD factory. The world is producing more PhDs that ever before. Is it time to stop? *Nature, 472,* 276–279.

Deem, R., Mok, K. H., & Lucas, L. (2008). Transforming higher education in whose image? Exploring the concept of the 'world-class' university in Europe and Asia. *Higher Education Policy, 21,* 83–97.

European University Association Council for Doctoral Education (EUA-CDE). (2010). Implementing the Salzburg principles. *PhdCentre.* http://www.phdcentre.eu/inhoud/uploads/2018/02/EUANewsIssue10_ LYpublicatieHS.pdf

European University Association. (2005a). *Doctoral programmes for the European knowledge society: Results of EUA doctoral programmes project 2004 – 2005.* European University Association. https://www.eua.eu/ publications/reports/doctoral-programmes-for-the-european-knowledge-society.html

European University Association. (2005b). *Salzburg II – Recommendations: European universities.* European University Association.

Falola, T., & Aderinto, S. (2011). *Nigeria, nationalism and writing history.* Boydell & Brewer.

Fatunde, T. (2008, March 30). Nigeria: Lecturers without PhDs to lose their jobs. *University World News.* https://www.universityworldnews.com/post.php?story=20080327105613634

Gunasekara, C. (2006). Reframing the role of universities in the development of regional innovation systems. *Journal of Technology Transfer, 31*(1), 101–113.

Kwiek, M. (2004). The emergent European educational policies under scrutiny: The Bologna Process from a Central European perspective. *European Educational Research Journal, 3*(4), 759–776.

Matas, C., & Poyatos, P. (2012). Doctoral education and skills development: An international perspective. *Revista de Docencia Universitaria, 10*(2), 163–191.

Mbamalu, M. (2018, December 3). UNN turns out highest number of PhD graduates in Nigerian history. *The Guardian.* https://guardian.ng/news/unn-turns-out-highest-number-of-ph-d-graduates-in-nigerian-history/

McGloin, R. S., & Wynne, C. (2015). *Structural changes in doctoral education in the UK: A review of graduate schools and the development of doctoral colleges.* UK Council for Graduate Education. https://doi.org/10.13140/RG.2.1.4397.8321

Melin, G., & Janson, K. (2006). What skills and knowledge should a PhD have? Changing preconditions for PhD education and post-doc work. In U. Teichler (Ed.), *The formative years of scholars* (pp. 79–84). Portland Press.

Muerza, V., & Larrode, E. (2018). Driving factors and implementation mechanisms for quality assurance in the Spanish PhD adaptation to the Bologna process: Experience in mechanical engineering. *Literacy Information and Computer Education Journal, 9*(2), 2907–2915.

Muller, S. (2012, September 20). More PhDs are not the answer. *Mail & Guardian.* https://mg.co.za/article/2012-09-20-more-phds-are-not-the-answer

National Universities Commission (NUC). (2019). Nigerian universities. *National Universities Commission. 19th November 2018 Bulletin.*

Obafemi Awolowo University. (2021). About OAU. *Obafemi Awolowo University.* https://oauife.edu.ng/about-oauife/

Odunsi, W. (2021, November 2). NUC names 198 federal, state, private universities in Nigeria [Full list]. *Daily Post.* https://dailypost.ng/2021/11/02/nuc-names-198-federal-state-private-universities-in-nigeria-full-list/

Okamoto, M., & Matsuzaka, H. (2015). Role of leading programmes in doctoral education: A new type of leadership education in the sciences at the University of Yiogo, Japan. *Education Sciences, 5*(1), 2–9. https://doi.org/10.3390/educsci5010002

Olaniyi, O. (2022, February 8). Strike: FG owes varsities N880 billion revitalisation fund, says ASUU. *Punch.* https://punchng.com/strike-fg-owes-varsities-n880bn-revitalisation-fund-says-asuu/

Research Councils UK. (2010). *Review of progress in implementing the recommendations of Sir Gareth Roberts, regarding employability and career development of PhD students and research staff: A report for Research Councils UK by an independent review panel.* https://publications.aston.ac.uk/id/eprint/16899/1/RobertReport2011.pdf

Roberts, G. (2002). *SET for success: The supply of people with science, technology, engineering and mathematics skills. The report of Sir Gareth Roberts' review.* https://dera.ioe.ac.uk/id/eprint/4511/1/robertsreview_in-troch1.pdf

Saint, W., Hartnett, T. & Strassner, E. (2003). Higher Education in Nigeria: A Status Report. *High Education Policy* 16, 259–281 https://doi.org/10.1057/palgrave.hep.8300021

Salzburg II Recommendations. (2010). *European universities' achievements since 2005 in implementing the Salzburg principles.* European University Association.

Shaw, D., & Elgar, B. (2013). The relevance of relevance in research. *Swiss Medical Weekly, 143*(1920). https://doi.org/10.4414/smw.2013.13792

Statista. (2018). Leading countries by gross research and development (R&D) expenditure worldwide in 2018. *Statista.* https://www.statista.com/statistics/732247/worldwide-research-and-development-gross-expenditure-top-countries/

Talby, M. (n.d.). *Doctoral education in France* [PowerPoint slides]. https://yerun.eu/wp-content/up-loads/2018/11/FRANCE-M-TALBY.pdf

Teferra, D. (2014). Charting African higher education – Perspectives at a glance. *International Journal of African Higher Education, 1*(1), 9–21.

Teferra, D. (2015). Manufacturing and exporting excellence and 'mediocrity': Doctoral education in South Africa. *South African Journal of Higher Education, 29*(5), 8–19.

The Nation. (2018, September 20). Revisiting the Needs Assessment Report. https://thenationonlineng.net/revisiting-the-needs-assessment-report/

The Nigeria Higher Education Foundation. (n.d.). *Ahmadu Bello University.* https://www.thenhef.org/partner-universities/ahmadu-bello-university/

Times Higher Education. (2019). *World university rankings 2019.* https://www.timeshighereducation.com/world-university-rankings/2019/world-ranking#!/page/0/length/25/sort_by/name/sort_order/desc/cols/stats

Trafford, V., & Leshem, S. (2009). Doctorateness as a threshold concept. *Innovations in Education and Teaching International, 46*(3), 305–316. https://doi.org/10.1080/14703290903069027

UK Quality Code for Higher Education. (2015). Characteristics statement: Doctoral degree. *QAA.* https://www.qaa.ac.uk/the-quality-code/characteristics-statements/characteristics-statement-doctoral-degrees

University of Ibadan. (n.d.). History. https://ui.edu.ng/content/history

University of Nigeria, Nsukka. (2013). *University of Nigeria research policy.* https://www.unn.edu.ng/wp-content/uploads/2015/09/UNN-RESEARCH-POLICY.pdf

University of Nigeria. (2018). *Postgraduate regulations.* University of Nigeria Press.

Van't Land, H. (2011). *The changing nature of doctoral studies in sub-Saharan Africa: Challenges and policy development opportunities at six universities in sub-Saharan Africa.* International Association of Universities. https://www.researchgate.net/publication/281619984_The_Changing_Nature_of_Doctoral_Studies_in_sub-Saharan_Africa

Witte, J. K. (2006). *Change of degrees and degrees of change: Comparing adaptations of European higher education systems in the context of the Bologna process* [Unpublished doctoral dissertation]. University of Twente.

CHAPTER 5

The role of the doctoral qualification in socio-economic development: A case study of a university in Benin

Estelle Bancole-Minaflinou

Benin Republic is in West Africa. It has a population of 13 million. There are four public universities in Benin. The University of Abomey Calavi (UAC), the University of Parakou (UP), the Agricultural University at Ketou (UK) and the National University of Sciences, Technologies, Engineering and Mathematics of Benin (UNSTIM). In 2022 more than 711 candidates were registered in seven doctoral schools in the country. The doctoral programme offers further education that helps a student become an expert in their field. A doctoral programme typically takes three to five years to complete and involves independent study and research in a focused area of interest. Doctoral programmes in Benin include course work and research that culminate in a final dissertation.

The **University of Abomey-Calavi** is the principal public university in Benin. The University comprises six university centres across the country, each housing a variable number of faculties, schools or institutes, and chairs. It has 40 training and research entities (TRE), including 20 schools or institutes, eight faculties, three chairs and nine doctoral schools. Student enrolments in 2021 amounted to 68 472. The university has 944 academic staff members.

1. Introduction

For a long time in Benin and many other African developing countries, primary and secondary education were understood as the key to development and poverty alleviation due to the 2000 World Bank policy document (World

Bank, 2000). The World Bank renounced this position not long after, recognising higher education's importance for socio-economic promotion. So, for the past two decades, local postgraduate enrolment both in master's and PhD programmes has grown steadily to become an expanding sector.

The belief that such programmes should be central to Benin's development efforts, by offering the potential of training highly skilled staff that can bring about needed changes for better governance and sound management, quickly turned into a 'nightmare'. This ultimately led to the 'Actes des Conférences du Collège des Ecoles de l'Université d'Abomey-Calavi' conference in 2018, the aim of which was to take the bull by the horns by striving for effective solutions.

The British Council and the German Academic Exchange Service (DAAD) in collaboration with the African Network for Internationalization of Education (ANIE, 2018), undertook to investigate research and doctoral training across six sub-Saharan African countries. The study shed light on the progress being made and mainly the challenges cropping up regarding the growing quality of PhD provision (Cross & Backhouse, 2014). Though Benin was not included in the sample, conditions in this country seem unexceptional. Tight budgets that lead to poor research capacity, poor quality supervision, weak internet access, poor equipment and libraries, compounded by massive expansion have naturally lowered the quality of higher education which results in weak research output and ultimately to unemployment or informal work. Apparently, these hurdles look like signs of failure. But if the battle of producing better trained graduates that can positively impact economic development and prosperity in this part of the world is to be won, these hurdles must be addressed.

The present chapter aims first to investigate and explore the perceptions of doctoral students and supervisors about the quality of current doctoral programmes. Second, a programme is designed that can stand the chance to meet the practical demand of the labour market, by bridging the gap between academic education and professional employment. For this to have better results, why not build this right into the lower levels of higher education qualification (i.e. diploma certificates and bachelor's degrees)? In fact, the professional trajectory envisioned for PhD holders, that is, to be employed as professors at universities, has changed in recent years because many PhD graduates find work outside academia (and research institutions). That raises the question: can – and should – doctoral level studies also be designed to prepare graduates for employment outside academia (Ortega & Kent, 2018)?

The main objective of this study is to assess the value of doctorate programmes to decision-makers and the general public in Benin by finding a new approach to postgraduate education (at master's and doctoral levels) to train future professionals, including researchers, by generating knowledge that can contribute to development and transformed into innovation and wealth creation.

Generating from the twofold purposes, the present study attempts to answer the following questions:

- What are the supervisors and doctorate students' perceptions about the current situation of doctoral programmes in Benin?
- What doctoral programmes can meet the students' professional needs and the demand of the labour market first and as a result help drive development?

Quantitative and qualitative data were collected to provide insights into these questions. Ethical clearance to use the data in this publication was granted by the Research Ethics Committee of Stellenbosch University (Project number 2273).

1.1 Background

As a former French colony, Benin inherited its educational system from France. Benin educational authorities have sought to give this system its own identity since independence in 1960. The medium of instruction is still French but English has been introduced and taught across the seven years of proficiency level as a compulsory subject. The universities (state and private), which house all the units of higher education, are organised into faculties, professional institutes and doctoral schools.

With the introduction of the licence/master/doctorate (LMD) structure (Décret No 2010-272 du 11 Juillet 2010), the system was reshuffled. The main objective is to use modern methods of training to facilitate the mobility and professional integration of lecturers and students. It offers the opportunity of aligning the training at university level with market needs while involving possible future employers inside and outside academia and making the whole process flexible, even in the case of doctoral graduates in research, or other institutions, outside academia. The implication is that both instructors and students should adopt a more professional approach to teaching, learning, evaluation, and management, emphasizing innovative and effective methods.

Most of the universities in Benin teach English across the different levels and the largest one, the University of Abomey-Calavi, was officially declared bilingual in 2003 (cf. the Orientation Law of the National Education 2003-17) including faculties, institutes and doctoral schools. There are nine such organisational units in the University of Abomey-Calavi, including the Pluridisciplinary Doctoral School of Humanities, Communication and Languages, which is the setting of this research according to the 2016 rectorate by-law.

The fields of study housed in this school are geography and territory management, sociology and anthropology, linguistics and communication, psychology and educational sciences, anglophone studies, history and archaeology, modern letters, and philosophy. In each of these fields, a master's programme of one year and a doctoral programme of three years are offered. During a period of almost two decades, 2004 to 2019, many doctoral and master's degrees were awarded in these eight fields of study.

Though there is no official source yet, it can be observed that many of the graduates are unemployed or just doing informal jobs. Some of these graduates have complained that, apart from the current unemployment due to economic recession, there are discrepancies between their profiles, their skill sets, and the needs of the job market.

The following is an overview of the situation of higher education in other parts of the world which can be instructive for elaborating on the Benin case.

2. Literature review

2.1 Doctoral programme management: Perceptions of doctoral students and supervisors

The past few decades have seen a worldwide increase in doctoral programmes training, and Africa is no exception. Cloete et al. (2018) provide evidence of the issue through their HERANA project profiling eight African universities. The statistical data were revealing. They believe that universities can be instruments for development agendas, but through sharing expertise and capacity-building, rather than through the production of new scientific knowledge. In fact, according to the study, governments, policymakers and university leaders believed that doctoral education could be a driver of economic development and a generator of solutions to the many developmental challenges of African countries. Solutions had to be found to contribute to ongoing research output, evolving from the traditional apprenticeship models to more collaborative ones (McKenna, 2017). In Europe, doctoral education is seen in terms of the Lisbon Strategy as a major contributor "to become the most competitive and dynamic knowledge-based economy in the world, capable of sustainable economic growth with more and better jobs and greater social cohesion" (European Parliament, 2009).

However, Pyhältö et al. (2016) found that there is sometimes a misfit between doctoral students themselves and their working environment in terms of the wrong department, issues with supervisors and uncertain career prospects that ultimately result in student attrition. They also found that between supervisors and doctoral students there are not always similar perceptions of the factors that contribute to a successful doctoral process. For instance, while students put more emphasis on social support and interaction with researchers, supervisors have identified funding, and student characteristics such as motivation, internal locus of control and self-direction as key ingredients for completing a doctoral degree. In addition, they contend that at times, student needs are not accurately provided for under supervision. For instance, a supervisor offering person-focused or pastoral support, where students are looking more for support with the project management. Discrepancies such as these may contribute to student dissatisfaction with their supervision and may have an impact on completion rates.

In fact, a poor relationship between supervisors and doctoral students can affect the whole doctoral project negatively. So, a key element to successful doctoral studies is good relations between the candidate and the supervisor. Frick et al. (2014) report various strategies supervisors can use at different stages of the doctorate process to support and mitigate risks by making the doctoral programme a human training programme that enhances criticality and creativity.

2.2 Professionalization of doctorate programmes

Because of the many challenges higher education is facing worldwide and in sub-Saharan Africa, professionalization of the training itself in terms of the alignment between university education and training and the world of work or professions outside universities appear unavoidable.

Do Africans only need to produce graduates who possess skills needed to secure good jobs and be able to commercialize research or effective leaders and professionals who can generate knowledge that can contribute to the developmental needs of a country? (Frick et al., 2017). Caution must be taken here, for the issue is more complex than one can expect and calls for nuance. There is no doubt that not all research findings can be commercialized, or all PhDs be translated directly into 'jobs'. Certainly, some PhDs in some fields do indeed lead to patents and commercialization, but the situation differs significantly depending on the fields of study and skills training.

This gives rise to many models to make doctoral education more responsive to new labour and educational market demands. Here again there are strongly different views on the issue. Barnacle (in Frick et al., 2017) believes that considering the purpose of the PhD from a purely economic point of view promotes a *consumerist orientation* to education and removes candidates from their socio-cultural context and plays down their roles as responsible and creative scholars. As for Frick et al. (2017), they wonder what will become of the future of the PhD, which is supposed to be a forward-looking process of knowledge production, if industry partners are allowed to lay claim to what suits them and or is relevant to their needs, or in determining PhD processes and products.

So, with the skills development movement of the early 1990s, stemming from dissatisfaction with education–job match, employers' discontent with the type of education produced by universities and ultimately to find solutions to poor resourcing of the sector worldwide, universities were forced to review their higher education offerings, mainly in master's degrees. (Chevalier, 2000)

The skills proposed by some European universities in this regard may seem compatible with the Salzburg Principles (2005). Seven categories of doctorate skills were identified by (Poyatos, 2012). Some were classical ones such as 'ethics and social understanding' and 'research skills and awareness' but some were more relevant to the fast-moving world, such as 'time management', including 'writing and publishing skills'. To be more productive, other skills such as 'teaching personal effectiveness/development', 'team working and leadership', and 'career management' are also considered important in the training of graduate students, as well as the development of 'entrepreneurship and innovation' though used at lower levels of university education (Irish Universities Association, 2008).

The Catholic University of Leuven, Belgium (2012) promotes the acquisition of doctoral skills development to help doctoral students gain employment by helping them to evaluate their competence on certain 'non-academic skills' and 'transferable skills' such as 'communication and management'. The 'transferable skills' are divided into five categories: (i) intellectual competencies, (ii) self-management, (iii) relational competencies, (iv) leadership and change management, and (v) academic and technical competences (Gatfield, 2005).

Considering information generated by an Erasmus-funded project on the modern doctorate, Lee (2018) isolated some of its features. She argues that the modern doctorate focuses on knowledge transfer as well as knowledge creation and includes the professional doctorate where the focus is on practice but not restricted to that. It allows research methods that other programmes might consider unacceptable such as action research (Armsby et al., 2017). Muller (2009) identified this modern doctorate as a transformational process which includes notions of employability outside academia that focus on knowledge transfer as well as knowledge creation.

The Standards and Guidelines for Postgraduate Studies in East Africa, developed by the Inter-University Council for East Africa (IUCEA 2018), aim to harmonize and enhance the quality of higher education and research across the region. The guidelines focus on fostering collaboration and ensuring consistency in postgraduate programs among East African universities.

In sub-Saharan Africa, including Benin, postgraduate unemployment, specifically among doctoral than master's or bachelor's graduates, has been and remains a real challenge and concern for all stakeholders in the field. The widely known causes are poor quality and relevance of qualifications, lack of quality staff, lack of skills sought by employers and the discrepancy between university education and the world of work (ANIE 2018). The ANIE study put forward eight key conclusions and recommendations among which featured the following: quality of programmes must not be jeopardised in the context of rapid expansion; higher education systems need to seek balance between concentration and diffusion of doctoral programmes; countries should aim for a broad disciplinary spread in doctoral studies; strong linkage should be developed between universities, communities, industry and government.

Kelly (2014) identified possible challenges to the quality of doctoral education in some African countries, namely corruption in governance and management as well as in student admissions, including cheating in examinations, sexual harassment by academic and supervisor staff and plagiarism in theses and publications.

A developing country like Benin is far from being an exception. Therefore, there is an urgent need to improve doctoral education, to develop knowledge that may help solve local problems and eventually drive development.

3. Methodology

The current study is exploratory in nature, considering the experience, perceptions and attitudes of the supervisors and enrolled graduate students and alumni of the Pluridisciplinary Doctoral School of Humanities, Communication and Languages at the University of Abomey-Calavi in Benin. Challenges evident in current practices were identified to shed light on a type of supervision with relevant goals that stands the chance to address developmental needs. A qualitative method was used. This consisted of conducting interviews to gather participants' views, attitudes and perceptions about current practices and suggested changes. The second phase used a quantitative method, that is questionnaire administration to both enrolled graduate students and alumni of the school.

3.1 Sample

In the sampling design used for this study two types of participants were identified:

i) eight supervisors, one from each of the eight study fields hosted by the school.
ii) and twenty postgraduate students: ten alumni and ten enrolled doctoral students.

The research was conducted in 2019 in the doctoral school where I am the deputy director, head of academic affairs.

3.2 Instrumentation

Interviews

The aim of the qualitative data analysis is to achieve a thorough understanding of the phenomenon under investigation. Qualitative interviews were chosen "to seek in-depth understanding about the experiences of individuals and groups, commonly drawn from a sample of people, selected purposively" (Scott & Usher, 2006, p. 147). So, a face- to-face, individual, audio-taped interview with the researcher was organised. All the interviews were conducted within a week. To minimize dropout and because of their busy and tight schedules, I chose to interview the eight supervisors, who willingly voiced their perceptions and attitudes in response to the questions listed below in a fair-play atmosphere. Some of the questions, probes, prompts and intuitive questions were formulated based on the researcher's own experience as a supervisor in the school. Each interview lasted twenty to thirty minutes. This open-ended interview method was designed to compensate for the limitations of the self-completion questionnaire method. Postgraduate students were not interviewed because of time constraints.

The questions related to:

i)   Supervisors' self-assessments of their supervisory work (adapted from Lee & Kamler, 2007). The following issues were raised: availability/enthusiasm; building a scientific and social community; critical thinking; skill development; networking; mentor for life.

The questions were:

- Have you been available and enthusiastic about your job as a supervisor despite the hurdles?
- Do you think that building a scientific and social community should be part of supervisory work and how can this be built into the job?
- How far do you use critical thinking as part of your supervisory skills?
- Do you think it is part of our job to introduce our students to scientific networking?
- Do you think that mentorship for life should be part of our supervisory work?
- What changes can you suggest in our doctoral programmes in Benin that can address the developmental needs of the country? Or how can our supervision strategies be improved so that they could result in more employable graduates and address developmental needs?

Questionnaire

Based on the purpose of the study and the two research questions, the investigator developed two questionnaires that were completed by ten postgraduate students and ten alumni of the school.

Graduate students' questionnaire: The participants were asked to fill in a questionnaire containing seven items. This questionnaire comprised of Likert-scale items and three or four multiple item questions. The items were as follows: satisfaction with doctoral studies; purpose in undertaking these studies; relationship with supervisor(s); supervisor contribution; expected challenges; knowledge and skills needed for a relevant qualification and finally suggested changes. Ten questionnaire sheets were distributed but only eight were completed and collected. (Refer to the questionnaire in Addendum A)

Alumni questionnaire: The participants were asked to fill in a similar question-naire, but for two questions, which are about the current professional challenges related to their doctoral studies; and the knowledge and skills (the attributes) needed by for doctoral graduates to contribute to the achievement of the developmental goals of the country. (Refer to the questionnaire in Addendum B). Ten (10) questionnaires were distributed but only eight were ultimately collected.

3.3 Data collection and analysis procedures

Data collection lasted one week to allow participants enough time to reflect carefully before responding to the questionnaire. The items were analysed according to their nature and graphs were designed to illustrate the data to highlight the two main research questions.

To ensure the content validity and reliability of the instruments used, the investigator discussed the issues at stake with experienced supervisors who had worked in the field. They were asked to judge the appropriateness and relevance of each instrument item, bearing in mind the overall purpose of the study. This exercise led to the reformulation or cancellation of some questions in the questionnaires for clarity and conciseness.

4. Results

The results of this study have shed light on the two research questions. They are presented, analysed and interpreted below.

4.1 Interview results

The data are drawn from interviews with eight (8) supervisors from each field of study. Some quotations were deliberately included to make raw data available and to illustrate the different issues.

Table 1: Supervisors' self-assessment results

Issues discussed	N = 8	Per cent
Availability/enthusiasm	5/8	62.5%
Building a scientific & social community	3/8	37.5%
Critical thinking (active questions)	2/8	25.0%
Skills development (work-focused skills)	2/8	25.0%
Networking (introducing students to scientific network)	1/8	12.5%
Mentor for life	4/8	50.0%
Total	8	

Though it is not common to, for example, use percentages in analysing qualitative data such as interview recordings – because in nature there is no quantification or very little – I chose to use this method so that a broad view of a social reality can be seen as an external objective reality.

The interview results show that, notably, most of the interviewed supervisors (62.5%) shared that, not only were they available to their doctorate students but they were enthusiastic as well, despite the various hurdles. Very few of them (25%) were able to integrate critical thinking into their supervisory designs and strategies. In fact, Minaflinou (2015) found that to mould students to face the challenges of the 21st century, the life and work-focused skill of critical thinking should be part and parcel of the instructional strategies right from the lower levels of learning. However, this study recommends for example that in this part of the world, new assessment modes should be found in the academic field at university level, that go beyond recalling or restating memorized information. Many interviewees confessed that more effort is needed to introduce these components below doctorate level.

Lee (2018) identified critical thinking as one of the approaches of the modern doctorate as it emphasises intellectual rigour, offers opportunities for thinking in new ways, encourages the ability to analyse and recognise flaws in arguments and is identified by the supervisor's intent to analyse and enable the candidate to analyse what is being planned or presented.

Only three out of the eight supervisors interviewed were aware that building a scientific and social community offers a golden opportunity to promote collaboration through exchange of best practices. Since access to the internet still needs improvement, only one supervisor reported having introduced his students to their scientific network. Half of the interviewees said they are still in contact with their previous students and are aware that they should be their mentor for life.

The following are three samples of the supervisors' quotations. They are expressive of their perceptions.

> I'm not satisfied with my supervisory works. I wish I had more time to invest into it. The workload is a handicap ... My deep conviction is that the work is not properly done and therefore has not been yielding the expected dividends. We need regular training and more sharing to break our own isolation, for instance setting up a supervisors' forum. We cannot blame students alone ... . There are many hurdles today. We need to reshuffle our doctoral programmes to make them meet our challenges among which unemployment. (Prof. Guy [pseudonym], supervisor, my own translation)

I enjoy my supervisory work in spite all the challenges … Building a scientific and social community through a scientific network is a very good idea. Our tasks are manifold and we need to be committed to the job. Our main key challenges is how to make our doctoral programme relevant to local, regional and continental needs by promoting innovations and entrepreneurship in our students. Sustainable development should be our main priority. Our programme needs change! (Prof. Kodjo [pseudonym], supervisor)

My job as a supervisor is one of the most exciting and demanding one as well. Apart from the many constraints we've been battling with, our main challenge is our own training in this world of perpetual change. I can see why our educational authorities are putting pressure on us. Policy shapes practices. Our practice should change so as to make our doctoral programmes a key instrument to a sustainable development. Deep reflections are needed in the field for effective actions to be taken. (Prof. Sylvia)

4.2 Results of doctorate students and alumni questionnaires

An effort was made to compare the alumni and enrolled doctoral students' results. The following figure shows the comparison between both groups on the question of how they understand the purpose of doctorate studies.

Figure 1: Purpose in undertaking doctorate studies

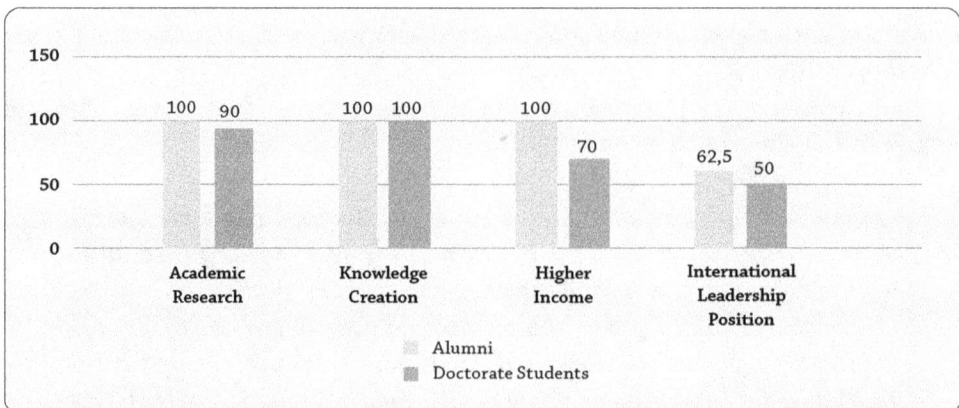

Apart from the variable of 'reaching international positions' which scored average (62.5 and 50%), all the other variables 'academic research and lecturing position', 'contributing to knowledge creation', and 'a ladder to attain a higher income' scored highly (100%, 90%, 70%). So, nearly all the respondents see the purpose of PhD studies in a similar manner.

Figure 2: Level of satisfaction

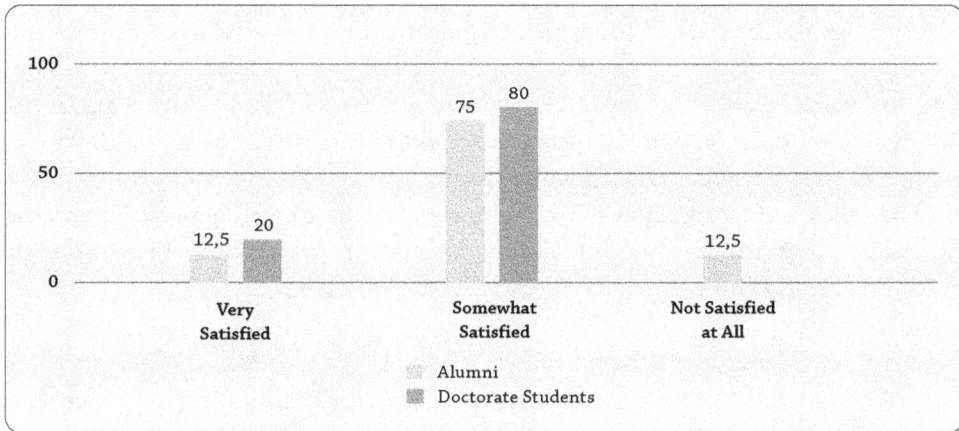

As for the level of satisfaction, both types of students were somewhat satisfied (75 and 80%). Very few of them (12.5 and 20%) were 'very satisfied' or 'not satisfied at all'. The level of satisfaction is average.

The process of effective and rewarding supervision requires that the supervisor knows and plays their role. The following figure shows the relationship between both types of students.

Figure 3: Relationship with the supervisor

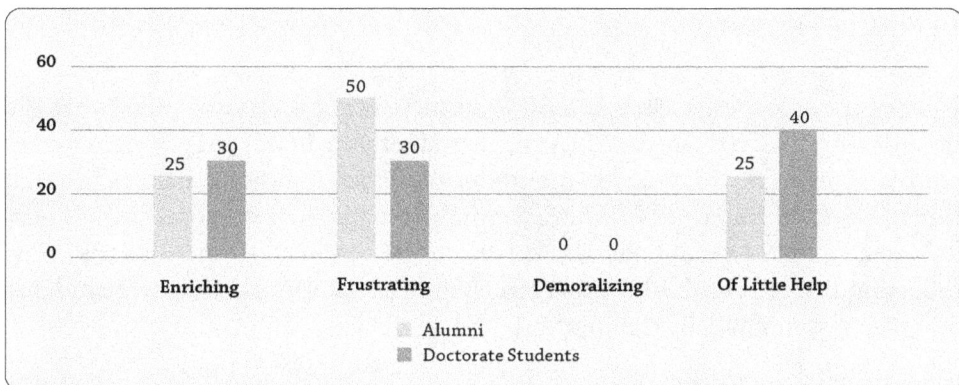

Both alumni and doctorate students found that their relationship with their supervisors was 'frustrating' (50 and 30%), while few of them found it 'enriching' (25 and 30%) and up to 40% of enrolled students and 25% alumni described it as 'of little help'.

To the question regarding the extent to which the supervisor contributed to the completion or the advancement of the thesis, 75% and 60% indicated that it is was 'some extent', while 25% and 30% admitted it to be a 'minimal extent' and only 30% and 25% suggested that it was to 'a great extent'. Evidently, supervisory work in this part of the world still needs improvement to be effective. I, as deputy director in charge of academic affairs, with the head of the school and a select team of supervisors, have been engaged in deep reflections in the last few years on effective changes that could be submitted to the educational authorities for approval and implementation.

The following figure shows how far in the opinion of the 18 respondents the doctorate programmes of both types of students prepared them for knowledge, attributes, skills and behaviour needed for the labour market.

Figure 4: Knowledge and skills needed

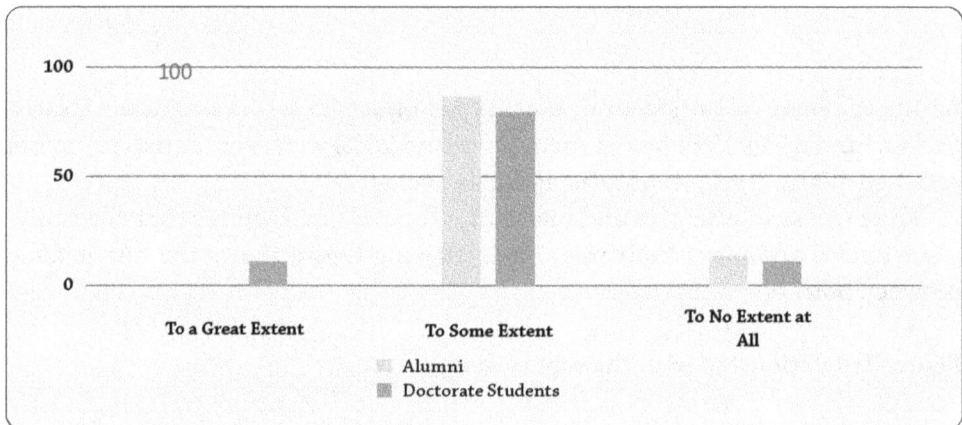

Most of these students (70% and 65%) admitted that they were aware that the qualification has not prepared (former students) or is not preparing (current students) primarily to meet job market needs. They indicated that preparation for the needs of the world of work is appropriate for their doctoral studies only 'to some extent'. None of the alumni chose the option 'to a great extent'. The following figure reveals the expected challenges of present doctoral students and the current challenges of alumni.

Figure 5: Expected and current challenges

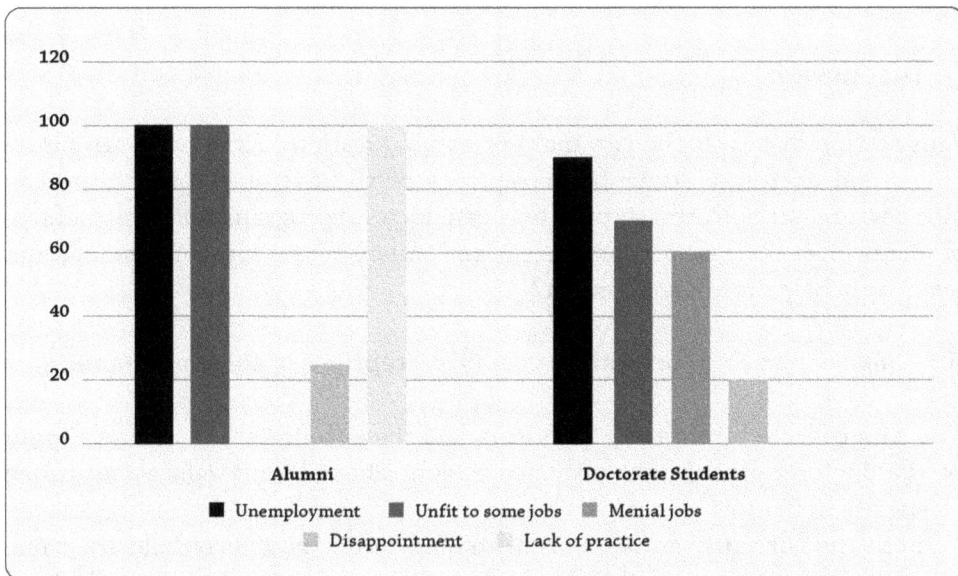

Nearly all the variables (unemployment, unfit for some jobs, opportunities for only menial jobs, lack of practice) scored very high. Alumni scored 100%; 100%; 100%, while disappointment scored 20%. Doctorate students scored (90%, 85%, 65%, while disappointment was 20%).

All were aware of the challenges to overcome. Fortunately, 'disappointment' scored very low (25%; 20%). It means that though they are aware of the apparent hurdles, these people were still optimistic and expected that if some changes were implemented, changes in terms of programmes, improved supervisory strategies, government policy that can shape good practice, a new dawn could be expected.

Figure 6 shows that all the respondents (100%) confessed that they 'strongly agree' that changes are unavoidable.

4.3 Limitations

Some limitations should, however, be identified. First, only humanities and social sciences fields of study were considered. It would have been more advantageous to investigate hard sciences disciplines that use different paradigms. Second, the investigation was conducted through a relatively small sample:

eight supervisors and eighteen PhD holders and PhD candidates. A larger sample could have yielded more representative results.

5. Discussion

This section discusses the two main research questions: first, what are supervisors and doctorate students' perceptions of the doctorate programmes in this doctoral school? And second, how can doctoral programmes help graduate students meet their professional needs and satisfy labour market demands and eventually help drive development?

5.1 Supervisors and doctorate students' perceptions of the programme

The data collected from the supervisors and the enrolled students and alumni of the doctoral school have provided insight about higher education in one university in Benin.

Both the currently enrolled students and recent graduates held the same view about the purpose of the PhD. Their purpose in undertaking doctoral studies was to have an academic research and lecturing position, to contribute to knowledge creation, to attain a higher income and to reach international leadership positions. This finding is backed up by Blume (1995, p. 30–31) and Heen (2002, p. 85) who contend that the outcome of doctoral research should enable graduates to find employment, prepare them for academic careers and develop generic research or other skills or even prepare them for careers outside of the academy. It is a matter of concern that few of these Beninese graduate students have the ambition to apply their competencies in international leadership positions in their field. Is it a lack in self-confidence or ambition? The supervisors who were interviewed maintained that the PhD programme currently lacks work-focused skills. The problem is how to equip doctoral students with transferable skills and specific skills so that they can undertake consulting jobs, for example, and eventually occupy senior appointments in government, in NGOs, in research organisations, in industry and business, and in universities.

The level of satisfaction of doctoral students and recent graduates with the quality of their PhD programmes is average probably because of the many hurdles to overcome among which is the relationship with the supervisor. Most of the doctoral students and graduates found it frustrating and of little help, but not demoralizing. In fact, ineffective interaction with the supervisor leads to negative research experience. The finding corresponds with published literature (Cross & Backhouse, 2014; Pyhältö et al., 2015; McKenna, 2017). This is

Figure 6: Suggested changes

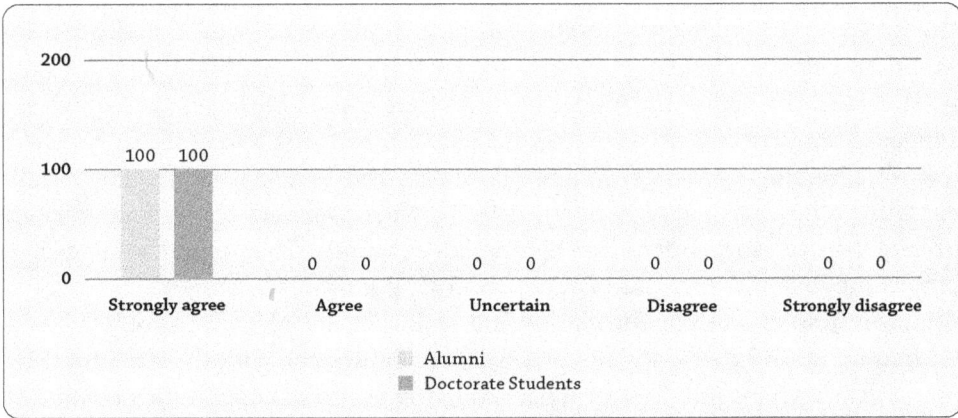

confirmed by most of the supervisors interviewed in this study who maintained that not only have they not been able to build a scholarly and social community which is key to doctoral education success today, but even introducing students into the scientific network seems unfeasible. It is not surprising, therefore, that few students indicated that their supervisor contributed greatly to their thesis advancement or the completion of their PhD studies. So, playing the role of mentor for life seems, according to some respondents, not to be part of the agenda of their supervisors. This is not surprising because the traditional apprenticeship model for doctoral supervision, still widely practised, is ineffective to meet the challenges of a developing country like Benin. The importance of a scientific and social community in a doctoral programme cannot be overlooked, for all students need to feel part of a supportive and inclusive environment to feel safe enough to participate and have a sense of being seen, listened to and valued. It is an arena where students can take risks and test out new ideas (McKenna, 2017). Hence the urgent need for continuous improvement of doctoral education to meet the needs of an employment market wider than academia (Ortega & Kent, 2018).

5.2 The doctoral programme's contribution to socio-economic development

The data collected in this study show that most supervisors maintained that the development of work-focused skills is not officially built into their training programmes. Recently graduated PhD holders indicated their doctoral qualification had not enabled them to attain the knowledge needed, attributes, skills and behaviour to help plan and manage their own career development. The current doctoral students are of the same view, and they expressed that if changes could be made over the short term to improve the situation, the benefit would be welcomed by all.

However, the prevailing model assumes that at the PhD level, candidates are supposed to have already acquired academic knowledge and skills at master's level (Université d'Abomey-Calavi, 2018). But the reality is that many candidates have not had equal opportunities as they probably come from various undergraduate programmes and diverse backgrounds. Therefore, the suggested programme should integrate course work, the aim of which is to establish a common base of subject knowledge and skills for all, so that those who have limited research experience and other shortcomings can gain insight into good research principles and best practices and any required competence needed in the workplace.

Meanwhile, in reviewing some innovative responses to the challenge of delivering good doctoral education in Africa, from the introduction of 'sandwich' programmes to collaborative models, Cross and Backhouse (2014) contend that such innovation is not only in the curricula and structures of the programmes, but in the judicious use of partnerships to compensate for resource limitations, to strengthen the capacity to lobby for change.

In Benin, it may entail introduction of course work in the form of seminars, workshops, exchange programmes, online or distance learning to the PhD programme of the school, resulting in "a shift from the master-apprentice model to the professional model of doctoral education" (Bartelse et al., 2007, p.7).

A one-year probation will be made compulsory for each candidate with a project to be submitted at the end that contributes in a productive way to the enterprise development. This project should be part of the requirements of the final thesis defence. It means that more emphasis must be put on the development of entrepreneurship and innovation skills for doctorate students to contribute to local needs and, as a result, drive socio-economic development. Such proposed professional development of doctoral candidates can play a role in paving the way for a wide range of career choices by bridging the gap between training and the job market.

For this to be possible, an academic and social community that provides a supportive and collegial environment and a combination of supervision and mentoring strategies must be built. This may call for two supervisors, an academic and a professional one who work hand in hand for a common shared purpose (Samuel & Vithal, 2011). The suggested new model of supervision would require training of supervisors. In fact, the interview data revealed that the supervisors recognise the need for regular supervisory training. In our fast-paced world, even experienced supervisors need training to keep up to date, for the field of research ethics and intellectual property is a growing one (Turner, 2015). Supervisor training/development activities may include online or distance programmes (e.g. CREST programmes), short seminars/ workshops, empowerment programmes, informal experience, resource and expertise sharing, supervisors' forums (as suggested by one of the interviewed supervisors), opportunities for supervisor group reflections etc. In other words, a platform must be set up for all supervisors to exchange best practices and provide opportunities to build up or rejuvenate regional and international part- nerships with funding organisations. To be effective today, supervision must be a collective effort in an atmosphere of trust, collaboration and support.

These suggestions for the renewal of the doctoral programme will proba- bly be widely welcomed but achieving them would require concerted effort. Fortunately, the educational authorities in Benin are aware of ethical issues, quality assurance and innovation. Two agencies, the Agence Béninoise de l'Assurance Qualité de l'Enseignement Supérieur (ABAQES) and the Agence Béninoise de Valorisation de la Recherche et de l'Innovation Technologique (ABeVRIT) were recently rejuvenated and given the mandate of upholding and enhancing high standards and best practices and to popularizing research in higher education in Benin (Décret No 220-342 du 20 mars 2016; Loi No 94-009 du 28 juillet 1994).

It is recommended that the doctoral programme changes suggested in this chapter are submitted to these bodies to be validated, popularized and inte- grated into general policies for doctoral schools.

Further research must be carried out on the correlation between PhD training and employment for instance: What type of research should doctoral candidates undertake, for what practical problems and for what solutions?

6. Conclusion

Improving doctoral education in a developing country so that it can play a role in social- economic development is a real challenge. This study has tried to shed light on the state of doctoral programmes in one of the doctoral schools in Benin. The findings from the supervisors, current graduate students and alumni of the school showed the following: the stakeholders agree that the situ- ation of doctoral education in Benin is at a low ebb and needs urgent change for quality improvement, so that high-level graduates who can contribute to the country's development by helping to address challenges and initiate innovations can be available.

In this chapter, I have introduced a new, more professional doctoral programme that integrates course work and professional probation into the curricula to improve its chances of meeting the needs of an employment market wider than academia.

References

ANIE (African Network for Internationalisation of Education). 2018. Building PhD capacity in Sub-Saharan Africa. https://www.britishcouncil.org/sites/default/files/h233_07_synthesis_report_final_web.pdf

Armsby, P. C., Costley, C., & Cranfield, S. (2017). The design of doctorate curricula for practising professionals. *Studies in Higher Education*. Advance online publication. https://doi.org/10.1080/03075079.2017.1318365

Arrêté Ministériel No 270 MESRS/DC/SGM/DAF/DGES/R-UAC/CCJ/SA 8503GG18. (2018, May).

Arrêté No 2012-712/MESRS/CAR/DC/SGM/DGES/R-UAC/R-UP/SA. (2012, October 12).

Barnacle, R. (2005). Research education ontologies: Exploring doctoral becoming. *Higher Education Research & Development, 24*(2), 179–188.

Bartelse, J., Oost, H., & Sonneveld, H. (2007). Doctoral education in the Netherlands. In S. Powell & H. Green (Eds.), *The doctorate worldwide* (pp. 64–76). The Society for Research into Higher Education and Open University Press.

Blume, S. (1995). *Problems and prospects of research training in the 1990s.* Centre of Australia, Adelaide, Australia.

Chevalier, C. (2000). *Graduate over-education in the UK.* Centre for the Economics Education. London School of Economics and Political Science.

Cloete, N., Bunting, I. & Van Schalkwyk, F. 2018. Research Universities in Africa. African Minds.

Cross, M., & Backhouse, J. (2014). Evaluating doctoral programmes in Africa: Context and practices. *Higher Education Policy, 27*(2), 155–174. https://link.springer.com/article/10.1057/hep.2014.1

Décret No 220-342. (2016, March 20). Portant création, organisation et fonctionnement de l'Agence Béninoise de l'Assurance Qualité de l'Enseignement Supérieur.

Décret Portant Organisation et Fonctionnement du LMD dans l'Enseignement Supérieur au Bénin No 2010-272. (2010, July 11).

Frick, B. L., Albertyn, B. L., & Bitzer, E. M. (2014). Candidates, supervisors, and institutions: Pushing postgraduates' boundaries. In E. Bitzer, R. Albertyn, L. Frick & F. Kelly (Eds.), *Pushing boundaries in postgraduate supervision* (pp.1–7). SUN PRESS.

Frick, L., McKenna, S., & Muthama, E. (2017). Death of the PhD: when industry partners determine doctoral outcomes. *Higher Education Research & Development, 36*(2), 444–447.

Gatfield, T. (2005). An investigation into PhD supervisory management styles: Development of a dynamic conceptual model and its managerial implications. *Journal of Higher Education Policy and Management, 27*(3), 311–325. https://www.tandfonline.com/doi/full/10.1080/13600800500283585

Heen, E. F. (2002). Research priorities and disciplinary cultures: Friends or foes? A cross-national study on doctoral research training in economics in France and Norway. *Higher Education Policy, 15*(1), 77–95. https://www.sciencedirect.com/science/article/abs/pii/S0952873301000241

Irish Universities Association. (2008). *Irish universities' PhD graduates' skills.* https://www.iua.ie/wp-content/uploads/2019/09/Graduate_Skills_Statement.pdf

IUCEA (Inter-University Council for East Africa). (2018). *Standards and Guidelines for Postgraduate Studies in East Africa.* Kampala: IUCEA.

Kelly, T. (2014). *Tech hubs across Africa: Which will be the legacy makers?* The World Bank.

Lee, A. (2018). How can we develop supervisors for the modern doctorate? *Studies in Higher Education, 43*(5), 878–892. https://www.tandfonline.com/doi/full/10.1080/03075079.2018.1438116

Lee, A., & Kamler, B. (2007). Bringing pedagogy to doctoral publishing. *Teaching in Higher Education, 13*(5), 511–523. https://www.tandfonline.com/doi/full/10.1080/13562510802334723

European parliament. (2009). Briefing note for the meeting of the EMPL Committee 5 October 2009 regarding the exchange of views on the Lisbon Strategy and the EU cooperation in the field of social inclusion. www.europarl.europa.eu/meetdocs/2009_2014/documents/empl/dv/lisbonstrategybn_/lisbonstrategybn_en.pdf.

Loi No 2003-17. (2003, November 11). Portant orientation de l'éducation nationale en République du Bénin.

Loi No 94-009. (1994, July 28). Portant création, organisation et fonctionnement de l'Agence Béninoise de Valorisation de la Recherche et de l'Innovation Technologique et des Offices à caractère social, culturel et scientifique.

McKenna, S. (2017). Crossing conceptual thresholds in doctoral communities. *Innovations in Educational and Teaching International, 54*(5), 472–480. https://www.tandfonline.com/doi/full/10.1080/14703297.2016.1155471

Minaflinou, E. (2015). Promoting critical thinking skills in EFL university students in Benin. *International Journal of English Language and Literature Studies, 10*(10), 200–210. https://archive.aessweb.com/index.php/5019/article/view/433

Muller, J. (2009). Forms of knowledge and curriculum coherence. *Journal of Education and Work, 22*(3), 205–226. https://www.tandfonline.com/doi/full/10.1080/13639080902957905

Ortega, S. T., & Kent, J. D. (2018). What is a PhD? Reverse-engineering our degree programs in the age of evidence-based change. *The Magazine of Higher Learning, 50*(1), 30–36. https://www.tandfonline.com/doi/full/10.1080/00091383.2018.1413904

Poyatos, M. C. (2012). Doctoral education and skills development perspective. *REDU - Revista de Docencia Universitaria, 10*(2), 163–191. https://doaj.org/article/453de028d1ed442eba72d4a154eeaaa1

Pyhältö, K., Vekkaila, J., & Keskinen, J. (2012). Exploring the fit between doctoral students' and supervisors' perceptions of resources and challenges 'vis-à-vis' the doctoral journey. *International Journal of Doctoral Studies, 7*, 395–314. https://www.informingscience.org/Publications/1745

Samuel, M., & Vithal, R. (2011). Emergent framework of research teaching and learning in a cohort-based doctoral programme. *Perspectives in Education, 29*(3), 76–87. https://journals.ufs.ac.za/index.php/pie/article/view/1697

Scott, D., & Usher, R. (2006). *Researching education: Data, methods, and theory in education enquiry.* Continuum International Publishing Group.

The Catholic University of Leuven, Belgium. (2012). *Research skills development for curriculum development and assessment.* KU Leuven.

Turner, G. (2015). Learning to supervise: Four journeys. *Innovations in Educational and Teaching International, 52*(1), 86–98.

UK Quality Code for Higher Education. (2015). *Characteristics statement.* Southgate House.

Université d'Abomey-Calavi. (2018). *Actes des Conférences du Collèges des Ecoles Doctorales de l'Université d'Abomey-Calavi.* Rectorat.

World Bank. (2000). *Higher education in developing countries: Peril and promise.* World Bank.

ADDENDUM A

Doctorate students' questionnaire

Dear Students,

I'm sending this questionnaire to you to seek your opinions about the role of the doctoral qualification in the socio-economic development of Benin, as part of the fulfilment of the requirement of an end-of-training assignment in the field of research in doctoral programme. Feel free, and be as truthful as possible, to tick the options that reflect best your viewpoints. This will go a long way to improve practice in our field of research. In advance, thank you.

1. What is your purpose in undertaking doctoral studies?
   a. For academic research
   b. For knowledge creation
   c. For higher income
   d. For international leadership

2. What is your relationship with your supervisor?
   a. Satisfied
   b. Somewhat satisfied
   c. Not satisfied at all

3. How can you qualify your relationship with your supervisor?
   a. Enriching
   b. Frustrating
   c. Demoralizing
   d. Of little help

4. How far has your doctorate programme prepared you for knowledge, attributes, skills, behavior needed for the labour market?
   a. To a great extent
   b. To some extent
   c. To no extent at all

5. What are your foreseen challenges?
   a. Unemployment
   b. Unfit for some jobs

    c. Menial jobs
    d. Disappointment
    e. Lack of practice

6. If changes are implemented, hope is still possible.
    a. I strongly agree
    b. I agree
    c. I'm uncertain
    d. I disagree
    e. I strongly disagree

ADDENDUM B

Alumni's questionnaire

Dear Students,

I'm sending this questionnaire to you to seek your opinions about the role of the doctoral qualification in the socio-economic development of Benin, as part of the fulfilment of the requirements of an end-of-training assignment in the field of research in doctoral programme. Feel free, and be as truthful as possible, to tick the options that reflect best your viewpoints. This will go a long way to improve practice in our field of research. In advance, thank you.

1. What is your purpose in undertaking doctoral studies?
    a. For academic research
    b. For knowledge creation
    c. For higher income
    d. For international leadership

2. What is your relationship with your supervisor?
    a. Satisfied
    b. Somewhat satisfied
    c. Not satisfied at all

3. How can you qualify your relationship with your supervisor?
    a. Enriching
    b. Frustrating
    c. Demoralizing
    d. Of little help

4. How far has your doctorate programme prepared you for knowledge, attributes, skills, behavior needed for the labour market?
    a. To a great extent
    b. To some extent
    c. To no extent at all

5. What are your current challenges?
    a. Unemployment
    b. Unfit for some jobs

    c. Menial jobs
    d. Disappointment
    e. Lack of practice

6. If changes are implemented, hope is still possible.
    a. I strongly agree
    b. I agree
    c. I'm uncertain
    d. I disagree
    e. I strongly disagree

CHAPTER 6

The MPhil/PhD degree at the University of Mauritius: Time to diversify and adopt other models of doctoral degrees?

Meera Manraj

The **Republic of Mauritius**, a group of islands in the Indian Ocean on the eastern side of Africa, has a 1 278 000 (in 2023). There are 10 publicly funded higher education institutions (HEI) and 30 private higher education institutions (HEIs) in Mauritius (Higher Education Commission in Mauritius). Four public institutions have the power to award doctoral degrees. In 2019, out of 18 372 new entrants into tertiary education, 15.6% and 8.3% enrolled at postgraduate level in public and private HEIs respectively, including 202 doctoral candidates.

The **University of Mauritius**, established in 1965, comprises 7 faculties, employs 276 academic and 623 support staff. In 2020/2021 the university had 9 321 students (20.6% on a part-time basis) of whom 193 were MPhil or PhD students, and one MPhil and 27 doctoral degrees were awarded (2020-2021 Annual Report).

1. Introduction

The average annual growth of doctorates awarded has increased worldwide (Cyranoski et al., 2011) mainly in countries that see educated workers as a key to economic growth. South Africa is considered a regional hub in graduate education on the African continent (Teferra, 2015) as it provides training both to local and PhD graduates from other African countries. The situation is quite different in Mauritius as the production of PhD graduates seems to stagnate even though the country aspires, according to its policymakers in 2006, to develop into a knowledge hub (Cloete et al., 2011).

The University of Mauritius (UoM) (established in 1965) is the main and oldest public tertiary public institution in the country. It offers the traditional supervised MPhil/PhD by thesis programme in all its seven faculties, namely, the Faculty of Science, the Faculty of Agriculture, the Faculty of Engineering, the Faculty of Social Sciences and Humanities, the Faculty of Law and Management, the Faculty of Information, Communication & Digital Technologies, and the Faculty of Medicine and Health Sciences (established in September 2020). The UoM has continued the tradition of Commonwealth universities where students usually register on a full-time or part-time basis for an MPhil, MPhil/ PhD programme after the bachelor's degree, or, more rarely, directly for a PhD programme. Organisation of the doctoral programme follows an apprentice-ship model and is thesis based. The average annual growth in doctoral output from 2001 to 2015 at UoM was estimated at 2%, the lowest among the eight African universities included in the HERANA project (Bunting et al., 2017, p. 40). The average annual growth in research publications over the same period at the UoM was also amongst the lowest. Whereas doctoral graduate numbers stagnated between 2001 and 2015 at the UoM (17 in 2001, 15 in 2011 and 21 in 2015), the number of taught master's graduates increased over the same period (69 in 2001, 396 in 2011 and 351 in 2015) (Bunting et al., 2017, p. 32).

In this chapter, I shall first make a few comments about the history of doctoral education in the world and the current situation regarding the prevalent types of doctoral studies. I shall describe the situation at the UoM based on data from its published annual reports of activities available from 2019/2020 to 2002/2003.[1] I shall propose a few suggestions regarding alternative formats of doctorates that may be realistically feasible and helpful in remedying the current situation of low doctoral production at the UoM in light of trends in doctoral education occurring in most parts of the world. The chapter will conclude with a summary of activities that are advised for good doctoral supervision practice.

---

1 https://www.uom.ac.mu/index.php/about-us/publications/report-on-uom-activities-factsheets.

2. History of the doctorate and models of PhD

2.1 The German and American models, and PhD by publication in 19th and 20th centuries

'Doctor' and 'master' were synonyms up to the 12th century in Europe and were not linked to research. These titles allowed individuals to teach (Hargreaves-Mawdsley, 1963 cited in Academic Apparel, n.d.). The doctoral degree that was developed in 1806 at Humboldt University, Germany, combined teaching and research. It was obtained upon completion of several years of research apprenticeship and submission of a dissertation. That was the traditional doctoral degree by thesis (German model) which was considered the highest academic degree.

The PhD qualification that was first offered by Yale University in the USA in the mid-19th century differed from the German model as it consisted of blended course work and a PhD thesis (Matas, 2012). Thus, it came to be known as the American model. The PhD qualification was offered in the early 20th century by Oxford University in the UK, then in Canada and Australia. Both German and American models co-existed in universities across the world. For much of the 20th century there were marked differences between science-based graduate programmes in the USA and elsewhere. Course work and research were an integral part of both master's and doctoral programmes in the USA and Canada, whereas European institutions privileged hands-on research and research training, usually to the exclusion of course work in doctoral programmes (Kehm, 2007). Doctoral programmes, which were of three-year duration in European universities, were longer in the USA, typically between four to six years. More institutions around the world have evolved curricula closer to the US and Canadian models, with blended course work and research in the past couple of decades.

A new trend occurred in the UK in the 1960s when the PhD by publication was introduced. This format, which is popular in some European countries and in Australasia, is examined on the basis of publishing one or more peer-reviewed academic paper(s), accompanied by an overarching introduction, discussion and conclusions (Matas, 2012).

2.2 Reforms as from the 21st century

In the late 20th century, several countries followed the example of the USA, where a national survey on doctoral learning experiences of students in

1999 had been carried out. The survey found that the research training was not comprehensive and not effective at preparing students for careers they could pursue in academia and outside of academia, and, alarmingly, it was not effective in preparing students to become researchers (Matas, 2012). A wave of doctoral education reforms ensued in various countries after surveys were conducted on the careers of doctoral graduates.

Germany redesigned its doctoral education with the creation of graduate schools teaching transferable skills through structured programmes to increase the quality and the relevance of doctoral education and research training in what was coined the 'third cycle' of studies in the framework of the Bologna process (Kehm, 2007). A trend of introducing learning outcomes frameworks and assessment into doctoral education, which previously only focused on undergraduate learning, began in the USA. This was in response to calls for aligning doctoral training with the career needs of students irrespective of their future, whether in academia (only 15% of PhD graduates secured academic appointments in 2006 in the USA) or elsewhere, and to make the learning outcomes of doctoral degree programmes more explicit and more student-centred (Ortega & Kent, 2018).

National qualification frameworks in Europe, Australia and Canada provided guidelines for the definition of doctoral degrees, placing emphasis on the creation of new knowledge through research. Parallel to the USA, the Lumina Foundation, which emphasises the importance of learning frameworks (Travers et al., 2019), provided a definition of the doctoral degree: Level 8 (the highest level) describes a PhD degree holder as someone "who demonstrates competencies for obtaining research findings in a scientific subject or for the development of innovative solutions and procedures in highly complex and novel problem situation within a field of occupational activity" (Ortega & Kent, 2018).

The UK innovated with the introduction of three new doctoral education models which included the 'professional doctorate', the 'practice-based doctorate', and the 'new route PhD' to reach more national and international students (Matas, 2012).

- The professional doctorate targeted working professionals and was based on a combination of course work and a supervised research project that was more applied and work-focused and smaller than the traditional PhD. An example of such endeavour in UK was the recruitment in 2011 of the first cohort of so-called 'Industrial PhD students' by the University of Strathclyde. These students were hosted at Glaxo-Smith-Kline (GSK) for the majority of their PhD project which was in an area directly aligned with GSK's business and discovery projects (Allen, 2016).

- The practice-based doctorate aimed to reach artists and was based on a supervised research project in the performing arts. This type of doctorate assessed a creative work and a thesis which was shorter than the traditional thesis and included context and reflections of the doctoral student.
- The new route PhD aimed at an international doctoral student population, it provided research training, personal and professional development opportunities, and formative assessment based on course work (Matas, 2012).

Doctoral education reform in the UK was also based on inclusion of at least two weeks of training per year in transferable and generic skills for all doctoral and postdoctoral researchers, to improve their employability prospects (Matas, 2012). In a survey performed in the UK, employers ranked researchers' relative competences in the following order: *data analysis, problem solving, drive and motivation, project management, interpersonal skills, leadership, and commercial awareness* (Matas, 2012, p. 171). It is to be noted that reforms that occurred in the UK were not necessarily adopted by universities in its former colonies (including Mauritius) which mostly retained traditional models of PhD training.

In trying to speed up and expand knowledge production to keep ahead in the international knowledge innovation race; to participate successfully in the global knowledge economy; as well as for universities to improve their place in the international university rankings doctoral students' publications are increasingly being financially rewarded by most governments (Matas, 2012). Thus, the model of the PhD by publication has become more appealing than ever in countries like Australia (Powell, 2004).

2.3 Situation in Africa and in Mauritius

The first doctorates were awarded by South African universities from 1899 (Herman, 2017). Other sub-Saharan African universities set up doctoral programmes later after achieving independence around the mid-20th century, Universities that were modelled on the institutions of their former colonizers.

The Higher Education Qualifications Sub Framework (HEQSF) of South Africa (2013) described the submission requirements for the doctoral degree, whose duration was to be for two years minimum full time after a master's degree: "submission of a thesis, with possibility of submitting publications or creative work". Thereafter the Council on Higher Education in South Africa

(CHE, 2018, p. 13–14; Botha et al., 2021, p. 164) described the minimum threshold for graduate attributes to be achieved at doctoral level. Attributes at doctoral level considered in the Doctoral Qualification Standard were "specialised knowledge of a discipline, specialised knowledge of a specific area of research, insight into the interconnectedness of the topic of research with other cognate fields, ethical awareness in research and professional conduct and an original contribution to the field of study".

Other definitions of the doctoral degree were provided in 2015 by the Inter-University Council for East Africa (IUCEA), such as in the East African Qualifications Framework for Higher Education (EAQFHE), and more recently, in the Standards and Guidelines for Postgraduate Studies in East Africa in 2018. The IUCEA is responsible for the coordination and harmonization of postgraduate degrees in East African countries but does not have accreditation or regulatory powers (Botha et al., 2021, p. 161).

The University of Mauritius offers the MPhil or PhD degree as in some other Commonwealth universities. Three other public universities in Mauritius also offer doctoral studies. Information on doctoral studies offered at the four institutions is summarised in Table 1.

Table 1: Brief description of research degrees currently offered by 4 public universities in Mauritius2

Public Tertiary Institutions	University of Mauritius (UoM)	University of Technology, Mauritius (UTM)	Université des Mascareignes (UDM)	Open University of Mauritius (OUM)
Set up through Parliamentary Acts	7 December 1965	21 June 2000	28 May 2012	12 July 2012
Type of doctoral degrees offered	MPhil, MPhil/PhD, or PhD (rare cases)	MPhil, MPhil/PhD, or PhD (directly)	MPhil or MPhil/ PhD or PhD	PhD (MPhil/PhD very rarely) DBA: professional doctorate
Areas of research	Many disciplines (across the 7 faculties and centres)	Management, tourism, applied mathematics, modelling and sustainable development	Engineering, IT and management	Business administration, Finance and investment, law and management

---

2 Sources: https://udm.ac.mu/research/doctoral-school-ecole-doctorale/ http://www.utm. ac.mu/files/sthug/Regulation/Research%20Degrees/booklet.pdf https://www.uom.ac.mu/ Images/Files/Regulations/MPhilPhD/2021_2022/chap1.pdf https://www.open.ac.mu/ dbaphd-programme-document-for-jan-2022-intake/

Public Tertiary Institutions	University of Mauritius (UoM)	University of Technology, Mauritius (UTM)	Université des Mascareignes (UDM)	Open University of Mauritius (OUM)
Entry requirements	For MPhil or MPhil/ PhD: 1st or upper 2nd class BSc Honours or taught master's degree. For PhD: MPhil degree (or MA by Research/MSc by Applied Research)	For MPhil or MPhil/ PhD: at least upper 2nd class Honours or master's degree For PhD: MPhil Degree or a master's degree by Research in the field	For MPhil or MPhil/ PhD: at least upper 2nd class Honours degree For PhD: MPhil or a master's degree in a related subject area	For DBA: A masters- level degree, MBA or specialist MA or M.Sc. in a related area. For PhD: A master's- level degree in the related area
Admission process	Applications are first processed by the doctoral school; research proposal is assessed by its Higher Degrees Committee. Final approval for registration is by the Teaching and Research Committee of UoM, then implementation is at the faculty level (6 monthly progress reports, external assessors for transfer reports and theses etc.).	Application and preliminary proposals are first processed by the head of school who provides a letter of offer after which the student attends courses on research methods, ethics and quantitative and qualitativeresearch. Final proposal is submitted within 6 months for consideration by the Research Degrees Committee prior to confirmation for MPhil and PhD Registration.	Applications and research proposals (format available online) are sent to the head of the doctoral school of UDM.	Applicants do not submit their research proposal up front in either the DBA or PhD. They benefit from course work in the first semester (PhD) or first year (DBA) of registration, this is followed by a supervised stage where the doctoral student develops a research proposal that is submitted to the OUM Research Committee for review and approval.
Duration of studies	MPhil: 2 to 3 years (FT), 3 to 4 years (PT) MPhil/PhD: 3 to 5 years (FT), 3½ to 7 years (PT) PhD (direct): 2 to 4 years (FT), 3 to 5 years (PT)	MPhil: 2 to 3 years (FT), 3 to 5 years (PT) MPhil/PhD: 3 to 5 years (FT), 4 to 7 years (PT) PhD: 1½ to 5 years (FT), 3 to 7 years (PT)	MPhil: 2 years (FT) MPhil/PhD: 3 years (FT), 5 years (PT)	DBA: 3 to 6 years PhD: 3 to 8 years

Public Tertiary Institutions	University of Mauritius (UoM)	University of Technology, Mauritius (UTM)	Université des Mascareignes (UDM)	Open University of Mauritius (OUM)
Degree course organisation	Apprenticeship model and thesis-based The doctoral school organises transferable skills seminars for PhD students. Student notifies dean of faculty, with the approval of their supervisor(s), of their intention to submit a transfer report. Faculty Research Committee approves selection of external assessors.	Apprenticeship model and thesis-based Student is supervised by a supervisor (2 max.). Supervisor interacts with student and submits undertaking that transfer report, or thesis is acceptable to the Higher Degrees Committee (HDC).	Apprenticeship model and thesis-based Student supervised by a director of studies. The doctoral school organises specialist courses and transferable skills seminars for PhD students.	DBA: Structured courses in the 1st year to develop learners' expertise in use of research in to explore professional practice and submission of supervised research work as a written DBA thesis. PhD: structured course work in the 1st semester on research, systematic literature review. Supervised research after final proposal is approved by OUM and submission of a thesis.
Assessment process Conditions for awarding degree	Two (overseas) external assessors are appointed for MPhil transfer report or PhD thesis. No viva voce. A board of examiners (BoE) makes recommendations based on both EEs' reports: For MPhil transfer report: BoE may recommend upgrade to PhD or award of MPhil degree (the first positive recommendation received from one EE is sufficient for upgrade to PhD). For PhD thesis: Need for one publication in Web of Science journal before PhD thesis is sent to the external assessors. BoE recommends award of a PhD (or corrections or resubmission).	MPhil transfer report examined through viva by a MPhil transfer assessment panel. MPhil/PhD thesis is assessed by a MPhil/PhD examination panel (including 2 external assessors) + face-to-face or online oral examination.	PhD thesis is examined by 2 external assessors + viva voce	DBA: Assessment is through review of the DBA thesis + viva voce. PhD: Assessment takes the form of a review and/or by an oral 'defence' of the thesis, conducted in person or by live video link. PhD degree is awarded to successful students. All PhD students are required to have published at least two papers in peer-reviewed journals before being allowed to submit their final thesis.

Public Tertiary Institutions	University of Mauritius (UoM)	University of Technology, Mauritius (UTM)	Université des Mascareignes (UDM)	Open University of Mauritius (OUM)
Number of registered students (most recent)	171 per annum on average in the last 18 years	30 MPhil/PhD students were registered in 2008	26 (9 enrolled in 2014, 6 in 2017, 11 in 2020)	Started offering PhD and DBA in 2013. Has offered 56 PhD and 18 DBA to date. No student is enrolled in MPhil/PhD
Output	297 since 2002 (235 PhD); 16 per year in the last 18 years	Not available	Total of 8 (5 PhD in 2020, 3 in 2021)	

FT: Full-Time; PT: Part-time; DBA: Doctorate in Business Administration; EE: External Assessors

3. Trends in doctoral production at the University of Mauritius

In the last three decades, the University of Mauritius has offered programmes providing the following possibilities for enrolment in postgraduate programmes by research: MPhil or MPhil/PhD or PhD, on a part-time or full-time basis. It also offered master by research programmes in the last decade such as the MA by Research (social sciences) or MSc by Applied Research (technology and sciences), which are "tailor- made programmes of demand work-based research type, they emphasise independent study over taught components". The MPhil or MPhil/PhD or PhD programmes of UoM do not involve any course work, they are based on the apprenticeship model and assessed upon submission of a transfer report and/or of a thesis. Entry requirements for the MPhil and MPhil/PhD programmes are common: having a first or upper 2nd class BSc Honours or a taught master's degree. Entry requirements for the PhD programme are having an MPhil degree or another postgraduate degree by research (MA by Research or MSc by Applied Research).

Few students choose to register for an MPhil programme without any future intention of registering for a PhD. In that case they submit an MPhil dissertation at the end of the research study period for assessment by two external assessors for the award of an MPhil degree. Up to now, even fewer students were able to register directly for a PhD degree. Most students choose to register in the MPhil/PhD programme, where their registration can be upgraded to PhD after successful submission of an MPhil transfer report. If the MPhil transfer report is unsatisfactory, the student may be requested to submit an MPhil thesis for the award of an MPhil degree (exit degree).

A taught postgraduate masters' degree is not deemed acceptable for entry into the PhD programme at the University of Mauritius and at the University of Technology, Mauritius (Table 1). The situation is different at Université des Mascareignes and the Open University of Mauritius which accept the registration of students with a "master's degree in a related subject area" in their PhD programmes. The four public universities have their own individual guidelines regarding the offer of doctoral degrees, the duration of doctoral studies and assessment formats. There has been to date no development of doctoral standards and guidelines for doctoral education at the national level as in other countries or regions.

To study the trend in doctoral production from 2002 to 2020, I extracted data on ongoing MPhil/PhD registrations, new MPhil/PhD enrolment and the number of MPhil or PhD graduates from the annual reports of activities that are publicly available for the period extending from 2002/2003 to 2019/2020.

Figure 1 shows the number of ongoing MPhil/PhD registrations (students registered either in the MPhil or PhD phases of their studies), new doctoral enrolments (either in MPhil or MPhil/PhD or PhD only), MPhil and PhD graduates (numbers of MPhil graduates and PhD graduates are combined), and PhD graduate output at the University of Mauritius from 2002 to 2020. MPhil graduates comprise those who enrolled in the MPhil programme only and those who had enrolled in the MPhil/PhD programme but were not upgraded to PhD and had to submit an MPhil thesis.

The number of ongoing MPhil/PhD students registered per faculty or centre in the period 2002 to 2020 is shown in Figure 2. The annual output of MPhil and PhD graduates (numbers combined) per faculty from 2002 to 2020 is shown in Figure 3. The cumulated MPhil and PhD graduate output over 18 years in the different faculties of the University of Mauritius (between 2002 and 2020) is illustrated in Figure 4.

- The total number of ongoing MPhil/PhD students registered at the University of Mauritius peaked at a maximum of 199 in 2005-2006, it decreased between 2007 and 2016 then increased again from 2016 to around 170 per year.
- Those fluctuations mostly reflect annual enrolment of new doctoral students over the same periods. New doctoral enrolment (MPhil or MPhil/PhD), which was above 30 per year between 2002 and 2006, decreased in 2006, stagnated for 10 years and then rose in 2017 to above 30 per year (peaking at 50 in 2017).
- The number of MPhil or PhD graduates (combined numbers) grew slowly from an annual average of 9.8 per year between 2002 to 2006, to an

**Figure 1: Number of ongoing MPhil/PhD registrations, new MPhil/PhD enrol-
ment, MPhil or PhD graduate output (combined), or PhD graduate
output at the University of Mauritius from 2002 to 2020**

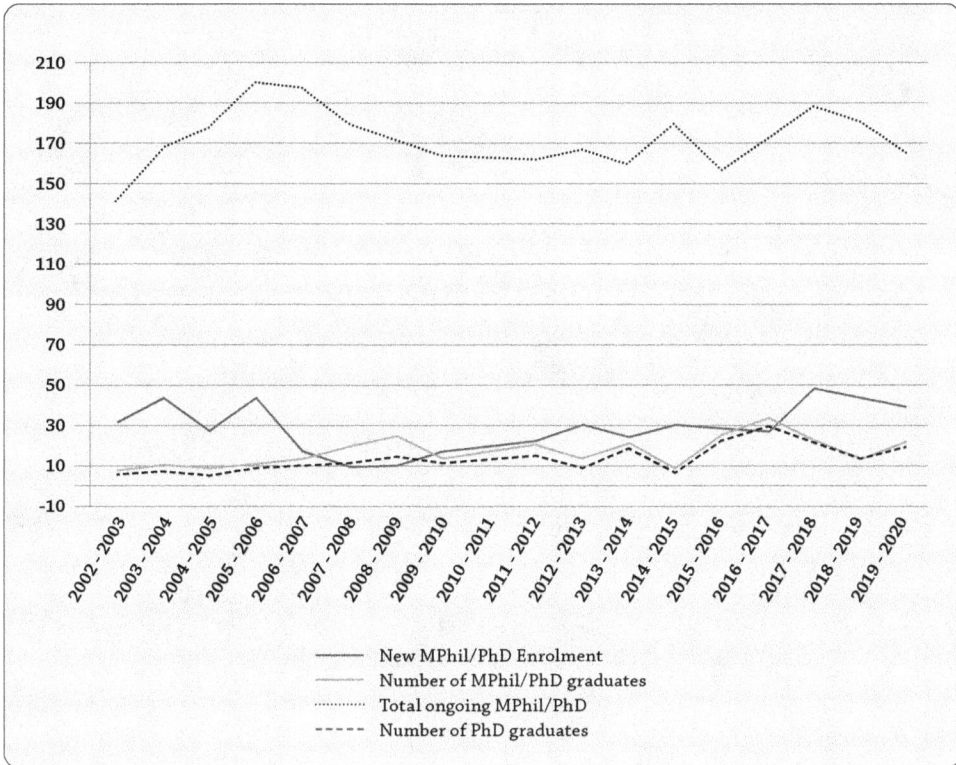

annual average of 16.8 between 2007 and 2014, and an annual average of
22.8 graduates between 2015 and 2020. The maximum number of MPhil
or PhD graduates was 33 in 2016-2017.

- The number of PhD graduates grew slowly from an average of 6 per year
  between 2002 to 2006, to an average of 12 PhD graduates between 2007
  and 2014, and an annual average of 21 PhD graduates between 2015 and
  2020 (17% increase over the 18-year period). The maximum number of
  PhD graduates at UoM was 29 in 2016-2017.

- Since 2015, an important decline has been noted in the number of ongoing
  MPhil/PhD students registered at the Faculty of Science. The decline has
  been even steeper since 2017, with the number of registrations in 2019-
  2020 being at its lowest since 2002 (only 24 students when that faculty
  had 50 students registered on average in the period 2002-2019).

Figure 2: Number of ongoing MPhil/PhD students registered per faculty or centre in the period 2002 to 2020

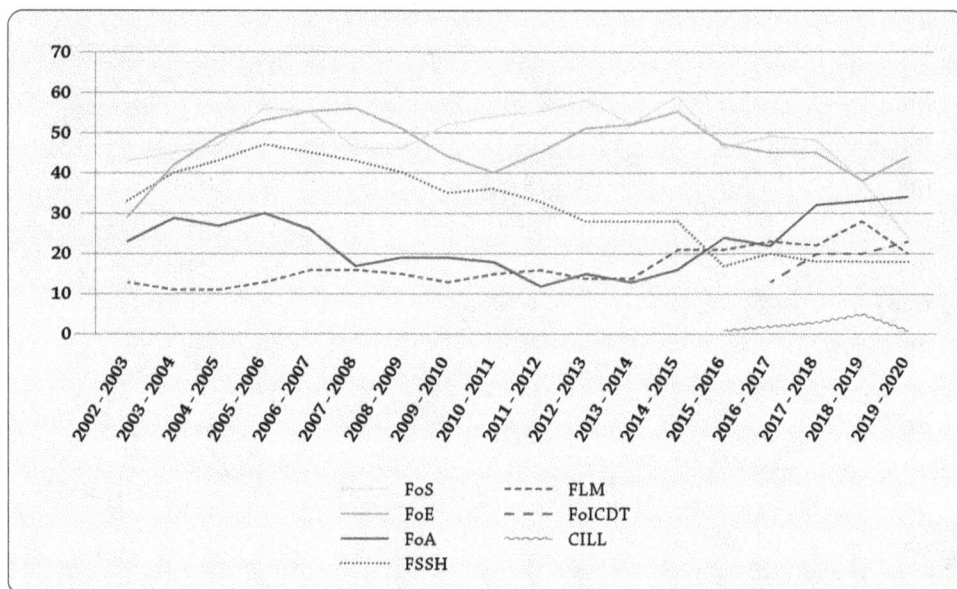

FoS: Faculty of Science; FoE: Faculty of Engineering; FoA: Faculty of Agriculture; FSSH: Social Sciences & Humanities; FLM: Faculty of Law and Management; FoICDT: Faculty of Information, Communication & Digital Technologies (newly set up Faculty); CILL: Centre for Innovative and Lifelong Learning

- A gradual and steady decline has been observed since 2006 in the number of ongoing registered students at the Faculty of Social Sciences and Humanities (32 registered on average for the period of 20 years, while the average number of registered MPhil/PhD students at the faculty in the last five years was 18, representing a 56% decrease in numbers).
- The number of MPhil/PhD students registered fluctuated around 47 on average at the Faculty of Engineering over the period 2002-2020, the number of students registered in that faculty in 2020 was higher than in 2002.
- The number of MPhil/PhD students registered at the Faculty of Agriculture was 27 on average between 2002 and 2006. It declined to an average of 17 doctoral students from 2007 to 2016, and that number has increased to 33 on average between 2017 and 2020 (94% increase).

- The number of MPhil/PhD students registered at the Faculty of Law and Management, which was 14 on average between 2002 and 2014, increased to 22 between 2015 and 2020 (57% increase).
- The number of MPhil/PhD students registered at the Faculty of Information, Communication & Digital Technologies (which was set up in 2015) averaged 19 per year between 2016 and 2020.
- There were very few doctoral students registered at the Centre for Innovative and Lifelong Learning (average of 2 between 2015 and 2020).

Figure 3: Annual output of MPhil and PhD graduates (combined) per faculty from 2002 to 2020

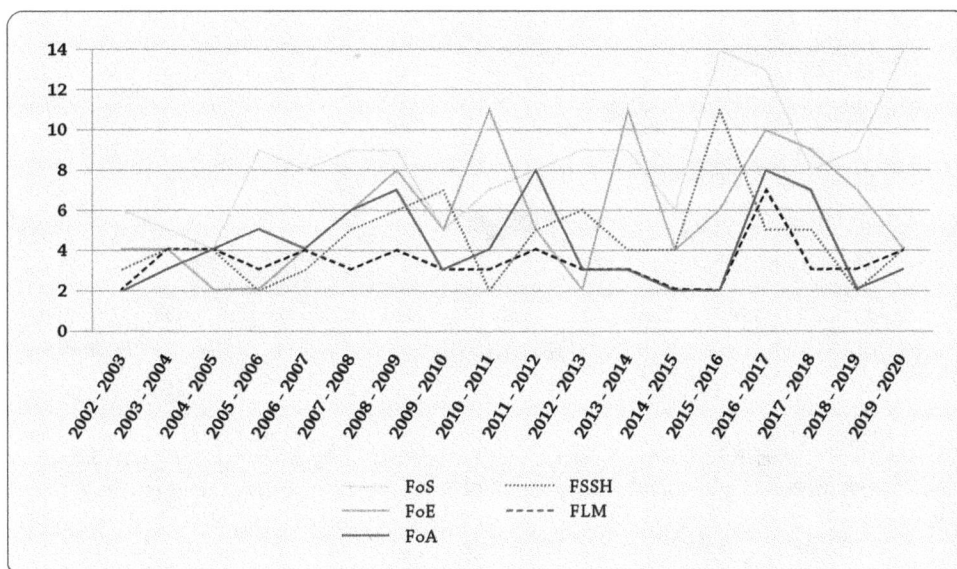

FoS: Faculty of Science; FoE: Faculty of Engineering; FoA: Faculty of Agriculture; FSSH: Social Sciences & Humanities; FLM: Faculty of Law and Management

- The average MPhil and PhD graduate output in the period 2002 to 2020 was 16.5 for the whole University of Mauritius (UoM).
- The Faculty of Science had the highest number of graduates from 2002 to 2020, it produced 39% of UoM graduates, with an annual average of 5.2 graduates from 2002 to 2014, and an annual average of 9.6 graduates between 2015 to 2020 (85% increase).
- The Faculty of Engineering produced 23% of UoM graduates, with an annual average of 3.8 graduates between 2002 to 2020.

- The Faculty of Social Sciences & Humanities produced 15% of UoM graduates, with an annual average of 2.6 graduates between 2002 to 2020.
- The Faculty of Agriculture produced 13% of UoM graduates, with an annual average of 2.2 graduates between 2002 to 2020.
- The Faculty of Law and Management produced 8% of UoM graduates, with an annual average of 1.4 graduates between 2002 to 2020.

Figure 4: Cumulated MPhil and PhD graduate output over 18 years in the different faculties of the University of Mauritius between 2002 and 2020

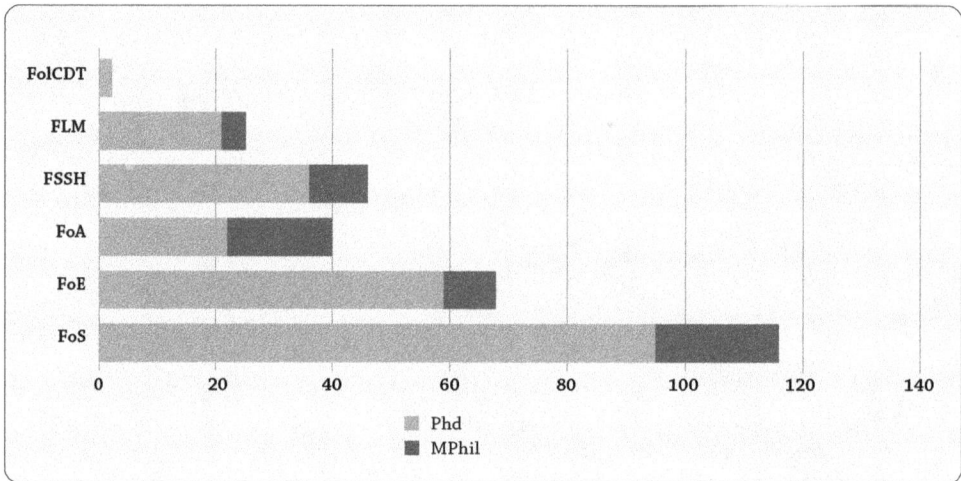

FoS: Faculty of Science; FoE: Faculty of Engineering; FoA: Faculty of Agriculture; FSSH: Social Sciences & Humanities; FLM: Faculty of Law and Management; FoICDT: Faculty of Information, Communication & Digital Technologies

- 2 PhDs were awarded for the first time in 2019-2020 at the recently set up Faculty of Information, Communication & Digital Technologies (March 2017).
- A total of 297 UoM students graduated with research degrees (MPhil or PhD) between 2002 and 2020, 62 MPhil (21%) and 235 PhD (79%).
- The ratio of MPhil to PhD at UoM in the period extending from 2002 to 2020 (all faculties combined) was thus around 1:4.
- The MPhil to PhD ratio was around 1:4 in the Faculty of Science and in the Faculty of Social Sciences & Humanities, it was lower both in the Faculty of Law and Management and in the Faculty of Engineering. The ratio of MPhil to PhD was much higher in Faculty of Agriculture (1:1).

- When only PhD graduate output was considered: the Faculty of Science had the highest proportion of graduates (40% of all graduates) followed by the Faculty of Engineering (25%), Faculty of Social Sciences & Humanities (15%), and Faculty of Agriculture and Faculty of Law and Management (9% each).

3.1 Estimation of dropout rates for students registered in the MPhil/PhD programme in the period 2002 to 2020

The best method to measure the doctoral graduate output efficiency at the UoM in the period between 2002 to 2020 would have been to apply a cohort-analysis methodology to individual student records with information on enrolment and graduation (Cloete et al., 2015, p. 77). Data that would have enabled cohort-tracking at the UoM are, however, not available to date. Therefore, I tried to provide a rough estimate of the proportion of students who dropped out of doctoral studies across the university each year by calculating a ratio of observed/expected number of MPhil/PhD registrations every year. We found that the proportion of students who had not yet graduated and still registered in the MPhil/PhD programme, decreased by 4% every year on average in the period 2002 to 2020. We did not have access to information that would have enabled us to estimate that proportion in the different faculties.

To look for the proportion of students who dropped out of the MPhil/PhD programme each year, I calculated a ratio where the observed numbers of ongoing MPhil/PhD registrations in an academic year [ObsNb(Y)] is divided by the expected numbers of ongoing MPhil/PhD registrations in the same academic year [ExpNb(Y)]. I calculated the expected number of ongoing MPhil/PhD registrations in an academic year using a simple operation involving numbers observed in the previous academic year (ongoing MPhil/PhD registrations, new enrolments and number of graduates):

ExpNb(Y)= ObsNb(Y-1) + ObsEnr(Y-1) – ObsGrd(Y-1)

Where:
ExpNb(Y): Expected number of students (Nb) registered in the current academic year (Y)
ObsNb(Y-1): Observed number of students (Nb) in the previous academic year (Y-1)
ObsEnr(Y-1): Number of new students enrolled (Enr) in the previous academic year (Y-1)

ObsGrd(Y-1): Number of students who graduated (Grd) in the previous academic year (Y-1)

ObsNb(Y): Observed number of students (Nb) registered in MPhil/PhD in the current academic year (Y)

I calculated the ratio between observed and expected of ongoing MPhil/PhD students for every academic year: [ObsNb(Y)]/ [ExpNb(Y)].

The results from calculating the ratio between observed and expected of ongoing MPhil/PhD students for every academic year are shown in Table 2. The ratio averaged over the 18-year period was 0.96. This means there was an annual average decrease of 4% in number of ongoing MPhil/PhD students registered at the University of Mauritius in the period between 2003 and 2020.

Summarily, from the data collected on numbers of doctoral students, doctoral enrolment and graduate output at the University of Mauritius between 2002 and 2020, I observed the following:

1. The number of ongoing MPhil/PhD students registered at the University of Mauritius:
   - has not increased, and seemed to have remained stable with an annual average of 171 over the 18-year period. The dropout rate was around 4% every year.
   - seemed to follow the trend in new annual doctoral enrolment during the same period, which was 28 on average, this number dropped between 2006 and 2012, and rose as of 2016.
2. The number of ongoing MPhil/PhD students registered in the different faculties:
   - had decreased sharply in the Faculty of Science over the last 5 years.
   - has decreased more gradually in the Faculty of Social Sciences & Humanities over the last 10 years.
   - had increased steadily in the Faculty of Agriculture over the last 3 years.
   - has also increased in the Faculty of Law and Management over the last 3 to 5 years.
   - has remained stable in the Faculty of Engineering.
3. MPhil and PhD graduate output increased quite slowly at the University of Mauritius from 8 per year at the beginning to 23 per year at the end of the 18-year period:
   - the annual graduate output averaged over 18 years was 16.5 per year, with 40% of doctoral output from the Faculty of Science, 25% from the Faculty of Engineering, 15% from the Faculty of Social Sciences &

Humanities and 9% from the Faculty of Agriculture and the Faculty of Law and Management.
- the ratio of MPhil to PhD was around 1:4 in most faculties, except in the Faculty of Agriculture where the MPhil graduate number was similar to that of PhD output.

Table 2: Observed and expected numbers of students registered every year in MPhil/PhD

Academic Year	New MPhil/ PhD Enrolment	Number of MPhil/PhD graduates	Observed number of ongoing MPhil/PhD	Expected number of ongoing MPhil/PhD	Ratio Observed/ Expected
2002-2003	31	7	141	-	-
2003-2004	43	10	167	165	1.01
2004-2005	27	8	177	200	0.89
2005-2006	43	11	199	196	1.02
2006-2007	17	13	197	231	0.85
2007-2008	10	19	178	201	0.89
2008-2009	10	24	171	169	1.01
2009-2010	17	13	163	157	1.04
2010-2011	19	17	163	167	0.98
2011-2012	22	20	161	165	0.98
2012-2013	30	13	166	163	1.02
2013-2014	24	20	159	183	0.87
2014-2015	30	8	179	163	1.10
2015-2016	28	25	156	201	0.78
2016-2017	27	33	172	159	1.08
2017-2018	48	22	188	166	1.13
2018-2019	43	13	180	214	0.84
2019-2020	39	21	164	210	0.78

4. Explanatory factors for the low PhD output at the University of Mauritius

The low output of PhD graduates is not due to high dropout rates (4%) but rather to the low enrolment rates which could be explained by several factors: lack of research funds, lack of equipment, scarcity of potential supervisors, delays when applications were managed by individual faculties, perception that MPhil/PhD is a lengthy and difficult journey.

4.1 Lack of research funding

We observed a drop in the number of new MPhil/PhD enrolments between 2006 and 2012, and a rise in numbers as of 2016. Funding for doctoral research by academic staff which was available before 2002 from the World Bank Higher and Technical Education Project (World Bank, 1999) had allowed an important number of academic staff to engage in doctoral degrees. Scarcity of research funding between 2006 and 2012 probably explains the drop in new enrolments of MPhil/PhD students during this period. Research funding available to academic staff at UoM was reported as being low compared to South African universities in the study by Cloete et al. (2011). The authors hypothesized that the chronic lack of research funds and high teaching workloads probably impacted on the weak outputs in doctoral graduates and research publications (Cloete et al., 2011, p. 105) and concluded: "The university will have to do a serious rethink of incentives if it wants to become a knowledge producer that can contribute significantly to an engine of development approach."

Funding prospects have improved considerably since 2015 with various research schemes made available to academic staff and researchers in public tertiary institutions by the Higher Education Commission of Mauritius and scholarships for full-time and part-time MPhil/PhD students.

Monetary rewards for research publications in Web of Science journals were made available in public tertiary institutions but doctoral supervisors at UoM were not remunerated and did not benefit from lower teaching workloads compared to those who did not supervise doctoral students. Academic development schemes at UoM were less well developed than at the University of Technology of Mauritius (UTM, 2018) where academic staff were encouraged to pursue their MPhil/PhD studies and were sponsored through a financial policy that allowed them to meet with their supervisors and to attend conferences.

Apart from better funding prospects, the rise in enrolment of new doctoral students was probably due to the change in the processing of applications that began in 2016. Instead of being managed by faculties where excessive bureaucracy often led to delays in enrolment of new MPhil/PhD students, applications were managed by the UoM doctoral school and the UoM Higher Degree Committee which made the application process more efficient.

The numbers of new registrants did not decline drastically, even with the offer of MPhil/PhD degrees by other public universities in Mauritius such as the University of Technology of Mauritius, the Université des Mascareignes and PhD degrees by the Open University of Mauritius which started recruiting students mid-2012. The time-to-degree is usually quite long for those registered in the MPhil/PhD degree at UoM for several reasons that will be discussed later, much longer than the 4.7 years in South Africa.

4.2 *Availability of potential supervisors*

The ratio of doctoral graduates to permanent academic staff at UoM was very low (as low as 2.8%) in 2001. The upgrading of the university's staff and facilities was an objective of the World Bank Higher and Technical Education Project (1999), which was scheduled to take effect as of September 1995. The overall outcome was judged unsatisfactory as only 67 out of a total of 158 staff targeted took advantage of this opportunity according to the World Bank Higher and Technical Education report (1999, p. 15). The situation improved in 2007 compared to 2001, with 45% of UoM's permanent academic staff having doctorates as their highest formal qualifications in 2007 (Cloete et al., 2011).

As per the *Report on the Activities of UoM* for the academic year 2018-2019, 56% of permanent academic staff were PhD holders, while an additional 40% were enrolled in doctoral studies in July 2019. The situation regarding the availability of potential supervisors seems therefore to have improved over the last two decades. In terms of research publications, UoM's output was low with a ratio of publication units per permanent academic staff at 0.13 in 2007. This was well below the ratio of 0.50 which had been set as a target for South Africa's research universities. The latter performed rather well in terms of bibliometric analysis in the fields of tropical medicine, infectious diseases and agriculture (Mouton & Blanckenberg, 2018).

The possibility of academics increasing their income through consultancies, and important teaching workloads of academic staff also explain the modest improvements in doctoral output in the past two decades. PhDs produced were mostly academics trying to improve their career prospects, even if it usually took a long time to complete as part-time students.

The traditional PhD which is the only model of doctoral study currently available at the UoM relies heavily on individual research supervisors. A doctoral education model that relies heavily on supervisors may have the major disadvantage of high levels of doctoral attrition (Matas, 2012). As described in a Carnegie-sponsored study, there is a need for new doctoral education options such as apprenticeship with several faculty members, as such intellectual communities would foster the development of new ideas and encourage intellectual risk taking (Walker et al., 2008, p. 11).

4.3 Other hurdles for postgraduate studies at the University of Mauritius

Lack of networking with other overseas institutions to overcome isolation resulting from being an island state, and sharing of best practices, also contributed to low research output. Tight fluctuating budgets resulting in lack of investment in new equipment and poor maintenance of existing equipment were also deterrents for new doctoral student enrolments.

4.4 The two-step process in MPhil/PhD programme

The MPhil/PhD which is offered at the UoM is also offered by two other public universities in Mauritius. It is a research programme which involves the traditional apprenticeship model and does not include any structured course work. It involves submission of an MPhil transfer report which is assessed by external assessors before the student can be registered for the PhD studies. Award of the PhD degree is conditional upon submission of a thesis that is assessed by two independent external assessors, the thesis can be submitted only if the student has at least one paper accepted in a Web of Science journal.

I did not observe a high attrition rate based on our calculations on ratios between observed and expected numbers of registered MPhil/PhD students from one year to the other. However, in a case study of doctoral studies at UoM published in 2010 (Cloete et al., 2011, p. 104), concerns were raised that very few of the MPhil/PhD students registered at the University of Mauritius appeared to move into full doctoral studies. I also observed that students registered in the Faculty of Agriculture seemed to struggle and progressed to the doctoral phase much less often than in the other faculties. It is to be noted that the same degree is offered in all disciplines in the different faculties of the University. It has been argued elsewhere that some types of PhD such as the 'practice-based doctorate' seemed to be preferred in arts and humanities, while the 'professional doctorate' was preferred in Engineering and other scientific fields, all helping in the creation of new knowledge which is the main purpose of doctoral research (Matas, 2012).

4.5 Arguments against the current MPhil/PhD format performed as a two-step research degree using the master-apprenticeship model without any prior structured course work

The MPhil/PhD degree at the UoM and in two other public universities (UTM, UdM) is a doctoral programme of studies that is currently performed in two steps or phases. A student registered full-time in such studies needs to produce a successful upgrading report after having performed two to three years of research to be registered in the PhD phase of their doctoral programme for at least another 2 years. MPhil/PhD students do not benefit from any structured course work that would provide them with tools such as research methodology, research design, research ethics, research management as well as scientific writing skills. The responsibility for transforming them into early researchers and scholars lies wholly on their supervisors.

The goal of doctoral education is to cultivate the research mindset, to nurture flexibility of thought, creativity and intellectual autonomy through an original research project (not through two smaller projects). The PhD student becomes a scholar through a process and not merely for having produced an upgrading report followed by a written thesis that is judged to be up to standard. In line with the first Salzburg Principle (European Ministers Responsible for Higher Education, 2007), it is the practice of research that creates this mindset.

The learning objectives of the MPhil and PhD programmes at UoM are more or less the same, the assessment criteria are very similar, except that the PhD student is expected to make an original contribution. Most students have an obligation to register for the MPhil/PhD degree and undertake their research apprenticeship in two phases. No two supervisors at UoM would have the same perception of what is expected from the students, yet the responsibility currently lies with the supervisor to decide when a student is ready for an upgrade. There are technical difficulties when there is a need for a second research question to be worked on after the upgrade report and when research funding has already been spent on the first project. There is a risk of dropping out of the programme after having produced the first upgrade report.

In an era where there are many holders of taught master's degrees, a structured PhD programme would be ideal. In that type of PhD programme, students would acquire, through course work, the generic skills and tools needed for postgraduate research, which would also help them develop and defend a research proposal in the first year. When the research proposal is accepted, students would benefit from guidance from supervisors who are experts in specific areas and disciplines for a period of 3 years if they are full-time students. This is the doctoral model that is currently adopted by the Open University of Mauritius.

5. Our recommendations for the introduction of a structured PhD programme at UoM

There are postgraduate studies scholars who maintain that the master–apprenticeship model is outdated, and that the models with course work provide a more structured doctoral learning environment, in which the doctoral student may not feel so isolated (Matas, 2012, p. 179).

If we believe that doctoral education is important for increasing the research capacity of the university and its reputation and ranking based on the number of scholarly publications, and contributing to the knowledge economy (Cloete et al., 2015), it is time to consider other models of doctoral study apart from the supervisor-centred traditional PhD by thesis currently required at the University of Mauritius. UoM regulations would need to be adapted regarding doctoral education programmes and their specific modes of assessment. Other processes such as doctoral applications, admissions, submission of research proposals, supervision, thesis submission, viva, etc. would be common.

1. I recommend that a 1 + 3 type of model for a full-time PhD programme at UoM be adopted, with a first year of PhD pre-registration comprising structured course work through which the students will benefit from training in generic skills that would increase their employability such as training in research methodology, research design, research ethics and integrity, research management as well as in scientific writing skills. Before the end of that year, they should have written a research proposal that they would have to defend to be granted permission to proceed with their full registration. Once the research proposal is accepted full-time students can spend 3 additional years for their PhD research and learn to master skills specific to the field they engage in with their supervisor/ supervisors. Students with the required academic ability, dedication and passion for scholarship are less likely to drop out if they have acquired the self-confidence through the initial coursework and after they have successfully defended their research proposal. A more structured phase of qualification for a doctoral degree is meant to reduce dropout rates and provide more efficiency (Kehm, 2007).

   The UoM doctoral school would be ideally suited for providing coordination of the structured course work and facilities for preparation and submission of research proposals by the doctoral candidates.

2. Instead of the traditional thesis-only model, the PhD by publication (Badley, 2009) could be an interesting alternative model of doctoral

assessment to adopt as it would encourage students to learn to write for publications in reputable scholarly journals in their areas of expertise. It can consist, for example, of refereed publications that bear on the literature review, on the methods that are appropriate for the doctoral research, and on results of qualitative or quantitative research. Students then write an overarching manuscript with an introduction, and an interpretation of the findings from the three publications and conclusions from the PhD research (Smaldone et al., 2019). There would be a need for an online viva as our small island is thousands of kilometres away from the universities of our external assessors. Since the advent of Covid-19 and the attendant difficulties experienced by higher education institutions throughout the first two years of the pandemic (Salmi, 2020), flexibility in assessment with use of digital communication has become widespread.

The PhD by publication could prove to be beneficial for the UoM in the medium to long term as an increase in the production of peer-reviewed papers, which was described as low (Bunting et al., 2017, p. 41), may contribute to enhanced ranking of the academic institution.

Prior to publications, a memorandum of understanding (MoU) should be set up between supervisee and supervisor(s) to establish a basis for a productive working relationship. The document should specify details on management of the project (meetings and communication, timelines and progress reports, submission of work to supervisor, feedback and revision, expected outputs (articles), expectations around intellectual property (expectations regarding authorship, ownership of data), expectations regarding skills and knowledge, expectations regarding funding, work, ground rules and regulations, mechanisms for dealing with disputes, managing co-supervision. Since an MoU is not legally binding, there would be no consequences if it is not respected by any one party. However, such a document that makes objectives and expectations of all parties very clear could help in preventing potential future disputes from occurring.

3. The team co-supervision model in the traditional apprenticeship model of PhD by thesis or in new PhD models. Since there are sometimes only a few PhD holders capable of supervision in some departments, in the proposed structured (1+3) PhD programme, having supervising committees (including PhD graduates with a variable mix of experience regarding doctoral supervision) in the 'Poles of Excellence' recently created at UoM could be possible. The latter group of academic researchers who apply for research grants to carry out multidisciplinary research and who are ready to provide research projects to doctoral students. This can promote the

inclusion of the doctoral students as early researchers in a community of scholars, provided that constructive feedback is provided by co-supervisors to students, it would also promote enculturation of doctoral students in their discipline. Apprenticeship with several faculty members (thesis committee) would stimulate the development of new ideas and intellectual risk taking would be encouraged through such intellectual communities (Walker et al., 2008, p. 11).

4. The professional doctorate in the Faculty of Engineering, with possibilities of submitting a portfolio instead of the traditional single, lengthy but narrowly focused doctoral dissertation. The portfolio could consist of a collection of shorter research reports, held together by a linking paper that helps to articulate the thesis. Some authors argue that the portfolio is appropriate for the professional doctorate which focuses on improvement in the professional workplace, and that the key issues to be considered are coherence and significance (Maxwell & Kupczyk-Romanczuk, 2009).

5. The practice-based doctorate based on a supervised research project in the performing arts, would be appropriate in the Faculty of Social Sciences and Humanities where students may be called upon to produce a work in creative arts or multimedia works. They could submit a portfolio of their creative works together with a thesis showing their ability "to contextualise that knowledge or performance so as to demonstrate to peers how it contributes to the development of the subject in its content, its methods and/or its means of communication" (UKCGE, 1997, p. 27).

6. Training in doctoral supervision could be provided by the UoM Doctoral School

As doctoral supervision is viewed as a specific and specialized type of professional work, it is very important to provide professional development for doctoral supervisors, as this would lead to improvements in the quality of doctoral education in an international and competitive higher education sector (Halse & Malfroy, 2009) and it could lead to lower attrition rates (Lee, 2008). Powell and Green (2007, p. 253) view doctoral supervision as an "act of pedagogy, not of research", as doctoral students are learning "about how to do research".

7. What is considered good supervision practice?

Supervisors should learn to accompany students on their doctoral journeys and adapt their supervisory style with the phase of the doctoral journey (Gatfield,

2005). Supervision style usually starts with a 'laissez-faire' approach, when the student is extensively reading literature to identify a research topic, then a 'directorial' style is used when the student needs to consider research design and methods, followed by a 'contractual' supervisory style. 'Pastoral' style is needed whenever the student needs compassionate support.

Research supervision pedagogy is different from that of teaching undergraduates because the doctoral student is expected to reach a level of knowledge mastery superior to that of their supervisor (Wisker, 2005). At the beginning of the research, at the time of reading the literature before and while writing the research proposal, good supervisors should encourage students to construct a reading map to create links between themes derived from interpretation of scientific information read on the research subject. This way they should be better able to identify concordant and discordant information as well as identify current gaps in information they could work on as research topics. Good supervisors should insist that students write throughout their doctoral journey as the learning only happens when they write (Thomas, 2016).

Students should be provided with enough support and compassionate rigour in a research environment to liberate them from the supervisory relationship, ultimately, and facilitate their development as early researchers in their own right. Mutual trust and a non-threatening relationship lead to better student satisfaction than hierarchical relationships (Van Rooij et al., 2019).

More workshops in basic bibliometrics for all students and emerging scholars are needed (Mouton & Valentine, 2017). Students should also be appraised of the principles and responsibilities summarised in the Singapore Statement on Research Integrity (SSRI) that are intended to promote integrity in research and responsible research practice. The SSRI was developed at the 2nd World Conference on Research Integrity held in Singapore and was released for global use on 22 September 2010 to guide the responsible conduct of research.

Supervisors should have research knowledge and related skills, as well as management and interpersonal skills. They need to have multiple qualities as managers: innovative, problem solver, resource-oriented, work-focused, technical expert, decisive and dependable and a reflective learner who integrates all the other qualities (Vilkinas, 2002). They should give feedback in a timely manner, as effective feedback was identified by students and supervisors as the most important strategy by which students learned to write (Aitchison et al., 2012).

There is a need for well-informed and systematic pedagogies for writing development in all doctoral programmes. Written feedback helps in the development of doctoral students' academic competencies (Carter & Kumar, 2017).

Supervisors should take care to include diversity in their comments when providing feedback on students' writing (Hyatt, 2005): they should include positive comments in their feedback so as to foster a good academic and social relationship with the students, developmental comments to help students with subsequent work, structural comments, stylistic comments, content related comments (with positive, negative evaluations or non-evaluative summaries of aspects of the written material), methodological comments (on the approach, procedures, and process in conduct of the research).

7.1 UoM should endeavour to be involved in the Consortium for Advanced Research Training in Africa

The Consortium for Advanced Research Training in Africa (CARTA)'s goal is to increase the use of inter-institutional collaboration in order to build research capacity of doctoral students and to strengthen university systems to lead and conduct research on critical areas around public and population health in the African region.

Northern collaborating partner institutions provide expertise to CARTA fellows and supervisors, organise workshops for practical training on grant writing, grant management, etc. Southern collaborators provide an online teaching platform to improve on the writing skills of the African academy. We believe that UoM would greatly benefit if it became a member of this consortium.

8. Conclusion

The University of Mauritius currently offers the MPhil/PhD by research which is assessed through submission of a doctoral thesis a few years after a successful upgrading report submitted at the end of the MPhil study. The low doctoral output observed over the last 2 decades seems to be due to low doctoral enrolment, and not so much on a high attrition rate (4%). To increase doctoral output, other types of PhD models developed elsewhere in the world should be considered to attract potential students. Assessment should be diversified by allowing the traditional PhD by thesis, the PhD by publication and the submission of a portfolio for professional doctorates or practice-based doctorate in creative arts.

Instead of requesting all doctoral applicants to register for MPhil/PhD by research through submission of a research proposal without having benefitted from any prior training in generic skills, they should be provided structured training in their first year as PhD pre-registration trainees by the doctoral school to enhance their research skills. They would afterwards embark on their individual doctoral journeys in their specific disciplines to make an original contribution to their field of study through their research projects. The doctoral school should also coordinate supervisory training for prospective PhD supervisors.

Moreover, there is a need for the development of doctoral standards and guidelines for the harmonization of doctoral education at a national level, given that PhD graduates enjoy the same privileges irrespective of the length and difficulty of their doctoral journeys at the different public higher education institutions.

References

Academic Apparel. (n.d.). *History of academic degrees: Origin of the bachelor's, master's, and doctorate*. https://www.academicapparel.com/caps/History-Academic-Degrees.html

Aitchison, C., Catterall, J., Ross, P., & Burgin, S. (2012). 'Tough love and tears': Learning doctoral writing in the sciences. *Higher Education Research and Development, 31*(4), 435–447. https://doi.org/10.1080/07294360.2011.559195

Allen, D. (2016). Where will we get the next generation of medicinal chemists? *Drug Discovery Today, 21*(5), 704–706. https://doi.org/10.1016/j.drudis.2016.04.012

Badley, G. (2009). Publish and be doctor-rated: The PhD by published work. *Quality Assurance in Education, 17*(4), 331–342. https://doi.org/10.1108/09684880910992313

Botha, J., Muria, M., Ozgoren, M., & Wilde, M. (2021). Quality doctoral education in Africa: A question of setting the right standards? In P. Rule, E. Bitzer, & L. Frick (Eds.), *The global scholar: Implications for postgraduate studies and supervision* (pp. 123–136). African Sun Media.

Bourke, S., & Holbrook, A. P. (2013). Examining PhD and research masters theses. *Assessment & Evaluation in Higher Education, 38*(4), 407–416. https://doi.org/10.1080/02602938.2011.638738

Bunting, I., Cloete, N., & Van Schalkwyk, F. (2014). *An empirical overview of eight flagship universities in Africa: 2001–2011. A report of the Higher Education Research and Advocacy Network in Africa (HERANA)*. Centre for Higher Education Transformation.

Bunting, I., Cloete, N., & Van Schalkwyk, F. (2017). *An empirical overview of emerging research universities in Africa: 2001–2015. A report of the Higher Education Research and Advocacy Network in Africa (HERANA)*. Centre for Higher Education Trust.

Carter, S., & Kumar, V. (2017). 'Ignoring me is part of learning': Supervisory feedback on doctoral writing. *Innovations in Education and Teaching International, 54*(1), 68–75. https://doi.org/10.1080/14703297.2015.1123104

Cloete, N., Bailey, T., Pillay, P., Bunting, I., & Maassen, P. (2011). Key findings from the eight African case studies: Mauritius and the University of Mauritius. In N. Cloete, T. Bailey, P. Pillay, I. Bunting, & P. Maassen (Eds.), *Universities and economic development in Africa* (pp. 100–112). HERANA and Centre for Higher Education Transformation.

Cloete, N., Mouton, J., & Sheppard, C. (2016a). The demand for a doctorate: Global, African and South African contexts. In N. Cloete, J. Mouton, & C. Sheppard (Eds.), *Doctoral education in South Africa: Policy, discourse and data* (pp. 1–26). African Minds.

Cloete, N., Mouton, J., & Sheppard, C. (2016b). The demand for improved efficiency. In N. Cloete, J. Mouton, & C. Sheppard (Eds.), *Doctoral education in South Africa: Policy, discourse and data* (pp. 64–76). African Minds.

Cyranoski, D., Gilbert, N., Ledford, H., Nayar, A., & Yahia, M. (2011). Education: The PhD factory. *Nature, 472*(7343), 276–279. https://doi.org/10.1038/472276a

Council on Higher Education (CHE). (2018). *Qualification standard for doctoral degrees*. Council of Higher Education. https://www.sun.ac.za/english/learning-teaching/learning-teaching-enhancement/APQ/Documents/Higher Education Legislative Frameworks/CHE/CHE Policies/CHE_Qualification Standard_Doctoral Degrees_Nov 2018.pdf

European Ministers Responsible for Higher Education. (2005). *The European higher education area - Achieving the goals* [Communiqué]. EHEA. https://ehea.info/Upload/document/ministerial_declarations/2005_Bergen_Communique_english_580520.pdf

Gatfield, T. (2005). An investigation into PhD supervisory management styles: Development of a dynamic conceptual model and its managerial implications. *Journal of Higher Education Policy and Management, 27*(3), 311–325. https://doi.org/10.1080/13600800500283585

Herman, C. (2017). Looking back at doctoral education in South Africa. *Studies in Higher Education, 42*(8), 1437–1454. https://doi.org/10.1080/03075079.2015.1101756

Higher Education Commission of Mauritius. (n.d.). *Research schemes and scholarships*. https://www.hec.mu/research_schemes_scholarship

Hyatt, D. F. (2005). 'Yes, a very good point!': A critical genre analysis of a corpus of feedback commentaries on Master of Education assignments. *Teaching in Higher Education, 10*(3), 339–353. https://doi.org/10.1080/13562510500122222

IUCEA (Inter-University Council for East Africa). (2018). *Standards and guidelines for postgraduate studies in East Africa*. IUCEA. https://www.iucea.org/mdocs-posts/standards-and-guidelines-for-postgraduate-studies-in-east-africa/

Johansson, C., & Yerrabati, S. (2017). A review of the literature on professional doctorate supervisory styles. *Management in Education, 31*(4), 166–171. https://doi.org/10.1177/0892020617734821

Kehm, B. M. (2007). Quo vadis doctoral education? New European approaches in the context of global changes. *European Journal of Education Research, Development and Policy, 42*(3), 307–319. https://onlinelibrary.wiley.com/doi/10.1111/j.1465-3435.2007.00308.x

Lee, A. (2008). How are doctoral students supervised? Concepts of doctoral research supervision. *Studies in Higher Education, 33*(3), 267–281. https://doi.org/10.1080/03075070802049202

Matas, C. P. (2012). Doctoral education and skills development: An international perspective. *Revista de Docencia Universitaria, 10*(2), 163–191. https://doaj.org/article/453de028d1ed442eba72d4a154eeaaa1

Maxwell, T. W., & Kupczyk-Romanczuk, G. (2009). Producing the professional doctorate: The portfolio as a legitimate alternative to the dissertation. *Innovations in Education and Teaching International, 46*(2), 135–145. https://doi.org/10.1080/14703290902843760

Mohamedbhai, G. (2018, March 30). *What do the next 10 years hold for higher education?* University World News. http://www.universityworldnews.com/article.php?story=20180327074736612

Mouton, J., & Valentine, A. (2017). The extent of South African authored articles in predatory journals. *South African Journal of Science, 113*(7-8), 1–9. https://journals.co.za/doi/pdf/10.17159/sajs.2017/20170010

Mouton, J., & Blanckenberg, J. (2018). African science: A bibliometric analysis. In C. Beaudry, J. Mouton, & H. Prozesky (Eds.), *The next generation of scientists in Africa* (pp. 13–20). African Minds.

Odendaal, A., & Frick, B. L. (2018). Research dissemination and PhD thesis format at a South African university: The impact of policy on practice. *Innovations in Education and Teaching International, 55*(5), 594–601. https://doi.org/10.1080/14703297.2017.1284604

Open University of Mauritius. (n.d.). *Postgraduate level courses leading to the award of a master's degree*. https://www.open.ac.mu/postgraduate-level-courses-leading-to-the-award-of-a-masters-degree/

Powell, S., & Green, H. (Eds.). (2007). *The doctorate worldwide*. The Society for Research into Higher Education and Open University Press.

Smaldone, A., Heitkemper, E., Jackman, K., Woo, K. J., & Kelson, J. (2019). Dissemination of PhD dissertation research by dissertation format: A retrospective cohort study. *Journal of Nursing Scholarship, 51*(5), 599–607. https://doi.org/10.1111/jnu.12504

Teferra, D. (2015). Manufacturing - and exporting - excellence and "mediocrity": Doctoral education in South Africa. *South African Journal of Higher Education, 29*(5), 8–19. https://journals.co.za/doi/abs/10.10520/EJC182521

Thomas, D. (2016). *The PhD writing handbook*. Palgrave Macmillan.

Trafford, V., & Leshem, S. (2009). Doctorateness as a threshold concept. *Innovations in Education and Teaching International, 46*(3), 305–316. https://doi.org/10.1080/14703290903069027

Travers, N. L., Jankowski, N., Bushway, D. J., & Duncan, A. G. (2019). *Learning frameworks: Tools for building a better educational experience*. Lumina Foundation. https://www.luminafoundation.org/resource/learning-frameworks/

UK Council for Graduate Education (UKCGE). (1997). *Practice-based doctorates in the creative and performing arts and design*. Retrieved from https://ukcge.ac.uk/assets/resources/4-Practice-based-doctorates-in-the-Creative-and-Performing-Arts1997.pdf

Université des Mascareignes. (n.d.). *Research: Doctoral school (École doctorale)*. https://udm.ac.mu/research/doctoral-school-ecole-doctorale/

University of Mauritius. (n.d.). *Report on the activities of UoM for the academic year 2018-2019*. https://drive.google.com/file/d/1eZa0JCAkBdn3RYdY3911x8o3fUHR02Q-/view

University of Mauritius (n.d.). *MPhil/PhD Regulations 2021-2022*. https://www.uom.ac.mu/index.php/study-at-uom/current-students/regulations/mphil-phd

University of Technology of Mauritius (UTM). (2018). Audit report. http://www.tec.mu/pdf_downloads/pubrep/UTM_Audit_Report010618.pdf

Van Rooij, E., Fokkens-Bruinsma, M., & Jansen, E. (2019). Factors that influence PhD candidates' success: The importance of PhD project characteristics. *Studies in Continuing Education, 43*(1), 48–67. https://doi.org/10.1080/0158037X.2019.1652158

Vilkinas, T. (2002). The PhD process: The supervisor as manager. *Education + Training, 44*(3), 129–137. https://doi.org/10.1108/00400910210424337

Walker, G. E., Golde, C. M., Jones, L., Conklin-Bueschel, A., & Hutchings, P. (2008). Moving doctoral education into the future. In G. E. Walker, C. M. Golde, L. Jones, A. Conklin-Bueschel, & P. Hutchings (Eds.), *The formation of scholars: Rethinking doctoral education for the twenty-first century* (p. 1–18). Jossey-Bass/Carnegie Foundation for the Advancement of Teaching.

World Bank. (1999). *Implementation completion report Republic of Mauritius industrial and vocational training project (loan 3401-MAS), education sector development project (loan 3578-MAS), higher and technical education project (loan 3859-MAS)*. https://documents1.worldbank.org/curated/en/304411468110074054/pdf/multi-page.pdf

Agostinho Neto University: An appraisal of the contexts and processes of doctoral production

Paulo Conceição João Faria

Angola has a population of about 32 million. Higher education (HE) in Angola emerged a year after independence from Portugal in 1975 with the creation of the University of Angola. On 24 January 1985 the University of Angola was renamed Agostinho Neto University (UAN) in honour of the country's first president and the UAN's first chancellor. The country has 85 higher education institutions, 27 public and 58 private. In 2020, postgraduate courses were offered at 25 institutions, amounting to 141 master's and 11 doctoral programmes. In 2019, a total of 6 217 students were enrolled in these postgraduate programmes, including 187 doctoral candidates (GEPE/MESCTI, 2020).

1. Introduction

This chapter analyses the processes of doctoral production at the University Agostinho Neto (UAN) in Luanda. Particularly, it will assess the doctoral training processes in three faculties. This analysis requires a thorough understanding of the existing context and the research environment at the institution. This chapter acknowledges the connectivity between the university and the world of work outside universities, for instance, business, industry, government, NGOs, etc. Equally, it is aware that different countries have different trajectories, patterns and standards of development in higher education (HE), which can sometimes hinder or enable this connectivity. While this connectivity is of great importance for its potential to prompt empirically relevant studies, it is paramount to pinpoint the differences between (a) the connectivity between the university and the existing spheres of productivity and (b) the university's internal context and processes. It is worth highlighting that "existing spheres of productivity" refers to the world of work outside universities, for instance, business, industry, government, NGOs, etc. So, the differences between the two lies in the fact that (a) refers to external considerations and (b) to internal considerations, that is, within the university. This chapter focuses on the latter to assess how context and processes influence doctoral production at the UAN.

As the oldest public university in Angola, UAN cannot be dissociated from a broader social and political milieu that presents two faces: on the one hand, it helps to define UAN as production source of cutting-edge knowledge, and on the other hand it functions as a stumbling-block for the achievement of this goal. In this Janus-like context, UAN currently faces a moment of reckoning and soul searching. It needs to reinvent itself from being a passive recipient of state revenue to a regional and internationally integrated institution taking action to unleash its human resources to the outside world, through joint research projects and through student mobility plans across African universities and elsewhere in the world. To achieve that, it would not just require networking and integration, but also a set of policies directed at bringing the best out of the UAN and to establish national authorities for national higher education like South Africa's Council on Higher Education (CHE) and Namibia's National Council for Higher Education (NCHE).

Although the chapter will also address the issue of the establishment of national authorities, my main purpose is to conduct a critical appraisal of the contexts and processes of doctoral production at the UAN. I do that in five sections. The first section gives a brief overview of the relevant literature. The second presents a critical account of the UAN research environment and identifies factors that are impacting negatively on the researcher's motivation. The third describes the UAN as a politically contested space, for it is often perceived more as a domain of power and control than a context conducive for the autonomous production of innovative and applicable knowledge. The fourth section surveys the key points in Angolan legislation that sustain the provision of doctoral education. The last section builds on information collected at the UAN's three faculties – social sciences (FCS), economics (FECUAN) and law (FDUAN) – to explain how context and process influence doctoral production.

2. National and institutional contexts for doctoral education in Angola

Contexts and research processes are the springboards of doctoral production. This often relies on two intertwined axes: doctoral training tailored towards the candidate's research needs and the role played by the supervisor. The supervisor is presented in the critical scholarship literature on doctoral supervision as no longer a distant master with sole responsibility for quality outcomes (Cloete et al., 2015), but above all a "facilitator of students' journey' from 'apprentice' or 'novice' to 'master'" (Bastalich, 2017, p. 1146; Kehm, 2007, p. 315). Seeing the doctoral student as a permanent learner makes sense when 'the student is expected to acquire knowledge of the research process, and supervisors and others facilitate the research process, and reflection on the research process, to ensure a "capacity" for future innovation' (Bastalich, 2017, p. 1146).

Thus, doctoral production becomes an integrated and ever increasingly evolving process, whereby the providers, beneficiaries, policymakers, government institutions and independent higher education bodies have a significant role to play in meeting five policy discourses which, according to Cloete et al. (2015:81ff), drive[s] and influence[s] the production of PhD in South Africa – quantity, transformation, efficiency, quality and internationalization.

The authors were careful to mention that trends in growth of doctoral enrolments and graduates co-exist in tension and contradictions (Cloete et al., 2015:178). The five policy discourse functions as a signpost for HE stakeholders and highlights the importance of getting the right balance between context, processes and expected outcomes. This should be taken as a conscious measure for avoiding or at least reducing the negative impacts of what MacGregor (2013:1) refers to as a 'conundrum', namely 'in order to produce more doctoral graduates, more PhD supervisors are needed, but in order to have more supervisors, more PhDs are needed'.

Where there seems to be an interplay between policies and practices, there is also an independent body established in many countries to audit and ascertain that the doctoral research regulations are adhered to coherently and harmoniously. This can work and makes sense in the South Africa context where one of the functions played by the CHE and Higher Education Qualifications Framework (HEQF) is to audit institutional policies. However, in the Angolan context there is currently no such independent national authority to assure quality of doctoral education provided across the universities and to check the soundness of the policies set by the ministry for HE.

Only in June 2022 was the National System for the Quality Assurance of the Higher Education (SNAES) in Angola launched by the Ministry of Higher Education, Science, Technology and Innovation. The goal is to foster a culture of quality in higher education by implementing assessments that drive the continuous improvement of expected quality standards across all components of the system, integrating rigor into institutional processes.

SNAES would conduct the assessment through four instruments or guides: (1) the guide for auto-assessment of the institutions of higher education and courses or programmes; (2) handbook for external assessment of higher education institutions, courses or graduate and postgraduate programmes; (3) handbook for the external assessment of courses or graduate and postgraduate programmes, and (4) handbook on the procedures for the accreditation of institutions of higher education, courses or graduate and postgraduate programmes (Cristovão, 2022).

The institution mandated to implement the SNAES was the National Institute for Assessment, Accreditation and Recognition of Higher Education Studies (INAREES). It is important to note that the legal framework that redefined the technical and organisation structures of INAREES and approved the regulations for the auto-assessment of courses or programmes and HEI was enshrined in the Presidential Executive Act 306 of 2020 and Presidential Decree Act 108 of 2020 (Republic of Angola, 2020a). This begs the question: why has it taken two years for the ministry to launch the SNAES? It is known that INAREES has been under intense public scrutiny for taking a year or more to issue recognition certificates to those who have completed any degree courses.

The normal waiting time to issue recognition certificates was 15 days for internal students and 60 days for those who had studied abroad. The main reason often echoed is related to lack of financial and human resources (Jornal de Angola, 2022, Editorial). The launching of the national system of quality assurance to all academic levels has the potential of becoming a trigger factor for change in HE, but the question is whether the INAREES will be strong enough to withstand the culture of impunity of powerful corporate entities who might deploy partisan influences in government or the incumbent party-state ranks to bend the regulations to protect business interests in HE.

Hence, the challenges related to the INAREES boil down to Bitzer's question, 'Who checks the checkers?' (Bitzer, 2016, p. 281), and this remains unanswered. Nevertheless, the Angolan context is ridden with a raft of legislation, presidential decrees and regulations. But it severely lacks a coherent system that serves the national interest and not a system that would just defend and work for the *status quo,* with higher tuition fees for profit-seekers.

There is a view that competitive advantage is more likely granted to those who undertake doctoral education. Yet, the main purpose of doctoral education is "to prepare students to become researchers" and therefore 'doctoral education structures' (Matas 2012, pp. 165–169) are paramount to assure "quality and efficiency in higher degree education" (Bastalich 2017, p. 1145). Two key principles can be derived from this discussion. First, the supervisor plays a role in the development of their doctoral candidates' talents. The second element lies in the recognition of the important role of institutional structures and processes in doctoral education. Here the idea of structures underlies the viewpoint that practices are rooted in a set of beliefs on how a chain of durable values, principles and procedures are applied and ultimately integrated within a given institutional setting as the cause and condition for HE stakeholders carrying out transformative action.

This points toward the fact that universities – particularly the case of UAN – are sometimes prone to absorb the authoritarian values of the dominant political structures under which they operate. Thus, if this structure is deviant, then the meaning and importance it might attribute to the five-policy discourse mentioned above diminishes, with the result that the university as a whole is sometimes likely to drift away from its core purposes and social responsibilities.

The need for structure in doctoral education and training calls for resources such as funding, expertise for taught components and supervision capacity and facilities available for research (Baptista et al., 2015, pp. 60–61; Frick et al., 2010). This view is held in most societies with advanced, autonomous and independent higher education systems. However, the supervisor's capacity to deliver on doctoral research outcomes can be compromised by the demands of the everyday struggle to meet all their responsibilities.

As for UAN, inefficient supervision is often the explanation for a lag in doctoral production. Judging from the existing data on doctoral enrolments and progression at UAN one can see the scale at which the situation is getting out of control with the increase in the number of doctoral enrolments versus the lower number of graduates who obtain their doctorates in the expected time. Besides insufficient duration of time allowed for doctoral studies, resources for research such as a library and internet access are a major barrier that doctoral candidates must learn to live with.

They tend to do so either by resorting to private means or face the risk of stagnation on the course of their doctoral studies. Doctoral training at the UAN is predominantly the professional doctorate combining course work and a supervised research project, as defined by Matas (2012, p. 165). Yet against the backdrop of IAU-ACUP optimism on the recognition of the PhD in Africa, one would be more inclined to acknowledge that, unfortunately, the PhD has not yet been fully recognised as an essential asset to contributing to the 'knowledge economy' in Angola, nor does the Angolan government "know how to evaluate competencies of PhD holders as well as the relevance of what they can contribute to society" (AU-ACUP, 2012, p. 20). Why is this the case?

There are at least three pieces of evidence to support this claim. First, for access to the public sector, having a master's (MA) or PhD does not make the holders stand out above other competitors who only hold bachelor's degree (BA) because the ministry of work, pension and social security gives preference to holders of first degrees for access into the public sector. It is certainly a challenging reality which defies international practice. Nonetheless, both MA and PhD can still apply for jobs, but if they were admitted then they would not earn more than their BA colleagues. MA and PhD holders are expected to work in academia where they can earn a competitive wage, per section 9 (1) of the Executive Decree Act 140 of 2021 (Republic of Angola, 2021). This also seems to be a challenge in Europe and non-European countries where, according to Kehm, non-academic labour markets for PhD holders are still rather limited or non-existent (Kehm, 2007, p. 310).

Second, fluidity between the political sphere and university causes the university to be perceived as a nursery for ministerial careers in government. For example, under the administration of president João Lourenço from the People's Movement for the Liberation of Angola (MPLA), the president appointed the rectors and vice-rectors of public universities, in accordance with section 12 (g) of the Presidential Higher Education Executive Act 90 of 2009 (Republic of Angola, 2009). This happened with Maria do Rosário Bragança Sambo and Maria Antonieta Baptista, formerly the UAN's rector and vice-rector for scientific research, who were appointed as cabinet ministers for higher education, science, innovation and technology, and for fishery and sea, respectively, by the president of the republic and MPLA party.

Third, the party encroachment has seen the university turn into an arena for asserting political allegiances for the reward of social status and goods. Despite its pledge to offer quality education and promote meritocracy, the university is still lagging behind in its purpose to deliver on critical thinking and socially applied knowledge. In these circumstances it would be too optimistic to expect UAN to play its full role as a space that is able to "generate jobs by balancing and integrating three aims: first, meeting the practical demands of the labour market, second, producing new knowledge through research by more doctoral-level scientists and finally, producing well-rounded and engaged citizens through teaching" (Friesenhahn, 2014:1).

Nevertheless, there have been positive signals, as will be discussed later in this chapter. One such positive was the previous administration's resolve to foster significant reforms in the HE as expressed in the National Development Plan adopted in 2018 (Plano de Desenvolvimento Nacional, PDN). The PDN pledges four key objectives for higher education, namely, to (1) "improve the network of higher education institutions,

(2) increase the courses, graduates, (3) increase the offers of postgraduates and (4) better the quality of teaching provided by strengthening master's and doctorate results (PDN, 2018b, p. 74). To attain these objectives the government set as a main target "reinforcing higher education with 772 new masters and 125 new doctors trained abroad by 2022" (PDN, 2018b, p. 85).

The plan was ambitious, and its consequences were not free of contradictions. In early January 2019 the Angolan Council of Ministers, *Conselho de Ministros*, gave a green light for the government to send Angolan doctorate students to the, so to speak, 'most prestigious universities in the world'. The data on the implementation of the targets set in 2018 were presented in the Angolan Government National Report on the Mandate Review, RNBM, Relatório Nacional de Balanço do Mandato 2017-2022.

For the period between 2018 until the first semester of 2022, the RNBM shows that 433 students were selected as part of the implementation of the annual programme of sending 300 undergraduate and master's high academic achievers to the best universities around the world. A total of 153 students were sent to the best universities, mainly in Portugal, Brazil, the UK, USA, Russia and Canada. Nonetheless, the report highlights that it is yet to proceed with sending out candidates selected in 2021 as well as other scholarship recipients from previous years. Furthermore, the report listed the conditions for sending a group of 12 PhD candidates and 3 postdoctoral that were already created under the project of development of science and technology. There was a total of 183 PhD and 931 master's degree holders (Republic of Angola., 2022b , p. 43).

This raises several significant questions at first glance. The RNBM report does not state where these 183 PhD and 931 MA degree holders have been trained and how many years, they took to complete the degrees. The RNBM brings to light a host of major issues that affect Angola's higher education system, including the lack of coherent, objective and accessible information on enrolment and progression of candidates as will be shown below for the three UAN faculties. Moreover, doctorate programmes require more time for candidates to complete and in most cases, as highlighted in the three UAN faculties, the candidates can take twice as much as the normal time mandated by law. In general, MA courses have a duration of 4 semesters with a maximum completion period of 3 years, whereas the doctorate courses last for 4 to 5 years.

A report by Expertise France, a French organisation implementing the European Union-funded Program of Support of High Education in Angola (UNI. AO), paints a rather challenging context. It states that since 2020, among the 168 official postgraduate courses created and published in the *Official Gazette* of Angola, 11 (7%) courses were doctoral, 16 (9%) were professional courses and 141 (84%) courses were at master's level. What stands out here is the growing demand for MA courses, with noticeably lower offers for doctoral courses. The reason provided in the report is the shortage of PhDs with both the necessary skills and expertise required to teach at doctoral level (Expertise France, 2022, p. 18). The data also show that overall, offers of postgraduate courses are greater in public institutions, which account for 60% of 101 courses, compared to private institutions, which account for 40% of 67 courses (Expertise France, 2022, p. 20).

The report raises an interesting point which may help in further scrutinizing the reliability and accuracy of the government's triumphant announcement that it had produced 183 PhDs and 931 MAs supposedly in 4 years. This relates to the short period of time in which both PhD and MA holders were produced. Normally, doctoral courses offered either by 9 public institutions or by 2 private institutions struggle with an acute lack of trained PhD scholars to train new PhDs. In that case, one would expect this problem to have improved slightly as HE absorbs the newly graduated PhDs and MAs referred to in the RNBM report.

Nonetheless, the government could have sent 300 doctoral candidates abroad. However, one thing that reveals the government's wishful-thinking and misconceptions about the Angolan HE system's shortcomings lies in the difficulty of explaining how it met the target of producing 183 doctorates, let alone 931 MAs, from 2018 to 2022. Another issue emerging from the PDN was its silence regarding domestic doctoral candidates. They exist and they are clogging up the system at the UAN's FCS, FECUAN and FDUAN as shown in Tables 1.3, 1.4 and 1.5. The underlying challenges begin when policymakers presume that the formulation of new, HE training policy would necessarily lead to a system-wide reboot, as if there were no doctorate courses already being offered in the country.

In fact, the outlook of doctoral production at UAN faculties demonstrates a reality of institutional neglect and utilitarian measures that resort to making money from PhD candidates. One of these measures relates to the high tuition fees charged by the higher education institution (HEI). For instance, the results of an inquiry conducted by Expertise France with the 90 coordinators of post-doctoral courses shows that "annual costs of tuition fees are AKZ 1 521,500 that equates roughly USD 3,554 for the specialisation courses of minimum duration of a year, AKZ 923,872.35 (USD 2,158) for the MA courses and AKZ 1 466,666.67 (USD 3,426) for doctorate courses. Nonetheless, the tuition fees are greater in private institutions, where the candidates are charged AKZ 2 730,000 (USD 6,377) for specialisation courses" (Expertise France, 2022:18).

The Angolan Catholic University (UCAN) offers three new MA courses for which each candidate must pay a tuition fee of AKZ 2 400 000 (USD 5 606) a year. The issue of fee discrepancy between public and private institutions results in a context charactarised by income generation opportunities and an "academic capitalist knowledge/learning regime", according to Knight and Slaughter's accounts, and it can divert the institutional focus away from ensuring the quality of university functions (Knight, 2008, p. 25–26; Slaughter, 2020, p. 15). Also, there is a belief that the university is an "agent of change and development" (Knight & Sehoole, 2013, p. 1; Jowi et al., 2013, p. 11–14; Langa, 2013, p. xi) wherein cooperation and competition define higher education at the height of globalization (De Wit, 2011, pp. 244–245).

Does Angola's national higher education system encourage competition among public and private institutions to create an environment conducive to generating cutting-edge knowledge, moving beyond profit-driven motives and mercantile approaches within higher education and fostering cross-national collaboration? While the UAN encourages cooperation through its partnerships with several well-established and international institutions, including New Lisbon University, University of Lisbon, Université Paris Panthéon Sorbonne, Sapienza Università di Roma, Universidad Complutense Madrid, Lisbon University, Portuguese Catholic University and the University of South Africa, it is hard to demonstrate how these linkages help to improve or enhance the UAN's postgraduate research practices and profile. Furthermore, competition should have as an end-goal the establishment of objective and measurable criteria for monitoring and evaluation to warrant quality and effective management of courses delivered by the faculties. Despite good intentions, research context can trump the resolve for change.

3. Research question and reflections on the research context

This chapter wrestles with the question: To what extent do context and process affect doctoral production at the UAN? To address this question, brief field research was conducted within the UAN's Department for Scientific Research and Postgraduate Studies and across the UAN's faculties of social sciences, economics and law, which offer doctorate courses. The UAN has as its core institutional rationale teaching, research and production carried out across seven faculties, namely science, social sciences, law, economics, engineering, humanities and medicine.

The vice-rector for scientific research and postgraduate studies would in theory oversee UAN's Department for Scientific Research and Postgraduate Studies (DICEP) for the whole university. In reality, there is no direct linkage between the rectorate's DICEP and the faculties' departments for research and postgraduate studies as regards monitoring and to serve as institutional-level mechanisms for oversight and quality assessment. In contrast, each faculty possesses a department for scientific research and postgraduate studies of its own that seems to operate in isolation, except for occasional reporting to the office of the UAN director of DICEP based in the rectorate who reports to DICEP vice-rector, who ultimately liaises with the National Directorate and Secretary for Higher Education in the Ministry of Higher Education, Science, Technology and Innovation (MESCTI). On some occasions the DICEPs sideline the rectory and report directly to the ministry.

Field research enabled me to acquire the most accurate data possible on

1. the number and gender of students enrolled in doctoral courses,
2. the number of doctoral candidates allocated to each supervisor,
3. the number of doctoral candidates that successfully submitted and defended their theses from each year of enrolment in the doctorate courses offered by the UAN faculties of social sciences, law and economics, and
4. the number of doctorate candidates working on the doctoral projects.

Field research intended to generate data can get bumpy and be time-consuming, which demands extra levels of resilience and people skills. The following three steps illustrate the challenges that were encountered during the process of gathering empirical information:

• **Step 1**: The researcher had to meet the UAN director for scientific research and postgraduate services (DICEP) to get his authorization for access to information from the faculties of social sciences, law and economics offering PhD courses in sociology, social psychology, anthropology, history, political science and social media; public law and private law; and economics and management. As is standard practice in research involving data collection within public or private institutions, a written letter of permission was required.

• **Step 2**: Once permission was given to the researcher, UAN's DICEP instructed the faculties to send the data to the DICEP who then handed it to the researcher. However, the data was mostly incomplete. The researcher then had to engage directly with the respective faculties to access the data. The bureaucratic procedures underlying the process reflect a context where data collection serves as a means of exerting power, determining both access and dissemination.

Moreover, the DICEP clearance letter stated the researcher's affiliation with the university and the reason for seeking authorization to conduct research and to obtain data at the UAN. Once the formal letter was issued one would assume that the researcher would not encounter more impediments from anyone. But to get to this stage the researcher had to engage the UAN vice-rector for scientific research and postgraduate studies once more, who instructed the DICEP director to authorize data collection. It took 2 weeks before the application for a credential was issued by the DICEP.

- **Step 3:** In his engagement with the faculties, the researcher presented a copy of the DICEP letter to the dean of the faculty since this was a condition set by the DICEP before the faculties could provide the information. It was then found that the information was scattered in different files, from those recording the data about doctorate courses, doctoral candidates to the partnership contracts between UAN's faculties and the Portuguese universities such as Lisbon New University and the Institute of Economy and Management. However, there were no accurate records demonstrating both the supervision process and candidate satisfaction with the quality of doctoral training and supervision experienced at the faculties, let alone record of the existing challenges regarding international cooperation, in terms of delivering doctoral outputs.

Interestingly, this context also illustrates a deeper social stigma and fear of potential political punishment, which in a way works as a deterrent to creativity and concomitantly serves as a kind of public prescript for survival and self-preservation. It is also a reflection of the inefficient processes that sustain the view that doctorate context matters a lot as it reveals the UAN showing perilous signs of being locked up in a political quagmire of its own making. A view held by the author of this chapter, as university context can in turn hamper doctoral production outputs. In sum, the research processes and structures at UAN are inefficient: there was no proper process for submitting an application for and obtaining permission; the DICEP services were very inefficient, requiring repeated visits; and when the information was provided it was incorrect or incomplete.

4. The UAN - beyond politicization

Notions of a 'resilient authoritarian regime', the Portuguese 'colonial legacy' and higher education trajectories are intertwined and define the broader research context at UAN. At this point one would wonder why, instead of helping enable the development of a full-fledged higher education system, UAN is entangled in a dominant party quagmire. HE in Angola is still a new phenomenon that only emerged a year after independence from Portugal in 1975 with the creation of the University of Angola (*Universidade de Angola*, UA). On 24 January 1985 the UA became Agostinho Neto University (UAN), named after the country's first president and the UAN's first chancellor (Almeida et al., 2022, p. 128; Langa, 2013, p. 6; Jowi et al., 2013, p. 15).

President Agostinho Neto (1977) defined the UAN's mission as

> to serve the revolution and fight against the remnants of the Portuguese colonialism; help to implant a just and progressivist society; to produce national cadres endowed with new consciousness, and who'd be able to work as the agents of a new society that will strive to fulfil the popular democracy [translated by the author, Faria].

Therefore, the rise of independent Angola's first public university as part of the national higher education system was more concerned with furthering nationalistic purposes than devising policies that would have promoted the quality of research education and subsequently help with harnessing critical-thinking skills (Yranoski, 2011). In fact, in Angola, party-dominant structures continue to define the campus as well as hinder academic freedoms and autonomy.

The context at the UAN has worsened since the university's establishment for the following three reasons: first, the higher education trade union fought against the government of former president of Eduardo dos Santos. Dos Santos's government had established in its Executive Act 90 (12) of 2009 that the government ought to appoint the governing bodies of the universities, proposed by the minister for higher education and based on three candidates elected by the assemblies of their respective institutions (Republic of Angola, 2009). The likely reason was that the legislation was tailored to control and discipline individuals perceived as critical of the regime's dominance over higher education. On the other hand, it seemed like an artefact to reward the scholars loyal to the status quo. Nevertheless, it took almost two and a half decades before new legislation defending a contested election of the UAN rector and vice-rectors, faculty deans and vice-deans came to effect in June 2022.

These officials were elected in May and June 2022 by the representatives of academic groups within the faculties, including the professors, researchers' assistants, postgraduate students, and students' association (UAN, 2022). Prior to this breakthrough on the tortuous path towards academic freedom, there had been no elections for positions in public university executive entities, because the then president dos Santos retained for himself the powers to appoint them. The higher education trade union criticized the decision to appoint these bodies as unconstitutional, claiming it reduced the pursuit of quality in higher education to nothing more than a "mirage" (José, 2015) Thirdly, governing higher education through presidential decree reflects a tension between efficiency, stability, and the president's discretionary decision-making.

The strict control over higher education began to ease during the first term of President João Lourenço's administration, as he, under pressure from unions, permitted all nine public universities and their respective faculties to hold elections (Angop, 2022). Before the elections, the UAN had since 2017 been run by an interim rector, Pedro Magalhães, who had been appointed by president Lourenço alongside Maria Antonieta Baptista as vice-rector. Later Maria Antonieta Baptista left this position to take up a ministerial post for fishery and sea, and automatically became a member of the MPLA political bureau, leaving the vice-rector post vacant. Magalhães rose to the top of UAN hierarchy after Maria do Rosário Sambo was appointed minister of higher education, science, technology and innovation.

Beyond the pledges for a relative liberalization of the national higher education system (NHES) lie two sets of challenges. The first has to do with a huge imbalance between the limited number of university staff holding PhD degrees and an increasing number of doctoral candidates. According to the Angola 2016 High Education Statistical Bulletin (2016, pp. 13–17) there were 64 HEIs in Angola, of which 24 are public and 40 private institutions. In addition, 18 were classified as universities (8 public and 10 private), 41 were classified as institutes (11 public and 30 private) and 4 higher education public schools.

However, when adding up the national data scattered in the RNBM as shown in Table 1, one notices that, at time of data collection, Angola had 87 HEI nationwide. However, in 2020 the Angolan government "abolished and fused 12 public HEI in unprecedented efforts to reorganise the higher education network to avoid the disbursement of finance and encourage the sharing of human resources" (Expansão, 2020).

Table 1: HEI by type and nature

HEI	Public	Private	Total
Academy	1	-	1
Higher Schools	4	-	4
Higher Institutes	12	37	49
Polytechnic Institutes	2	9	11
Universities	11	11	22
TOTAL	**30**	**57**	**87**

Sources: Anuário Estatístico (2018a) and Relatório National de Balanço (2022).

According to the Social Statistical Yearbook, there were 11 433 lecturers in Angola's HE system in 2019 (2 574 female and 8 859 male) (Anuário de Estatísticas Sociais, 2022a, p. 75). The proportion of staff with master's degrees in 2016 was 33.3%, with 1 708 holders of master's and doctoral degrees employed by public universities and 1 209 by private institutions. Whereas the academic staff with doctorate degrees was 9.8%, that is 601 doctorate holders in public universities and 237 for all private universities.

Since the HE Statistical Yearbook began publishing this data in 2016, there has been systematic and reliable information to illustrate the evolution of HE staff according to degrees. Nevertheless, the existing information which is scattered and hard to verify accounts for the production of 183 PhDs and 931 MAs from 2018 to 2022 (RNBM, 2022, p. 43). Despite this limitation, one should give the benefit of the doubt and recognise that the HEI system did manage to bring newly graduated BA, MA and PhD holders into the system, surpassing the figures in Table 2 below.

Table 2: National higher education teaching staff in 2019

Indicators	Gender		Total
	Female	Male	
No. Lecturers	2 575 (22,5%)	8 858 (77,4%)	**11 433**
Lecturers MA holders	1 025 (39.84%)	3 054 (34.48%)	**4 079 (35.69%)**
Lecturers PhD holders	250 (9.71%)	987 (11.15%)	**1 237 (10.83)**

Source: Anuário Estatístico (2019) (adapted and completed by the author)

The table could be problematic to interpret, for it mixes numbers and percentages. However, it is possible to make the calculations and complete the table. Table 3 below provides an overview of the persistent dominance of lecturers with bachelor's (BA) degrees. For instance, where the number of lecturers is 8 405 (2016), 10 198 (2017), 10 441 (2018) and 11 433 (2019), there would respectively be 3 755 (2016), 4 613 (2017), 4 716 (2018) and 5 224 (2019) lecturers with either MA or PhD degrees. The pattern that springs out shows that the number of lecturers with BAs is consistently higher than the number of lecturers who are MA holders, and the number of PhD holders in Angola's HEI is even lower in comparison to the two former categories of lecturers.

Table 3: BA holding lecturers in Angola's HEI

Year	No. BA holders	Total lecturers
2016	4 650	8 405
2017	5 585	10 198
2018	5 725	10 441
2019	6 209	11 433

Sources: Anuários Estatísticos 2016–2019

In sum, the figures on Tables 2 and 3 show three conflicting realities. The first betrays a higher education system which has been expanding both in type and nature. The second depicts a condition of protracted deficit of lecturers to respond to pressing demands for HE degrees and courses. Furthermore, a third reality emerges from the data of the Bulletin of Social Statistics: that out of a total 319 295 students enrolled in HEI in 2019, 151 946 (47.5%) were female and 167 349 (52.5%) male (Anuário de Estatísticas Sociais, 2022a, p. 70).

A second observation relates to a comment made by Maria de Rosário Sambo, the minister of higher education, science, technology and innovation. She said that the national scientific environment reflects that

> there is scientific research, but it is still weak, compared with other SADC countries. We have a huge potential to avert this reality, if we are able to properly manage the human, the financial resources and above all we shouldn't be megalomaniacs. We should instead try to focus on the objective to produce science with a pragmatic sense. (Voz de Angola, 2017)

Furthermore, she asserted "we need to diagnose bad practices and make an effort to root them out progressively with a change of mind and behaviour" (Voz de Angola, 2017).

Sambo's remarks should have rung alarm bells about a serious mix-up between the causes and the effects of bad practices. Clearly, these could be comprehended as an effect of the entanglement of the national higher education system with the omnipresence of the party-state regime. In such a context, the possible production of scientific knowledge is constrained, even if this is conducted with pragmatism, as there is a clear and growing gap between a set of policies and the contexts in which the researchers find themselves. A closer look at the UAN shows an imbalance of strategies, policies and available resources for providing quality doctoral training. The next section looks at some government legislation to ascertain how it establishes the process for doctoral provision.

5. Government legislation on doctoral training

The key challenge for HE is not the lack of legislation to regulate the system, but the lack of implementation of coherent mechanisms for quality assurance across different HEIs and within each university, across different faculties. In fact, the doctoral research process does follow an orderly defined set of procedures and guidelines on the nature of the doctorate, the role of doctoral supervisors and the defined goals and competences a PhD candidate ought to acquire throughout the process.

This section discusses some of the legislation in order to indicate the general institutional guidance on doctoral education.

Legislation on HE and doctoral studies in Angola is based on two presidential acts: Presidential Executive Act 90 of 2009 (Republic of Angola, 2009) and Presidential Executive Act 29 of 2011 (Republic of Angola, 2011). Each act establishes the procedures and norms necessary to regulate the universities. According to Section 24 of the Presidential Executive Act 90 of 2009 (Republic of Angola, 2009), postgraduate studies comprise two categories: the academic route for MAs and PhDs and the professional route.

The professional route aims to improve and expand the technical and vocational skills of postgraduate students. Additionally, the same legislation specifies the maximum completion time for MAs as two years, and four to five years for PhDs. The PhD is viewed as a

> training and research process that consists of strengthening, widening and deepening scientific abilities of BA and MA holders through research and a written thesis, which ought to be original and with the potential to make contributions to universal scientific heritage.

Subsequently Section 21 of the Presidential Executive Act 29 of 2011 reiterates the overarching government policy on PhD education as a

> process of training and of research, which endows the candidates with BA and MA degrees with a vast and deep scientific competence, resulting with

a production of thesis whose content must be innovative and constitute to universal knowledge. (Republic of Angola, 2011)

In this process, the PhD students are expected to do course work during the first two years of doctoral study to acquire research skills. For this purpose, different faculties have different types of modules crafted in accordance with the nature and objectives of each doctoral programme. That is the case with doctoral programmes in UAN's faculties, namely, social sciences, economics and law. These share the same processes and procedures regarding the writing of an original thesis, which happens after the student has successfully defended the doctoral research project.

Moreover, Section 26 of the Presidential Executive Act 29 of 2011 (Republic of Angola, 2011) on supervision specifies three key procedures: first, for the doctoral candidates to produce the thesis they must be supervised by professors or researchers holding a PhD degree and affiliated to the institution where the doctoral candidate is enrolled. The supervision could be provided in a system of co-supervision. However, it spells out that this model must be referred to clearly in the candidate doctoral project as well as stating the strategies for co-supervision. Second, it specifies that only those lecturers and researchers with PhDs should supervise theses. HEI could seek to establish agreements or contracts with other institutions for adequate supervision of doctoral candidates. Lastly, supervisors must inform and update the scientific councils of their faculties every semester on the key milestones and progress of the theses.

Clarity about the role and purposes of supervision makes a big difference when it comes to meeting the target of graduating more doctoral candidates within the expected timeframe. In this section it will be shown that the outlook on doctoral production is negative as there has not yet been a single doctoral graduate from the doctoral courses offered by FCS, FECUAN and FDUAN since their start. It will be shown that underlying causes for this failure relate to context and bad institution practices that ultimately are tied to the dysfunctional equilibrium between legislation and implementation of policies by the faculties. It is worth bearing in mind that this gap between policy and implementation is also a major challenge in many other African countries with consolidated academic and research cultures. It does not help much to have a set of excellent policies if the capacity and will to implement them properly is lacking. There is also a need for a fully independent and autonomous body to provide oversight as well as audit policies and assure efficiency and quality, as in most other countries in the world (CHEA, 2022; INQAAHE, 2022).

6. UAN's doctoral production outlook

This section draws from the data collected at the UAN's three faculties – social sciences (FSC), economics (FECUAN) and law (FDUAN). To help further illustrate the status of doctoral production at the UAN, the data were pooled together from disparate sources of information provided by each faculty's DICEP (documents and internal memos) as well as exchanges with staff members of DICEP in each faculty. As will be made clear, there is a common thread running through the data conveyed below. However, it would be misleading to claim that the profit-driven approach, reflected in the high fees of AKZ 3,500,000 (approximately USD 8,121.53) per PhD candidate, has turned doctoral candidates into mere "golden geese," causing faculties to neglect or abandon their primary responsibility of fostering doctoral research and production.

Tables 4, 5 and 6 depict a context of stagnation in doctoral production. The tables offer an overview of enrolment and progression patterns in three of UAN's biggest faculties, FCS, FECUAN and FDUAN, by conveying four sets of information about (a) the number of doctoral candidates (PhD) according to gender; (b) doctoral candidates from the first cohort in 2012, the second in 2016 and the third in 2020; (c) number of PhD enrolments per supervisor; (d) number of doctoral theses handed in; and (e) the number of vivae held per year.

Table 4: FCS: PhD in social sciences enrolment and progression 2012, 2016 and 2020

FCS	PhD Enrolments by Gender		PhD Enrolments per Supervisor	Theses Handed In by 2020	Vivae per Year		
	F	M			2019	2020	2022
PhD in 2012	10	13	5	3	1	1	1
PhD in 2016	8	18	5	-	-	-	-
PhD in 2020	11	50	5	-	-	-	-
TOTAL	29	82	-	3	3		
	111						

Source: Data from DICEP – FCS

The FSC started offering a doctoral programme in social sciences in 2012 with 23 enrolments, plus 26 and 61 enrolments in 2016 and 2020 respectively. That gives a total of 111 enrolments over the whole period, of whom 29 were female and 82 male candidates. FCS seems to allocate five candidates to each supervisor. This means that the faculty would need at least 22 lecturers/professors holding PhDs to be able provide adequate supervision and combine it with heavy teaching loads. In general, the candidates are mature students, who hold full-time jobs with state institutions, government departments such as defence and security, as well as the banking sector, and some are UAN staff as well as in the private sector.

PhD candidates have struggled to meet the mandatory completion time, and this factor combined with the challenges of coping with the pressure of finding the right balance between working life, private life and studies, leaves the doctoral student less time to do research. Moreover, the same challenges are encountered by supervisors who so often can barely, as Cloete et al. (2015:112) argue, facilitate the student to become an independent professional researcher and scholar possessed of a set of cognitive and meta-cognitive skills. In these circumstances, only 3 doctoral candidates, out of 23 who have been enrolled since 2012, have managed to submit their theses and had successful vivae.

The doctoral pipeline at UAN is therefore clogged and consequently, doctoral production rates remain low. In this case there is no clarity nor the slightest possible estimate as to when 20 candidates from the first cohort will manage to complete their doctoral studies, let alone those from the second and third cohorts. A key problem observed here relates to the lack of good record keeping on who's supervising who and, more importantly, there was no file or data about the supervisor six-monthly report accounting candidate progression or drop out. This practice is just one among many which seems to indicate that the regulations of the government on doctoral supervision are not complied with at UAN.

Table 5: FECUAN: PhD in economics 2015 and PhD in management 2015, 2016 & 2017

FECUAN	PhD enrolments by gender		PhD enrolments per supervisor	Theses handed in by 2020	Vivae p/Year		
	F	M			2019	2020	2022
PhD in management 2015	5	21	1-2	6	-	-	-
PhD in economics 2015	5	16	1-2	2	-	1	-
PhD in management 2016	2	15	1-2	2	-	-	2
PhD in management 2017	2	18	1-2	-	-	-	-
TOTAL	14	70	-	10	3		
	84						

Source: Data from DICEP – FECUAN

FECUAN started offering doctoral programmes in economics in 2015, forging institutional cooperation with two Portuguese institutes, the Portuguese Public University Institute (ISCTE) and the Lisbon School of Economics and Management (ISEG). FECUAN outperformed FCS and FDUAN as it saw 10 doctoral candidates who handed in their thesis for jury review. Most of those, around 8, were enrolled in 2015 and 2016 from the first and second cohorts in management. However, only 2 doctoral candidates went on to pass the viva in 2022, whereas 4 out 6 PhD candidates in management were waiting for the viva in 2022, and 1 PhD candidate had the thesis refused by the jury with strong recommendations, and the other was still waiting to hear the jury's assessment.

There were 2 doctoral candidates from the first cohort in economics, who submitted the thesis, one underwent the viva successfully in 2022. Overall, 81 doctoral candidates had yet to submit the thesis and do the viva. According to the data provided by DICEP "on average 17 lectures in FECUAN supervise between one and two PhD candidates" (FECUAN, 2022). This suggests that most doctoral students lacked supervisors, with DICEP highlighting the poor organization of the database on doctoral production.

However, lower output in doctoral production in management and economics has been subject to different interpretations. The faculty could have produced its first doctorate prior to 2022, but the "candidate was found guilty of plagiarizing his thesis by the FECUAN's internal review committee before commending it to UAN's rector for viva" (Personal communication, 2019). The student was advised to rewrite his thesis.

Table 6: FDUAN: PhD in public and private law 2011 and 2017

FDUAN	PhD Enrolments by Gender		PhD Enrolments per Supervisor	Theses Handed In by 2020	Viva per Year
					2020
	F	M			
PhD in public law 2011	3	12	NRA	-	0
PhD in private law 2011	2	9	NRA	4	4
PhD in public law 2017	2	14	NRA	-	0
PhD in private law 2017	3	19	NRA	-	0
TOTAL	10	54	-	4	4
	64				

Source: Data from DICEP – FDUAN

The faculty of law (FDUAN) enrolled their first cohort of doctoral programmes in public and private law. Taken together, there were 26 doctoral candidates enrolled in the two courses in 2011, 5 female and 21 male. There were 4 doctoral candidates in private law, who had vivae in 2020. This was a significant achievement for the FDUAN that could be a positive stride towards ending its 9-year drought in doctoral output. Nonetheless, there were 60 candidates yet to complete the thesis. In DICEP's view "3 candidates were nearing to the end" (Personal communication, 2022). Matters became even more complicated when the faculty DICEP was unable to supply a record of the number of PhD candidates per supervisor, and no information was available on the progress of these candidates, despite the fact the law programme had more than a decade of experience running doctorate courses.

Here an anecdote about the experience of one PhD candidate is worth retelling. The jury to recommend the candidate to reformulate in 6 months after the candidate's first viva attempt on 20 June 2017. Only in 2020 was the candidate able to give the viva a second attempt, and then they had to complete the viva via Skype as the supervisor, a professor at the University of Coimbra in Portugal, was unable to travel to Luanda. With regard to the second cohort in 2017, it shows an increasing demand for the doctoral programme.

The doctorate in public law gained one more student, but the number of female candidates dropped to two compared to the first cohort; whereas the PhD in private law added one more female student and the number of male candidates jumped from nine to 19 in 2017. As mentioned before, no information was made available to the researcher to determine what the supervision load is within the doctoral course of the FDUAN. Finally, this study has found that there were some discrepancies between what the written regulations and norms say about the obligation of supervisors to inform the faculty scientific council on their doctoral candidates' progress and the actual recording of this information on file. This issue seems to stand out as a common shortcoming among the faculties.

On the whole, the low doctoral production rates demonstrate that these faculties share common challenges. There is a gender gap. The number of male candidates is significantly higher than the female candidates in all three faculties. In the Faculty of Social Sciences, the first female has yet to complete their PhD, and this faculty had more female doctoral candidates than the faculties of economics and law.

UAN's faculties share the challenge of an inadequate information management system, to record who is supervising who, data on the doctorate candidates, and data on the quality of training and supervision. This is certainly an issue that independent bodies such as the NCHE and HEQE need to address and enable the faculties to contribute to doctoral production. Currently the contexts and processes exhibit many deficiencies that hinder the UAN's contribution to increasing in PhD graduates across the whole Angola HE system. Moreover, the total number of doctoral candidates stood at 249 in 2022 for just three faculties. It will certainly continue to increase steadily, but the UAN must undertake deep assessment to revamp or fail to become a driver of innovation and development.

7. Conclusion

Angola's HE system straddles the crossroads of deep reforms to ensure, on the one hand, an alignment between the demand for doctoral education and training, and on the other hand, the need to deliver quality research and supervision across postgraduate courses.

Three of UAN's faculties, FDUAN, FCS and FECUAN, started offering doctoral training from 2011, 2012 and 2015 in fields such as public law, private law, management and economics. Since then, these faculties enrolled 259 PhD candidates, of whom 10 obtained doctoral degrees, whereas the greatest part are still stuck in the pipeline despite twice exceeding the 5-year period allowed for doctoral studies by the legislation. Below are some of the issues that might contribute to UAN's producing too few doctoral graduates:

- The political context of secrecy and bureaucracy puts pressure on the data gathering process. Access to information that in normal circumstances would be publicly accessible is protected behind walls of secrecy, wherein DICEP operates as the gatekeeper of information that is only made available to researchers if they obtain a clearance letter from the deputy vice-chancellor.
- There is no set of guidelines for submitting an application for permission to access data. DICEP services were often inefficient. Repeated visits and requests were needed to get information and when it was finally made available, it was either incomplete or incorrect. Thus, the lack of a proper process propels the researcher to seek personal contacts that may help them with obtaining data. Having a good network of contacts at the academic level proved to be crucial for access to the higher education statistical bulletins of 2017, 2018 and 2019 from the ministry of higher education, science, technology and innovation.
- The doctoral training *conundrum* (MacGregor) shows a reality where the growing demand for doctoral degrees is met with a low number of PhD

degree holders. This unbalanced reality threatens the chances of any HEI having enough PhD supervisors.

- Institutional neglect within the faculties – with rare exceptions from the FECUAN – is fueled by an inadequate and deficient organisational model of doctoral training. The current model at UAN is representative of what Kehm (2007, p. 314) calls a "chair holder logic" rather than an "institutional logic".

One could add the entrenched partisan sense of belonging shown by the top managers – ministers, rectors, vice-rectors, deans and doctoral courses directors – whose membership to the incumbent MPLA party plays out as a free ride to move in and out of HEI ranks.

The dean of a faculty or the director of doctoral courses would either belong to the MPLA central committee or be a member of the national parliament for the incumbent party or even a much-trusted pair of hands for the 'securitised state' (Roque, 2021). PhD candidates were piling up, receiving poor or unaccounted supervision. This blackspot is assumed to be dealt with silently, in a way that would prevent any potential negative publicity against the regime. Doctoral candidates are caught up in this context. They are expected to pay tuition fees regardless of the fact that the faculty lets them down persistently.

Suffering in silence is often the only way of overcoming doctoral research challenges. For the sake of development, society-based knowledge and HEI's reputation, there will have to be a constructive and steady way out of these pitfalls. A solution to that would become possible when the key HE stakeholders coalesce around the belief that "the generation of the new knowledge has become an important strategic resource" for any society, be it developed or underdeveloped (Kehm, 2007, p. 308). The only way that may help Angola's higher education turn doctoral research into the "trigger of economic growth and innovation" (Kehm, 2007, p. 315; Jowi et al., 2013, pp. 17–21), will be to adopt a more systemic, structured and innovative model that works for the benefit of doctoral students, researchers and state institutions.

For that purpose, the academic production context needs a major "paradigmatic change in higher education policymaking, which implies first, the shift from the institutional to system logic, focusing on the structure and configuration, and second the shift from chair holder logic to the institutional logic" (Kehm, 2007, p. 314). In this case, such shift would require the introduction of a doctoral school at UAN faculties as a key strategy "to provide more efficiency, i.e., get higher number of doctoral candidates more rapidly through this phase" (Kehm, 2007, p. 309).

Equally, doctoral schools need to ensure good practices and constructive approaches towards research and postgraduate studies across UAN faculties, where each DICEP shows a reality of doctoral studies of its own making. In addition, a doctoral school could help to improve the practices of supervision as well as act as a coordinating body for the whole university which could foster intra-doctoral school continuous engagement to improve: (a) teaching and learning and curriculum development (Botha, 2020, p. 1801); (b) harmonise doctorate programmes; (c) monitor supervision arrangements; (d) control progress of doctoral candidates; (e) "launch a 'central management information office in which complete sets of institutional data would be stored' and made available" (Botha, 2020, p. 1797), and (f) foster a collaborative research and knowledge production community system (Sehoole & Jowi, 2020, 1899; Botha, 2020, p. 1798).

Such a new institution and organisational system at UAN's doctoral school could also help in defining criteria to determine the knowledge and skills with which doctoral candidates enter their studies and subsequently find ways to match them up with relevant institutional facilities, funding and range of initiatives that could harness cross-regional institutional mobility. All these should liaise with domestic quality assurance bodies such as INAREES and the International Network for Quality Assurance Agencies in Higher Education (INQAAHE).

In a context in which there are not enough supervisors to match the growing number of doctoral candidates, a one-to-one supervision model might not properly deliver doctoral production, but the faculties would greatly benefit from a "shared supervision or *co-tutelle* arrangement" (Kehm, 2007, p. 308). The doctoral schools may also introduce supervisory panels composed according to their respective research subjects and expertise. This could be attained as long as there was an increase in partnership opportunities and

> *strengthened relations between African universities through collaboration, exchange and the development of supportive frameworks to strengthen capacity to deal with [the continent's] own circumstances and develop plat-forms for international engagements.* (Jowi et al., 2013, p. 24)

A cross-continental engagement could not only expose Angolan doctoral candidates to new and more competitive environments, but also foster institutional drive and commitment to developing excellent and innovative doctoral programs. This would enable Angola's higher education institutions to capitalize on the opportunities offered by internationalization (Jowi et al., 2013, pp. 27–28). Both PhD candidates and UAN doctoral academic staff would be compelled to embrace a competition mindset for research funding, rather than relying heavily on the government's dwindling resources.

This chapter argued that UAN's context and processes are currently detrimental to doctoral production, for a number of reasons. UAN cannot be completely dissociated from Angola's past and most recent political trajectory. Here, so often politics trump UAN's chances of becoming a locus of knowledge production through doctoral research. The process for doctoral production is clearly codified in presidential decrees and faculties. Yet, there is a big gap between policy ideals and actual practice.

The chapter found that the lack of accountability, the institution's lack of independence to apply checks and balances, and the existence of bureaucratic posturing and political entanglement cast a shadow over doctoral provision.

References

Almeida, C. G., Sá, A. L. & Faria, P. C. J. (2022). We got a taste for protest! Leadership transition and political opportunities for protest in Angola's resilient authoritarian regime, In Sanches, E. R. (Ed.), *Political protest, political opportunities, and change in Angola*. London & New York: Routledge, 128–145.

Angop Angola Press. (2018). PR Orienta realização de eleições universidades públicas. https://www.portaldeangola.com/pr-orienta-realizacao-de-eleicoes-nas-universidades-publicas/

Baptista, A., Frick, L, Holley, K., Remmik, M., Tesch, J., Âkerlind, G. (2015). The doctorate as an original contribution to knowledge: Considering relationships between originality, creativity, and innovation. *Frontline Learning Research*, 3 (3). Special Issue, 55-67.

Bastalich, W. (2017). Content and context in knowledge production: a critical review of doctoral supervision literature. *Studies in Higher Education*, 42 (7), 1145-1157.

Botha, J. (2018). "Institutional research and themes, southern Africa". In Shin, J.C. & Teixiera, P. (eds.), *Encyclopedia of international higher education systems and institutions*. Dordrecht: Springer.

Cloete, N., Mouton, J., & Sheppard, C. (2015). *Doctoral Education in South Africa – Policy, Discourse and Data*. Cape Town: African Minds.

Da Costa, J. V. F (2022). *HE Statistical Yearbook 2017, 2018 & 2019*, e-Mail to P. C. J. Faria, 12 July.

De Wit, H. (2011). Globalisation and Internationalisation of Higher Education. *Revista de Universidad y Sociedad del Conocimiento (RUSC)*, 8 (2). 241-248.

Expansão. (2020). Reorganização extingue e funde 12 instituições públicas de ensino superior. https://expansao.co.ao/universidade/interior/reorganizacao-extingue-e-funde-12-instituicoes-publicas-de-ensino-superior-97631.html

Expertise France-UNI.AO/MESCTI. (2022). *A pós-graduação em Angola: Situação e perspectiva para a criação de novos cursos*. https://ciencia.ao/images/noticias/Docs/Programa_UNIAO_verso_digital.pdf

Faria, P. C. J. (2022). Request for supplementary data for the publication of book chapter, Email to R. Maia 24 June. Available: paulocjfaria12@gmail.com.

Fernando, P. F. (2022). *Personal communication*, e-Mail to P. C. J. Faria.

Frick, L. Albertyn, R. & Rutgers, L. (2010). The Socratic method: adult education theories. *Acta Academica Supplementum* (1), 75-102.

Friesenhahn, I. (2014). *Making higher education work for Africa: Facts and figures*. https://www.scidev.net/global/features/higher-education-africa-facts-figures/.

José, M. (2015). Angola: Nomeação de reitores posta em causa. https://www.voaportugues.com/a/angola-no-meacoes-de-reitores-postas-em- causa/2855288.html.

Jornal de Angola. (2022). INAAREES leva anos a reconhecer certificados. https://www.jornaldeangola.ao/ao/noticias/detalhes.php?id=397371.

Jowi, J. O, Knight, J. & Sehoole, C. (2013). Internationalisation of African Higher Education: Status, Challenges and Issues, in J. Knight & C. Sehoole (eds.), *Internationalisation of African Higher Education: Towards Achieving the MDGs*. Rotterdam, Boston & Taipei: Sense Publishers, 11-31.

Kehm, B. M. (2007). Quo Vadis Doctoral Education? New European Approaches in the Context of Global Changes. *European Journal of Education*, 42 (3), 307-319.

Kiala, S. (2022). *Personal communication to author*. e-Mail to P. C. J. Faria.

Knight, J. & Sehoole, C. (2013). Introduction, in J. Knight & C. Sehoole (eds.), *Internationalisation of African Higher Education: Towards Achieving the MDGs* Rotterdam, Boston & Taipei: Sense Publishers, 1-10.

Langa, P. V. (2013). *Higher Education in Portuguese Speaking African Countries: A Five Country Baseline Study*. Cape Town: African Minds.

MacGregor, K. (2013). Africa: Emerging ideas for building PhD training capacity. *University World News*. https://www.universityworldnews.com/post.php?story=20131215083542491.

Maia, R. (2022). *Personal communication to author*. e-Mail to P. C. J. Faria.

Matas, C. P. (2012). Doctoral education and skills development: An international perspective. *Revista de Docencia Universitaria*, 10 (2), 163-191.

Republic of Angola. (2009). *Presidential Higher Education Executive Act 90 of 2009*. Luanda. Government Printer.

Republic of Angola. (2011). *Presidential Executive Act 29 of 2011*. Luanda. Government Printer. Republic of Angola. 2016. *Anuário Estatístico*, HE Statistical Yearbook, Ministério do Ensino

Superior, Ciência, Tecnologia e Inovação (MESCTI), Gabinete de Estudos, Planeamento (n.d.). Luanda. Governo de Angola.

Republic of Angola. (2017). *Anuário Estatístico*, HE Statistical Yearbook, Ministério do Ensino Superior, Ciência, Tecnologia e Inovação (MESCTI), Gabinete de Estudos, Planeamento, Cabinet of Studies, Planning Statistics. Luanda. Governo de Angola.

Republic of Angola. (2018a). *Anuário Estatístico*, HE Statistical Yearbook, Ministério do Ensino Superior, Ciência, Tecnologia e Inovação (MESCTI), Gabinete de Estudos, Planeamento, Cabinet of Studies, Planning Statistics. Luanda. Governo de Angola.

Republic of Angola. (2018b). *Plano de Desenvolvimento Nacional*, PDN, Ministério da Economia e Planeamento. Luanda. Governo de Angola.

Republic of Angola. (2019). *Anuário Estatístico*, HE Statistical Yearbook, Ministério do Ensino Superior, Ciência, Tecnologia e Inovação (MESCTI), Gabinete de Estudos, Planeamento, Cabinet of Studies, Planning Statistics. Luanda. Governo de Angola.

Republic of Angola. (2020a). *Presidential Decree Act 108 of 2020*. Luanda: Government Printer.

Republic of Angola. (2020b). *Presidential Executive Act 306 of 2020*. Luanda: Government Printer.

Republic of Angola. (2021). *Presidential Executive Act 140 of 2021*. Luanda. Government Printer.

Republic of Angola. (2022a). *Anuário de Estatísticas Sociais 2015-2019*, Social Statistics Yearbook, Instituto Nacional de Estatística, INE, Divisão de Estatísticas Sociais. Luanda. Governo de Angola.

Republic of Angola. (2022b). *Relatório Nacional de Balanço de Mandato*, RNBM 2017-2022. Luanda. Governo de Angola.

Roque, P. C. (2021). *Governing in the Shadows: Angola's securitised state*. London: Hurst.

Sehoole, C. & Jowi, J. O. (2020). Internationalization of Higher Education, Africa in Teixeira, P.N. & Shin, J. C. (eds.). *The International Encyclopedia of Higher Education Systems and Institutions*. Dordrecht: Springer. 1898-1901.

Slaughter, S. (2020). Academic Capitalism, Evolution and Comparisons, in Teixeira, P. N. & Shin, J. C. (eds in chief). *The International Encyclopedia of Higher Education Systems and Institutions*. Dordrecht: Springer. 6-16.

Tadeu, C. (2022). *Personal communication to author*. e-Mail to P. C. J. Faria.

The Council for Higher Education Accreditation (*CHEA*) (n.d.). https://www.chea.org/.

The International Network for Quality Assurance Agencies in Higher Education (*INQAAHE*). (n.d.). https://www.inqaahe.org/.

Universidade Agostinho Neto (UAN) (2022). *A Nossa História*, Presidente Agostinho Neto Speech, 12 September 1977 at the inauguration ceremony of the UAN vice-rector. https://uan.ao/sobre-uan/historia

Voz de Angola. (2017). Ministra do Ensino Superior admite que investigação científica em Angola é fraca. http://vozdeangola.com.

CHAPTER 8

The role of doctoral supervisors in addressing the problem of predatory publishing in francophone sub-Saharan Africa

Kokouvi Edem N'Tsoukpoe

Burkina Faso is in West Africa, with a population of 22 million. It is home to 122 higher education and research institutions, including 7 public universities and 12 other public institutions, (DGESS/MESRSI, 2022). In 2020/2021, the total student population in the country was 190 218, with 36.6% female. In 2020/21 there were 3 600 doctoral candidates in Burkina Faso (1.9% of total enrolment).

Located in Ouagadougou, the **International Institute for Water and Environmental Engineering (2iE)** was established as a higher education and research institute in 1968-1970 by 14 French-speaking countries in West and Central Africa. It specializes in areas such as energy, water and sanitation, civil engineering and hydraulics, and sustainable development. 2iE currently has 1 500 on-site students, including 60 PhD candidates. The 2iE is a Center of Excellence of the West African Economic and Monetary Union (UEMOA), the Economic Community of West African States (ECOWAS), NEPAD and the World Bank.

1. Introduction

Publish or perish has become today the motto for success in any respectable research institute. This has given rise to various unethical publication practices in sciences including salami slicing (the incremental publishing of noncomprehensive papers on the same topic) and publication in predatory journals.

Predatory journals and publishers can be defined as journals and publishers that exploit the gold open- access model to profit from scholarly publishing in a dishonest way, without or with cursory peer-review, while charging publication fees to authors (Beall, 2016; Fovet-Rabot & CIRAD, 2021). This open access model exhibits a clear conflict of interest: the more papers the journal publishes, the more money it gets (Beall, 2017).

Since its introduction, the term 'predatory journals' has been a subject of debate, particularly considering the ongoing adaptation of journals accused of unethical practices. A reason for this is that these dubious, fraudulent, questionable, or pseudo-journals encompass a wide range of misconduct. Therefore, a move away from the term 'predatory' has been suggested and a distinction between 'deceptive' and 'low-quality' journals has been promoted (Eriksson & Helgesson, 2018). This view has been confirmed by a recent global study by the InterAcademy Partnership (IAP) (2022), who describe a spectrum of predatory behaviours ranging from "fraudulent journals" to "questionable quality journals" (InterAcademy Partnership, 2022, pp. 28–32). Another reason is that many academics, driven by the pressure to publish at any cost, are often fully aware of the nature of their dealings, resulting in a relationship that is less about predator and prey and more about a new and ugly symbiosis (Kolata, 2017; Darbyshire et al., 2020). For the sake of simplicity, the term 'predatory journals' is used in this chapter since it is directed at the global scientific community.

Universities and research institutes in sub-Saharan Africa countries are no exception to this phenomenon (Andoh, 2017; Mouton & Valentine, 2017). According to the study of Demir (2018) on researchers who published in predatory journals in 2017, the greatest number and share (84%) of researchers were from developing countries. Three African countries (Nigeria, Egypt and Kenya) are among the top 20, with Nigeria as the second highest contributor, just behind India. An earlier analysis of articles published in predatory journals in 2013 had already ranked India and Nigeria as the two countries with the highest contributions to predatory journals (Xia et al., 2015). Regarding Nigeria, besides various reasons indicated by Xia et al. (2015), the major reason behind the phenomenon is that academics are financially rewarded for publications, through academic promotion, in international journals regardless of the quality of the journal (Demir, 2018).

If no francophone countries in sub-Saharan Africa appear in the aforementioned studies, it is not because predatory publication practices are unknown in these countries. This absence is probably due first to the low publication output in these countries (see Figures 1 and 2), who face various challenges in research and innovation. Publications in sub-Saharan francophone countries counted for only 0.01% of the worldwide publications in 2015 in journals indexed in the Web of Science and represent only 2.75% of publications in sub-Saharan Africa (Figure 2). Of course, predatory journals are not, a priori, catalogued in Web of Science but the very low number of publications from francophone African countries in this widely trusted citation database is an indicator of low publication output.

One also may infer that scholars from these countries prefer publishing elsewhere, including those who may see a form of neo-colonialism in the international publishing system which is heavily weighted towards North America, Europe and the English language (InterAcademy Partnership, 2022; Adomi & Mordi, 2003). It could also be that their publications mostly do not meet the generally accepted scientific standards, at least those of the leading scientific publishers and their academic partners.

Nevertheless, the publication output of the sub-Saharan Africa region has more than doubled during the period 2003-2012, according to a joint study of the World Bank and Elsevier (World Bank & Elsevier, 2014). Our discussion here is not about whether these standards or citation databases (such as Web of Science and Scopus) are relevant to the African context or not, a topic that is discussed elsewhere (Mavhunga, 2017; Piron et al., 2017). The point is how to make sure that contributions from sub-Saharan francophone countries, even small, are of a sufficient quality that would be useful for development. One possible way would be to promote scientific excellence and integrity by, for instance, tackling the issue of publication in predatory journals.

In francophone Africa, the African and Malagasy Council for Higher Education (CAMES), created in 1968 in the wake of the old Malagasy and African Common Organisation (OCAM) (Guèye 2008), is the institution in charge of coordinating the higher education and research systems in these countries with the ideal of harmonizing higher education and research in Africa. Among other things, CAMES ensures the evaluation and the promotion of academic staff, the lecturers-researchers (enseignants-chercheurs) of the 19 member countries in a harmonized system. In the two latest researcher promotion reports of CAMES in the "Mathematics-Physics-Chemistry" field(s), the assessment boards mention that there is a "net progress in the improvement of the quality of applications and this explains the performance of the results obtained" (CAMES / Comités Consultatifs Interafricains, 2016, 2018). While the quality of applications improves, one may wonder whether the relevance (to society) of the content of the presented works improves. Indeed, for a large part, the promotion and career management of teachers-researchers in this area is based on the number of publications (CAMES, 2018). In this way, publication has over

Figure 1: Number of publications in Web of Science from various countries in 2011

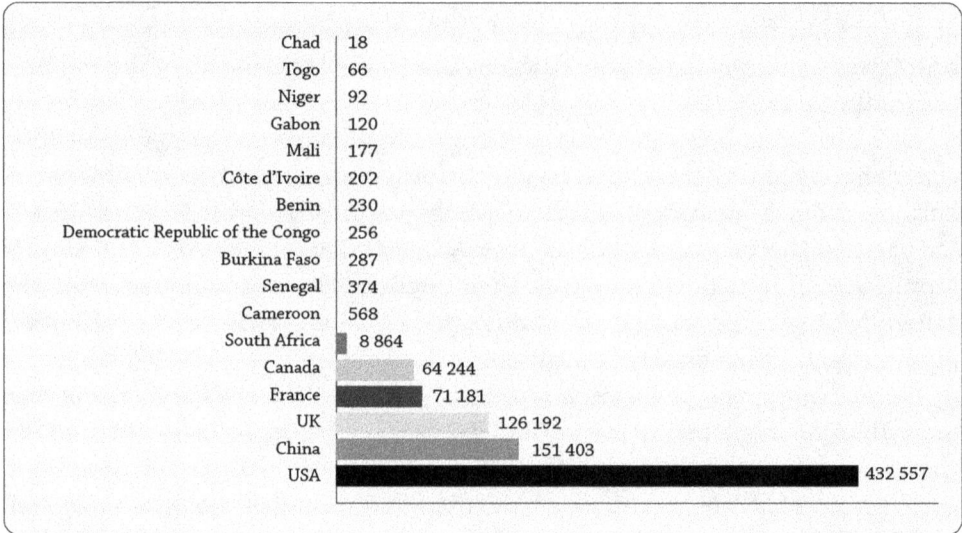

Chad	18
Togo	66
Niger	92
Gabon	120
Mali	177
Côte d'Ivoire	202
Benin	230
Democratic Republic of the Congo	256
Burkina Faso	287
Senegal	374
Cameroon	568
South Africa	8 864
Canada	64 244
France	71 181
UK	126 192
China	151 403
USA	432 557

Source: Piron et al. (2017)

Figure 2: Number of publications in the world as inventoried in Web of Science in 2015

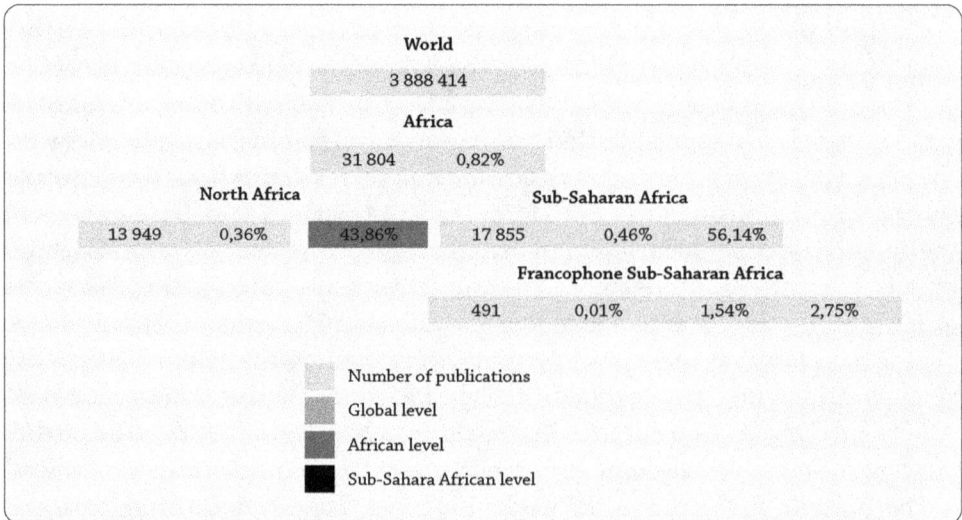

World
3 888 414

Africa
31 804   0,82%

North Africa   Sub-Saharan Africa
13 949   0,36%   43,86%   17 855   0,46%   56,14%

Francophone Sub-Saharan Africa
491   0,01%   1,54%   2,75%

Number of publications
Global level
African level
Sub-Sahara African level

Source: Mboa Nkoudou (2016)

time become the purpose of research activity, with lower priority accorded to the content and the relevance of the research work.

In this context, predatory journals and publishers appear to be very attractive for a community of scholars in francophone Africa who often experience language barriers, besides the other challenges that they share with their African colleagues of anglophone countries. There is a danger that research can become an industry for publications and that it does not necessarily serve any public interest through contributions to socio-economic development. Predatory journals have offered academia in these countries the opportunity to publish low-quality research papers within a short time to meet the requirements for academic promotion. Although the extent of the phenomenon in these countries has not yet been investigated, the issue of whether publication in predatory journals is jeopardizing the efforts to improve quality of research is raised here.

African countries prioritize research and innovation in their development policies and strategies (African Union Commission, 2014; World Bank & Elsevier, 2014). African governments have fully acknowledged science, technology and innovation as pillars for the development of the continent and that knowledge production and dissemination are key factors for human capacity building and economic growth. Therefore, there is an increasing demand from stakeholders that research that is partly or fully supported by public funding should demonstrate its expected societal impact even if it is a small amount of funding (FONRID, 2013; Bornmann, 2013). These legitimate aspirations cannot be met by poor-quality research and an inefficient science information system. It is therefore urgent to find solutions to issues such as publishing in predatory journals to make enduring contribution and impact through science and innovation to the sustainable development of these countries.

As someone responsible for training and capacity building of PhD candidates at a doctoral school, my contribution in this chapter is mostly related to the context of PhD research and publication, including the role of doctoral supervisors in guiding their candidates to avoid predatory journals and to publish their research in appropriate journals. It is mostly influenced by my experiences in the science, technology, engineering and mathematics (STEM) departments of institutions in francophone sub-Saharan Africa. This STEM domain appears to be the most affected by the curse of scientific misconduct (Edwards & Roy, 2017) and publishing in predatory journals (Mouton & Valentine, 2017). Since the behaviour of the supervisors themselves is an important factor in doctoral students' enculturation into the principles and practices of the scientific community, it is also important to consider what determinants in the environment of the supervisor affect their publishing behaviour and how this environment could possibly be changed or improved. Why do scholars in francophone sub-Saharan Africa publish in predatory journals? How could the issue be addressed and what could be the role of PhD supervisors in his regard? This chapter attempts to answer these questions considering the local context constraints and potentials and to provide insights for stakeholders, including supervisors, for practical implementation.

2. Why do academics in francophone sub-Saharan Africa publish in predatory journals?

Among various reasons underlying publication in predatory journals (Demir, 2018), two have often been mentioned by colleagues: (1) the low quality of research output, which means that it does not qualify for publication in repu-table journals, and (2) the fact that publications are required for promotion. Although poor English language proficiency is recognised as one of the reasons leading to paper rejection in reputable journals (Joshi, 2014), it is not the primary reason.

This chapter does not aim to cover or examine extensively the reasons for the poor quality of the research system and output in francophone sub-Sa-haran Africa. Rather, it reviews some aspects directly related to PhD theses. There are numerous other reasons for the low-quality research output. First to mention are funding issues and how the long duration of PhD studies exacer-bates this problem. It is hard to complete a high-quality PhD with limited and erratic funding, a very common situation in countries with limited funding available for research and development and with poor research infrastructure. Without funding from the state, research agencies, or universities, the studies of many doctoral candidates are funded personally or through the help of family. In many universities, PhD candidates have to pay laboratory fees for their annual registration, an amount that is ten to fifteen times the minimum wage (Université de Lomé, 2017; Université Abomey-Calavi - ED- SDI, 2020; Université Joseph Ki-Zerbo, 2021). Without any scholarship and funding, it is hard to expect high-quality research output. Some of the papers produced from such research eventually end up in predatory journals after multiple rejec-tions by reputable journals. In institutions where students are provided with scholarships, most theses are undertaken without any funding for the research itself, so it sometimes happens that a candidate cannot complete the required experimental work.

The absence of funding has been shown to significantly affect the duration of PhD studies: students who benefit from scholarships are likely to complete their doctoral studies in a shorter time (International Association of Universities, 2011). In many higher education institutions in francophone Africa, the regulated time for the completion of a PhD thesis has been aligned to the regulated time in France (i.e. three years). This duration has been adopted by various higher education institutions in Africa without accounting for the differences in the research environments of France and that of most African countries. For a STEM research department, it may take more than two years to obtain and prepare the equipment for the experiments, mostly, but not only, due to procurement procedures which are relatively time-consuming and complex in francophone sub-Saharan Africa (Mkandawire & Association of African Universities, 2022; Bouvier et al., 2004) as compared to neighbouring countries. In 2021, for instance, it took me 10 months between the transmission of specifications to our procurement office and the delivery of a pyranometer, a simple device costing about EUR 300 and readily available for purchase online. I know a PhD student who has completed 3 years of PhD study without getting the equipment ordered at the beginning of her study period. Furthermore, during the study the equipment may need to be serviced or repaired by a service provider in Europe or the USA. That is another factor that impacts duration of study, especially in these times when security reasons prevent some providers from travelling to some areas of the continent, for example the Sahel region.

The capacity and workload of faculty members, who supervise PhD research, is another issue. Due to the reduced number of supervisors and the drastic increase in the need for supervisors, non-trained or insufficiently experienced young researchers find themselves in the position of supervisors along with a large number of teaching hours and services to be provided. They have to attend to activities that draw their attention away from scientific discovery and analysis so that their support to PhD students may become practically non-existent. Issues may then arise with the research methodology. The relevance of the research topics in the context of the literature may even sometimes be questioned.

Promotion concerns both PhD students and supervisors. In most countries in francophone sub-Saharan Africa, publication is required to obtain the defence approval for a PhD. Therefore, PhD candidates need to have a paper published during their doctoral study (Bureau Afrique de l'Ouest – AUF, 2014, p. 68; Université de Yaoundé II, 2018, p. 7; CERPP/Université Abdou Moumouni, 2020, p. 9; Université de Lomé, 2020; Institut 2iE, 2023). When the research output is poor, especially in a context where the number of years to PhD completion is limited by limited resources, publication in predatory journals is seen as an attractive option. Some of the predatory journals publish articles within a very short time after submission (sometimes even within a few days (Kpenavoun Chogou, 2021; Avlessi, 2022)). It even happens that articles are reverse dated (i.e. the publication date precedes the submission date). The qualification system of CAMES (2018) has set a minimum number of publications for promotion to a higher level. For example, to become an assistant professor (*maitre-assistant*), a lecturer needs a minimum of two publications and a minimum length of service of two years. The only specification regarding the journals is that they need to be peer-reviewed journals. Predatory journals usually claim that they satisfy this requirement. So, with the option of a (very) short time from submission to publication offered by predatory journals, why would a candidate choose to publish in a reputable journal with high standards and the risk of rejection of their work? It is very easy to use the 'services' of a predatory journal.

To become associate professor (maître de conference), an assistant professor (maître-assistant) needs a minimum of five publications and a minimum length of service of three years as maître-assistant. Three of the articles need to be published in journals indexed in citation databases (e.g. the list of citation databases made available online by the STEM sections of CAMES (CAMES / CTS MPC & STI du CAMES, 2019)) and the other two only need to be published in peer-reviewed journals. When candidates are considered for promotion, it is not uncommon to see that almost all the publications were published in the year of application, as I and colleagues of mine have experienced while evaluating applications for promotion. Indeed, some months or weeks before the application deadline, applicants who have not achieved the minimum required publications + 1 article (to be on the safe side since one or more articles may be rejected for any reason during evaluation) will simply submit several 'papers', sometimes an extended abstract of a master's thesis with inconsistent results to predatory journals, instead of waiting for the next year to submit their application. Sometimes the first three authors would pay the publication fees and submit the papers that will then be published within a few days, irrespective of their quality. Because there is no published CAMES list of neither predatory nor accredited journals, publication in predatory journals has become a normal and quick way to promotion.

Since PhD students do not always have experience with rigorous peer-review process during their studies, their supervisors may convince them that high-grade journals are reserved only for institutes in developed countries.

Such students may then pass on that culture later in their own supervision of PhD candidates.

3. Recommendations to address the problem of predatory publishing by doctoral candidates

A number of measures to ensure doctoral dissertation quality or standards have been proposed in the literature. However, some may be hard to implement in our francophone Africa context due to the lack of resources (human and financial, material, i.e. time). In the following paragraph, we focus on measures mostly based on my own experience and from the literature study.

One of the first solutions is to raise the subject of predatory journals among researchers: "academics and students have to recognise that they have a responsibility to ensure that their own research and publication practices comply with the highest standards of quality and integrity in scientific research. This responsibility does not lie solely on government and agencies" (Mouton, quoted by Haq-Williams (2021:1). Pointing out the harm to science and to society in general caused by predatory journals (Fovet-Rabot & CIRAD, 2021) may be useful. Own its own, however, this solution is unlikely to be effective since publishing in predatory journals has become a form of science corruption in an environment with already worrying levels of science corruption (Edwards & Roy, 2017). In the same manner as the curse of corruption in general seems not to have been eradicated only by consciousness-raising and better knowledge, it would be hard to expect to solve the problems of science corruption without specific measures that deter or discourage people from choosing predatory publishers. Corruption is not unique to the academic world. The CAMES system has been severely criticised for high levels of corruption (Rahimy & Lalèyè, 2018). In addition, we should not forget that the sustainability of predatory publishing entities is supported by academia who may cooperate with them as 'editors', and members of their 'editorial boards', 'reviewers' or 'authors' even though supporting predatory journals has been clearly stated as a form of research misconduct (ALLEA, 2017). Public denunciation of the behaviour of individuals, as has been the case for plagiarism, might prove deterrent (Fovet-Rabot & CIRAD, 2021). One problem is that, sometimes, a person may be added as co-author to these kinds of papers without being informed, as predatory journals tend not to conduct author verification prior to the publication of articles.

To tackle the problem at the root, there is a need to attend to the causes, mainly the issue of poor research quality. Enhancing the quality of research in Africa is an issue that is beyond the scope of this chapter because it is a rather broad issue, especially when it comes to research funding. A number of actions could however be undertaken without raising significant resources. These actions may be considered by the doctoral schools.

3.1 Duration of PhD study

Although there is pressure for shorter completion times (time-to-degree) globally (EUA-CDE, 2022), a rational discussion between doctoral schools and researchers in Africa and also with funding agencies is needed to agree on a reasonable and viable duration for PhD studies in Africa, depending on the research areas, instead of simply taking over the European, especially the French, practice. According to statistics of various universities in sub-Saharan Africa, full-time PhD students in these countries are likely to complete their studies within 4 to 5 years (International Association of Universities, 2011). In their proposal of ways to address academic corruption, Edwards and Roy (2017:51) noted, *inter alia*, "the overemphasis on quantitative metrics, competition for limited funding, and difficulties pursuing science as a public good". Pressure to shorten the duration of the PhD studies can have a negative effect on the achievement of these essential objectives.

3.2 Training and support for PhD candidates and supervisors

There is a serious need for sufficient training opportunities to be provided, especially when it comes to the transferable skills expected of a PhD holder. It would be ideal to incorporate these training opportunities into a credit validation system (CAMES, 2017, p. 19). According to the framework for doctoral school assessment and evaluation of CAMES (2017, pp. 7, 10), these transferable skills include the production of new knowledge and new scientific tools, the development of innovative solutions, solving complex problems, knowledge of communication and transmission, working in a team and in a network and adaptation to various professional contexts. It is particularly important to support PhD students in acquiring the following skills: writing skills, research paper writing, responsible research conduct, research project management, scientific English, research supervision. Skills training opportunities for their students would reduce the workload of supervisors so that they can focus on the content of the theses and methodology. The number of PhD students per supervisor needs to be capped, although this may be difficult in some institutions. Training for PhD supervisors is very important and the ability to supervise a PhD thesis should no longer be taken for granted based merely on the fact that somebody holds a PhD. As the number of these doctoral graduates has significantly and rapidly increased in the African context (Mohamedbhai, 2014a; British Council, German Academic Exchange Service (DAAD) & African Network for Internationalization of Education (ANIE), 2018), there is a need for well-prepared doctoral supervisors in order to achieve quality human resources. The need for doctoral graduates who are well-prepared to face global challenges and to deal with the challenges and difficulties of this environment at African universities is critical. The fact that a significant part of the themes of these trainings are transversal means that they may be organised jointly by doctoral schools located in the same region. This could reduce the problems of resources and logistics.

3.3 Monitoring committee

A monitoring team, including external members to be added to the supervision team with the mandate of annually evaluating student progress, can be an important instrument to limit dropout and to shorten time-to-degree. It can also play a role in terminating the studies of students in cases where it is clear that the output is not going to be of sufficient quality within the specified period and when it is clear that the PhD candidate does not have the capacity to complete the study. It is better for our research system to have a lower number of high standard researchers instead of a large number of low standard researchers. However, terminating a PhD study may have legal complications, especially in the case of PhD students holding three-year contracts linking them as research fellows to a higher education institution. Another factor to be considered when a decision is made to terminate PhD study before completion is what to do when that study was funded as part of a larger research programme. Would the supervisor then be expected to complete the research in order to meet the contractual agreement with the funder?

3.4 Examination committee

Currently, supervisors propose examiners, but the selection and appointment of the members remain the sole responsibility of the doctoral school. The examination committee needs to be as objective as possible to guarantee an independent examination. According to a recent case reported by Darbyshire et al. (2020, p. 137), *a PhD examiner returned a PhD thesis containing multiple publications, because all of the included publications were published in predatory journals. [...] Had this examiner not been diligent and meticulous enough to spot this duplicity and act upon it, a new PhD would have been created who assuredly did not deserve the highest of academic awards.*

It is important to make sure that from the time the examinations committee is appointed until the defence, there is no contact between the committee members and the PhD student or their supervisor regarding his submitted thesis. As proposed by the Association of Francophone Universities (Bureau Afrique de l'Ouest – AUF, 2014, p. 36), the head of the doctoral school may be assisted in the approval process by a 'thesis curator', an experienced researcher devoted to deeper evaluation of the examiner proposal and examination of the reviews of the rapporteurs (examiners). The supervisors may attend the defence but should not be part of the decision of the committee, they should even leave the jury room and not take part in the deliberation. Instead of requiring a journal publication as acceptable for the PhD defence, a practice that is shifting the responsibility of evaluating a PhD thesis from universities to journal editors, Kirchherr (2018) states as ideal that a PhD candidate would complete their PhD when they have made a difference in the real world. Because "a difference in the real world" may be difficult to evaluate or be understood in different ways (Esterhuyse, 2019, p. 13), especially when it comes to basic research, it is in the first place the supervisors who play a key role, and then also the examinations committee.

3.5 Price cap of the Article Processing Charge or no publication fee policy

The ongoing open access transformation leads to business models mainly based on article processing charges or publication fees as a revenue source for academic open access publishers (Jahn & Tullney, 2016; Schönfelder, 2020). As already mentioned, this open access model exhibits a clear conflict of interest since the more papers the journal publishes, the more money it gets (Beall, 2017). Predatory journals take advantage of this transformation by charging publication fees with no correlation to the editorial services offered since their target is primarily the collection of article processing charges from authors. Limiting the amount of money that could be 'invested' in a publication may be a way of achieving a more virtuous system. For instance, the German Research Foundation (DFG) as part of its funding activities for open-access funding at German universities imposes a price cap of EUR 2 000 per article

(DFG, 2021b). Between 2005 and 2015, the average payment was EUR 1 298 per article, based on data from 30 German universities and research organisations (Jahn & Tullney, 2016).

I would argue that it is unethical to pay up to EUR 2 000 as page fees for a publication in a journal, especially considering that such an amount represents more than 30 times the minimum monthly wages in most francophone sub-Saharan countries. This is the range of the amount of research grants offered by various regional agencies in West Africa (e.g. Association of African universities, 2017; ECOWAS Centre for Renewable Energy and Energy Efficiency, 2020). A capping of the maximum amount of page fees per article needs to be debated but the target should be to cover the costs associated with publication and not for journals to make profits. I suggest that a maximum cap of EUR 200 per article would be reasonable, based on the open-access publication fee of USD 200 applied by *Scientific African* (2022), an open access journal published by Elsevier for the Next Einstein Forum. This is line with the publication fee of EUR 150 per article charged by the Revue Africaine et Malgache de Recherche Scientifique, a consortium of nine journals published by CAMES (Service de la communication du CAMES, 2022a). Although it may not be feasible, because many high-reputation journals do charge page fees (not only predatory journals), but the supervisor may also even opt for not paying for any journal publication and allow PhD students to publish only in journals that do not charge for publications. This is a policy that the French National Centre for Scientific Research is currently promoting by inviting its researchers to no longer pay for publication (CNRS Info, 2022). To ensure fair access to the publications, the authors may publish in the existing free-of-charge open-access journals (these journals are mostly financially supported by research funding institutions) or archive online author accepted manuscripts when the papers are not published in an open-access journal.

3.6 List of predatory journals

A list of predatory journals may be kept and regularly updated by the doctoral school and only publications in the listed journals would be accepted as admissible for a PhD defence. As a first guide, Beall's list of predatory journals may be used. It could be refined in the framework of a dialogue with the researchers who are involved in the doctoral school. Alternatively, doctoral candidates could be encouraged to check a list of criteria for what is and is not considered a predatory journal before submitting a paper to any journal. At this stage, support from their supervisors is crucial. Before submission, it may be necessary for the thesis supervisor to validate the journal, particularly when publication fees are involved. In case of funding requests for publication, even when it would come from research project funding, these checks need also to be performed by the thesis curator. It is also recommended that an evaluation agency such as CAMES and the universities themselves keep a regularly updated list of predatory journals.

3.7 List of accredited journals

After facing intense pressure from his employer, the University of Colorado, and fearing for his job, the famous librarian and associate professor, Jeffrey Beall decided to shut down his blog and related platforms (Beall, 2017). Beall, his colleagues and his university experienced constant harassment from publishers and standalone journals constantly tried various means of getting off the lists (Beall, 2017). Beall's experience illustrates the complexity of the decision to publish a blacklist, including legal challenges. So, instead of limiting the work to listing predatory journals, CAMES could consider drawing up a list of accredited journals for its different domains. This is an idea that has been implemented by various scientific communities worldwide, for example in France, especially within the social sciences and humanities community (HCERES, 2014), they have created a list in which journals are categorised and available online (HCERES, 2021a). For instance, the sub-community for economics and management adopted a list (HCERES, 2021b) that is an amalgamation of a list from the French National Centre for Scientific Research (Section 37 (Économie / Gestion) du Comité National de la Recherche Scientifique, 2020) and a list compiled by the French National Foundation for Companies Management Academic Education (FNEGE) (Collège scientifique de la FNEGE, 2019). The elaboration of the list of the FNEGE has built upon the strong foundations of other entities such as EJL (Netherlands), CABS (UK), VHB (Germany), ABDC (Australia), etc. (Collège scientifique de la FNEGE, 2019). Journals that do not belong to the list may submit an application for this purpose. Interestingly, local ('national') journals published in French are also included in this list and even in top positions. The HCERES list of the social sciences and humanities community includes 14.3% of journals published in French, although about 35% of francophone journals indexed in Scopus and Web of Sciences are not included in this HCERES list (Chartron & Le Guilloux, 2020).

On the African continent, South Africa (Department of Higher Education and Training (DHET), 2022) and Algeria (Université Mouloud Mammeri de Tizi-Ouzou & Direction Générale de la Recherche Scientifique et du Développement

Technologique (DGRSDT), 2021), to name only these, have also created lists of accredited journals that are annually updated, while Algeria is also keeping an updated list of predatory journals list (Université Mouloud Mammeri de Tizi-Ouzou & Direction Générale de la Recherche Scientifique et du Développement Technologique (DGRSDT), 2021). As in France, the South Africa's DHET also maintains a list of accredited South African journals, designed to promote and support high-quality local journals. Ethiopia has achieved very interesting results in its fight against predatory journals, by adopting a national journal evaluation and accreditation system that is used to promote scholarly publishing in Ethiopia with international standards (InterAcademy Partnership, 2022, p. 102). In Algeria, separate lists of the accredited journals accepting publications in Arabic and journals in Scopus accepting publications in Arabic are also provided, to underline the importance of publishing in the researcher's first language (Université Mouloud Mammeri de Tizi-Ouzou & Direction Générale de la Recherche Scientifique et du Développement Technologique (DGRSDT), 2021) and the associated necessary recognition, as it has been stressed by FNEGE in France (Collège scientifique de la FNEGE, 2019, p. 6).

On its website, CAMES has released tips on how to identify and avoid publishing in predatory journals (Service de la communication du CAMES, 2022b). Although CAMES has no 'blacklist' or 'whitelist' for journals, its STEM section has released a non-exhaustive list of indexation databases (CAMES / CTS MPC & STI du CAMES, 2019) where no publication in an indexed journal could be rejected, based on the quality of the journal. CAMES has a total of nine scientific journals (Service de la communication du CAMES, 2022c) for all of its thematic areas, published by the Conference of Rectors of Francophone Universities in Africa and the Indian Ocean (CRUFAOCI). None of these journals are recognised as indexed journals by CAMES. This situation calls for a strategy to promote these journals to support local scholarly publishing and also publishing in French. Because the editorial teams cover a large region, there is a large potential to quickly reach or maintain international standards in these journals. CAMES promotion programme candidates could be invited to publish at least one paper in this series.

Both 'black' and 'white' list approaches have been criticised (Beall, 2017; InterAcademy Partnership, 2022) in favour of a spectrum approach, because blacklists are disliked by publishers while whitelists have substantial limitations (Beall, 2017). However, I would argue that a 'black' or 'white' list approach could be relevant in the CAMES context where almost nothing has previously been established. Adoption of a spectrum approach that could provide opportunities for dubious local journals to establish and implement internationally accepted scientific publishing standards could be the next step.

Beyond these reflections, the arguments of Altbach and de Wit (2018) are also worthy of consideration by higher education authorities in francophone African countries. They suggest that not all universities should be research-intensive institutions:

> *In the United States, for example, perhaps 200 out of more than 3,000 post-secondary institutions are serious research universities. The Russell Group of research-intensive universities in the United Kingdom has 24 members out of a total of some 140 total universities. And in Australia, the Group of Eight is only a small proportion of the higher education sector. Most universities that are not research-intensive should, and largely do, focus on teaching. Faculty members should be rewarded for good teaching and for service to society and industry and not for research.*

In francophone Africa the development and implementation of such a differentiated higher education system would require the creation of a parallel system to the current mandate of the CAMES. Such a differentiated system could separate a research career from a teaching career, which does not mean that teaching would not be supported by research. This idea has also been promoted by Mohamedbhai (2014b), former secretary general of the Association of African Universities (AAU). However, this would raise another issue: can we afford to sacrifice a part of our already very limited human resources for research to teaching only? On the other hand, by doing that we could have at least some people who are actually focused and devoted to scientific research with clearer and easier monitoring of progress in research and higher quality research output. However, further discussion of the debates on the research/teaching nexus (Tight, 2016) in higher education systems is beyond the scope of this chapter.

Incentives for academic career advancement mainly based on publications have led to questionable practices (Edwards & Roy, 2017). The evaluation of the research for a researcher's career advancement should be made via a 'summa scientifica', a kind of integration of the overall research contribution over a longer period (of at least ten years for instance), disregarding how many articles were published during that period. Furthermore, the introduction of a feasible system to monitor and record the societal impact of research in the field of STEM could also be considered. A first draft of these societal impact indicators may be drawn from the list of 'Faits observables' (observable facts) in the assessment criteria of HCERES (French High Council for Evaluation of Research and Higher Education (HCERES), 2014). In this way, research evaluation would not in the first place be done by journal editors or publishers but by universities. This needs to be implemented throughout the career of the researcher in order to de-emphasise output in favour of outcomes, and privilege quality instead of quantity.

Doctoral supervisors can play a key role in addressing the problem of predatory publishing in francophone sub-Saharan Africa not only through guidance and monitoring with regard to predatory journals, but also in setting an example through their own publication behaviour and more broadly, their behaviour as scientists in all respects. An improvement of the CAMES research evaluation system would be very supportive for them, and to doctoral schools, who have to include the topic as a serious component of the training of Africa's future researchers.

References

Adomi, E. E., & Mordi, C. (2003). Publication in foreign journals and promotion of academics in Nigeria. *Learned Publishing, 16*(4), 259–263. https://doi.org/10.1087/095315103322421991

African Union Commission. (2014). *Science, Technology and Innovation Strategy for Africa (STISA-2024)*. https://au.int/sites/default/files/newsevents/workingdocuments/33178-wd-stisa-english_-_final.pdf

ALLEA. (2017). *The European Code of Conduct for Research Integrity* (Revised ed.). https://www.allea.org/wp-content/uploads/2017/05/ALLEA-European-Code-of-Conduct-for-Research-Integrity-2017.pdf

Altbach, P. G., & de Wit, H. (2018). Too much academic research is being published. *University World News*. https://www.universityworldnews.com/post.php?story=20180905095203579

Andoh, H. F. (2017). *The uptake of doctoral thesis research in Ghana* [Doctoral dissertation, Stellenbosch University]. https://core.ac.uk/download/pdf/188220813.pdf

Association of African Universities. (2017). *Small Grants for Theses and Dissertations – Call for Applications: Issued September 2017*. AAU Blog. https://blog.aau.org/small-grants-theses-dissertations-call-applications-issued-september-2017/

Avlessi, F. (2022). *Formation sur l'identification des revues prédatrices* [YouTube video]. https://www.youtube.com/watch?v=LnkAEKo-ysE

Beall, J. (2016). Essential information about predatory publishers and journals. *International Higher Education, 0*(86), 2–3. https://doi.org/10.6017/ihe.2016.86.9358

Beall, J. (2017). What I learned from predatory publishers. *Biochemia Medica, 27*(2), 273–278. https://doi.org/10.11613/BM.2017.029

Bornmann, L. (2013). What is societal impact of research and how can it be assessed? A literature survey. *Journal of the American Society for Information Science and Technology, 64*(2), 217–233. https://doi.org/10.1002/asi.22803

Bouvier, M., Esclassan, M.-C., Orsoni, G., Bouhadana, I., & Gilles, W. (2004). *La gestion de la dépense publique dans les pays de l'Afrique francophone subsaharienne*. Paris, France. https://www.diplomatie.gouv.fr/IMG/pdf/Mise_en_ligne_rapport_pages_interieures.pdf

British Council, German Academic Exchange Service (DAAD), & African Network for Internationalisation of Education (ANIE). (2018). *Building PhD Capacity in Sub-Saharan Africa*. https://www.britishcouncil.org/sites/default/files/h233_07_synthesis_report_final_web.pdf

Bureau Afrique de l'Ouest - AUF. (2014). *Livre blanc des Ecoles Doctorales en Francophonie*. https://www.auf. org/wp-content/uploads/2015/02/Livre_Blanc_ED_BAO_V2-FINAL-web.pdf

CAMES. (2017). *Référentiel d'Évaluation des Écoles Doctorales du CAMES (REED-CAMES)*. https://www.le-cames.org/wp-content/uploads/2019/06/Referentiel-Evaluation-Ecoles-Doctorales-CAMES.pdf

CAMES. (2018). *Guide d'évaluation des enseignants-chercheurs et chercheurs (GEE-CC) dans le cadre des comités consultatifs interafricains (CCI)*. https://www.jstm.org/wp-content/uploads/2015/09/CAMES-criteres_2017_2021.pdf

Cape Peninsula University of Technology (CPUT). (2022). *Library guides: For Researchers: Accredited Journals 2012–2022*. https://libguides.library.cput.ac.za/c.php?g=628041&p=4382005

CERPP/Université Abdou Moumouni. (2020). *Livret de l'étudiant-CERPP*. Retrieved June 18, 2023, from https://www.cerppniger.org/images/pdf/Guide_de_l_tudiant_08_07_2020.pdf

Chartron, G., & Le Guilloux, C. (2020). Regard sur la publication scientifique francophone : Le cas des revues. Retrieved June 18, 2023, from https://hal.science/hal-03154433v1/document

CNRS Info. (2022). Le CNRS encourage ses scientifiques à ne plus payer pour être publiés. Retrieved June 18, 2023, from www.cnrs.fr/fr/cnrsinfo/le-cnrs-encourage-ses-scientifiques-ne-plus-payer-pour-etre-publies

Collège scientifique de la FNEGE. (2019). *Classement des revues scientifiques en sciences de gestion*. Retrieved June 18, 2023, from www.lgco.iut-tlse3.fr/wp-content/uploads/FNEGE-2019.pdf

Darbyshire, P., Hayter, M., Frazer, K., Ion, R., & Jackson, D. (2020). Hitting rock bottom: The descent from predatory journals and conferences to the predatory PhD. *Journal of Clinical Nursing, 29*(23–24), 4425–4428. https://doi.org/10.1111/jocn.15516

Demir, S. B. (2018). Predatory journals: Who publishes in them and why? *Journal of Informetrics, 12*(4), 1296–1311. https://doi.org/10.1016/j.joi.2018.10.008

DFG. (2021a). *Guidelines and supplementary instructions: Open access publication funding* (DFG form 12.21 – 01/22). Retrieved June 18, 2023, from www.dfg.de/formulare/12_21/12_21_en.pdf

DFG. (2021b). How does the DFG support open access in infrastructure funding? Discontinued programme "Open Access Publishing". Retrieved June 18, 2023, from www.dfg.de/en/research_funding/pro-grammes/infrastructure/lis/open_access/infrastructure_funding/index.html

ECOWAS Centre for Renewable Energy and Energy Efficiency. (2020). *Call for proposals: Research grant program for policy research*. Retrieved June 18, 2023, from www.ecreee.org/procurement/call-proposals-research-grant-program-policy-research

Edwards, M. A., & Roy, S. (2017). Academic research in the 21st century: Maintaining scientific integrity in a climate of perverse incentives and hypercompetition. *Environmental Engineering Science, 34*(1), 51–61. https://doi.org/10.1089/ees.2016.0223

Eriksson, S., & Helgesson, G. (2018). Time to stop talking about "predatory journals." *Learned Publishing, 31*(2), 181–183. https://doi.org/10.1002/leap.1135

Esterhuyse, H. W. (2019). Understanding the societal impact of research through productive interactions and realist theory-based evaluation: Select cases of agricultural research in South Africa (Doctoral dissertation). Stellenbosch University. Retrieved May 24, 2022, from https://scholar.sun.ac.za/bitstream/handle/10019.1/107014/esterhuyse_societal_2019.pdf

FONRID. (2013). *Guide d'élaboration des projets du Fonds National de la Recherche et de l'Innovation pour le Développement (FONRID)*. https://lefaso.net/IMG/pdf/guide_d_elaboration_des_projets_fonrid.pdf

Fovet-Rabot, C., & CIRAD. (2021). *Eviter les éditeurs prédateurs / Publier et diffuser*. https://doi.org/10.18167/coopist/0036

Guèye, P. (2008). Migration and education: Quality assurance and mutual recognition of qualifications: The Senegalese case. In *Expert Group Meeting on Migration and Education: Quality Assurance and Mutual Recognition of Qualifications* (pp. 1–10). UNESCO. https://unesdoc.unesco.org/ark:/48223/pf0000179851

Haq-Williams, A. (2021). Predatory publishing is a threat to scientists' integrity. *University World News: African Edition*. https://www.universityworldnews.com/post.php?story=20210825130429207

HCERES. (2014). *Critères d'évaluation des entités de recherche : Le référentiel du HCERES.* Haut Conseil de l'évaluation de la recherche et de l'enseignement supérieur. https://www.hceres.fr/sites/default/files/media/downloads/Hceres_campagne_2016_2017_Criteres_evaluation_Entites_Recherche.pdf

HCERES. (2021a). *Guide des produits de la recherche et activités de recherche.* https://www.hceres.fr/fr/guides-des-produits-de-la-recherche-et-activites-de-recherche

HCERES. (2021b). *Liste des revues et des produits de la recherche HCÉRES pour le domaine SHS1: Économie et gestion.* https://www.hceres.fr/sites/default/files/media/files/liste-des-revues-et-des-produits-de-la-recherche-hceres-shs1-eco-et-gestion.pdf

Institut 2iE. (2023). *Formation doctorale internationale.* https://www.2ie-edu.org/formation/formation-doctorale-internationale/

InterAcademy Partnership. (2022). *Combatting predatory academic journals and conferences.* https://www.inter-academies.org/sites/default/files/2022-03/1.%20Full%20report%20-%20English%20FINAL.pdf

International Association of Universities. (2011). *Changing nature of doctoral studies in sub-Saharan Africa: Challenges and policy development opportunities at six universities in Sub-Saharan Africa.* https://www.researchgate.net/publication/281619984

Jahn, N., & Tullney, M. (2016). A study of institutional spending on open access publication fees in Germany. *PeerJ, 4*, e2323. https://doi.org/10.7717/peerj.2323

Joshi, Y. (2014). Can poor English affect the publication and impact of research? *Editage Insights.* https://www.editage.com/insights/can-poor-english-affect-the-publication-and-impact-of-research

Kirchherr, J. (2018, August 9). A PhD should be about improving society, not chasing academic kudos. *The Guardian.* https://www.theguardian.com/higher-education-network/2018/aug/09/a-phd-should-be-about-improving-society-not-chasing-academic-kudos

Kolata, G. (2017, October 30). Many academics are eager to publish in worthless journals. *The New York Times.* https://www.nytimes.com/2017/10/30/science/predatory-journals-academics.html

Kpenavoun Chogou, S. (2021). Sur l'identification des revues prédatrices dans le processus de publication des résultats de recherche. *Projetsoha.* https://urlz.fr/fLDL

Mavhunga, C. C. (Ed.). (2017). *What do science, technology, and innovation mean from Africa?* Cambridge, MA: MIT Press.

Mboa Nkoudou, T. H. (2016). Le Web et la production scientifique africaine : Visibilité réelle ou inhibée ? *Projetsoha.* https://www.projetsoha.org/?p=1357

Mkandawire, S., & Association of African Universities. (2022). *ACE impact progress and update.*

Mohamedbhai, G. (2014a). Massification in higher education institutions in Africa: Causes, consequences, and responses. *International Journal of African Higher Education, 1*(1). https://doi.org/10.6017/ijahe.v1i1.5644

Mohamedbhai, G. (2014b). Mettre l'accent sur la recherche au service du développement, pas sur les classements. *SciDev.net.* https://www.scidev.net/afrique-sub-saharienne/opinions/mettre-l-accent-sur-la-recherche-au-service-du-d-veloppement-pas-sur-les-classements/

Mouton, J., & Valentine, A. (2017). The extent of South African authored articles in predatory journals. *South African Journal of Science, 113*(7–8). https://doi.org/10.17159/sajs.2017/20170010

Piron, F., Diouf, A. B., Dibounje Madiba, M. S., Mboa Nkoudou, T. H., Ouangré, Z. A., & Rhissa Achaffert, H. (2017). Open access seen from francophone Sub-Saharan Africa. *Revue Française des Sciences de l'Information et de la Communication, 11.* https://doi.org/10.4000/rfsic.3292

Rahimy, M. C.-D., & Lalèyè, O. O. M. (2018). Le Cames, une nébuleuse qui entrave l'essor du Bénin et de l'Afrique [CAMES, the nebula that hampers the development of Benin and of Africa]. *Secret des Arts.* Cotonou, Bénin.

Schönfelder, N. (2020). Article processing charges: Mirroring the citation impact or legacy of the subscription-based model? *Quantitative Science Studies, 1*(1), 6–27. https://doi.org/10.1162/qss_a_00015

Scientific African. (2022). *Scientific African: Guide for authors.* https://www.elsevier.com/journals/scientific-african/2468-2276/guide-for-authors [2023-06-18]

Section 37 (Économie / Gestion) du Comité National de la Recherche Scientifique. (2020). *Categorization of journals in economics and management*. https://www.conicyt.cl/fondecyt/files/2013/05/Categorization-of-journals-in-Economics-and-Management1.pdf [2023-06-18]

Service de la communication du CAMES. (2022a). Présentation de la série « Sciences juridiques et politiques » la revue RAMReS (CRUFAOCI). *Lundi CAMES, 393*. https://www.lecames.org/presentation-de-la-se-rie-sciences-juridiques-et-politiques-la-revue-ramres-crufaoci/ [2023-06-18]

Service de la communication du CAMES. (2022b). Les revues prédatrices : Comment les reconnaître et les éviter ? *Lundi CAMES, 393*. https://www.lecames.org/les-revues-predatrices-comment-les-reconnai-tre-et-les-eviter/ [2023-06-18]

Service de la communication du CAMES. (2022c). Présentation des 9 séries de la revue RAMReS (CRUFAOCI). *Lundi CAMES, 393*. https://www.lecames.org/presentation-des-9-series-de-la-revue-ram-res-crufaoci/ [2023-06-18]

The World Bank & Elsevier. (2014). *A decade of development in sub-Saharan African science, technology, engineering and mathematics research* (No. 91016). https://documents.worldbank.org/curated/en/237371468204551128/A-decade-of-development-in-sub-Saharan-African-science-technology-engi-neering-and-mathematics-research [2023-06-18]

Tight, M. (2016). Examining the research/teaching nexus. *European Journal of Higher Education, 6*(4), 293–311. https://doi.org/10.1080/21568235.2016.1224674

Université Abomey-Calavi - ED-SDI. (2020). *Droits d'inscription en doctorat* (N/R 145/D/ED-SDI). https://www.edsdi.uac.bj/uploads/doc/283.pdf [2022-05-25]

Université de Lomé. (2017). Arrêté n° 040/UL/P/SG/2017 du 18 octobre 2017, fixant le montant des frais de formation dans les grades de Master de Doctorat et au Diplôme d'Études Spécialisées (DES) à l'Université de Lomé. https://univ-lome.tg/sites/default/files/2019-08/Arrete_Nouveaux_Frais_Master_Doctorat_DES_UL.pdf [2023-06-18]

Université de Lomé. (2020). Arrêté n° 046/UL/P/SG/2020 du 13 août 2020, portant conditions et modalités d'organisation d'une soutenance de thèse de doctorat à l'Université de Lomé.

Université de Yaoundé II. (2018). *Décision n°18/317/UYII/CAB/R/VREPDTIC/DAAC du 21 juin 2018 portant organisation des études doctorales à l'Université de Yaoundé II*. https://www.univ-yaounde2.org/wp-con-tent/uploads/D%C3%A9cision-Etudes-Doctorales.pdf [2023-06-18]

Université Joseph Ki-Zerbo. (2021). *Communiqué. Recrutement en première année de thèse de doctorat unique dans les écoles doctorales de l'université Joseph Ki-Zerbo*. https://ujkz.bf/wp-content/uploads/2021/08/Recrutement-2021-2022-1re-A-de-Th%C3%A8se-de-doctorat.pdf [2023-06-18]

Université Mouloud Mammeri de Tizi-Ouzou & Direction Générale de la Recherche Scientifique et du Développement Technologique (DGRSDT). (2021). *Revues indexées*. https://www.ummto.dz/revues-in-dexees/ [2023-06-18]

Xia, J., Harmon, J. L., Connolly, K. G., Donnelly, R. M., Anderson, M. R., & Howard, H. A. (2015). Who publishes in "predatory" journals? *Journal of the Association for Information Science and Technology, 66*(7), 1406–1417. https://doi.org/10.1002/asi.23265

CHAPTER 9

Project management as an enabler of doctoral completion

Isabel Meyer

South Africa has a population of 62 million. The country has 26 public universities with a total enrolment of 1.1 million students. Doctoral enrolments in South Africa have increased from 9 994 in 2008 to 23 588 in 2020 (CHE, Vitalstats). During the period 2000-2018, a total of 32 025 doctoral students graduated at South African universities. Annual doctoral graduates increased from 972 in 2000 to 3 339 in 2019 (SciSTIP, Tracer Study).

Stellenbosch University became an independent university in 1918, tracing its origins to the Theological Seminary of the Dutch Reformed Church (est. 1859) and Stellenbosch College (est. 1880). The university has ten faculties located on four campuses (in Stellenbosch, Bellville, Cape Town and Saldanha). In 2021 it had 1 400 academic staff members and 32 471 students, including 1 611 doctoral candidates, and 310 doctoral degrees were awarded. The first doctoral degree was awarded by Stellenbosch University in 1923, in physics.

The **Council for Scientific and Industrial Research (CSIR)** is a national research and development organisation in South Africa, established in 1945. The CSIR undertakes directed, multidisciplinary research and technological innovation that contributes to the improved quality of life of South Africans. The CSIR's shareholder is the South African Parliament, held in proxy by the Minister of Higher Education, Science and Innovation.

---

1. Introduction: The pressure to comp(l)ete

The pressure on the national ability to deliver PhD graduates is multidimensional. At the institutional level, the pressure to complete doctoral studies is driven by a focus on resource optimisation and efficiency, the financial benefits of completion, and the costs of non-completion (Backlund, 2017). At the individual level, the implications on the student's wellbeing, as well as the financial, psychological, and opportunity costs of non-completion are relevant (Backlund, 2017; Herman, 2011).

In a broader national context, a link appears to exist between the need to develop PhD graduates and the state of economic development. In the African context, the need for increased higher education enrolment rates and increased completion rates of high-quality PhDs is motivated from the perspective of higher education as an enabler of economic development (Mohamedbhai, 2018; Mouton, 2010; Nakwenya, 2018). In contrast to the economic development pressure experienced in developing contexts, the developed world seems in some instances to be grappling with an 'excess' PhD students, who are 'abused' at the hands of supervisors as cheap, competent labour to bolster the personal research output of accomplished researchers (*The Economist*, 2016). In other cases, supervisors are pressured to improve their PhD delivery rates to retain their own positions in an increasingly competitive labour market (Carter, 2017). Research on PhD completion rates confirms relatively high dropout rates in the African context (e.g. Mouton, 2010; Herman, 2011), and as such supports the need to develop a systemic ability to consistently deliver doctoral graduates *of good quality* (Mouton, 2010). However, the reasons for high dropout rates are poorly researched and not well understood (Herman, 2011).

Regardless of the reason for increased pressure on completion rates, it is accepted that this pressure is changing both the focus of PhD studies and the quality of learning (Khosa, 2019). The spectrum of needs for PhD development across developing and developed economies, as well as the personal and institutional-level pressures on PhD completion, begs the question of what the desired outcome should be for increased PhD delivery rates and, hence, what mechanisms are appropriate to facilitate such increased delivery. By focusing on supporting PhD completion for the mere sake of completion, participating in the academic pipeline, or preparing candidates for contributions to industry would position the role of project management in different ways.

This chapter is based on the assumptions that PhDs in Africa are indeed a necessary enabler of economic development, that the capacity of the continent for sustainable delivery of PhDs should be bolstered, and that mechanisms are required to achieve this. It explores the role of project management as a tool to enhance African education systems' PhD throughput rate while also developing the capability to deliver high quality research in support of economic development.

The assertion is that, by incorporating rigorous project management approaches in the PhD journey, the student should not only complete the PhD in time for the sake of attaining the degree and for managing institutional pressures, but also develop a valuable skillset for the delivery of high-quality research that adds value in either academic or industry contexts. The skillset required to manage the PhD research project competently has the potential of developing a workforce that is better able to manage high-quality research in industry and academia and in so doing can contribute to improved economic development.

This chapter is exploratory in nature. It provides a brief overview of current perspectives on project management as an enabler of PhD completion (section 2) and reflects on potential value addition to the doctoral journey through project management (section 3). Finally, some concluding remarks and recommendations for future research are made (section 4).

2. From the literature: Some perspectives and practices

A brief literature review was undertaken to assess views on project management approaches in doctoral supervision. In line with the purpose of outlining the landscape of available literature on the topic, a scoping review approach was adopted (Arksey & O'Malley, 2005; Grant & Booth, 2009). On the ProQuest Educational Database, the current author searched literature published since 2015 featuring the full search terms (doctoral supervision) AND (project management) in the abstract, and located only 2 articles of relevance (Backlund, 2016; Katz, 2018). A broader search identified some (but not a significant number) additional work that addresses project management (as part of broader investigations, rather than as sole focus). This low article identification rate indicated a gap in research that explicitly addresses the role of project management in doctoral supervision. However, some empirical work was identified that provides insight into the current practices and perceptions of supervisors and students on the role of project management in doctoral supervision, as well as the role of project management from an institutional perspective. It is notable that the role of project management in African PhD studies is not widely addressed in the literature. Some general observations are reported here. The purpose and role of project management, the perceptions of supervisors and students, and the relevant elements are summarised.

2.1 To what end and in what role?

Studies cite the following as reasons for adopting project management practices in doctoral supervision:

- increased pressure on academic institutions to deliver, and the increased complexity of managing multiple doctoral candidates (Backlund, 2017).
- a need to alleviate supervisory pressure, improve efficiency, and provide support for the delivery of quality work in environments of increased job insecurity (Carter, 2017); and
- a high workload (Roets, 2017).

Project management is identified as a key challenge in doctoral supervision, in both STEM and non-STEM disciplines (Carter, 2017).

Other motivations in support of project management approaches extend beyond these institutional pressures. For example, some authors position project management as a precondition for and enabler of collaborative supervision across academic–industry collaborations, where a lack of formal process between more than one supervisor for a single student has been identified as a supervisory gap (Maguire, 2018). At a personal development level, Schulze (2012) argues that students' ownership of their projects would facilitate power and self-transformation. The latter two focus areas point to a role for project management in PhD supervision that extends beyond alleviation of immediate institutional pressures.

Project management as a skill for future research management is rarely addressed in literature, except Katz (2016), who points out that academia lags relative to (high tech) industry in the adoption of project management methods for research project management. Similarly, Buckland (2016) refers to an inertia in the uptake of project management skills in the highly individualised academic world.

The potential outcomes of an increased focus on the role of project management in PhD supervision is summarised in Figure 1.

2.2 Perspectives on project management in supervision

Bøgelund (2015) highlights three perspectives on knowledge production, namely academic, market, and changing society perspectives, and indicates through empirical work that supervisors who take an academic perspective do not consider project management to be important.

Figure 1: Some potential outcomes of improved project management

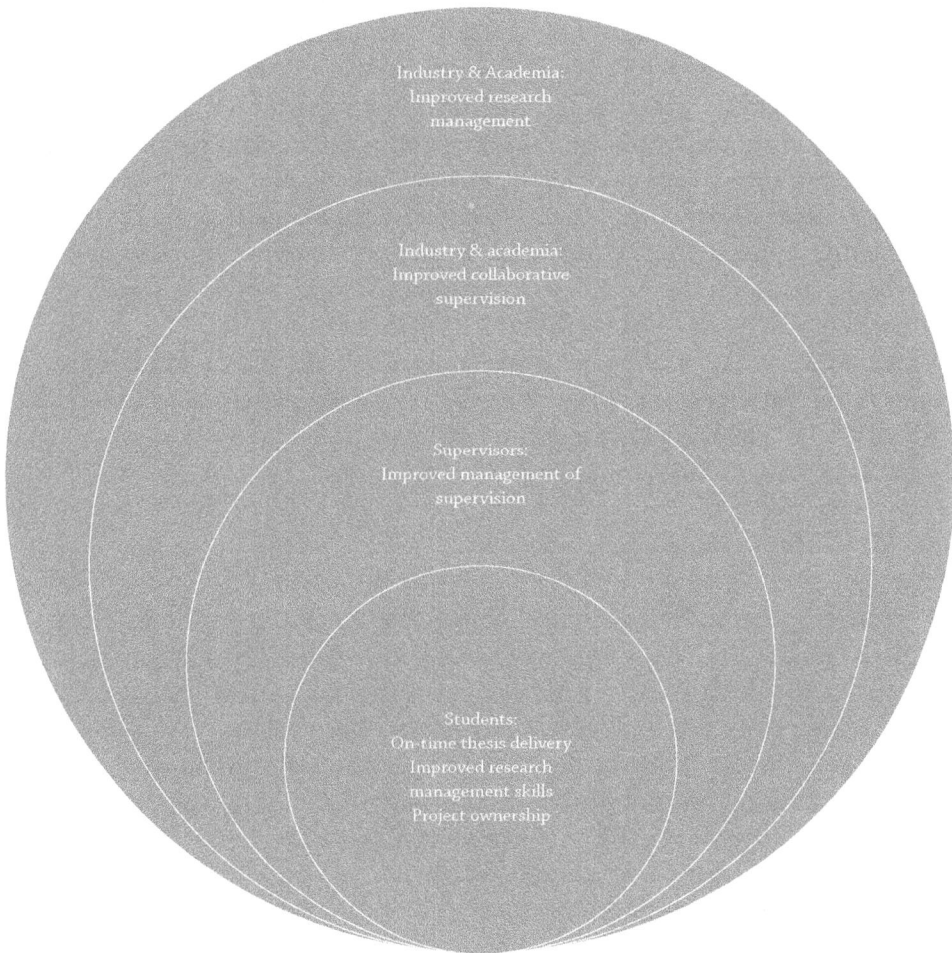

Industry & Academia:
Improved research
management

Industry & academia:
Improved collaborative
supervision

Supervisors:
Improved management of
supervision

Students:
On-time thesis delivery
Improved research
management skills
Project ownership

Source: Author

Work by Katz (2016) indicates that the majority of doctoral candidates have neither training nor expertise in research project management. In a study of 1 470 Israeli and Western European candidates, most participants (in excess of 55%) considered doctoral research as a project, while 95% of them had not had any training in research project management (Katz, 2016). More than 30% considered their supervisor a good manager. Backlund (2016) indicated that, in cases where students did have project management experience, they found it difficult to translate this to the research management environment. Further, students expect supervisors to provide structure and facilitate the project management of their research, including time management (Khosa, 2019).

In a study of more than 1 000 Spanish students, González-Ocampo and Castelló (2019) collected positive and negative experiences of doctoral supervision from students. In their study, the following experiences were categorised as aspects of project management: funding and resources, guaranteeing quality, guidance, and giving career advice. Students did not rank project management as a significant contributor to their overall supervisory experience.

Similarly, Saleem (2018) identified project management as the least satisfactory of six supervisory skills, as perceived by students, in a survey of the experiences of 422 supervisees from 12 Pakistani universities.

Despite the relatively low project management skills and abilities of PhD students as indicated above, work by Buckland concluded that supervisors and students "have a common desire to learn about project management" (Buckland, 2016, p. 918).

2.3 Elements of project management

Project management, in its broadest form, aims to define, schedule, and coordinate a number of different activities towards a predefined goal. A research project fits the definition of a project, since it is concerned with a task that has a definite start and end point, works towards a goal, and has constrained resources (Katz, 2016). In studies that investigate project management as an element of doctoral supervision, the definitions of project management are not necessarily clearly defined. The diverse concepts that are identified as elements of project management in doctoral supervision, as highlighted by this brief literature review, are summarised below:

Table 1: Elements of research project management as identified in the literature

Reference	Focus	Elements of project management (concepts as listed in the article)
Backlund (2016)	How doctoral students experience a project perspective on doctoral studies, with the aim of improving effectiveness and efficiency	• Project control • Project organisation • Project methods and tools • Goal-setting • Stakeholder and uncertainty management

Reference	Focus	Elements of project management (concepts as listed in the article)
Carter et al. (2017)	Exploration of supervisors' experiences of project management, communication, and writing	*Outcomes of project management for supervisors:* • Learning about the topic • Increased passion for the discipline • Satisfaction of launching the career of an emerging researcher • Overseeing a challenging research design • A satisfying aspect of academic work
González-Ocampo & Castelló (2019)	Analyse students' significant supervisory experiences and relate them to coping strategies	• Funding and resources • Guaranteeing quality • Guidance • Giving career advice
Katz (2018)	Empirical assessment of the project challenges and management skills of doctoral candidates	• Meeting constraints of quality, time, scope, and budget • Planning and environmental control • Stakeholder analysis and understanding • Uncertainty and risk reduction
Keller et al. (2018)	Conceptual underpinnings of a PhD in health sciences, based on translation of European guidelines for enhanced quality of PhD education	• Planning and structuring of research • Organisation of infrastructure and logistics • Quality assurance
Manathunga	Intercultural supervision	• Transaction-based • Mitigates power imbalances • Focused on logical, sequential steps • Goal-focused

Source: Author

The summary points to the diverse perspectives on elements of project management in doctoral supervision. From his review of the application of project management in doctoral supervision, Backlund (2016) points out that project management seems to be interpreted rather simplistically, without clear definition of concepts, incomplete adoption of formal project management principles, and an over-focus on roles. Further, Katz indicates that their work did not encounter any references to the use of a holistic project management framework in doctoral research management (Katz, 2016).

3. Value addition through project management

The previous sections briefly highlighted the current state of limited use of formal project management principles in doctoral research supervision, and summarised potential positive outcomes of adopting project management principles for the individual, supervisor, academia, and industry. However, a focus on research project management is positioned by some researchers as a negative practice in the generative and creative context of doctoral studies.

The author is of the opinion that, for project management to add value to the doctoral process, it should be positioned relative to, and customised for, the broader supervisory context. Some thoughts in the debate between project management as either an enabler of delivery, or enabler of a creative process, are explored here, as well as its role in enabling improved supervision.

3.1 Delivery vs. creative research

A key theme centres on an overly task- and output-focused approach to doctoral supervision at the cost of a high-quality research product — in other words, the tension between product and process.

Kandiko and Kinchen (2014), in their exploration of the focus of doctoral supervision on product vs. process, highlight the five supervisory strategies of Lee (2008), namely, functional, enculturation, critical thinking, emancipation, and developing a quality relationship. The functional supervisory style resembles traditional project management and is positioned as having a task focus with low personal support (Lee, 2008; Kyrö et al., 2019). It is depicted as an environment that academics are comfortable with, since it clearly reflects their functional responsibilities (Goede, 2017). Further, it is considered optimal in achieving timely completions of research output and is favoured by both supervisors and students — as found in a study of New Zealand and Australian accounting students (Khosa, 2019).

Kandiko and Kinchen (2014) proceed to warn that pressure for increased output rates leads to an overfocus on a functional approach to the detriment of a more holistic supervisory strategy. The concern is echoed by Manathunga (2015, p. 3), who emphasises that an (almost transaction-based) project management approach "excludes the unpredictable, creative or surprising outcomes and obstacles possible in research".

The call for balance between process and product is extended somewhat in empirical work by Löfström and Pyhältö (2015), who indicate that different expectations of doctoral supervision pose an ethical dilemma in which supervisors approach ethics from a project management perspective, whereas students expect concern at a personal and work-related level.

Bastalich (2015) argues that a perception exists among supervisors that lending too much help would undermine aspects such as a candidate's autonomy and originality of work; this leads to supervision taking on a project management rather than a critical engagement role (Bastalich, 2015). This further supports the view of project management as a rigid, non-creative endeavour in a research undertaking.

3.2 Project management as an enabler of improved supervision

In addition to facilitating delivery, the role of project management in facilitating improved supervision is worth exploring.

Boehe (2016) positions the quest for scientific originality as being in conflict with structured, controlled project management, and defines appropriate supervisory styles for environments of differing process and product-related contingency factors (see Figure 2). This model provides a basis for linking the process component of the research to appropriate project management styles on a spectrum, from a dominant controller to an equal collaborator (Boehe, 2016).

Figure 2: Supervisory styles and contingency factors (Boehe, 2016)

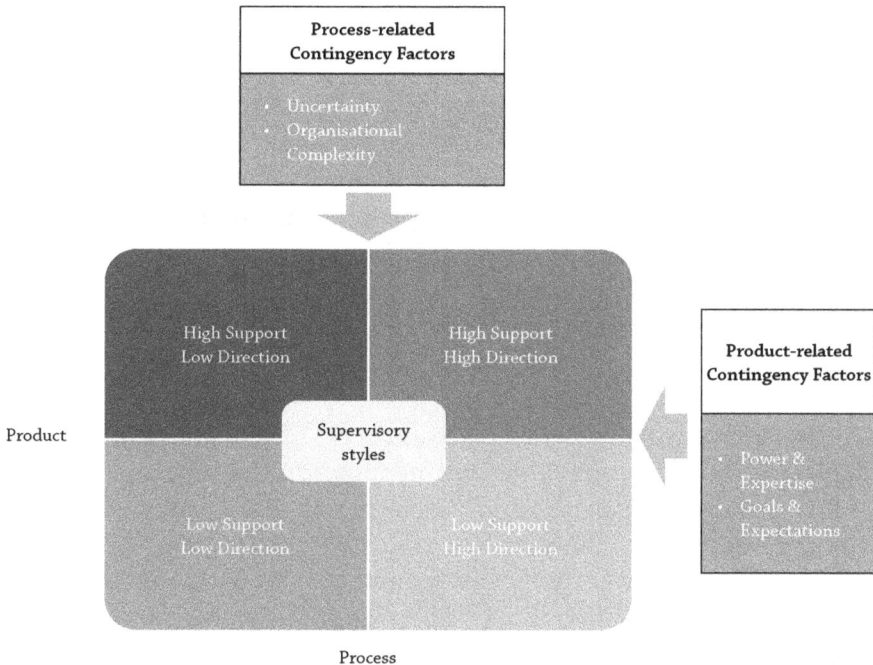

A similar presentation is that of Riikka (2019), who relates different supervisory styles to different communication practices and levels of personal investment (see Figure 3).

Figure 3: The link between supervisory praktice and communication/relation-ship building (Source: Kurö et al., 2019)

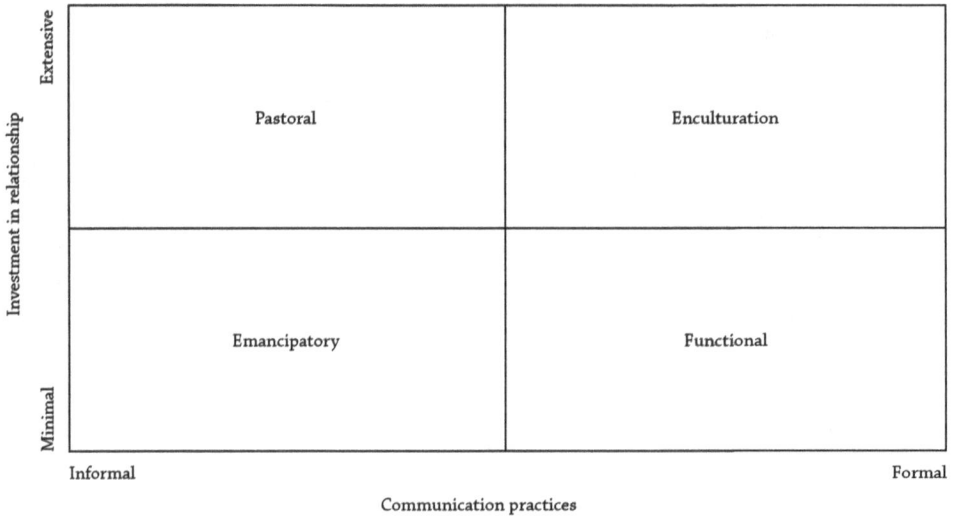

This important approach of linking supervisory styles to the process nature of doctoral supervision succeeds in contextualizing project management as not merely a mechanical action, but as an interactive process that can be influenced by supervisory style, and that hence has the potential to support doctoral research as a creative process.

A further effort to link project management to supervisory approaches is provided by Mayeza (2018), who considers enculturation as a supervisory approach that should include pedagogical strategies to enable project management.

Lin (2018) builds on the work of Manathunga (2011, 2014) in highlighting that supervisors find the project managementapproaches recommended by academic institutions as inadequate in addressing the complex environment of intercultural supervision. Further, Khosa (2019) found that a supervisory approach such as enculturation has the potential to deliver on-time research, include group supervision to reduce supervisory pressures, and develop performance outcomes for supervisors and students. By implication, these approaches have the potential to deliver on what the functional approach is trying to achieve, but with more flexibility and support for creative endeavours. Saleem (2018) argues for the development of candidates' understanding of the research process, in addition to knowledge development, in a PhD programme, and argues that a static supervisory framework will lead to missed deadlines and higher dropout rates.

3.3 Linking project management to supervisory models

Recent work has highlighted the need to better equip supervisors for the supervisory task and identified the following aspects as a means of managing the workload: project management, time management, and additional supervisory styles (Roets, 2017). However, while principles are transferable from traditional project management to research project management, some customisation is required (Buckland, 2018).

In an effort to bring these concepts and recommendations closer to a means of supporting practice, researchers are integrating project management into larger models of doctoral supervision or doctoral programme structures. These could in future be extended to provide a practical means of integrating project management into the broader supervisory context. Some examples are as follows:

Table 2: Models of supervision that integrate project management

Reference	Focus	Programme structure or elements
Keller et al. (2018)	Basel approach for PhD candidates in health sciences	Project management is included in one pillar of three competency areas, as follows: • knowledge and scientific competencies; • organisation and management competencies (including project management); and • leadership and personal competencies
COSTA (2019)	Postgraduate research coaching model	A structured framework of learning and development in postgraduate research, presented as a five-step process (project management not explicitly included, but a strong process focus is present): • Concepts (research language) • Objectives (research proposal) • Situation (literature review) • Tact (methods and presentation) • Assessment of impact (evaluation and defence)
Vilkinas (2005)	Learnings from leadership and management fields for research supervision, presented as the modified Competing Values Framework	The modified competing values framework identifies eight operational roles for the supervisor, each addressing different outcomes in four quadrants, as well as that of integrator: • Human commitment: mentor, facilitator • Expansion, adaptation: innovator, broker, • Maximisation of output: producer, director • Consolidation, continuity: monitor, coordinator • Integrator: delivers across quadrants
Careers Research and Advisory Centre (University of Queensland, 2022)	Vitae Researcher development framework, based on empirical data to identify the characteristics of excellent researchers	Characteristics are expressed as four domains and twelve sub-domains. Domains include the following: Domain A: Engagement, influence, impact Domain B: Personal effectiveness Domain C: Research governance and organisation Domain D: Engagement, influence, and impact

Source: Author

It is notable that the models integrate, or have the potential to integrate, project management skills as part of a broader framework. However, the detailed application of project management principles is not necessarily outlined. Adaptability of these models to different contexts is recommended. For example, it is recommended that limited modules of the Basel model are applied in resource- constrained environments, but that project management remains an essential component (Keller, 2018). A notable coaching, management, and leadership focus is present, while the COSTA model has a strong process focus.

Summary

African economies are under growth pressure and increased doctoral completion rates are seen as a means of strengthening the academic pipeline. However, the capacity for delivering on the increasing demand for doctoral supervision is limited. Mechanisms are sought to enhance doctoral graduation rates, with project management as one potential instrument.

A very brief review of the literature provides preliminary evidence that project management as an enabler of improved doctoral supervision does not receive extensive attention as a research topic, that the definition of project management in doctoral supervision is unclear and can benefit from further exploration, and that supervisors and students do not pursue project management broadly and rigorously as a key enabler of improved supervision.

This review positions project management as an enabler of improved efficiency in thesis delivery, as a means of enabling supervisors to coordinate better across multiple students, and as a means of facilitating academia–industry supervisory collaborations. The ability to manage research projects in a well-founded manner has potential benefits in academic as well as industry settings. While the focus in academia is on improving the capacity to deliver graduates, industry could benefit significantly from research that is well planned, well managed, and delivered in a cost-effective manner. This could especially be beneficial in developing economies. However, while literature makes some reference to the enhanced capacity of doctoral graduates as research managers through project management (e.g. Katz, 2016; Buckland, 2016), this is not a dominant focal point in the debate to introduce project management as a core element of doctoral supervision.

While some interest in project management's role in doctoral supervision is clear from the literature, the definition thereof, and models of research project management, are not abundant. Some studies have linked supervisory styles to elements of project management, and others have expanded on this line of thought to develop supervisory models including a project management focus. Evidence could not be found of an extensive focus on African-centric models of supervision that include a focus on project management.

Future work could (a) confirm the prevalence and practices of supervisory project management on the African continent; (b) define key elements of supervisory project management that are relevant to the continent's academic and industry research demands; (c) develop appropriate supervisory project management models; and (d) identify skills development needs.

This chapter outlined some preliminary pointers to the current status of project management in doctoral supervision. It is based on a limited review of literature, which should be expanded substantially to confirm the identified pointers.

References

Arksey, H., & O'Malley, L. (2005). Scoping studies: Towards a methodological framework. *International Journal of Social Research Methodology, 8*(1), 19–32. https://doi.org/10.1080/1364557032000119616

Backlund, F. A. (2017). Project perspective on doctoral studies – A student point of view. *International Journal of Educational Management, 31*(7), 908–921.

Bastalich, W. (2017). Content and context in knowledge production: A critical review of doctoral supervision literature. *Studies in Higher Education, 42*(7), 1145–1157. https://doi.org/10.1080/03075079.2015.1079702

Boehe, D. M. (2016). Supervisory styles: A contingency framework. *Studies in Higher Education, 41*(3), 399–414. https://doi.org/10.1080/03075079.2014.927853

Bøgelund, P. (2015). How supervisors perceive PhD supervision: And how they practice it. *International Journal of Doctoral Studies, 10*, 39–55.

Carter, S., Kensington-Miller, B., & Courtney, M. (2017). Doctoral supervision practice: What's the problem and how can we help academics? *Journal of Perspectives in Applied Academic Practice, 5*(1).

Costa, K. (2019). Introduction to the C.O.S.T.A. postgraduate research coaching model – A complementary approach to supervision. In *Proceedings of the Fourth World Conference on Qualitative Research* [online]. https://www.researchgate.net/publication/337939696_INTRODUCING_THE_COSTA_POSTGRADUATE_RESEARCH_COACHING_MODEL_-_A_COMPLEMENTARY_APPROACH_TO_SUPERVISION_ABSTRACTS_BOOK_OF_THE_4_th_WORLD_CONFERENCE_ON_QUALITATIVE_RESEARCH [2023, June 16]

The Economist. (2016, December 27). Why doing a PhD is often a waste of time. *The Economist* [online]. https://medium.economist.com/why-doing-a-phd-is-often-a-waste-of-time-349206f9addb [2023, June 16]

Goede, R., & Taylor, E. (2016). Using critical systems thinking in emancipatory postgraduate supervision. In *Proceedings of the 59th ISSS Annual Meeting*, Berlin.

González-Ocampo, G., & Castelló, M. (2019). How do doctoral students experience supervision? *Studies in Continuing Education, 41*(3), 293–307. https://doi.org/10.1080/0158037X.2018.1520208

Grant, M. J., & Booth, A. (2009). A typology of reviews: An analysis of 14 review types and associated methodologies. *Health Information & Libraries Journal, 26*, 91–108. https://doi.org/10.1111/j.1471-1842.2009.00848.x

Kandiko, C. B., & Kinchin, I. M. (2012). What is a doctorate? A concept mapped analysis of process versus product in the supervision of lab-based PhDs. *Educational Research, 54*(1), 3–16. https://doi.org/10.108 0/00131881.2012.658196

Katz, R. (2016). Challenges in doctoral research project management: A comparative study. *International Journal of Doctoral Studies, 11*, 105–125. http://ijds.org/Volume11/IJDSv11p105-125Katz2054.pdf [2023, June 16]

Keller, F., et al. (2018). How to conceptualize and implement a PhD program in health sciences—the Basel approach. *Journal of Medical Education and Curricular Development, 5*, 1–8.

Khosa, A., Burch, S., Ozdil, E., & Wilkin, C. (2019). Current issues in PhD supervision of accounting and finance students: Evidence from Australia and New Zealand. *The British Accounting Review.* https://doi. org/10.1016/j.bar.2019.100874

Kyrö, R., Walsh, N., Martin, T., & D'Agostino, C. (2019). *What determines supervision style? Introducing the key players.* Lund University. Retrieved from https://portal.research.lu.se/files/65822554/Kyro_etal2019_ report_Whatdeterminessupervisionstyle_Introducingthekeyplayers.pdf

Lee, A. (2008). How are doctoral students supervised? Concepts of doctoral research supervision. *Studies in Higher Education, 33*(3), 267–281. https://doi.org/10.1080/03075070802049202

Lim, W. K. (2018). *Intercultural doctoral supervision: Barriers and enablers in international PhD students' cultural adaptation and academic identity formation in an Australian university* (PhD thesis). School of Business UNSW Canberra, Canberra: UNSW.

Löfström, E., & Pyhältö, K. (2015). "I don't even have time to be their friend!" Ethical dilemmas in PhD supervision in hard sciences. *International Journal of Science Education, 37*(16), 2721–2739. https://doi.org /10.1080/09500693.2015.1104424

Maguire, K., Prodi, E., & Gibbs, P. (2018). Minding the gap in doctoral supervision for a contemporary world: A case from Italy. *Studies in Higher Education, 43*(5), 867–877. https://doi.org/10.1080/03075079.2018. 1438114

Mayeza, E., & Mpofu, N. (2018). 'A supervisor can make or break a student': Lessons learned towards building postgraduate supervision capacity at a South African university. *Journal of Educational Studies, 17*(1).

Manathunga, C. (2011). Moments of transculturation and assimilation: Post-colonial explorations of supervision and culture. *Innovations in Education and Teaching International, 48*, 367–376.

Manathunga, C. (2014). *Intercultural postgraduate supervision.* Routledge.

Roets, L., Botha, D., & Van Vuuren, L. (2017). The research supervisor's expertise or postgraduate student preparedness: Which is the real concern? *Africa Journal of Nursing and Midwifery, 19*(2), 1–10. https:// doi.org/10.25159/2520-5293/3740

Saleem, T., & Mehmood, N. (2018). Assessing the quality of supervision experiences in the different research stages at postgraduate level. *Journal of Education and Educational Development, 5*(2), 8–27.

University of Queensland. (n.d.). *Vitae Research Development Framework.* https://research.uq.edu.au/vitae-researcher-development-framework-rdf [2023, June 16]

CHAPTER 10

Doctoral supervision in the context of the physician scientist

Susan Williams

South Africa has a population of 62 million. The country has 26 public universities with a total enrolment of 1.1 million students. Doctoral enrolments in South Africa have increased from 9 994 in 2008 to 23 588 in 2020 (CHE Vitalstats). Between 2000 and 2018, a total of 32 025 doctoral students graduated at South African universities. Doctoral graduates increased from 972 in 2000 to 3 339 in 2019 (SciSTIP Tracer Study).

The **University of the Witwatersrand (Wits)** is located on two campuses in Johannesburg. It became an independent university in 1921, tracing its origins to the South African School of Mines established in 1896. Wits has produced four Nobel Prize recipients, including Nelson Mandela, who was a Law student at Wits from 1947-1949. The university has five faculties and 33 schools. In 2021 it had 1 174 full-time academic staff members and 42 175 students, including 2 470 doctoral candidates.

---

1. Introduction

The supervision of medical doctors undertaking doctoral studies has distinct challenges. This chapter seeks first to understand this group of researchers and then to explore these challenges. The term 'physician scientist' has been selected to refer to medical doctors who have training in research and spend a substantial proportion of their time on research.

Physician scientists, also called 'physician investigators', are part of the broader group of 'clinician scientists' (or 'clinician investigators') that also includes other clinical researchers like nurse scientists, dentist scientists, veterinarian scientists, and others. Although physician scientists are the specific focus of this chapter, the discussion applies to the broader group and would therefore be useful to readers in the wider medical field who work with clinician scientists/investigators.

This chapter will explore doctoral supervision as it relates to physician scientists. This group of researchers, who often have dual careers, is necessary for furthering medical research and will benefit from the doctoral journey. The doctoral journey, and doctoral supervision, of this group needs to be tailored to address specific challenges and to ensure that they acquire appropriate professional skills.

2. The need for physician scientists

Physicians have specific skills and attributes that make them ideally suited to conducting research. First, they have human contact with their patients and a deep understanding of the disease processes affecting them. They are therefore uniquely aware of patient concerns, patient needs, knowledge gaps and treatment burdens that may inform research directions (Ley & Rosenberg, 2005). Second, they are perfectly positioned to test hypotheses in clinical settings as well as to enroll patient participants in clinical trials. The physician with research training and expertise can complete this cycle by understanding the mechanisms and systems (be they laboratory or otherwise) through which research may be conducted to test hypotheses and analyse results. Ultimately the physician scientist may identify clinical challenges, research these challenges and analyse the findings, such that they may be returned to the bedside in true translational research (Dickler et al., 2007).

With the aid of physician researchers, research inquiry that begins in a clinical setting and leads to laboratory experimentation and discoveries may be translated into practical solutions for clinical medicine. The physician researcher can therefore act as a conduit between laboratory and patient (Cornfield et al., 2013). The enormous healthcare burdens Africa faces, in particular, require dedicated scientific research from appropriately trained clinical researchers (Kramer et al., 2015; Tette et al., 2020).

Despite the strong case for physician scientists and their ability to advance scientific discovery in clinical medicine, the proportion of medical doctors actively conducting research worldwide is very low (in 2011 only 1.6% of physicians in the United States were also active scientific researchers) (Garrison & Deschamps, 2014). This proportion has been declining over the last few decades

(Ley & Rosenberg, 2005; Hall et al., 2017, Garrison & Deschamps, 2014). This is in stark contrast to the state of doctoral studies in other fields worldwide (Cyranoski et al., 2011). In Africa, this is a specific concern, with very few clinically trained medical doctors pursuing research careers and poor support for physician scientists (Kramer et al., 2015; Grossman, 2016; Adefuye et al., 2018). A reduction in research scientists who are also trained clinicians threatens scientific advances in healthcare. The factors underlying the worldwide decline in the proportion of physician scientists, and the low numbers in Africa, are interrelated and sometimes indivisible issues related to funding, time, support and motivation (Adefuye et al., 2018).

An understanding of these motivators and challenges can provide a foundation for successful supervision of the physician scientist's doctoral studies to completion.

3. Challenges for physician scientists

Physicians are often discouraged from research-oriented careers because research is remunerated poorly in comparison with clinical work (McKinney, 2017). A career incorporating research is inherently riskier financially than a (financially) safe clinical career (Cornfield et al., 2013). Research is expensive and requires funding and this is in short supply worldwide. Furthermore, clinicians must compete with full-time scientists for this scarce funding. Full-time basic scientists tend to be better funded than their clinician scientist counterparts (Dickler et al., 2007). They frequently have better research and publication records, partly because they do not have clinical demands on their time, but also because laboratory research may be faster than clinical or translational research. The funding challenges are particularly evident for early-career clinician scientists, including doctoral students, who are further impacted by poor funding opportunities for their supervisors and mentors (Cornfield et al., 2013). This is compounded by poor support for unfunded junior clinical researchers by their medical schools. It appears that many medical schools are more likely to invest in the provision of clinical services that are much more lucrative (Cornfield et al., 2013). Medical schools are conflicted by simultaneously attempting to provide medical services while still furthering research in the resource-constrained health sector (Grossman, 2016).

Time is the next big challenge facing physician scientists. Clinical practice is demanding work and is time intensive. It frequently requires after-hours work and emergency calls. Research must compete on an uneven footing and frequently loses out to clinical demands (Lingard et al., 2017). The physician researcher is forced to battle to create protected time for research, a battle that is frequently lost. The time required for academic and administrative responsibilities further compounds the problem, as does any attempt to achieve a 'work-life' balance. Time is, consequently, also a challenge for the physician scientist supervisor, who is also confronted with all the aforementioned competing demands and must still find time for demanding doctoral supervision (Grossman, 2016).

Because so few physicians are also active researchers, the physician scientist's journey is often a lonely one. The isolated scientist may be demotivated as he addresses different career issues from those of his fellow clinicians and divisional chiefs (Cornfield et al., 2013). A lack of understanding of the importance of the research role of the physician scientist (and a disproportionate valuing of the clinical role) may result in poor research support at both departmental and institutional levels. This is further exacerbated by a lack of suitable mentors (Dickler et al., 2007).

An unrewarded (apart from financially) career may also be demotivating. Because physician scientists must divide their time between their clinical work and their research work, this may mean that they meet neither the targets for promotion on a research track nor on a clinical track (Cornfield et al., 2013).

4. Do physician scientists need a doctorate?

It is possible to be an active physician scientist without having a doctoral degree, however obtaining a doctorate provides numerous potential benefits.

From the outset, the doctoral journey ensures proper training in research methodology, such that the physician becomes skilled in critical evaluation, is properly equipped to design quality studies and to interpret the findings of these studies as they become an authority in their chosen field. Furthermore, the journey develops interpersonal skills, including communication and project and team management. Leadership is a key skill that is developed during the doctoral journey that translates into success for multidisciplinary research teams (Montalvo-Javé et al., 2016).

These benefits for the individual and research teams have knock-on benefits on the health system, where risk factors and disease trends may be identified, or new treatments developed. Additionally, physicians with a doctorate are more involved in teaching and the development of academic programmes (Montalvo-Javé et al., 2016). Together, these will enhance healthcare institutions. Better patient care and outcomes and more motivated staff are expected in research-active hospitals, that then have a higher academic profile and therefore attract a better calibre of academic staff (Ahmed et al., 2021).

Physicians with doctorates are much more likely to obtain grant funding than those without as evidenced by grant data from the National Institute of Health (NIH) in the United States (Hall et al., 2017; Dickler et al., 2007). This reflects a measurable consequence of the numerous benefits of the doctoral journey.

Doctorateness (Wellington, 2013) implies both the knowledge and skills the doctoral journey equips the physician scientist for a successful research career. The physician scientist with a doctorate has presumably reached a threshold, experienced liminality, developed the critical and analytical skills necessary to cross that threshold, has developed theorising skills and has made an original contribution (Trafford & Leshem, 2009). The very specific skillset inherent in 'doctorateness' may be achieved outside the formal degree environment, but with less predictability. The doctoral degree is still the most effective way of establishing physician scientists (Daye et al., 2015).

5. Format of the doctoral degree for physicians

In South Africa there are no simultaneous MD-PhD degrees available of the sort that are available in the United States, Canada and the United Kingdom. The doctoral journey therefore begins after the completion of medical training. This is not necessarily a disadvantage, since it appears that physicians obtaining PhDs after their primary medical training (as opposed to those who obtain simultaneous MD-PhDs or doctoral degrees followed by medical training) are more likely to pursue careers in biomedical research (Kearney et al., 2007). These more mature students may have already begun research careers that they wish to augment with their doctoral studies. Alternatively, they may have, through their clinical work, identified research questions in their selected fields and it is the desire to answer these that has led them to enroll for a targeted doctorate. Higher completion rates may result than for the younger student enrolling in an MD-PhD as a career choice without first having experienced clinical practice.

The unfortunate consequence of a qualified medical doctor pursuing doctoral studies is that the student is seldom a full-time student. Most clinicians are working in their chosen field. Even those working in academic departments are still predominantly undertaking clinical responsibilities. A PhD involving course work is therefore generally not an appropriate model.

I completed all my postgraduate training at the University of the Witwatersrand (Wits University) in Johannesburg, South Africa. At Wits, physician scientists typically complete a thesis-based doctorate although publication-based doctorates are rapidly gaining popularity. The latter have the advantage of focusing the research into smaller, publishable outputs that allow faster dissemination of scientific findings that might have clinical relevance. A valid concern with thesis-based clinical research is that it may, in fact, never be published. This has been corroborated by a 2012 review which found that a large proportion of doctoral projects in clinical research are not published (Caan & Cole, 2012). It further found that clinical doctoral students who completed a doctoral thesis and graduated on that basis were more likely to never publish their evidence than those who began publishing their clinical research before completing the degree (Caan & Cole, 2012). My own PhD was thesis-based and the advantage, for me, was that I did not have to rely on the very slow response rates of medical journals to complete my studies. However, writing the papers after I had graduated was difficult because I did not have graduation as a motivation, and I had reached a saturation point with my research. I wanted nothing more than to pack my research away and never look at it again. As a result, I encourage my students to pursue a publication-based degree or at least to write the thesis and publications simultaneously to ensure that their contribution reaches the broader scientific community.

6. Professional skills for the physician scientist

There are certain professional skills that the physician doctoral student should acquire during their doctoral journey. These include research methodology, grantsmanship, time management and human subject protection and research ethics knowledge and skills (Lingard et al., 2017).

Medical doctors receive very little research training during their undergraduate degrees (Dickler et al., 2007). At Wits University, where I studied, there is a research component incorporated into our postgraduate (master's) degrees. This degree, however, coincides with medical specialization, so the research component is often overwhelmed by the clinical component of the degree and the time intensive aspects of patient care. Before a physician can become a scientist, therefore, there is a need for some formal training in research methodology. The supervisor should be in a position to facilitate this training.

The aspirant physician scientist needs protected research time (Cornfield et al., 2013, Kramer et al., 2015). In South Africa, the South African Medical Research Council (SAMRC) offers clinician scientist PhD fellowships that provide a stipend for clinician PhD students, allowing them time away from their clinical responsibilities. The Discovery Foundation also offers fellowships and grants to physician scientists. The supervisor should have knowledge of these and other resources available to assist their students with negotiating the time and financial implications of pursuing a career incorporating research. This may assist with time management, but specific coaching with respect to time management skills is also an imperative that will be necessary for a post-doctoral research career.

Clinical research is expensive, and grant funding should be secured by the students themselves, unlike basic science research in well-funded research laboratories.

Grantsmanship is therefore a skill that requires formal training for the physician scientist to be successful (Daye et al., 2015). This goes beyond the actual process of writing a grant and includes learning about the sources, mechanisms and review processes of research grants (Back et al., 2011).

The supervisor is required to guide the student in the responsible conduct of research. Most physician scientists undertake clinical research involving human participants (Hall et al., 2017), and that means that particular care must be taken when considering the ethical implications of the research. Procedural, intrinsic and extrinsic ethical issues have been described that should be considered whenever embarking on research (Stacey & Stacey, 2012). An important intrinsic concern specific to physicians are the power dynamics of the physician–patient relationship, particularly when the patient is the study participant. The extrinsic issues of unintended consequences are very relevant for clinical research that may have far reaching consequences for disease-affected individuals as well as for the hospitals treating them and even national and international health sector stakeholders.

7. The role of the supervisor

The first role of a supervisor is to understand his or her own research identity (Guerin et al., 2015). My research identity is that of an ophthalmologist scientist, one of only five in the country (two graduated after me and two have nominally retired). My clinical expertise is in the sub-specialty of glaucoma and my research expertise is in genetics and glaucoma. And yet I am called upon to supervise any ophthalmologist wishing to pursue doctoral studies at my own institution, anywhere in the province and sometimes anywhere in the country, whether I have the relevant subject-specific expertise or not. Recognising my own limitations in this regard has been an important aspect of my development as a supervisor. My challenge is not unique among physician scientist supervisors, who are a scarcity in Africa (Grossman, 2016). In an acknowledgement of the potential pitfalls of supervising an unfamiliar topic or methodology, we should be prepared to consider co-supervision models and collaborations, not merely within the discipline (where we can consider collaborating with sub-specialist clinicians who may not be researchers but are subject experts) but within the broader scientific community (perhaps collaborating with basic scientists with specific methodological strengths). We need to be honest with our students about our own strengths and weaknesses if we are to provide them with the necessary support in their journey (Heyns et al., 2019).

Unfortunately, in instances where appropriately qualified supervisors are a scarcity, the supervisor may not have the luxury of selecting their students. The challenge of providing suitable support for a student whose research does not align with our own is only one aspect of this dynamic. Even more challenging is having a student 'foisted' upon us who may not even be a suitable doctoral candidate. In my own experience, expert physicians who have successfully completed specialist training may choose to pursue a doctorate simply because it seems like the logical next step in a life of studying. They may consider the doctoral road as another 'notch on the belt' in a life of scholarship, whereas I think that it is only the correct direction for a physician scientist intent on a career in clinical research. Learning to negotiate the tricky task of dissuading the unsuitable 'would-be' PhD candidate is a skill that could potentially trans-form our supervision, providing us with more time and capacity for appropriate students. I have not yet been successful in dissuading any student of mine from beginning doctoral studies. Nor have I had the courage to refuse to supervise a colleague, since that would prevent them from registering at my university (where the only barrier to pursuing doctoral studies for a physician is to have the agreement of a suitable supervisor). I hope that as I mature as a supervisor and possibly as my capacity to undertake supervision diminishes (based on the number of students I am currently supervising), that I learn these skills and can execute them with compassion.

The physician doctoral student, in this country, is a mature student. Typically, they have completed at least fifteen years of graduate and postgradu-ate studies. Supervising such a student has both advantages and disadvantages compared to the supervision of a young postgraduate. The advantages are that they are generally academically confident and dedicated students. The power dynamics of the supervision relationship are therefore less pronounced. They may even be reversed: for example, one of my students is the head of depart-ment at another university. Another trained me, clinically, when I was a student and is currently my clinical superior. In this setting the student may have very strong ideas and opinions with little regard for input from the supervisor. In this context particularly, although the same is true for any supervisory relationship, an unequivocal memorandum of understanding (MoU) is indispensable. If this is properly considered and negotiated, it can provide coherent guidelines for the relationship and provide security for both student and supervisor (Heyns et al., 2019). My first attempts at supervision were without the protection of an MoU and were fraught with misunderstanding. I shall not make that mistake again.

8. Supervisory models and styles

The traditional supervisory model for physician scientists is the apprenticeship model, although the co-supervision model is more frequently used nowadays. Co-supervision is particularly important where research is cross-disciplinary. This is frequently the case for clinical research, where the research may be part patient-based and part laboratory-based. Co-supervision, with both clinical supervisors and basic scientists, provides complementary expertise and supervisory skills (Yoon et al., 2013). This was my experience. My PhD was on the genetics of glaucoma. I had two supervisors, an ophthalmologist and a geneticist. Neither would have provided sufficient knowledge support on their own, but together their support was comprehensive. Likewise, I am now co-supervising an ophthalmologist together with a pathologist because my student's research incorporates tumour cytology. I can confidently leave the cytology component of his research to his co-supervisor and know that he is not being misguided by my weakness in that area.

Physician scientists need quality mentors (Lingard et al., 2017). This appears to be a shortfall of many physician scientist doctoral programmes because poor mentoring (or no mentoring) is a frequent complaint of physician scientists (Yoon et al., 2013). Most physician scientist supervisors tend to have directorial management styles when there is a need for a more contractual or even pastoral style (Gatfield, 2005). The doctoral supervisor should, preferably, be in a position to provide support outside the specific task-driven aspects of doctoral research. Mentoring skills can be learned (Lingard et al., 2017) and should be acculturated into any physician scientist supervisory programme. Effective mentorship of the physician scientist entails understanding the numerous challenges facing the physician doctoral student and working, together with the student, to find solutions. For example, the supervisor may be able to have some impact on the work environment by lobbying their medical school to improve the academic culture to respect research such that it is more nurturing of physician scientists (Dickler et al., 2007). The supervisor can help create a community of physician scientists, so that the doctoral students feel less isolated (Lingard et al., 2017). This can be cross-disciplinary, national and even international with the use of virtual meetings. Such multidisciplinary collaborations are an effective tool for increasing physician scientist productivity. Finally, the supervisor should understand the competing influences not only of demanding clinical work, but also of family and children since the student is usually an older student.

9. Conclusion

Doctoral supervision, the art of guiding a novice towards successful 'doctorateness', is arduous. The specific task of supervising a physician on their doctoral research journey has unique issues. Most of these issues are situational. Understanding the context of a split career and developing our own supervisory, mentoring and research skills will enable us to support the next generation of physician scientists.

References

Adefuye, A. O., Adeola, H. A., & Bezuidenhout, J. (2018). The physician-scientists: Rare species in Africa. *The Pan African Medical Journal, 29*.

Ahmed, M. H., Husain, N. E., & Elsheikh, M. (2021). Why Sudanese doctors should consider a research career or PhD degree after their postgraduate medical training. *J Public Health Emerg, 5*, 16.

Back, S. E., Book, S. W., Santos, A. B., & Brady, K. T. (2011). Training physician-scientists: A model for integrating research into psychiatric residency. *Academic Psychiatry, 35*, 40–45.

Caan, W., & Cole, M. (2012). How much doctoral research on clinical topics is published? *BMJ Evidence-Based Medicine, 17*, 71–74.

Cornfield, D. N., Lane, R., & Abman, S. H. (2013). Creation and retention of the next generation of physician-scientists for child health research. *JAMA, 309*, 1781–1782.

Cyranoski, D., Gilbert, N., Ledford, H., Nayar, A., & Yahia, M. (2011). The PhD factory: The world is producing more PhDs than ever before. Is it time to stop? *Nature, 472*, 276–279.

Daye, D., Patel, C. B., Ahn, J., & Nguyen, F. T. (2015). Challenges and opportunities for reinvigorating the physician-scientist pipeline. *The Journal of Clinical Investigation, 125*, 883–887.

Dickler, H. B., Fang, D., Heinig, S. J., Johnson, E., & Korn, D. (2007). New physician-investigators receiving National Institutes of Health research project grants: A historical perspective on the "endangered species." *JAMA, 297*, 2496–2501.

Garrison, H. H., & Deschamps, A. M. (2014). NIH research funding and early career physician scientists: Continuing challenges in the 21st century. *The FASEB Journal, 28*, 1049–1058.

Gatfield, T. (2005). An investigation into PhD supervisory management styles: Development of a dynamic conceptual model and its managerial implications. *Journal of Higher Education Policy and Management, 27*, 311–325.

Grossman, E. (2016). 'My supervisor is so busy...': Informal spaces for postgraduate learning in the Health Sciences. *South African Journal of Higher Education, 30*, 94–109.

Guerin, C., Kerr, H., & Green, I. (2015). Supervision pedagogies: Narratives from the field. *Teaching in Higher Education, 20*, 107–118.

Hall, A. K., Mills, S. L., & Lund, P. K. (2017). Clinician-Investigator Training and the need to pilot new approaches to recruiting and retaining this workforce. *Acad Med, 92*, 1382–1389.

Heyns, T., Bresser, P., Buys, T., Coetzee, I., Korkie, E., White, Z., & Mc Cormack, B. (2019). Twelve tips for supervisors to move towards person-centered research supervision in health care sciences. *Medical Teacher, 41*, 1353–1358.

Kearney, R. A., Lee, S. Y., Skakun, E. N., & Tyrrell, D. L. (2007). The research productivity of Canadian physicians: How the timing of obtaining a PhD has an influence. *Academic Medicine, 82*, 310–315.

Kramer, B., Veriava, Y., & Pettifor, J. (2015). Rising to the challenge: Training the next generation of clinician scientists for South Africa. *African Journal of Health Professions Education, 7*, 153–154.

Ley, T. J., & Rosenberg, L. E. (2005). The physician-scientist career pipeline in 2005: Build it, and they will come. *JAMA, 294*, 1343–1351.

Lingard, L., Zhang, P., Strong, M., Steele, M., Yoo, J., & Lewis, J. (2017). Strategies for supporting physician-scientists in faculty roles: A narrative review with key informant consultations. *Acad Med, 92*, 1421–1428.

McKinney, R. E., Jr. (2017). The daunting career of the physician-investigator. *Acad Med, 92*, 1368–1370.

Montalvo-Javé, E. E., Mendoza-Barrera, G. E., Valderrama-Treviño, A. I., Alcántara-Medina, S., Macías-Huerta, N. A., & Tapia-Jurado, J. (2016). The importance of master's degree and doctorate degree in general surgery. *Cirugía y Cirujanos (English Edition), 84*, 180–185.

Stacey, A., & Stacey, J. (2012). Integrating sustainable development into research ethics protocols. *Electronic Journal of Business Research Methods, 10*, 54–63.

Tette, E. M., Gyan, B. A., & Koram, K. A. (2020). Perspectives on research internships for medical students and young doctors in Ghana: An opportunity to replenish the stock of physician investigators? *Advances in Medical Education and Practice, 11*, 473.

Trafford, V., & Leshem, S. (2009). Doctorateness as a threshold concept. *Innovations in Education and Teaching International, 46*, 305–316.

Wellington, J. (2013). Searching for 'doctorateness.' *Studies in Higher Education, 38*, 1490–1503.

Yoon, J.-Y., Appleton, T., Cecchini, M. J., Correa, R. J., Ram, V. D., Wang, X., Ng, E., Speechley, M., & Wilcox, J. T. (2013). It begins with the right supervisor: Importance of mentorship and clinician-investigator trainee satisfaction levels in Canada. *Clinical and Investigative Medicine, E269–E276*.

CHAPTER 11

A reflection on doctoral supervision in the School of Natural Sciences at the University of Zambia

Wilma Sithabiso Sichombo Nchito

Zambia's population according to the last census is 19.6 million. The country has 9 public universities and 54 private universities with a total enrolment of 126 739 students. Doctoral enrolments in Zambia are still very low but are slowly increasing with more universities offering them. Figures collated by the Higher Education Authority are of PhD candidates and not those who have completed. The number of candidates registered for PhDs increased from 987 in 2020 to 1 325 in 2021 (HEA, The State of Higher Education in Zambia). The number of PhD graduates nationwide is not collated by any institution. In 2023 the University of Zambia graduated 71 PhDs which was the highest the institution had ever graduated.

The **University of Zambia** (UNZA) was established in 1966 through the University of Zambia Act. Established after independence, it was the first university in the country and was given the mandate of producing professionally trained human capital for the young nation. It currently has 12 faculties, 810 academic staff and over 14 676 students.

---

1. Introduction

The University of Zambia (UNZA) offers both undergraduate and postgraduate qualifications. As the oldest university in the country, it initially concentrated on undergraduate training to supply an educated workforce for the newly independent country. With time the university developed a few postgraduate programmes in some of its schools. The university has not had deliberate policies or plans for postgraduate education. Postgraduate training has generally evolved based on the interests and competencies of individual departments or schools. Historically, supervision was not closely monitored and directed by specific guidelines. This chapter considers the practice of supervision in one department in the School of Natural Sciences at the University of Zambia and outlines the benefits and pitfalls of the various supervision processes. The chapter provides a brief reflection on the prevailing situation in the institution and evaluates recent proposals that have the potential of transforming doctoral training. The chapter will also present some of the guidelines used for postgraduate training at the university, as they relate to the issues covered herein. Some Schools and individual programmes in the institution are better funded and have stronger collaborative relationships with external institutions that continue to guide and support doctoral training. Other schools have lagged behind and do not have adequate human resources to sustain doctoral training. The Department of Geography and Environmental Studies may not be the best example, but it represents a unit that has the potential to improve doctoral training in the institution. In my view it lies mid-point on the continuum in terms of the quality of doctoral training offered at UNZA.

When Zambia gained independence in 1964, the nation did not have an institution of higher learning. The colonial territory of Northern Rhodesia, as Zambia was known then, had contributed immensely to the creation and running of the University College of Rhodesia and Nyasaland that had strategically been located in Harare, Zimbabwe (then Salisbury, Southern Rhodesia) (Ajayi et al., 1996). The University of Zambia opened its doors in 1966 and in the early years, from 1966 to the mid-1980s, the university grew rapidly and gained momentum. Like other post-colonial universities on the continent, the University of Zambia set out to train professionals and expand the frontiers of knowledge in order to serve local economies (Knight, 2017). These new universities were also modelled on institutions of their former Western colonizers (Mohamedbhai, 2017). To make up for deficits in the education sector, funding was provided for the training of secondary school teachers at universities like the University of Zambia. Funding for research was limited but postgraduate studies were eventually introduced in most schools and departments in the mid-1980s.

This limited progress was dealt a major blow when the Zambianization policy which had initially started with secondary schools in the early 1980s was eventually actualised at tertiary level. Zambianization was envisioned from the inception of the university as it was argued that students needed to be taught by people with shared cultural backgrounds (Kashoki, 1994). It came out of the nationalisation policies that were aimed at ensuring that jobs which could be done by Zambian citizens were taken up by Zambian citizens. The country was also spending colossal sums of money on emoluments for expatriate staff who were paid more than the locals. At the time, the Zambian government, like her Tanzanian, Ugandan and many other counterparts, was guided by the global impression that tertiary education was a waste of money (Ajayi et al., 1996; Freisenhahn, 2014; Hayward & Ncayiyana, 2014). Therefore, the government was no longer willing to pay the high salaries of both academic and administrative expatriate staff.

The 1990s saw a revived drive to recruit and train staff, and the university sought external scholarships for potential staff, which was in line with the changes taking place globally (Friesenhahn, 2014). A staff development programme was launched to try and fill the gaps left by expatriate staff who had opted to leave at the end of their contracts. Training staff was simple enough but retaining them proved to be more problematic and the institution suffered a 'brain drain' of its brightest staff who did not return once they had been trained (Ajayi et al., 1996). By the late 1980s the situation was at its most critical due to the failing economy hence the increased recruitment in the early 1990s. Efforts were made to change the scholarship requirements and many sponsors ensured that once a programme of study ended, trained staff had to return to their home country. Those who were awarded scholarships also had to agree to be 'bonded' and had to return to their employers once their study programme was over. This, as well as the slowly improving economy, saw many academics trained abroad return to Zambia. Faculties which previously had depleted numbers were almost reaching or even exceeding establishment sizes. For instance, the Department of Geography and Environmental Studies (GES) dropped to only six members of staff in 1991 but has now exceeded the original establishment size of 18, with 21 academic members of staff. The improvement in staffing levels by the mid-1990s allowed some departments in the school to reintroduce the original MSc programmes which had started in the 1980s. The Department of GES revived its MSc programme around 1996 but did not fare very well due to long completion times and shortage in teaching staff since, at the time, though the staffing levels had increased many still did not hold PhDs. The department eventually introduced two new MSc programmes and shelved the old one in order to revise it. In the process a PhD was launched in 2003. The first PhD candidate in geography graduated after 10 years of study. This situation reflected what was taking place in the rest of the university.

Since then, doctoral training has definitely seen a rise at the university and the number of locally trained staff is increasing. A similar rise in PhDs is taking place in the new universities that have been founded in the past 10 years. It is not clear whether the causes of this are similar to the global rise in PhDs (Cyranoski et al., 2011). Wachira (2018) refers to this as unplanned expansion of tertiary education. This chapter intends to interrogate the doctoral supervisory roles pertaining to the School of Natural Sciences.

2. Background

2.1 The supervisory role

It is clear from existing literature that doctoral education is important for the development of the continent (Friesenhahn, 2014; Wachira, 2018). Certain preconditions must be met for education to be used as a driver of economic development, and well thought out postgraduate and research programmes are among them. The School of Natural Sciences' approach is that of the final research product constituting 'doctorateness' (Trafford & Leshem, 2009, cited by Bitzer, 2016). This 'product view' entails that there is minimum concern about the processes that take place in order to train the candidate and yet, according to Bastalich (2015, p. 1145), "supervision is key to both quality and efficiency in higher degree research". Griffiths et al. (1999) on the other hand consider the selection of a supervisor as the most 'influential' aspect of one's PhD. Their view stems from contexts where students are at liberty to select supervisors, which is not always the case. Clearly, supervision is very important whether the supervisor is selected by the candidate or not. Griffiths et al. (1999) consider the three important characteristics of a supervisor to be (i) expertise in the research area, (ii) showing support to student and, (iii) having a balance of creativity and criticism. Added to this list are those qualities presented by Vilkinas (2002) who in the competing values framework (CVF) model considers the supervisor as a manager who should have a variety of qualities and proficiencies. Whilst the supervisor's expertise is verifiable at the onset the other two are not quite obvious and this is where many problems emanate from. Supervisors need to know how and when to be supportive. Some do not know how to be mentors, or they simply overlook the role (Katz, 2015). Since supervision is not the only role that supervisors have, getting them to learn these skills may not be that easy since many universities assume that since the supervisor has a PhD they will learn from their own experience.

The styles and approaches of supervision that are predominant in an institution such as, laissez faire, pastoral, directional, contractual, functional, enculturation, critical thinking, emancipation among others (Lee, 2018, 2008;

Mouton et al., 2015; Gatfield, 2005), need to be reviewed from time to time to assess their effectiveness and relevance. The supervisory relationship is also one aspect which requires constant review and having an MoU (memorandum of understanding) between the student and supervisor is ingenious as it outlines the roles of both parties (Boughey & McKenna, 2019). However, since most supervisors would not have had training in adult education there needs to be a forum through which they can be taught different supervisory styles and approaches. It is the experienced supervisor who is able to identify when for instance a candidate is experiencing doctoral liminality (Keefer, 2015). Supervisors are also responsible for training their candidates in responsible conduct of research (RCR) (Titus & Ballou, 2013). Benderly (2003) included career development as a mentor's role beyond the usual feedback and advice. Lee (2018) also adds the aspect of supervisor training. Her assessment of a 2016 Training of trainers project for supervisors in Norway found that not only were participants encouraged to try out different pedagogical approaches but that as a result of the training many universities had instituted teams which oversaw supervisor development. This is the best way for universities to ensure their supervisors are fulfilling their roles accordingly and that candidates are getting the best guidance. The fact that supervision does not take place in a vacuum entails that it is complex and there cannot be only one recommended style or approach (Pyhältö et al., 2015).

2.2 PhD delivery in the School of Natural Sciences

From the time departments started offering PhDs, very little has been done to formulate the actual structure of the programmes. This implies that the value that doctoral education can add to our knowledge economy is not taken into consideration (Mouton et al., 2015). This was around when the World Bank had shifted its emphasis on education towards higher education so in terms of funding, a few master's students were able to receive funding from their employers. Unfortunately, there were no arrangements made to fund doctoral students, and the cost of postgraduate education has disproportionately been borne by the students themselves. Many potential candidates prefer to do their studies abroad because employers tend to give them paid study leave when one is studying abroad but expect the person to report for work when they study locally. This implies a current lack of understanding of the advantage of PhDs by employers. However, in some cases candidate's choice of subject is irrelevant to their line of work and therefore the employers do not deem it necessary to support them in their studies. A PhD as a qualification is still largely seen as only being relevant for academics.

The school suffers mainly from not having focused policy and approaches to doctoral learning, poor-quality supervisors, low institutional capacity, lack of funds and weak links to industry. The situation in the school to a large extent mirrors Bastalich's (2017) list of problems facing African scholarship. The other problem is that there has not been much, if any, research on doctoral education by the institution or by individual students so there is a dearth of information on doctoral education in general.

3. What needs to change and why?

Doctoral student supervision needs a major overhaul if doctoral education is going to contribute to the knowledge economy and the institution is going to train researchers and future academics. Among the several changes to doctoral studies necessary include admission processes as well as the management of the relationship between the supervisor and doctoral candidate. Admittedly, it is not always possible to screen candidates before admission (Mouton et al., 2015). There is definitely some level of training required for supervisors in order to increase their effectiveness (Lee, 2018). Supervisors often model their supervision on the supervision that they experienced during their own doctoral studies. As a result, bad experiences are often replicated. Supervisors need to be equipped with skills in how to give feedback and how to provide mentorship and support to their students.

Currently, students are assigned to supervisors who are conversant with or have an interest in their field. For the most part, supervisors volunteer and are not coerced to take on doctoral students. In some instances, the students seek out possible supervisors before registration and prospective supervisor and student agree on the possibility of working together once the student is accepted for the programme. This is helpful because it reduces the tension and uncertainty in the supervisor–student relationship. Mouton et al. (2015) are of the view that rigorous screening of candidates is important for effective and efficient supervision. The role of the supervisor has over the years not been given the attention needed to ensure that supervisors have the requisite skills. It appears there has been an assumption that once a member of staff has acquired experience in supervising at master's level, they should be able to do the same at the doctoral level, which is often not the case. The result has been a tortuous process for students and supervisors alike. This chapter will now consider this process from the application stage to graduation. Proposals for improvement will be presented at each stage.

3.1 Admission and funding

Prospective doctoral students are expected to look for advertisements of doctoral programmes of the School of Natural Sciences in the national newspapers and apply either online or in person. Online applications were introduced in 2020. At this stage some students will contact a member of staff to find out if there are possibilities for supervision. At this point the potential student may be advised to tweak their topic to suit the interests and competencies of available staff. This enhances the chances for the student's application to be successful and helps the future supervisor in preparing to receive a student. Those who do not approach the department before applying will sometimes have their application rejected because there is no one with the required competencies in their proposed field. Since they are not present to explain their flexibility or willingness to change topic, such students lose opportunities to study at the university. Some end up going to private universities which are more flexible, admitting students first and looking for supervisors second.

Admitting potential PhD candidates without engaging or screening them can be precarious for two reasons: first, no one in the department will claim candidates as their responsibility and such candidates may be forced upon unwilling supervisors. Second, this route holds the potential of the student not having the required competencies that could have been noted through prior engagement. Since departments in the school are understaffed, not admitting such students saves valuable time. Mouton et al. (2016) agree that it is not always possible to screen students before they are admitted. They reported that some faculties turn away 54 % of applicants. Admission, which previously has been all year round, has now been streamlined to twice a year.

Introducing a meeting with potential supervisors or heads of department as a prerequisite for doctoral applicants would be an instrumental part of a screening process. It is not easy for potential candidates to know whether the area of their interest has adequate staffing. This initial contact could help increase the number of doctoral students accepted in the school. A thorough screening of potential candidates is proposed as the best way forward. The Department of Geography and Environmental Studies has introduced pre-entry interviews with potential candidates. These have been done virtually and have given the department the opportunity of getting a better understanding of the potential candidate's research ideas. Potential candidates are requested to make a brief presentation and then they are asked questions by various members of the faculty. This method is not fool proof, and candidates have been taken on based on their presentation who have then gone on to not meet expectations. Two main questions asked during the interview are about the proposed candidate's motivation and whether they think they will have adequate time to do a PhD. If they are in full-time employment, they are asked if they will be able to get time off from work to pursue their studies.

The other way of resolving this problem is for the departments in the school to offer specified programmes as opposed to the current status of simply offering a PhD in geography, physics, chemistry, etc. Project funding enables some universities to link PhD programs to these initiatives, attracting students in specific fields. However, this approach is not applicable to the school. Typically, projects prioritize funding master's students due to the shorter duration of most projects, which usually span 2–3 years. There have been some projects which do this in a few other schools, but this is not the norm. This is an approach the school could seek to follow in attracting doctoral students. Funding of these projects also needs to be from within the country to ensure that the focus is relevant. Externally funded projects typically align with the funders' priorities, requiring the school to adapt its approach to fit within the framework of these projects. In order for projects to be developed the school needs to decide what it wants to achieve with doctoral education and concentrate on those fields which will benefit from research. For instance, most universities offering doctoral studies in geography will specify whether it is in human, physical, planning or earth sciences. This helps eliminate those students who do not have an interest in these fields. Some departments have distinct research groups which invite students to take up studies under teams of supervisors who have specific topics in mind. For a country with limited funding this is also a way of increasing research output.

The past three to four years have seen an introduction of a few scholarships offered at postgraduate level by the Ministry of Higher Education (MOHE). This is a very positive move. The scholarships try to target women in STEM, offering them 70% and the remaining 30% to male applicants. The total number offered in the 2019-2020 academic year were only 11, with 6 being at doctoral level and five for master's. The scholarships are tenable in any of the following fields: "Geology, Engineering, Bioinformatics, Biotechnology, Pharmacognosy, Forensics, Renewable Energy, Food Science, Agriculture, Nutrition, Pathology, Physics, Chemistry, Biology, Mathematics, Medicine, Veterinary Medicine, Mining, Fourth Industrial revolution courses (4IR) Nuclear Science and

Technology, Space Science and Technology and Education with Science subjects" (MOHE, 2019). The website goes on to say that

> is in line with the Ministry's long-term objective of promoting a cadre of researchers at postgraduate level, especially increased participation of women in Science and Technology studies for the purposes of lecturing in the universities or conducting research in the scientific institutions.

The aim is mainly to produce academics. It is not clear whether the ministry carried out a survey to create a database of available PhD programmes especially when one considers the inclusion of space science and technology. Public universities in their current state are not able to adequately offer such a programme. Apart from limited capacity in terms of manpower UNZA also lacks infrastructure dedicated to postgraduate training.

3.2 Supervisor allocation

Supervisors are allocated by departments either through the supervisor having met the prospective student and taken an interest in the subject matter or by the department's graduate committee meeting and deciding which supervisors would be suitable for the topics at hand. In other instances, students are assigned to supervisors and depending on the relationship the supervisor has with the head of the unit they may or may not accept the appointment as supervisor. A supervisor may be deemed suitable by the department even though they themselves may think otherwise. This relationship may not work if the supervisor is reluctant to take on the student from the start. The reasons could be a general lack of knowledge of the field of study, lack of interest in the field or heavy workload. If the targeted supervisor feels their head of unit may think they are being insubordinate, they will reluctantly take on the student. Progress is guaranteed to be slow in these instances. There has not been any formal training for supervisors and the only requirement is that the supervisor should have qualified for their own PhD two years prior to their supervising a student. Recently, the Directorate of Research and Graduate Studies (DRGS) has been working in conjunction with Vanderbilt University in the United States on a mentorship and supervision curriculum for lecturers. With the highly competitive academic landscape there is an urgency for improving the student experience at doctoral level. The university also envisions positioning itself as a postgraduate institution. There have also been moves to structure doctoral training across the whole university.

3.3 Improving the PhD process

The university has not had a standard structure for the PhD process. This has been identified as a problem contributing to slow graduate output. In 2020 the School of Veterinary Medicine, School of Medicine and School of Health Sciences started the process of developing structured PhDs. The School of Medicine additionally felt that mentoring skills were lacking amongst faculty members and in 2020 developed a mentoring curriculum for staff. These efforts have yielded results, leading to the adoption of the PhD framework as a university-wide process. This ensures that PhD students follow a structured program, including courses and assessments, before advancing to candidacy. Beyond establishing a standardized process, it was recognized that certain competencies often missing in applicants could be addressed and evaluated during the first year of study. This way, a student who lacked certain competencies could attain them before embarking on the doctoral process. It would also eliminate those who would not successfully complete the first year of assessments. The framework provides guidance on expected competencies, structure, admission requirements and progression. It also outlines the different types of PhDs that will be offered by the institution. Members of the Department of GES have collectively gone through the framework and developed the required course work to be undertaken by a student. Specific doctoral programmes have also been created, which is a deviation from past practice.

The fact of only a few students enrolling makes it easy for lonely student syndrome to set in from very early into their studies. This situation also makes it difficult to create a postgraduate community so that students can benefit from being in a group. It is difficult especially for a candidate who did not previously study in the school to find their feet. In most cases this loneliness comes about because there are usually no other students doing similar doctorate studies as most departments usually have one or two students. The student has no one to act as a sounding-board for their ideas and some supervisors do not have planned feedback sessions but instead ask candidates to drop off their work, and once they have read through it and made comments, they leave it for the student to collect. There is barely any contact between the two and therefore very limited supervision and mentoring. Training of supervisors is required so that they fully understand what is expected of them. It is hoped that the curriculum on supervision and mentorship will improve supervision in the institution. The intended purpose of the curriculum is to make supervisors aware of their roles and equip them with the skill to carry them out effectively.

3.4 Write up and submission

Once the supervisor and student feel that the work is ready the process of submission can begin. The student officially has to have a paper published in a refereed journal by the time they are submitting their work for examination, but this does not always happen. However, a published paper needs to be presented with the final thesis before the candidate can graduate. Despite this requirement, many supervisors are not aware of their role in the writing process. Aitchinson et al. (2012:440) report that those supervisors who try to assist their students to write often express "frustration, irritation and even anger over a student's writing", indicating that this is not a pleasant or easy task. The student should then submit an 'intention to submit' form at least three months before the actual submission. This is meant to allow time for examiners to be allocated. The supervisor is expected to submit a list of examiners who are ratified first by the department and then by the school. In some instances, supervisors are not aware of the requirements of the university, and this can cause delays. External examiners are not easy to find.

4. Conclusion

Castells's (1991) view of the university as an engine of development should guide universities in developing countries to think of the role their institutions should play in economic development (Mouton et al., 2019). In a brief survey of what members of the Department of Geography and Environmental Studies felt we were trying to achieve in our PhD programmes, all three members who responded stated that it was not clear what our doctoral studies were intended to achieve. When asked whether we needed to create specific programmes, all three respondents answered positively. This should be the starting point for the transformation of doctoral education in the school and the whole institution. Programmes should be aligned with research groups as well as with industry for increased relevance and for possible sponsorships. This will also help attract more students, which would make group work possible. Thereafter, training of supervisors is the next necessary step. The traditional supervisory methods practised in the school need to be revised to make them more practical and productive. All aspects of the PhD process need serious rethinking if the school is going to attract, retain and graduate doctorates who will be able to contribute positively to society and the economy.

References

Aitchison, C., Catterall, J., Ross, P., & Burgin, S. (2012). Tough love and tears: Learning doctoral writing in the sciences. *Higher Education Research & Development, 31*(4), 435–447. https://doi.org/10.1080/07294360.2011.559195

Ajayi, J. F. A., Goma, L. K. H., & Johnson, A. G. (1996). *The African experience with higher education.* Association of African Universities; James Curry.

Bastalich, W. (2017). Content and context in knowledge production: A critical review of doctoral supervision literature. *Studies in Higher Education, 42*(7), 1145–1157. https://doi.org/10.1080/03075079.2015.1079702

Benderly, L. B. (2003). Mentoring and PI productivity. In *Taken for granted: Issues perspectives, Postdoc Academic Americas.* https://doi.org/10.1126/science.caredit.a0700140

Bryan, B., & Guccione, K. (2018). Was it worth it? A qualitative exploration into graduate perceptions of doctoral value. *Higher Education Research & Development, 37*(6). https://doi.org/10.1080/07294360.2018.1479378

Cloete, N., Mouton, J., & Sheppard, C. (2015). *Doctoral education in South Africa: Policy discourse and data.* African Minds.

Cyranoski, D., Gilbert, N., Ledford, H., Nayar, A., & Yahia, M. (2011). The PhD factory. *Nature, 472,* 276–279. https://doi.org/10.1038/472276a

East, M., Bitchener, J., & Basturkmen, H. (2012). What constitutes effective feedback to postgraduate research students? The students' perspective. *Journal of University Teaching and Learning Practice, 9* (2). Available at http://ro.uow.edu.au/jutlp/vol9/iss2/7

Fraser, R., & Mathews, A. (1999). An evaluation of the desirable characteristics of a supervisor. In K. Martin, N. Stanley, & N. Davison (Eds.), *Teaching in the Disciplines/Learning in Context* (pp. 129–137). 8th Annual Teaching Learning Forum, The University of Western Australia.

Friesenhahn, I. (2014). Making higher education work for Africa: Facts and figures. Retrieved from https://www.scidev.net/global/education/feature/higher-education-africa-facts-figures.html

Gatfield, T. (2005). An investigation into PhD supervisory styles: Development of a dynamic conceptual model and its managerial implications. *Journal of Higher Education Policy and Management, 27*(3), 311–325.

Griffiths, A. W., Blakey, H., & Vardy, E. (2015). The role of supervisor and the impact of supervisory change during PhD. Retrieved from https://www.researchgate.net/publication/309487103_The_role_of_a_supervisor_and_the_impact_of_supervisory_change_during_your_PhD

Hampwaye, G., & Mweemba, L. (2020). Zambia. In Kotecha, P., Wilson-Strydom, M., & Fongwa, S. M. (Eds.), *A Profile of Higher Education in Southern Africa – Volume 2: National Perspectives* (pp. 105–114). SARUA.

Hayward, F. M., & Ncayiyana, D. J. (2014). Confronting the challenges of graduate education in Sub-Saharan Africa and prospects for the future. *International Journal of African Higher Education, 1*(1). https://doi.org/10.6017/ijahe.v1i1.5647

Hyatt, D. F. (2005). Yes, a very good point!: A critical genre analysis of a corpus of feedback commentaries on Master of Education assignments. *Teaching in Higher Education, 10*(3), 339–353.

Kashoki, M. (1994). The African university: Towards innovative management strategies for the 21st century. In *Higher education staff development.* UNESCO.

Katz, R. (2016). Challenges in doctoral research project management: A comparative study. *International Journal of Doctoral Studies, 11,* 105–125.

Keefer, J. M. (2015). Experiencing doctoral liminality as a conceptual threshold and how supervisors can use it. *Innovations in Education and Teaching International, 52*(1), 17–28. https://doi.org/10.1080/14703297.2014.981839

Knight, J. (2017). The concept and process of higher education regionalization. In J. Knight & E. T. Woldegiorgis (Eds.), *Regionalization of African Higher Education: Progress and Prospects* (pp. 11–28). Sense Publisher.

Lee, A. (2018). How can we develop supervisors for the modern doctorate? *Studies in Higher Education, 43*(5), 878–890. https://doi.org/10.1080/03075079.2018.1438116

Masaiti, G., & Mwale, N. (2017). University of Zambia: Contextualization of contribution to flagship status in Zambia. In D. Tefarra (Ed.), *Flagship universities in Africa* (pp. 467–506). Palgrave Macmillan.

Mouton, J., Boshoff, N., & James, M. (2015). A survey of doctoral supervisors in South Africa. *South African Journal of Higher Education, 29* (2), 1–22.

Nakweya, G. (2018). PhD training – Why African government funding is needed. *University World News.* Retrieved from http://www.universityworldnews.com/article.php?story=20180509132730221

Phyalto, K., Vekkaila, J., & Keskinen, J. (2015). Fit matters in the supervisory relationship: Doctoral students and supervisors' perceptions about the supervising activities. *Innovations in Education and Teaching International, 5* (1), 4–16.

Titus, S. L., & Ballou, J. M. (2013). Ensuring PhD development of responsible conduct of research behaviours: Who is responsible? *Science and Engineering Ethics.* https://doi.org/10.1007/s11948-013-9437-4

Vilkinas, T. (2005). The PhD process: The supervisor as manager. *Education and Training, 44*(3), 129–137.

Wachira, K. (2018). Higher education caught in a double bind. *University World News.* Retrieved from http://www.universityworldnews.com/article.php?story=20180328162530835

Woolston, C. (2019). PhDs: The tortuous truth. *Nature, 575*(7782), 402–406. https://doi.org/10.1038/d41586-019-03459-7

CHAPTER 12

Science doctoral students' perceptions of supervision at a Sudanese university

Ahmed Elsayed

Sudan is a country of nearly 1.9 million square kilometres, located in north-eastern Africa. In 2022 it had about 44 million inhabitants. Higher education in Sudan started in 1902 under British colonial rule. In 1951 the medical school was merged with the colleges and the combined entity was called Khartoum University College, since 1956 the University of Khartoum. By 2022 there were 29 public and 28 private higher education institutions in Sudan.

Alzaiem Alazhari University (est. 1993) comprises four campuses located in Khartoum North. It is a comprehensive university with 13 faculties, more than 18 000 students and more than 1 000 teaching and research staff members. In 2022 it had about 2 000 postgraduate students enrolled in 61 master's and 37 PhD programmes.

1. Introduction

It is well-documented that the quality of supervision has a significant impact on the learning experiences of doctoral candidates and their chances of success (Taylor et al., 2020). So, one would expect that there would be a large amount of literature about doctoral candidates' views on their supervision, which is the case in many countries in the Global North (for example Barnes & Randall, 2012; Pyhältö et al., 2015). However, literature on this topic in the African context is limited, including in the Sudanese context where this study is based. The chapter reports the results of a study on the perceptions of doctoral students of the supervision they received in the PhD in Science programme offered by Alzaiem Alazhari University (AAU) in Sudan.

My experience as a consultant clinician for three decades and an academic for the last two decades alerted me to the need to not only improve my own supervision practice, but also to contribute to the improvement of the PhD process in Sudan. The central issues are those raised by Cloete et al. (2015) on the contribution of the PhD to the knowledge economy in general and to a country's economy, and the PhD's contribution to the improvement of the quality of the university system.

Alzaiem Alazhari University (AAU), a public university in Khartoum, the capital of Sudan, was established in 1994 and currently has 17 faculties. It has an active postgraduate programme which, at the time of study in 2022, had about 2 000 students enrolled in 61 master's and 37 PhD programmes (AAU, 2022). These programmes are all based in the Faculty of Graduate Studies (FGS) of AAU where they are categorised administratively into sciences and humanities programmes. When the study was conducted, the science division had 117 doctoral students, and the humanities division had 450. The study reported here explored the perceptions and experiences of supervision of the 117 doctoral students in the sciences enrolled at AAU.

2. Literature overview

The Salzburg 1 Principles, which aimed at reforming doctoral education in Europe (European University Association, 2005), emphasise the critical role of supervision in the PhD process. Doctoral supervision is increasingly being recognised as a part of academia that merits research (Frick & Mouton, 2021). Sverdlik et al. (2018) highlight the vital role of supervision in the doctoral experience. Bastalich (2017) explains that supervision consists of the triad of the supervisor, a student, and the relationship between them. Bastalich (2017:1145) maintains that one aspect that can help to improve the quality of PhDs, is to solve what she calls the 'problem of supervision'. The resolution of this 'problem' lies in finding the best fit for the above triad as shown repeatedly in the literature by different authors (Barnes & Randall, 2012; Gatfield & Alpert, 2002; Helfer & Drew, 2019; Moxham et al., 2013, Pyhältö et al., 2015; Taylor & Beasley, 2005). For example, one suggestion given by Helfer and Drew (2019) to ensure this fit, is to appoint additional supervisors if a particular expertise is required in terms of the different models of supervision that could be followed instead of the traditional one-to-one supervision model (Lee, 2007, 2010; Kaguhangire-Barifaijo & Nkata, 2021; Olmos-López & Sunderland,

2017). Adrian et al. (2007) show that this fit encompasses a broad range of aspects, including expectations of the role of each party in the supervision process Having a memorandum of understanding (MoU) for the PhD process agreed on by the supervisor and the student which clearly sets out the roles and responsibilities of each party, builds on the literature that suggests the roles and responsibilities of each partner in the PhD process need to be carefully considered (Boud & Lee, 2007; Ives & Rowley, 2005; McCormack, 2004). Supervision involves students, and they are important as they are participants and also primarily responsible for the end product of the doctoral study.

Based on this overview of the literature, various authors emphasise the importance of PhD students' perspectives on their supervisors. Some studies found that PhD students are, in general, satisfied with the quality of their supervision (Mouton & Frick, 2019; Riaz et al., 2020), but the degree of satisfaction widely differs when different aspects of the supervision process are considered. Second, in countries such as Australia, where there are codes of practice for higher education research, students and supervisors are aware of their respective roles and responsibilities in the PhD process (Heifer & Drew, 2019). In countries where there are no codes of practice, this is not the case (Riaz et al., 2020). Third, there seem to be cultural differences in the expectations of students and supervisors, for example, students in countries such as the UK and in Australia primarily expect supervisor's expertise in their field of study and they are critical of the lack of involvement of the supervisors in the research process (Heifer & Drew, 2019; Sidhu et al., 2014). On the other hand, students in a country such as Malaysia expect a more personal involvement from the supervisor who would motivate them and boost their confidence, and they were more dependent on their supervisors in general (Sidhu et al., 2014).

Against this background, this study was conducted to assess the perspectives of doctoral students in the sciences at the AAU.

3. Background and methodology

The aim of the study was to investigate sciences doctoral students' perceptions of supervision processes and their experiences of supervision at Alzaiem Alazhari University. Specific aims included:

1. To describe a number of the pertinent characteristics of the sciences doctoral students enrolled at AAU.
2. To assess the perceptions of these students on the division of the responsibilities of PhD processes between themselves and the supervisors.

3. To identify how these PhD students chose their supervisors.
4. To determine these students' perceptions of their supervision.
5. To consider the implications for doctoral supervision in Sudan and beyond from the data generated.

Approval for the study was obtained from the Ethics Review Committee of AAU. All sciences doctoral students in the AAU's postgraduate division were telephonically contacted. The students who agreed to participate were sent a unique study number and a link to an online questionnaire via WhatsApp or email (depending on their preference).

The questionnaire adapted that of Heifer and Drew (2019) and translated it into Arabic. The questionnaire was pilot tested by first distributing it to five AAU senior supervisors for comments and second, by asking five university staff who had recently completed their PhDs to complete it and to share their comments with the authors.

The questionnaire itself is divided into five parts as follows:

Part A contained four questions about the PhD candidates themselves, eight questions about their doctoral programme (commencement, full/part-time, financing, etc.), a question about how often they meet their supervisors, and two questions about their knowledge of research and computers, and a question about their knowledge of statistics.

Part B contained 13 questions asking the participants who they thought was responsible for different parts of the PhD process. This was the widely used instrument developed by Kiley (1998, 1999). It entailed asking the students if they perceived the responsibility for the designated role as varying between being strongly the supervisor's responsibility to joint responsibility between the supervisor and student, to strongly the student's responsibility. The responses were compared to the responses from Australian students (as discussed in Heifer & Drew, 2019).

Part C asked participants their reasons for choosing a particular supervisor(s). This was also done in the instrument used by Heifer and Drew (2019) which was adapted from Garret (2006), who adapted it from the original developed by Golde and Dore (2001). I modified these questions by asking students to select the reason for choosing their supervisor(s) instead of ranking three reasons in descending order as per the original questionnaire.

Part D asked the participants their perceptions of their supervision on a Likert scale covering 22 different aspects, 14 of these were from the composite used by Heifer and Drew (2019) and the other 8 were added by the author and 5 senior AAU staff.

Part E asked participants to rate their supervisors, whether they ever thought of changing supervisors, and lastly, whether they would recommend their supervisors to others doing a project in the supervisor's area of expertise.

This chapter reports on a small-scale study that was conducted in the Postgraduate Deanery of one university in Sudan, therefore the findings cannot be generalized. Although care was taken to anonymise the responses, the position of both the researcher and the supervisor in the studied division needs to be taken into account in terms of the respondents' willingness to participate and be forthright in their responses. This consideration was taken into account in interpreting the results.

4. Results and discussion

From the records of AAU FGS, there were 117 PhD candidates in the sciences in 2022 (see distribution by colleges in Table 1). The study was conducted during the Covid-19 lockdown period, which was followed by a major Muslim festival and holiday (Eid al- Adha), both of which encouraged the movement of the population back to their rural villages where cell phone reception is usually not good. Therefore, when students were contacted by telephone, some numbers were found to be closed (presumed temporarily off- grid), seven numbers proved to be wrong, and two candidates had no contact details on file. A total of 62 students responded (54%). Table 1 provides a summary of the study population and their faculty affiliations.

Table 1: Summary of study population and their affiliations

Faculty	Total enrolled	Responded	Not responded	Closed or not answering	Wrong number	No number
Medical Technical*	14	10	4	0	-	-
Agriculture	14	6	4	3	1	-
Radiology	11	8	2	1	-	-
Laboratory	13	6	2	3	1	1
Urbandevelopment**	16	8	3	4	1	-
Public Health	14	6	5	1	1	1

Faculty	Total enrolled	Responded	Not responded	Closed or not answering	Wrong number	No number
Computer	17	10	4	2	1	-
Engineering	18	8	1	7	2	-
	117	62	25	21	7	2

* Medical technical includes nursing, midwifery, physiotherapy, and anaesthesia.
**Urban development includes demography, women's studies, urban planning, and environmental studies

Science students formed approximately 25% of the PhD students at the AAU. All the respondents were Sudanese and 38 (61.3%) of them were female. In terms of age, more than 69% of them were more than 36 years of age (with 43.5% of the total respondents being older than 40 years). The majority (62.9%) were staff members of universities, with 12 (19.4%) working in the public sector and 10 (16.1%) working in the private sector. The majority (74.2%) were doing their PhDs part-time, with 59.7% doing more than 11 hours of other work per week. Only 19 respondents (30.6%) were financed by the Federal Ministry of Higher Education, whilst 66.1% were personally financing their PhDs. This, however, may be due to some of them being expatriates working abroad and doing their PhDs partly at a distance (a common occurrence as local staff emigrate abroad where they are better remunerated).

In the PhD process itself, 53.2% had only one supervisor and the rest had 2 supervisors. A total of 79% were doing their PhD for more than a year, so it was not surprising that 88.7% of the respondents were in the data collection phase of their studies or beyond (analysing, writing or finished and waiting for the final examination). In response to the question of whether they had any study-related problems, 32.3% of the respondents reported problems in preparing their research proposals, and 51.6% of the respondents faced problems during data collection (which may indicate that the proposal was not prepared well enough to predict problems that could arise during data collection). This latter result is interesting given that 85.5% of the respondents rated themselves as good or very good at research before starting their PhD studies.

Only 42% of the respondents met their supervisors less than once every 2 months (this result needs to be interpreted against the stage of the research process, which was not done in the study). Upon asking participants about who they thought was responsible for the different roles in the PhD process (see Table 2), and comparing this to guidelines for higher research for Australian universities and the Australian students in the study of Heifer and Drew (2019), it became clear that there is a need to explicitly establish the roles and responsibilities of each party as the students evidently did not understand what their or their supervisors' roles and responsibilities were in comparison to their Australian counterparts.

Table 2: Sudanese students' perceptions of roles and responsibilities in the PhD process compared to Australian university guidelines (values in %)

Role	Who is responsible?			AAU	Aust. univs	Aust. stdnts
	Supervisor	**Both**	**Student**			
Selection of a topic	1.6	46.8	51.6	Stud/Bot	Both	Both
Deciding theoretical framework	27.4	62.9	9.7	Both	Both	Sup/both
Research timetable	24.2	51.6	24.2	Both	Stud	Std/both
Introduction to university facilities	45.2	30.6	24.2	Sup/both	Super	Sup
Introduction to university policies	61.3	24.2	14.5	Sup	Both	Sup
Arrange meetings	35.5	59.7	4.8	Both/sup	Both	Sup/both
Initiate communication	11.3	53.2	35.5	Both/std	Super	Sup/both
Check progress	33.9	61.3	4.8	Both/sup	Both	Sup/both
Timely finish	25.8	59.7	14.5	Both	Both	Sup/both
Supervisor sees all drafts*	46.8	45.2	8.1	Sup/both	Both	Sup
Supervisor assists in writing**	6.4	48.4	45.1	Both/std	Stud	Undetermined
Supervisor has final say***	71	24.2	4.8	Sup	Both	Sup
Emotional support****	48.4	37.1	14.5	Sup/both	Sup	Sup/both

Note: The first three columns show the results of this study, the fourth column is the summary of this study, and columns five and six are from Heifer and Drew's (2019) results.

Sup= supervisor; Stud = student

*Supervisor should see all written drafts or Student should only show supervisor if they want guidance

**Supervisor should assist in writing the thesis or it should be the responsibility of the student

***The supervisor has the final say in the standard of the thesis or the student

****Supervisor should provide emotional support or student should have their own support

In the absence of a memorandum of understanding between supervisors and candidates, Eley and Jennings (2005) argue that it is incumbent on the supervisor to meet with the candidate at the beginning of the doctorate and explain to them the different roles and responsibilities.

When asked about the reasons they chose their supervisors, 27.4% of the respondents indicated that they did not choose their supervisors themselves. The respondents who did have a choice, indicated a combination of reasons similar to both the Malaysian and UK students in the study of Sidhu et al. (2014), as 45% of the respondents in this study chose their supervisors by their reputation of being good supervisors, and 40.3% of the respondents chose their supervisors by virtue of their knowledge in the techniques and methods to be used in the research. Factors such as funding, doing interesting research projects and helping secure future jobs were of insignificant importance in the results found.

The next study objective was to ask the students about their assessment of their supervisor in different aspects of the PhD process. The results are summarised in Table 3 from the usual 5 Likert scale items were reduced to 3 categories (strongly agree and agree as positive, neutral, and strongly disagree and disagree as negative).

Table 3: Students assessment of supervisor in different roles (%)

Role	Positive	Neutral	Negative
Available when needed	84.1	11.1	4.8
Friendly	85.7	11.1	3.2
Respects students	92.1	7.9	0
Respects research ethics	93.6	6.3	0
Promotes critical thinking	71.4	27	1.6
Promotes good manners	87.3	11.1	1.6
Understands my difficulties	74.6	22.2	3.2
Provides additional relevant information	85.7	9.5	4.8
Guides topic selection	84.2	12.7	3.2
Helpful feedback	88.9	7.9	3.2
Timely feedback	76.2	19	4.8
Contributed in organisation & writing	58.7	14.3	37
Contributed in analysis* (36.5)	34.9	19	9.5
Contributed in collection of data on topic* (15.9)	31.8	33.3	19.1
Contributed in literature study* (14.3)	46	20.6	19.1
Contributed in data collection* (20.6)	27	30.2	22.3
I am happy with meetings	76.2	22.2	1.6
Encourages conference attendance	60.3	28.6	11.1
Encourages publications	65.1	27	7.9
Thinks about my goals	60.4	34.9	4.8
Motivator	66.7	31.7	1.6
Gives clear directions	87.3	11.1	1.6

Denotes that some participants had not reached this stage in the PhD process (the actual percentage of those who had not reached the stage is shown as a hyper script figure after the stage)

Taking the average satisfaction rate of the 18 out of the 22 parameters in Table 3, where there were no sizable number who had not finished that parameter, overall, sciences PhD students in AAU FGS were 78% positive about their supervisors, which is similar to what Riaz et al. (2020) found in a study done in Pakistan.

This positive level of satisfaction holds up, except in the following which are all the aspects where a negative plus a neutral response was given by more than 15% of respondents. These aspects include 'the supervisor is/does not':

1. Available when needed
2. Promote thinking
3. Understand difficulties
4. Guide topic selection
5. Provide timely feedback
6. Contribute in organisation and writing
7. Help in collecting background data about the topic or in the literature review
8. Encourage conference attendance.
9. Encourages the candidate think about their goals
10. Motivate the candidate
11. Confirm that the candidate is happy with their joint meetings

The last study objective was the students' rating of their supervisor (see Figure 1 below). The respondents were asked to subjectively rate their supervisors overall on a scale from 1 to 5, with 1 being very bad and 5 being excellent. More than half of the respondents (51.6%) rated their supervisors highly, while only 4.7% rated their supervisors a 2 out of 5, although 18.8% rated them at an equivocal 3 out of 5.

Despite the above favourable rating, 15.6% of respondents had thought of changing their supervisors at some stage, and 31.2% of the respondents

Figure 1: Rating of supervisors by their students

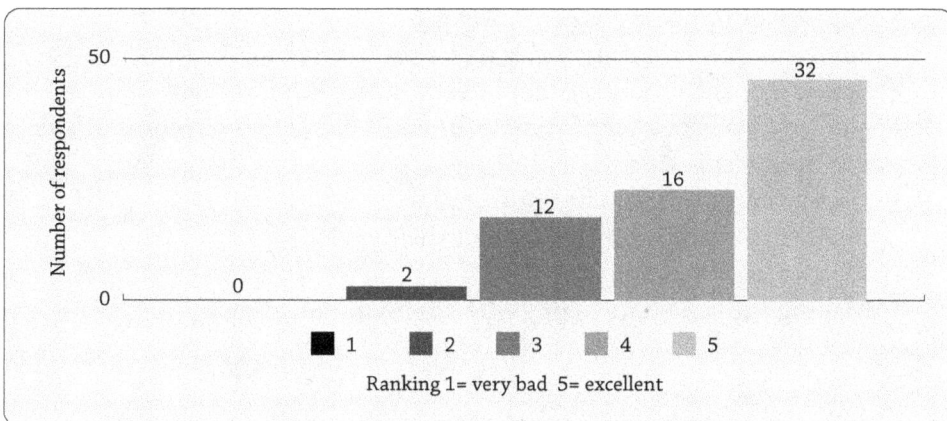

would either not recommend (10.9%) or may not recommend (20.3%) their supervisor(s) to other students pursuing research in the same field. This latter discrepancy could be explained by the fact that maybe students culturally tend not to criticize their seniors as noted before (see Elliot & Kobayashi, 2019).

5. Conclusion

This study looked at candidates doing their PhDs in the science section of the Postgraduate Deanery of Alzaiem Alazhari University. These students formed 25% of the total PhDs in the university and only 53% (62 out of 117) of them responded due to the havoc caused by the Covid-19 pandemic at the time. However, this study, being the first of its kind in the university (and most probably in the country), established a methodology and first pointers for further studies to clarify the questions it sought to answer.

The PhD candidates surveyed were mostly (61.3%) female and 69% were over 36 years of age and 63% were academic university staff. 74% were doing their PhDs part-time and 66% were self-financing. Of the PhD process itself, they shared how they encountered problems during the data collection and proposal preparation phases.

As for the respondents' opinions about their supervisors, they were generally positive but there were certain points, as mentioned in the results above, which if supported by larger studies would require remedial action. These points mostly revolve around two aspects:

1. Organisational aspects which include:
   - Availability of supervisor.
   - Supervisor guiding topic selection
   - Supervisor helping in collecting background material about the topic
   - Supervisor providing timely feedback
   - Supervisor contributing to organisation and writing
   - Supervisor encouraging candidates to attend conferences
2. Personal relations between supervisor and candidate in aspects such as:
   - Promoting thinking
   - Understanding candidates difficulties
   - Making the candidate think about their goals
   - Motivating the candidate
   - Making the candidate happy with their joint meetings

Many of the abovementioned points would need further study in bigger samples from more universities around the country to see if they are consistent and, if so, remedial action of some kind would need to be taken as mentioned in the recommendations below.

6. Recommendations

Some preliminary recommendations from this study:

- A compulsory memorandum of understanding (MoU) between supervisors and students must be introduced, which is to be implemented by the FGS administration. The MoU should contain all the points mentioned under 'organisational aspects' in the discussion above. This would ensure a clear delineation of the roles and responsibilities of the supervisors and candidates.
- Perceived deficiencies in organisation, literature study, data collection, analysis, and writing can be partly rectified by better training for supervisors as implemented in Australian universities (Kiley, 2011) by using techniques such as writing camps and group seminars.
- Encouraging supervisors to have regular meetings with their candidates and to ensure that they take care of the points mentioned under 'personal' in the conclusions above so that they cater for such things as motivating the candidates more and encouraging them to think about their medium- and long-term goals.
- The deficient areas in supervision in promoting thinking and understanding in students can be remedied by introducing courses for supervisors on supervisor–student relationships, as suggested by Kiley (2011). However, from my personal experience, mentoring students requires a lot of local cultural context, and before such courses are introduced, a lot of local research first has to be done to assess whether it could work.

References

Alzaiem Alazhari University (AAU). (2022). *Statistics*. Retrieved 31 May 2023, from http://aau.edu.sd/about/statistics/statistics

Adrian-Taylor, S. S., Noels, K. A., & Tischler, K. (2007). Conflict between international graduate students and faculty supervisors: Towards effective conflict prevention and management strategies. *Journal of Studies in International Education, 11*(2), 90–117. https://doi.org/10.1177/1028315306293532

Bastalich, W. (2017). Content and context in knowledge production: A critical review of doctoral supervision literature. *Studies in Higher Education, 42*(7), 1145–1157. https://doi.org/10.1080/03075079.2015.1079702

Barnes, B. J., & Randall, J. (2012). Doctoral student satisfaction: An examination of disciplinary, enrolment, and institutional differences. *Research in Higher Education, 53*(1), 47–75. https://doi.org/10.1007/s11162-011-9225-4

Boud, D., & Lee, A. (2005). 'Peer learning' as pedagogic discourse for research education. *Studies in Higher Education, 30*(5), 501–516. https://doi.org/10.1080/03075070500249138

Cloete, N., Mouton, J., & Sheppard, C. (2015). *Doctoral education in South Africa – Policy, discourse and data.* Cape Town: African Minds.

European University Association. (2005). *Salzburg 2005: Conclusions and recommendations.* Retrieved on 11 January 2023, from https://eua.eu/resources/publications/626:salzburg-2005-%E2%80%93-conclusions-and-recommendations.html

Eley, A., & Jennings, R. (2005). *Effective postgraduate supervision: Improving the student/supervisor relationship.* Berkshire: McGraw-Hill Press.

Elliot, D. L., & Kobayashi, S. (2019). How can PhD supervisors play a role in bridging academic cultures? *Teaching in Higher Education, 24*(8), 911–929. https://doi.org/10.1080/13562517.2018.1517737

Frick, B. L., & Mouton, J. (2021). Doctoral education as a field of global scholarship – An analysis of published research (2005–2017). In P. Rule, E. M. Bitzer, & B. L. Frick (Eds.), *The global scholar: Implications for postgraduate studies and supervision* (pp. 45–67). Stellenbosch: African Sun Media.

Garrett, R. U. (2006). *The quality of the doctoral experience in education at historically Black colleges and universities* (Doctoral dissertation). University of North Texas.

Gatfield, T. J., & Alpert, F. (2002). The supervisory management styles model. In *Proceedings of the 2002 Annual International Conference of HERDSA* (pp. 1–12). Perth, Australia.

Golde, C. M., & Dore, T. M. (2001). *At cross purposes: What the experiences of today's doctoral students reveal about doctoral education.* Philadelphia, PA: Pew Charitable Trusts. Retrieved from https://files.eric.ed.gov/fulltext/ED450628.pdf

Griffith University. (2019). *Code of practice for higher degree research candidates.* Retrieved on 8 August 2020, from https://policies.griffith.edu.au/pdf/Code%20of%20Practice%20for%20the%20Supervision%20of%20HDR%20Candidates.pdf

Helfer, F., & Drew, S. (2019). Students' perceptions of doctoral supervision: A study in an engineering program in Australia. *International Journal of Doctoral Studies, 14*, 499–524. https://doi.org/10.28945/4383

Ives, G., & Rowley, G. (2005). Supervisor selection or allocation and continuity of supervision: PhD students' progress and outcomes. *Studies in Higher Education, 30*(5), 535–555. https://doi.org/10.1080/03075070500249161

Kaguhangire-Barifaijo, M., & Nkata, J. L. (2021). A paradox in the supervision of doctoral candidates in Ugandan higher education institutions (HEIs). *International Journal of Educational Administration and Policy Studies, 13*(2), 76–84. https://doi.org/10.5897/IJEAPS2021.0689

Kiley, M. (1998). Expectations in a cross-cultural postgraduate experience. In *Proceedings of the 1998 Conference on Quality in Postgraduate Research: Managing the New Agenda* (pp. 189–202). Adelaide, Australia. Retrieved on 10 August 2020, from http://www.qpr.edu.au/Proceedings/QPR_Proceedings_1998.pdf

Kiley, M. (1999). *Expectations and experiences of Indonesian postgraduate students studying in Australia: A longitudinal study* (Doctoral dissertation). The University of Adelaide. Retrieved on 10 August 2020, from https://digital.library.adelaide.edu.au/dspace/bitstream/2440/19424/2/02whole.pdf

Lee, A. M. (2007). Developing effective supervisors: Concepts of research supervision. *South African Journal of Higher Education, 21*(4), 680–693.

Lee, A. (2010). New approaches to doctoral supervision: Implications for educational development. *Educational Developments, 11*(2), 18–23.

McCormack, C. (2004). Tensions between student and institutional conceptions of postgraduate research. *Studies in Higher Education, 29*(3), 319–334. https://doi.org/10.1080/03075070410001682559

Moxham, L., Dwyer, T., & Reid-Searl, K. (2013). Articulating expectations for PhD candidature upon commencement: Ensuring supervisor/student 'best fit'. *Journal of Higher Education Policy and Management, 35*(4), 345–354. https://doi.org/10.1080/1360080X.2013.812029

Name. (2022). Personal communication by the Dean of the Faculty of Graduate Studies to the author.

Olmos-López, P., & Sunderland, J. (2017). Doctoral supervisors' and supervisees' responses to co-supervision. *Journal of Further and Higher Education, 41*(6), 727–740. https://doi.org/10.1080/030987 7X.2016.1188902

Pyhältö, K., Vekkaila, J., & Keskinen, J. (2015). Fit matters in the supervisory relationship: Doctoral students' and supervisors' perceptions about supervisory activities. *Innovations in Education and Teaching International, 52*(1), 4–16. https://doi.org/10.1080/14703297.2014.981839

Riaz, M., Ashraf, M. N., & Butt, M. A. (2020). Research guidance experiences, expectations, and perceived learning outcomes of university students in Pakistan. *Pakistan Social Sciences Review, 4*(2), 436–448.

Sidhu, G. K., Kaur, S., Fook, C. Y., & Yunus, F. W. (2014). Postgraduate supervision: Comparing student perspectives from Malaysia and the United Kingdom. *Procedia - Social and Behavioral Sciences, 123*, 151–159. https://doi.org/10.1016/j.sbspro.2014.01.1419

Sverdlik, A., Hall, N. C., McAlpine, L., & Hubbard, K. (2018). The Ph.D. experience: A review of the factors influencing doctoral students' completion, achievement, and well-being. *International Journal of Doctoral Studies, 13*, 361–388. https://doi.org/10.28945/4113

Taylor, S., & Beasley, N. (2005). *A handbook for doctoral supervisors*. Oxford: Routledge.

Taylor, S., Kiley, M., & Holley, K. A. (Eds.). (2020). *The making of doctoral supervisors: International case studies of practice*. Routledge.

Wendy, B. (2017). Content and context in knowledge production: A critical review of doctoral supervision literature. *Studies in Higher Education, 42*(7), 1145–1157. https://doi.org/10.1080/03075079.2015. 1079702

Supervisory practices in the School of Therapeutic Sciences of the University of the Witwatersrand

Ané Orchard

South Africa has a population of 62 million. The country has 26 public universities with a total enrolment of 1.1 million students. Doctoral enrolments in South Africa have increased from 9 994 in 2008 to 23 588 in 2020 (CHE Vitalstats). Between 2000 and 2018, a total of 32 025 doctoral students graduated at South African universities. Doctoral graduates increased from 972 in 2000 to 3 339 in 2019 (SciSTIP Tracer Study).

The **University of the Witwatersrand** (Wits) is located on five campuses in Johannesburg. It became an independent university in 1922, tracing its origins to the South African School of Mines established in 1896. Wits has produced four Nobel Prize recipients, including Nelson Mandela who was a law student at Wits from 1947-1949. The university has five faculties and 33 schools offering over 3 000 courses. In 2021 it had 1 174 full-time academic staff members and 42 175 students, including 2 470 doctoral candidates.

1. Introduction

Supervisors are mentors and critical mediators for postgraduate (PG) candidates (Kamler, 2008; Maxwell & Smyth, 2011). However, the supervision journey may often be a challenging, lonely, uncertain and overwhelming one (Green, 2005; Wisker et al., 2007; Friedrich-Nel & Mackinnon, 2013; Cornér et al., 2019). Various publications exist on recommendations for what is expected of postgraduate candidates, the postgraduate degree experience, the different stages a postgraduate candidate undergoes, and the support that supervisors can offer their candidates (Vilkinas, 2002; Aitchison et al., 2012; Bruce & Stoodley, 2013; Pyhältö et al., 2015). However, there is not as much done to help novice supervisors deal with their own internal journey of challenges and uncertainty they may experience, or when they could achieve a level of confidence of more experienced supervisors (Green, 2005; Friedrich-Nel & Mackinnon, 2013; Cornér et al., 2019). Is a postgraduate degree a sufficient requirement for 'qualifying' to supervise a postgraduate? Especially considering that supervision of postgraduate candidates is accepted as a specialized skill (Chikte & Chabilall, 2016), when is one ready to be called a specialist in supervision? Is it the experience or a qualification that helps define this specialty? Does the experience or qualification affect one's style of supervision?

There are various styles (the way one chooses to interact with the candidate during supervision) and models (master–apprentice, co-supervision, team supervision, project supervision) of supervision (Bitzer & Albertyn, 2011; Grossman & Crowther, 2015). The supervision style and model can impact on the supervisor's experience, goals, expectations, and workload (Bruce & Stoodley, 2013), which can translate into the experience and mentoring the postgraduate candidate receives (Bruce & Stoodley, 2013). Based on my readings, supervisors seem to take on multiple roles. They must be able to motivate their candidates, demonstrate empathy and understanding, and establish clear boundaries regarding their supportive capabilities, and at the same time, they are expected to serve as guides and mentors, offering timely and ongoing feedback (Chikte & Chabilall, 2016). It is no wonder the journey is overwhelming.

At the start of 2020, I was feeling quite uncertain about my ability to supervise postgraduate candidates. I had observed many fellow researchers/supervisors, and they appeared so capable and confident. When did they become so confident? At the time of writing this chapter (2021), my experience was mainly around supervising Honours research projects, and co-supervising master's, which appears to be a popular route for novice supervisors to undertake (Grossman & Crowther, 2015). However, I had hoped that with time I would become more comfortable and experienced by observing the supervisory practices of my colleagues and drawing from the supervision I had received, and I would inevitably be ready to supervise on my own. As a novice supervisor I had so much uncertainty and wondered if it was normal, thus I sought to ask the School of Therapeutic Sciences to answer a few of my own questions.

2. Rationale

In this study, I wanted to determine the supervision styles and models prevalent in the School of Therapeutic Sciences and how those that supervise have come to supervise the way they do.

As a novice supervisor myself, I have found that there is a lot of uncertainty and feelings of unpreparedness (Vereijken et al., 2018) and my mind has been plagued with questions such as 'Will I figure out how to be comfortable in my supervision? Should I work in a team or co-supervise? Should I attend more courses?' It is beneficial for a novice to be supported and to explore these different approaches and develop their own supervisory pedagogy (Vereijken et al., 2018). Thus, this study was designed for me to explore the different options, and from these findings I could further reflect on what I have learned and decide on how best to advance with my own supervision.

3. Research question

What influences supervision knowledge and practice at the School of Therapeutic Sciences?

4. Aim

I aimed to survey the active postgraduate supervisors in the School of Therapeutic Sciences (part of the Faculty of Health Sciences at the University of the Witwatersrand) on their supervisory practices and readiness to supervise.

5. Objectives

To achieve my aim, the following objectives were set:

5.1. To compare the supervisory experience of the participants in the School of Therapeutic Sciences with their readiness/confidence to supervise.
5.2. To investigate the supervisory practices of the participants and compare this to the training received and experience.

6. Study design

Data collection was through a self-administered cross-sectional survey. The survey was designed by myself based on observations I had made from my own PG supervision and the courses I had attended. The survey was pilot tested by three colleagues before being distributed. The survey, consisting of 30 fields, was sent out via email to the School of Therapeutic Sciences and was available for a week.

7. Study site

The study was carried out at the University of the Witwatersrand, School of Therapeutic Sciences.

8. Study sample

A convenience sampling method was employed for the active postgraduate supervisors in the School of Therapeutic Sciences. The School of Therapeutic Sciences contains 382 members consisting of technicians, secretaries, lab assistants, support staff, lecturers, senior lecturers, associated professors and personal professors, and post-docs. Thus, not everyone on the available list of emails qualified as a potential supervisor, and not all lecturers supervise. Thus, I am unable to calculate the response rate. Reminders were sent three times.

9. Methods

The School of Therapeutic Sciences was asked via email to participate in the survey and complete the questionnaire. The email provided information about the study, a consent statement, and a link to an anonymous survey on REDCAP©. The survey incorporated both qualitative and quantitative questions. For questions where participants selected 'other', branched logic was incorporated.

Inclusion criteria:

- Only active postgraduate supervisors with a master's or PhD degree.
- Only active postgraduate supervisors of master's and PhD candidates were included (master's supervisors were included due to an expected small sample size due to size of the school).

Exclusion criteria:

- Supervisors that were not actively supervising.
- Lecturers that were not yet supervising. (A stop order was included in the survey for those that were not supervising).

10. Data analysis

The questionnaire was analysed using descriptive statistics. The t-test (comparison continuous and categorical variables) and p-value were calculated. The data were expressed as percentages in pie charts and bar graphs.

11. Results and discussion

Thirty-one (31) respondents participated in the survey, 2 were excluded by the stop order as they were not actively supervising. Thus, 29 participants were able to complete the survey.

11.1 Section A: Demographics

The first part of the survey contained demographic information related to rank and supervision of the participants. The participants were asked to select their levels as a lecturer (rank) and their highest degree. The majority of respondents were junior lecturers, followed by senior lecturers, and the smallest groups were the associated and personal professors. Each of the professors had a PhD, 19% of the junior lecturers had a PhD (and 19% were in the process of obtaining a PhD), and 75% of the senior lecturers had a PhD.

The years of experience between the ranks were reviewed and as can be expected, the professors had the highest number of years of experience, with the maximum being 25 years. The lowest number of years for postgraduate supervision experience was amongst the junior lecturers. All the associated and personal professors from the survey had supervised more than 20 PG candidates and were supervising both master's and PhD candidates. Based on the years of experience between the two, there is a p-value of 0.69, indicating no significant difference between the years of experience.

The years of experience between those classified junior lecturers and seniors has a p-value of 0.012, which indicates a statistical significance in the difference in years of experience. The p-value between the associated professors and senior lecturers is 0.399, which is not a statistically significant difference. Reasons may be attributed to the outliers in terms of years of supervision amongst the senior lecturer group and the professor groups. This was an interesting observation for me as I expected that all senior lecturers would have already been PhD holders. It was also interesting for me to notice an associate professor with 9 years of experience, although it is normal to on average reach a professorship in 10 years (UCT Newsroom, 2016). I was curious about the supervision model of this participant and saw that this participant preferred working in a team. There were quite a few supervisors with more years of experience, however, who were still senior lecturers, which highlights to me that there is a lot that may be gained from working in a team. It appears there is more opportunity for exposure to supervising PG candidates.

Because experience based on lecturer rank was not statistically significant, comparison was then done based on the number of PG candidates that had been supervised by the participants with the years of experience, and more statistically different p-values were calculated. Based on these statistics, from this group of participants, experience is better defined by number of PG candidates supervised, as opposed to the participant's rank. What I can then draw from these findings is that the years of supervision and number of PG candidates supervised is what contributes towards experience, despite one's ranking within the university.

11.2 Section B: Training, confidence, and readiness

Section B of the questionnaire focused on identifying how the participants came to supervise as they do (Figure 1) and their readiness for supervision. Participants were grouped according to the amount of PG candidates they had supervised/experience.

It is evident that the majority (20 participants) came to supervise as they do based on how they were supervised as postgraduate candidates. This is closely followed by observing how a colleague supervises. Interpretivist ontology conceives of our knowledge and meaning as constructed through social interaction (Vanson, 2014). Vygotskian thinking emphasises social involvement via communication, regarding social interactions and relationships between an individual with more knowledge and an individual with less knowledge as what constructs knowledge (Packer & Goicoechea, 2000; Lantolf & Poehner, 2008). The results presented in Figure 1, participants learning from their own supervisor, colleagues and training courses, would appear to support the interpretation that participants learned most of what they know through social learning.

Figure 1: Summary of how participants came to supervise as they do

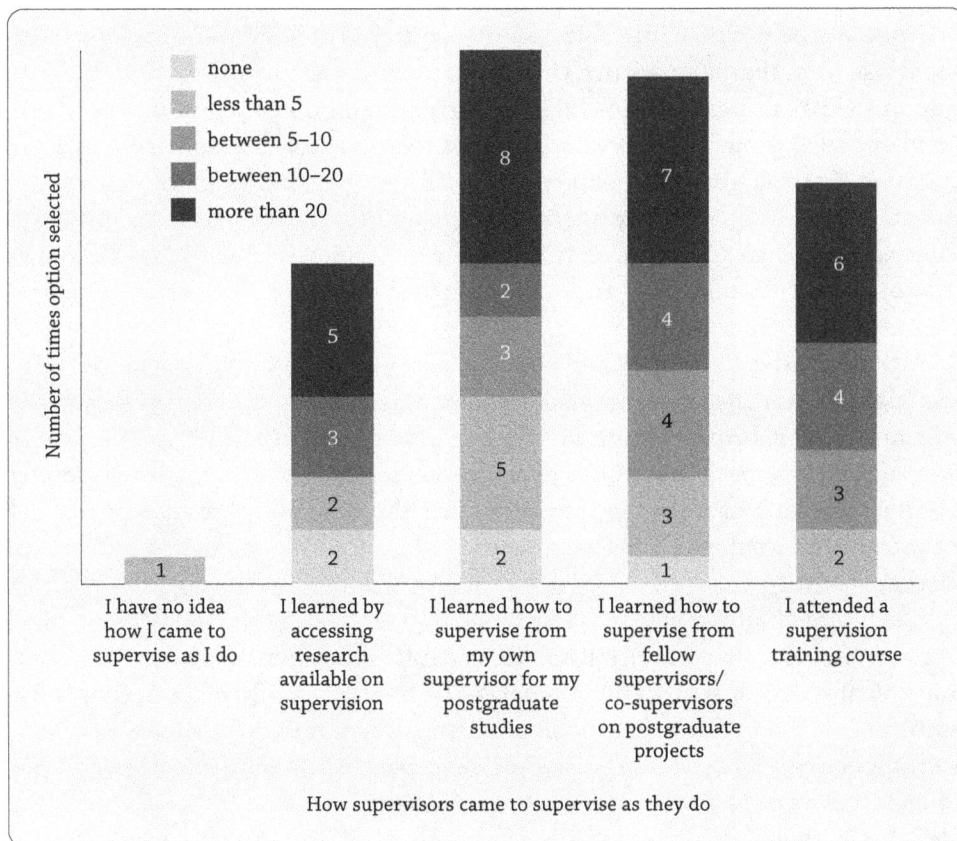

While a formal qualification for supervision is not required at my university to be eligible to supervise, training opportunities are available, such as in-house workshops or online certification courses for supervisors. The most attended training course was the Wits Centre of Learning and Teaching Development (CLTD) course, followed by the Faculty of Health Sciences course. This is a three-day course I had attended in 2018. It would appear that supervisors are more willing to attend an 'in-house' course than one offered by another university, according to my study.

The next question asked the participants to select the option that would best describe their readiness/confidence to supervise postgraduate candidates. The responses were compared to years of experience, the number of postgraduate candidates supervised and if a course had been attended (Figure 2). Two groups emerged, those newer to supervising (thus with 5 years or less of experience), and those with more than 5 years of experience.

None of the participants selected the option that they were 'not' ready to supervise. For the participants that are new to supervision, there is a variation in their readiness and confidence, with no relation to years of experience, number of PG projects supervised, and no relation to a course they may have attended. For the group of participants with more than 5 years of experience, the majority (89%) were confident in their ability to supervise, and 11% felt they were ready to supervise as first supervisor. Thus, it predominantly shows that confidence comes with an increase in years of experience and number of PG candidates supervised.

A finding that did not make sense to me is that several participants with less than 5 years of experience and had not attended any course had some level of confidence. It brings to mind the quote often attributed to Mark Twain *"To succeed in life, you need two things: ignorance and confidence"* and made me wonder whether the lack of a course may allow for the blissful ignorance of not yet knowing what we don't know, leading to confidence. An interesting subject for further study.

Readiness of all participants was compared to the way the participant came to supervise, and no correlation could be identified. When comparing the readiness of the participants to their supervision model, it could be seen that those with confidence in their supervision abilities predominantly supervised with a co-supervisor. This finding was not surprising to me, as supervising with co-supervisors or as a team appears to have many benefits (Hyrkäs et al., 2002; McCallin & Nayar, 2012), especially considering that it provides an opportunity for supervisors to learn from each other, address challenges together, increases confidence and strengthens one's own professional identity (Hyrkäs et al., 2002).

Overall, section B addressed my first objective. Readiness and confidence appear to mostly be related to experience in years, number of postgraduate candidates supervised, and supervising with peers. My advice to novice supervisors is to not be too hard on themselves. That confidence will come with time and experience, and working with a co-supervisor or in a team may be beneficial to their growth in confidence. Taking part in supervision courses can also help with confidence.

Figure 2: Readiness of participants for supervising PG candidates

Less than and equal to 5 years of supervision experience			
Years of supervision experience	No. of PG projects supervised	Postgraduate supervision course	Readiness for supervision
0	None		I am confident in my ability to supervise postgraduate students
0	None		I feel I may be ready to supervise postgraduate students as first supervisor
1	Less than 5		I am confident in my ability to supervise postgraduate students
1	Less than 5		I feel I may be ready to supervise postgraduate students as first supervisor
2	Less than 5		
2	Less than 5		I do not feel ready to supervise postgraduate students as first supervisor
3	Less than 5	CLTD*	
4	Less than 5		
4	Between 5-10	CLTD	I am confident in my ability to supervise postgraduate students
5	Less than 5	CLTD	
5	Between 5-10		I feel I may be ready to supervise postgraduate students as first supervisor

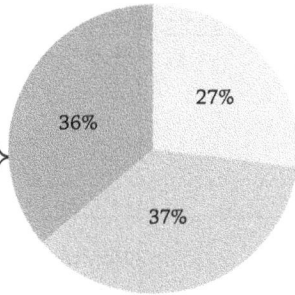

Readiness/confidence of supervisors with 5 or less years of experience

27%

36%

37%

(continued on next page)

Figure 2: (continued)

More than 5 years of supervision experience			
Years of supervision experience	No. of PG projects supervised	Postgraduate supervision course	Readiness for supervision
7	Between 5-10	CLTD	I am confident in my ability to supervise postgraduate students
8	Between 5-10	DIES/ CREST	
8	Between 10-20	CLTD and FHS	
9	Between 5-10		
9	More than 20	FHS	
9	More than 20	FHS	
10	Between 10-20	CLTD	
10	Between 10-20		
12	Between 10-20	FHS	
12	More than 20	CLTD and FHS	
13	More than 20		
14	More than 20	CLTD	
15	More than 20		I feel I may be ready to supervise postgraduate students as first supervisor
16	Between 10-20	FHS	I am confident in my ability to supervise postgraduate students
20	More than 20	Facilitator from Stellenbosch university	
20	More than 20		I feel I may be ready to supervise postgraduate students as first supervisor
20	More than 20	CLTD	I am confident in my ability to supervise postgraduate students
25	More than 20		

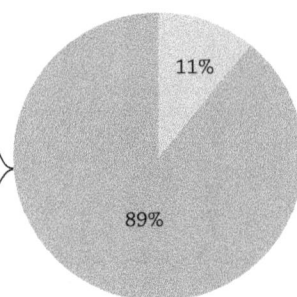

11%

89%

Readiness/confidence of supervisors with more than 5 years of experience

CLTD – Centre for Learning and Teaching Development Postgraduate Supervision Course (Wits), FHS – Faculty of Health Sciences Postgraduate Supervision Course (Wits)

11.3 Section C: Supervision style

For this section, I aimed to investigate the supervision model of the participants. Co- supervision is preferred by 65% of participants. For their reasons for choosing their supervision model of preference, the data were grouped according to descriptions most suited to the participant's reason to provide a summary.

There is no supervision model gold standard, and if one delves into the reasons given by the participants, their reasons for choosing their preferred model are idiosyncratic (Hyrkäs et al., 2002; McCallin & Nayar, 2012), just as different supervisors have their own views on what it is to be a supervisor, and what they want out of supervision (Pearson & Brew, 2002; Bruce & Stoodley, 2013), they also know with whom they would want to supervise.

From this study and readings (McCallin & Nayar, 2012), I am personally quite keen on the co-supervision and team model of supervision as it does come with the benefit of different perspectives, strengths and learning from each other, offers more support, and assists with the workload and responsibilities. To avoid encountering the issues mentioned by those that preferred supervising alone (delayed input from other supervisors, being excluded, blurred roles), I would consider drawing up a screening document for prospective co-supervisors, to assess their ability to contribute to the community of practice. Another thing to consider though is not making the mistake of including a co-supervisor out of friendliness and familiarity in the office. I had experienced a friendly colleague that came across as being a potentially beneficial co-supervisor for an Honours project. Unfortunately, the colleague's contribution was painfully lacking, and I would not consider co-supervision with this colleague again. However, if I reflect on this, I cannot consider the experience as a waste of a project and time considering it was completed within a year. It was a small price to pay for learning the lesson of not professionally trusting a colleague based on being familiar in the workplace. Thus, I would recommend including a potential co-supervisor in smaller projects first as a trial run. It definitely comes down a lot to trust with team members (Robertson, 2017), and I value being conscious of the downsides and the screening of potential co-supervisors. So, to avoid future issues, a screening document and supervisor agreement form specifying responsibilities and duties will be used going forward.

My next question regarded supervision style which included determining whether supervisors encouraged their postgraduate candidates to work in teams, how often the supervisors provided feedback, when writing was encouraged, methods of providing feedback and how participants provided advice to their candidates on their writing/concept. I also wanted to find out whether participants provided advice on time-management, scientific writing skills, and grammar. Lastly, participants' views on these subjects were compared to the participant's supervision model, highest degree, supervision experience (years and number of candidates), and how they came to their supervision practice. No trends could be identified.

Based on my findings, 76% of participants encouraged their candidates to work together, and fostered a sense of community. This provides candidates with the opportunity to support each other, bounce ideas off each other and give each other different perspectives. It also allows the candidates opportunities to discuss different concepts with each other in a way they are unable to do with their supervisors (McKenna, 2017). This is something I would encourage amongst my candidates. I experienced this when I was doing my master's and found it beneficial. I lacked this opportunity during my PhD study as I was the only candidate at the time.

Considering that learning only happens as we write (Boser, 2020), it would be best to encourage writing in the process of study, which thankfully 100% of the participants encouraged of their postgraduate candidates. On one of the supervision courses I had attended, the concept of the internal conversation was brought to my consciousness: while we write, we may often have a conversation with ourselves where we anticipate objections and calls for greater clarity. I was initially oblivious to the fact that I had done this, however, thinking back to my PhD and any publication I write, that internal conversation was/ is there! 'If I say this, would Prof. be fine with this?', 'Would this make sense to an external reviewer?', 'Oh, Prof. will probably ask me to elaborate on this point, so I had better do it now.' Writing encourages that internal conversation in the candidate. The sooner we can encourage our candidates to start writing and we provide feedback, the earlier they can be sensitized into considering the audience they are writing for as they write. The sooner the candidates work to 'answer' those internal voice question and conversations, redrafting may improve.

I found incorporating feedback using Socratic questioning (Frick et al., 2010) an extremely beneficial approach that I had learned in one of my courses. I had a conversation with one of my candidates where she was telling me how she was anticipating my questions, and how she was trying to answer them before submitting her draft. Thus, Socratic questioning seemed to also encourage the internal conversation. Early writing and timely feedback on drafts is encouraged (Postgrad.com, n.d.; Lee 2008)

The frequency of meetings and feedback may vary from taking place daily to once every six months and contributes towards the success of the candidate–supervisor relationship, which further promotes student resilience and satisfaction (Lee, 2008; Pyhältö et al., 2015; Cornér et al., 2017). In the School of Therapeutic Sciences, monthly meetings appeared to be the preferred frequency (Figure 3). A monthly meeting does seem a reasonable time for progress to be made by the candidate and allows the supervisor time to review the candidates submissions.

Figure 3: Frequency of feedback and meeting with postgraduate candidates, and reasons

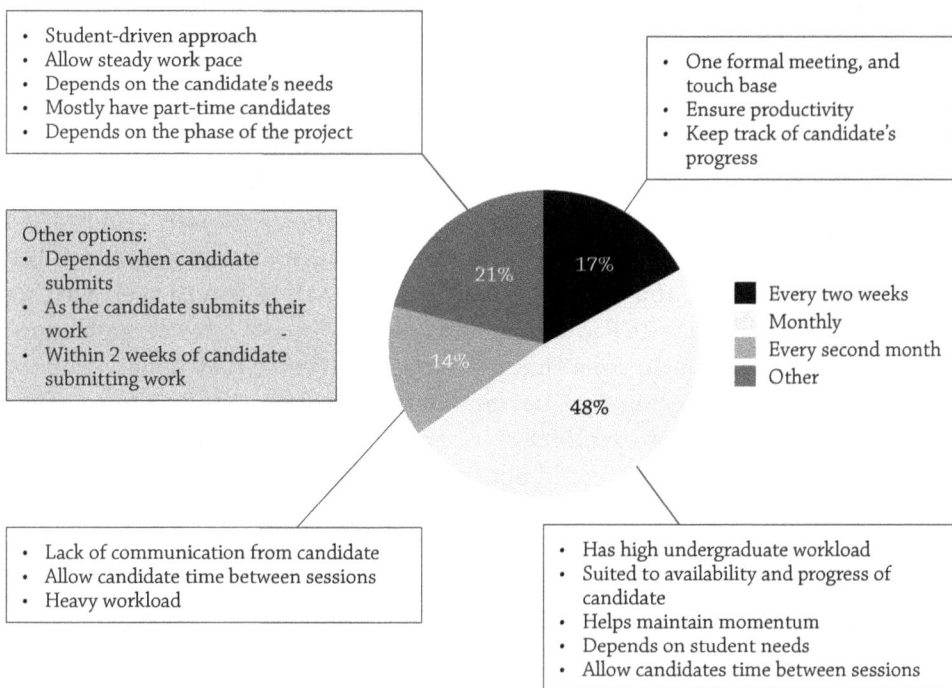

From my findings, it was evident that track changes and comments on the submitted draft, with a meeting to discuss the feedback, is the most practised form for providing feedback amongst the participants. No participant selected the options for: 'the candidate is told to rewrite the section (chapter/paragraph)' or 'face-to-face/online meetings only'. It's good to see that constructive feedback is the main method of feedback, and clearly tools such as track changes make this more possible.

Guidance on time management came through as something the majority of participants did, aligning with calls for supervisors to incorporate project management into their supervision practice (Vilkinas, 2002; Gatfield, 2005; Lee, 2008). Participants also predominantly guided their students in their scientific writing style. This is in line with 'good' supervisor practice which means involvement in the postgraduate candidate's scholarly writing (Gatfield, 2005; Lee, 2008; Hemer, 2012; Lee, 2018).

During a course I attended on postgraduate supervision, I was aback to learn that correcting candidate grammar is not encouraged. As a postgraduate candidate detailed attention was devoted to my grammar, thus I found this very difficult to accept. And it turns out 90% of the participants at the School of Therapeutic Sciences addressed grammar (Figure 4). A potential reason behind not correcting grammar is that it takes a lot of time. Even the student–supervisor agreement contract by the university stipulates that supervisors are not required to correct grammar. Having a history of research in the laboratory as I do, what I learned from my supervision was that grammar could be an indicator of attention to detail. Thus, poor grammar reflects badly on attention to detail in the lab. This is what was drilled into me as a postgraduate. Perhaps, it's only coincidence or confirmation bias, but I have noticed the negligence in the lab of a few candidates and students that do not pay attention to their writing grammar. I am still a novice supervisor and probably do not have enough exposure to draw strong conclusions that grammar negligence may equate to poor data collection. Considering that postgraduate candidates are becoming more diverse, having a student excellent at research in the laboratory but weaker on grammar, and vice versa, would not be unheard of. This would make for an interesting study.

The topic of grammar correcting has me conflicted, and I can only conclude that I need to find a balance. Going forward, I think my focus on grammar correcting should be in the beginning of the candidates writing process. When I would explain to the candidate why some attention needs to be given to grammar (adult learning theory states adults need to know the reason for doing something (Taylor & Hamdy 2013)), then do less editing the more they write. Emphasis can be placed on the importance of grammar in the beginning, then supervisors can refer students to grammar checkers or suggest that they have their work edited. The participants do at times also refer candidates for language editing or a library writing course, to an editor, or lend the candidate other resources. It is something that should be corrected and focused on by the candidate for their own growth in attention to detail. It should not affect the supervisor long term.

Figure 4: Whether participants provide feedback on the candidate's grammar and reasons

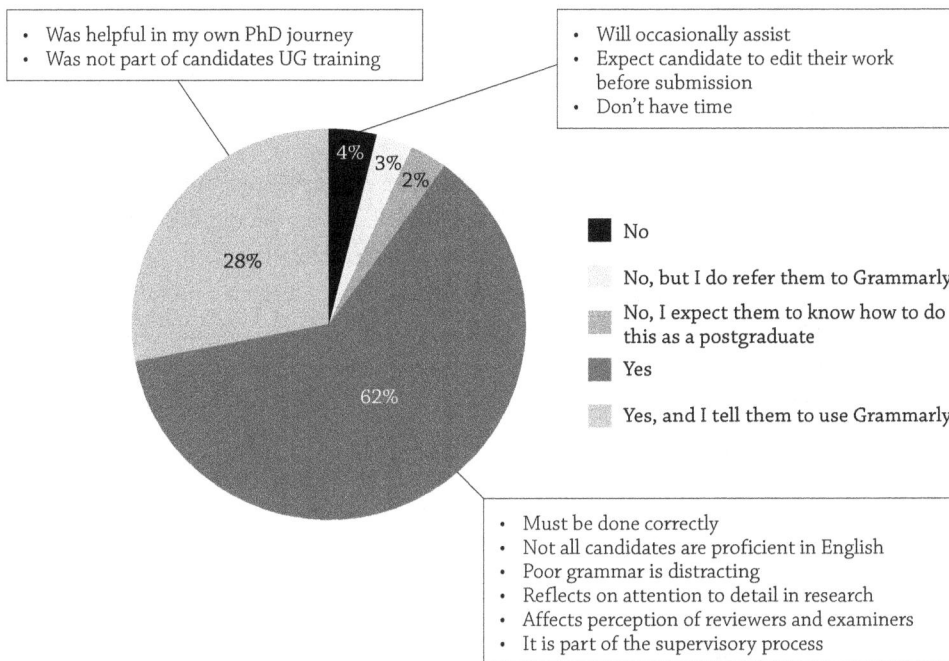

- Was helpful in my own PhD journey
- Was not part of candidates UG training

- Will occasionally assist
- Expect candidate to edit their work before submission
- Don't have time

- No
- No, but I do refer them to Grammarly
- No, I expect them to know how to do this as a postgraduate
- Yes
- Yes, and I tell them to use Grammarly

- Must be done correctly
- Not all candidates are proficient in English
- Poor grammar is distracting
- Reflects on attention to detail in research
- Affects perception of reviewers and examiners
- It is part of the supervisory process

For this section, supervision style was compared to the participant's supervision models, highest degree, supervision experience (years and number of candidates), and how they came to their supervision practice. No trends were identified.

Overall, section C addresses my second objective. Supervisory style of the participants was investigated and compared to supervisor model preference, experience and how they came to their supervision practice. Neither training, model, nor experience influence the supervisory style, and it came down to each participants' preference. This aligns with social theory which states that learning is constructed and occurs individually and collectively (Dee et al., 2006).

Limitations

This study may not be generalizable across the school and the university due to the number of people that responded. The time the survey was available may have also been too short.

After analysis of the results, there were a few questions I could have added, and for demographics I should have added the question of how long since participants had completed their PhD. I could not include age or sex of participants in my demographics as it would made identifying some of the participants possible.

12. Conclusion

To answer my research question (What influences supervision knowledge and practice at the School of Therapeutic Sciences?), I did a survey to explore supervision styles, readiness and confidence and compared them to experience in supervision. I learned that confidence is something that comes with years of experience and with the more postgraduate candidates one supervises. I am no longer as intimidated by the prospect of supervision as I was before. Readiness and confidence will come with experience, and I don't need to already be a specialist in supervision from the very start.

I have learned that we don't have to be lonely in the supervisory experience. I think these findings helped me with my own uncertainty about supervision. It is such a scary thing. And now being aware of the benefits of co-supervision and teams, I find I am not as scared. I have been co-supervising the last two years with two colleagues, as an opportunity to learn and be able to supervise on my own one day. Before, I had not realised I could approach other colleagues and have them supervise with me as a team. I can feel the mental confidence shift within myself that I am now not as reluctant to take on postgraduate candidates as first supervisor. I accept that I don't have to know everything, that my co-supervisor may know what I do not, and/or that we shall at least have company in figuring it out.

It is comforting to learn that no supervisor knows everything, that we do sometimes go beyond our own sphere of expertise, and that is ok. It is why we co-supervise or turn to each other for advice. Course attendance can positively influence confidence levels. Most supervisory styles are developed based on social learning, and each supervisor adopts their own preferences for how to supervise candidates.

Acknowledgements

I would like to acknowledge my head of department, Professor Yahya Choonara, for his guidance in reviewing my survey. He encouraged me to survey the school as opposed to just the department and provided me with constructive feedback. This was genuinely appreciated and used.

References

Aitchison, C., Catterall, J., Ross, P., & Burgin, S. (2012). 'Tough love and tears': Learning doctoral writing in the sciences. *Higher Education Research & Development, 31*(4), 435–447. https://doi.org/10.1080/072943 60.2011.598146

Bitzer, E. M., & Albertyn, R. M. (2011). Alternative approaches to postgraduate supervision: A planning tool to facilitate supervisory processes. *South African Journal of Higher Education, 25*(5), 875–888.

Boser, U. (2020). Writing to learn and why it matters. *The Learning Agency Lab.* https://www.the-learning-agency-lab.com/the-learning-curve/learn-better-through-writing/

Bruce, C., & Stoodley, I. (2013). Experiencing higher degree research supervision as teaching. *Studies in Higher Education, 38*(2), 226–241. https://doi.org/10.1080/03075079.2011.589684

Chikte, U., & Chabilall, J. (2016). Exploration of supervisor and student experiences during master's studies in a health science faculty. *South African Journal of Higher Education, 30*(3), 57–79.

Cornér, S., Löfström, E., & Pyhältö, K. (2017). The relationship between doctoral students' perceptions of supervision and burnout. *International Journal of Doctoral Studies, 12*, 91–106. https://doi.org/10.28945/3652

Cornér, S., Pyhältö, K., & Löfström, E. (2019). Supervisors' perceptions of primary resources and challenges of the doctoral journey. *International Journal of Teaching and Learning in Higher Education, 31*(1), 12–22.

Dee, L., Devecchi, C., & Florian, L. (2006). LSRC research report: Being, having, and doing: Theories of learning and adults with learning difficulties. Learning and Skills Network. https://www.lsneducation.org.uk

Frick, L., Albertyn, R., & Rutgers, L. (2010). The Socratic method: Adult education theories. *Acta Academica, 42*(2), 75–102.

Friedrich-Nel, H., & Mackinnon, J. (2013). Expectations in postgraduate supervision: Perspectives from supervisors and doctoral students. *Interim: Interdisciplinary Journal, 12*, 1–14.

Gatfield, T. (2005). An investigation into PhD supervisory management styles: Development of a dynamic conceptual model and its managerial implications. *Journal of Higher Education Policy and Management, 27*(3), 311–325. https://doi.org/10.1080/13600800500283783

Green, B. (2005). Unfinished business: Subjectivity and supervision. *Higher Education Research and Development, 24*(2), 151–163. https://doi.org/10.1080/07294360500062610

Grossman, E. S., & Crowther, N. J. (2015). Co-supervision in postgraduate training: Ensuring the right hand knows what the left hand is doing. *South African Journal of Science, 111*(1–8). https://doi.org/10.17159/sajs.2015/20140219

Hemer, S. R. (2012). Informality, power, and relationships in postgraduate supervision: Supervising PhD candidates over coffee. *Higher Education Research & Development, 31*(6), 827–839. https://doi.org/10.10 80/07294360.2012.658017

Hyrkäs, K., Appelqvist-Schmidlechner, K., & Paunonen-Ilmonen, M. (2002). Expert supervisors' views of clinical supervision: A study of factors promoting and inhibiting the achievements of multiprofessional team supervision. *Journal of Advanced Nursing, 38*(4), 387–397. https://doi.org/10.1046/j.1365-2648.2002.02261.x

Kamler, B. (2008). Rethinking doctoral publication practices: Writing from and beyond the thesis. *Studies in Higher Education, 33*(3), 283–294. https://doi.org/10.1080/03075070802062218

Lantolf, J. P., & Poehner, M. E. (2008). *Sociocultural theory and the teaching of second languages.* Equinox.

Lee, A. (2008). How are doctoral students supervised? Concepts of doctoral research supervision. *Studies in Higher Education, 33*(3), 267–281. https://doi.org/10.1080/03075070802049251

Lee, A. (2018). How can we develop supervisors for the modern doctorate? *Studies in Higher Education, 43*(5), 878–890. https://doi.org/10.1080/03075079.2017.1292013

Maxwell, T. W., & Smyth, R. (2011). Higher degree research supervision: From practice toward theory. *Higher Education Research & Development, 30*(2), 219–231. https://doi.org/10.1080/07294360.2010.511231

McCallin, A., & Nayar, S. (2012). Postgraduate research supervision: A critical review of current practice. *Teaching in Higher Education, 17*(1), 63–74. https://doi.org/10.1080/13562517.2011.607406

McKenna, S. (2017). Crossing conceptual thresholds in doctoral communities. *Innovations in Education and Teaching International, 54*(5), 458–466. https://doi.org/10.1080/14703297.2016.1173694

Packer, M. J., & Goicoechea, J. (2000). Sociocultural and constructivist theories of learning: Ontology, not just epistemology. *Educational Psychologist, 35*(4), 227–241. https://doi.org/10.1207/S15326985EP3504_2

Pearson, M., & Brew, A. (2002). Research training and supervision development. *Studies in Higher Education, 27*(2), 135–150. https://doi.org/10.1080/03075070220140040

Postgrad.com. (n.d.). How to write a master's dissertation or thesis: Top tips. *Postgrad.com*. https://www.postgrad.com/advice/exams/dissertations_and_theses/top_tips_writing_postgraduate_thesis/

Pyhältö, K., Vekkaila, J., & Keskinen, J. (2015). Fit matters in the supervisory relationship: Doctoral students and supervisors' perceptions about the supervisory activities. *Innovations in Education and Teaching International, 52*(1), 4–16. https://doi.org/10.1080/14703297.2013.868332

Robertson, M. J. (2017). Trust: The power that binds in team supervision of doctoral students. *Higher Education Research & Development, 36*(7), 1463–1475. https://doi.org/10.1080/07294360.2017.1321369

Taylor, D. C., & Hamdy, H. (2013). Adult learning theories: Implications for learning and teaching in medical education: AMEE Guide No. 83. *Medical Teacher, 35*(11), e1561–e1572. https://doi.org/10.3109/0142159X.2013.827652

UCT Newsroom. (2016, June 28). New professors share journeys and reflections. *UCT Newsroom*. https://www.news.uct.ac.za/article/-2016-06-28-new-professors-share-journeys-and-reflections

Vanson, S. (2014). What on earth are ontology and epistemology? *The Performance Solution*. https://theperformancesolution.com/earth-ontology-epistemology/

Vereijken, M. W., van der Rijst, R. M., van Driel, J. H., & Dekker, F. W. (2018). Novice supervisors' practices and dilemmatic space in supervision of student research projects. *Teaching in Higher Education, 23*(5), 522–542. https://doi.org/10.1080/13562517.2018.1451219

Vilkinas, T. (2002). The PhD process: The supervisor as manager. *Education + Training, 44*(3), 129–137. https://doi.org/10.1108/00400910210424201

Wisker, G., Robinson, G., & Shacham, M. (2007). Postgraduate research success: Communities of practice involving cohorts, guardian supervisors and online communities. *Innovations in Education and Teaching International, 44*(3), 301–320. https://doi.org/10.1080/14703290701486881

Reflections on cohort and thesis-by-publications approaches to doctoral supervision at Makerere University

Stephen Ojiambo Wandera

Uganda has a population of about 45 million people (UBOS, 2014) and 303 institutions of higher education, including 10 public and 16 private universities (UNCHE, 2023). Between 1970 and 2020, about 1 025 PhDs were awarded by four of the public universities in Uganda, Makerere University, Mbarara University of Science and Technology, Kyambogo University and Gulu University.

Makerere University was established as a technical college in 1922. It evolved into a university in 1949 and currently offers programs in various fields such as arts, social sciences, engineering, medicine, agriculture, and law. The University has about 40 000 students, including about 1 000 doctoral students in all its colleges. In 2023 doctoral degrees were awarded to 132 candidates.

1. Introduction

In this chapter, I present my reflections on my experience with doctoral training in a graduate programme organised and implemented using a cohort approach and based on the thesis-by-publication (TBP) format (see Frick, 2019; Niven & Grant, 2012). The approach has been tested at various universities in Africa including Makerere University Kampala (MAK), Uganda, under the Consortium for Advanced Research Training in Africa (CARTA) programme. CARTA is a capacity-building programme co-led by the African Population and Health Research Centre (APHRC), Nairobi, Kenya, and the University of the Witwatersrand, Johannesburg, South Africa (Ezeh et al., 2010b; Igumbor et al., 2022). Ten universities in Africa, including Makerere University, and ten universities elsewhere in the world (Europe and North America) are members of the consortium (CARTA, 2023). The programme offers population and public health fellowships for doctoral training and supervision using a cohort approach (Ezeh et al., 2010a; Igumbor et al., 2022).

I was a CARTA doctoral student in 2012-2016 (Cohort 2). In this cohort, we were four (out of 25) CARTA doctoral fellows from Makerere University. By 10 May 2023, a total of 21 PhD students from Makerere University had participated in CARTA (see Figure 1). Thus far a total of 225 PhD students have been trained in the CARTA programme, 142 have graduated from various universities and by the end of 2023, 83 were currently still studying (CARTA, 2023). During this period (2012-2020), a total of 544 doctoral candidates graduated at Makerere University (Etomaru et al., 2020, p. 43). I will argue in this chapter that the experiences gained in this programme can be of value to Makerere University in general, including and going beyond those students involved in the CARTA programme.

Figure 1: CARTA PhD students at Makerere University by cohort

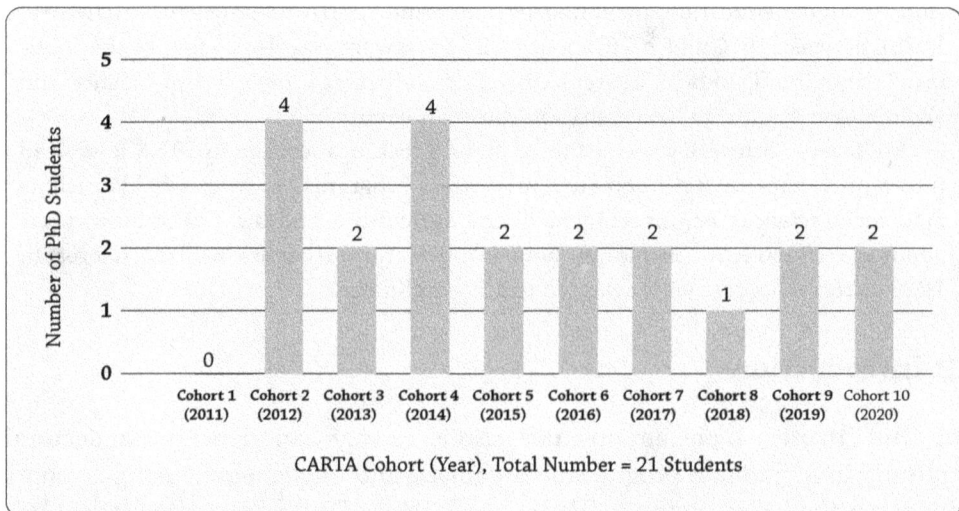

Source: CARTA

In terms of the TBP approach, PhD students are encouraged to publish journal articles during their participation in the training programme. To prepare and support CARTA fellows to meet this requirement, cross-cutting doctoral training courses in the form of four joint advanced seminars (JASes) are offered during the four years of the PhD programme.

Limited attention has been given to documenting the experiences of PhD students and supervisors following the TBP format and cohort approach in African universities. In this chapter I share an overview of the structure and activities of the CARTA programme, followed by a reflection on my experience as a PhD student (PhD fellow) in the CARTA programme. I conclude with observations and suggestions on how these approaches can be of value to doctoral education in the African context, particularly at Makerere University and beyond.

2. Methodology

In this chapter, I use autoethnography as a methodology to present my reflections on my experience of doctoral supervision. This methodology allows authors to use their experiences to explore specific topics (as in this case, a collaborative PhD programme), call attention to problematic cultural issues and practices, and offer reflections (e.g. fieldwork diaries). Autoethnographic projects use "selfhood, subjectivity, and personal experience (*auto*) to describe, interpret, and represent (*graphy*) beliefs, practices, and identities of a group or culture (*ethno*)" (Adams & Herrmann, 2020:2). I consider the institutional and professional contexts with the aim of obtaining better understanding through self-analysis, and reflect on institutional processes, as suggested by Pańkowska (2022). I use *critical* autoethnography, that is, "a process that involves a dialogue between the autoethnographer and study participants" (Pańkowska, 2022:1), through involving the other Makerere University PhD students who were also CARTA fellows at the time. Those fellows have reviewed the reflections I have presented in this chapter.

2.1 Cohort supervision using a thesis-by-publication format

Supervision models include the traditional master–apprentice model, team supervision, and group supervision (Agné & Mörkenstam, 2018; Carter et al., 2017). Cohort supervision is part of the group supervision model (Wilmot, 2021). Cohort supervision is an approach to supervision that extends beyond the traditional one-to-one supervision (apprenticeship) and the generic group supervision (one-to-many or many-to-one) models in the sense that a cohort of students works together in a structured programme for a designated period (Wilmot, 2021). There are two models of cohort supervision: (i) a cohort where one supervisor is assigned to a cohort of students, and (ii) a cohort with many, where a group of supervisors supervises a group of students (Choy et al., 2014; Wilmot, 2021). A cohort of students participating in the same programme shares five characteristics. First, the cohort has a defined, long-term membership of students who commence and complete a study programme together. Second, the students share a common goal that can best be achieved when the members are academically and emotionally supportive of each other. Third, they engage in a collaborative series of learning experiences. Fourth, the cohort follows a highly structured meeting schedule. Finally, the cohort forms a network of synergistic learning relationships that is developed and shared among members (Choy et al., 2014).

Cohort supervision has several benefits: it allows collaborative learning and mentorship in a structured programme; members of the cohort provide technical assistance and emotional and social support to one another as they pursue their doctoral studies (Agné & Mörkenstam, 2018; Choy et al., 2014; Holloway & Alexandre, 2012); it reduces academic isolation which often happens during PhD training (Hutchings, 2015); and continuous engagement with peers, supervisors and experts promotes nurturing and enculturation into the academic community and discipline (Jacobs, 2020; Wrigley et al., 2020). In the CARTA model, cohort supervision is practiced. Four joint advanced seminars over a period of four years, each lasting four weeks, are organised. Supervisors and fellows give feedback to one another to improve the quality of the PhD theses (Ezeh et al., 2010b).

However, cohort supervision also has some challenges and concerns. Conflicting and contradictory advice from a group of supervisors and students may be confusing to students. Dominant personalities of some supervisors and/or students might stifle the growth and progression of other students (Jacobs, 2020).

The thesis-by-publication (TBP) approach has become common in some universities for two reasons: (i) universities want to increase their scientific output and (ii) students aim to increase their competition in the marketplace (Guerin et al., 2015). TBP is a popular model used by universities in Australia and Scandinavian countries, and recently in some African countries (Niven & Grant, 2012). According to the 2016 Makerere University Doctoral Supervision Guidelines, PhD students aiming at a TBP may be examined based on a compilation of at least three (3) to five (5) papers published in refereed journals before students are allowed to participate in a public PhD defence as a final examination of their doctoral thesis (Makerere University, 2016).

Students are drawn to the TBP approach because they see it to fast-track their careers as researchers or academics (Mason & Merga, 2018b, 2018a). This rationale is not without challenges. For example, some students fall prey to predatory publishers and journals (Mouton & Valentine, 2017). Therefore, they need constant mentoring from experts and supervisors. The TBP also accelerates contribution to the body of knowledge. However, this model is not an option for all doctoral students. It is a tough challenge to publish at several peer-reviewed journal articles as an emerging researcher (Niven & Grant, 2012). To complete a thesis-by-publication, doctoral students need to acquire a skillset that includes writing skills, time management, and being technology savvy (Merga et al., 2019).

Continuous research capacity building is critical to the success of doctoral training. Makerere University runs cross-cutting seminars for PhD students. These seminars help build the skills of PhD students. During the CARTA training programme, four joint advanced seminars (JASes) are provided to build the research capacities of the doctoral fellows (Ezeh et al., 2010b; Igumbor et al., 2022). The seminars build the research and management capacities of PhD students (Igumbor et al., 2022). Table 1 summarises the focus of these JASes in CARTA training.

Table 1: Structure of the CARTA programme

Year	Joint advanced seminar (JAS)	Duration	Location	Content
Year 1 (March 2012)	JAS 1	4 weeks	African Population and Health Research Centre (APHRC), Nairobi, Kenya at Safari Park Hotel	Proposal development; Responsible Conduct of Research; Communicating research
November - December 2012	JAS 2	4 weeks	University of the Witwatersrand, Johannesburg, South Africa	Theoretical perspectives on research methodology & Quantitative data analysis (STATA) and Qualitative Data analysis (Nvivo)
Year 2 (2013)	No seminars		Students in their home countries	PhD candidates collect data
Year 3 (2014)	JAS 3	4 weeks	University of Ibadan, Ibadan, Nigeria	Data analysis (facilitators available for quantitative and qualitative analysis); Scientific writing
Year 4 (2015)	JAS 4	4 weeks	African Population and Health Research Centre (APHRC), Nairobi, Kenya at Safari Park Hotel	Grant writing and management; Policy influence (to develop policy briefs); Educator role (incl. curriculum design); Research leadership

2.2 Reflecting on my experience as a CARTA fellow

The PhD training programme at Makerere University uses doctoral committees in the supervision process. These committees consist of supervisors and other faculty members with expertise in the research area (often referred to as dissertation committees in other contexts) (Holloway & Alexandre, 2012). The CARTA fellows enrolled at Makerere University must also comply with this requirement. During my participation in the CARTA programme, I have learned different styles of supervision. I enjoyed the team approach to supervision. The doctoral committee members supervise either one or several PhD students. The doctoral committees guide and advise the student from the beginning to the end of the process. They recommend the appointment of external supervisors and academics who are external to the university.

During my PhD training in CARTA, I had an external supervisor based at the African Population and Health Research Centre in Nairobi, Kenya, who strongly supported and mentored me during the initial conceptualisation of the PhD, the development of the proposal, and my engagement with the relevant literature. During the CARTA training, we were encouraged to have external supervisors (external to the university where a PhD student is registered). The external supervisor provided additional support to several CARTA PhD students in the same or different cohorts.

As a graduate of CARTA, I had to sign a formal contract with my doctoral supervisors. This contract stated my roles and responsibilities as a student and those of the supervisors. In addition, the contract states the number of publications a student intends to publish as part of the thesis. Those terms and conditions made the supervision experience so smooth for the team. However, Makerere University had no standard contract or memorandum of understating (MoU) template for doctoral training. Students were expected to submit semi-annual progress reports which are signed by the student and the supervisor(s). Makerere is currently reviewing these processes.

Managing supervisor–student relationships is a critical factor in doctoral training (Lee, 2018). International policy frameworks such as the Bologna process, encourage the treatment of PhD students as colleagues, thus promoting collegial relations between supervisors and their supervisees (Verhoeven & De Wit, 2022). In many African universities, the master–apprentice model of supervision dominates (Wilmot, 2021). During my PhD studies, my supervisors were collegial in their interactions with me. Not only had they supervised me during the master's programme too, but I was also a faculty member during my postgraduate studies. We had already built a rapport. They used functional, relationship development, critical thinking, as well as emancipation approaches in the supervision process. In addition, during the CARTA doctoral training prorgramme, I received immense support and input from fellow CARTA doctoral candidates in the same cohort at Makerere University and from other participating universities.

Managing divergent ideologies, feedback, and viewpoints from supervisors (cohort of supervisors) and peers in the cohort is a common issue in cohort supervision (Govender & Dhunpath, 2011a). During the CARTA seminars, we received feedback from multiple supervisors who facilitated the sessions and cohort peers. There were instances of conflicting views about our proposals, methodologies, and manuscripts. This sometimes led to conflict of opinions among me and other students. The way of resolving this was to call for the opinion of the principal supervisor. Their opinion would sometimes be taken as the final direction for the thesis (Cornwall et al., 2019; Govender & Dhunpath, 2011b; McAlpine & McKinnon, 2013). When divergent opinions emerged among my supervisors, we would meet and discuss it, and we were able to reach an agreement for a way forward with the thesis.

Managing the expectations of both students and supervisors during PhD supervision is challenging. These expectations depend on the personalities of both students and supervisors. They are also deeply embedded in individual and institutional cultures (Turner, 2015a; Lee, 2018). Sometimes, students expect their supervisors to be personal friends, mentors, coaches, and directors at different points of the PhD process (Czigan, 2014; Makerere University, 2016; Lee, 2007; Turner, 2015b). However, it is not an easy task to find all these virtues in every supervisor. On the other hand, supervisors expect PhD students to be self-driven, highly motivated, and able to develop scientific independence (Turner, 2015a; Lee, 2018). In addition, students expect to be treated as colleagues, while some supervisors expect students to behave like apprentices in a workshop. Such mismatches and varying expectations easily breed tension and frustration when they are not met or fulfilled (Turner, 2015a; Lee, 2018). From my experience, my two supervisors were highly supportive.

My first/principal supervisor was like a father-figure to me. He was a mentor, a coach, and a guide. Following his advice helped me to overcome many obstacles during the PhD journey. Since I was the first student my supervisors were guiding to write a TBP, I was expected to be self-driven and consultative. I convened a meeting to agree on the structure of the TBP with my supervisors. They recommended that I visit the university library and the Directorate of Research and Graduate Training to find three to five other TBP theses and then we met to compare and discuss them. Following this discussion, we agreed on the structure and number of publications of my TBP.

Personality differences between the student and the supervisor can pose challenges. Temperaments affect human behaviour, expectations, as well as attitudes. For example, introverts find it a challenge to express their thoughts and emotions to outsiders, while extroverts can more easily do so (Czigan, 2014). Temperaments influence expectations from both students and supervisors. Perfectionist supervisors are highly critical of their students and set very high standards for them. My principal supervisor focused on milestones and deliverables – a functional supervision approach (Lee, 2018), and he is a perfectionist. He read every sentence and even rephrased every sentence when needed. He was strong on quantitative data and statistical analysis. He trained as a medical statistician. The co-supervisor was a critical reader. A good mix and synergy in the temperaments of supervisors and myself enabled me to go for the highest targets in doctoral training. I aimed to publish five journal articles and ended up with four done and one manuscript ready for submission (Wandera et al., 2014, 2015a, 2015b, 2015c).

Most of the PhD students in Makerere University's postgraduate programmes are part-time students, who are engaged in formal employment. This puts pressure on and makes demands on the students. It makes it more difficult for students to meet and interact regularly with their supervisors. Demands from employers and heavy workloads cause interruptions for varying periods in the research activities of many PhD students. Such experiences reduce the consistency and tenacity of the doctoral students (Lindén et al., 2013; White, 2003). PhD students are expected to be mature and to be able to guide themselves. Such an expectation by the supervisors sometimes leaves PhD students lacking these and similar abilities to fall through the cracks. I was admitted on a full-time basis, and I was granted study leave for three years (2013-2016) as a member of faculty at Makerere University. The PhD study leave granted me sufficient time to focus on the writing and the completion of the TBP on time. If Makerere University did not grant me study leave, I would not have finished the thesis in time. The TBP is an enormous endeavour with several rounds of peer review for manuscripts submitted to journal articles. If one does not have the time, there is no way they can finish in the allotted time. I completed my TBP in four years. I was only delayed by the external examination process, otherwise I would have completed in three.

At Makerere University, doctoral theses can follow either a monograph or thesis-by-publication format (Makerere University, 2016). Most students at Makerere University use the monograph format. However, those Makerere students participating in CARTA are encouraged to produce a thesis-by-publication. I decided to follow the TBP format. Universities in Africa set different rules to guide doctoral training, particularly the requirement of publications from doctoral students. Makerere University has a graduation requirement of three (3) to five (5) publications for those following a TBP format (Makerere University, 2016). This requirement is a serious challenge to PhD students who are normally novice researchers with limited knowledge and experience of scholarly publishing (Teferra, 2015). When not guided well, some fall prey to predatory publishing houses and journals (Mouton & Valentine, 2017; Titus et al., 2014, Welfare & Sackett, 2011). Peer review feedback from journal editors as well as the publication process after peer review usually take a long time. These delays are a major challenge for PhD students who have time and resource constraints. When I submitted the first manuscript to a journal, I received editorial comments that required gender-disaggregated analysis. It meant repeating all the statistical analysis three times for each level: univariate, bivariate and multivariate. That was an equivalent of writing three articles for each of the papers. I was frustrated and complained to one of my supervisors. She encouraged me to calm down, take time and address the comments. Eventually I managed to rewrite the entire article and included gender-disaggregated analyses in all the articles.

I had a CARTA cohort supervision network (facilitators and supervisors) that trained us on how to identify reputable journals in which to publish. The CARTA supervisors were supportive in identifying reputable journals. I learnt to use the journal finders of major publishers like Springer, Nature, BioMed Central and Taylor and Francis.

Timely feedback to doctoral students is expected in a cohort supervision model. One of the key critical aspects of supervisor–student relations is the turnaround time for written feedback to doctoral students (Aitchison et al., 2012; Hyatt, 2005; Kumar & Stracke, 2007; Turner, 2015a). I received timely written feedback from my supervisors. This is one of the best practices I would want to replicate in my career as a PhD supervisor. In the CARTA cohort, I benefitted a lot from other CARTA facilitators and fellows, including scholars from universities in other countries. They also gave timely feedback on manuscripts before they were submitted for publication. This 'in-house' peer review in CARTA was a great support to my work. During the joint advanced seminars, I received constructive comments from the cohort fellows and supervisors and facilitators on two manuscripts. Such timely feedback from the cohort fellows played a great role in my progress. I continue to use this approach in my work.

Linking theory to a PhD thesis is easier in a cohort supervision model. Several PhD students struggle with the literature review, with identifying conceptual thresholds, and with the application of theory and doing justice to the chosen methodological considerations (Badley, 2009). There is a need for constant capacity building on the role of concepts and concept mapping during the writing of the PhD thesis. How these concepts and theories apply to methods is a challenge, especially when engaged in mixed methods research (Creswell, 2013). During the doctoral training as part of the CARTA cohort, we would share our chosen theoretical frameworks with each other and were able to learn more from our peers. We reviewed and provided feedback to other students' theories and conceptual frameworks. I was able to tailor and adopt two theories to my PhD thesis after attending the seminars where other students presented their work.

The external examination process can delay the completion of a TBP. There are challenges associated with the process of external examination (Kiley, 2009), such as identifying reliable and available external examiners, preparing the final PhD thesis to be sent to the external examiners, the turnaround time for feedback reports, and payment of honoraria by universities that are resource constrained. This partly explains why the average completion time for doctoral training in many African universities, including Makerere University, is five years (Cloete et al., 2015). On average, our experience in CARTA is that feedback from external examiners ranges from three to nine months. This has implications for PhD completion time and rates at Makerere University.

2.3 Implications of cohort supervision and the TBP format for doctoral education at Makerere University

1. Makerere University currently does not provide a list of reputable journals for publishing the research of PhD students (like the list of accredited articles provided by the Department of Higher Education and Training in South Africa, see (SUN, 2023). There are various comprehensive journal databases listed on the Makerere University library portal. The lists of journals are updated annually. This is a best practice for academic libraries, which can be adopted elsewhere in Uganda. However, Makerere University still needs to develop a robust publications policy to guide both PhD students and members of faculty and to assist them in avoiding the pitfalls of publishing in predatory journals.

2. Critically, the CARTA cohort model emphasises the signing of supervision contracts or memoranda of understanding (MoU) between supervisors

and doctoral candidates (Ezeh et al., 2010b; Igumbor et al., 2022; Uwizeye et al., 2020). The use of contracts between students and supervisors should be made compulsory for all postgraduate students at Makerere University.

3. Makerere University also needs to improve its support for supervisors. For example, in the CARTA model, supervisors receive monetary reward when their supervisee completes the PhD in time. There is evidence that monetary rewards can improve throughput, however, they may also have unintended consequences (Muthama & McKenna, 2020).

4. Makerere University does not employ graduate research coordinators in all its schools. Graduate coordinators can help to allocate and prepare students for presentations, seminars, and public defences. Such arrangements may support mechanisms for PhD students as the former will be contact persons for the students. Currently, such coordinators exist at school and, sometimes, college level. There is a need to appoint such coordinators at departmental levels. Graduate coordinators are instrumental in supporting the cohort supervision model.

3. Conclusion

Only a few PhD students (21 in total) at Makerere University are CARTA fellows. Based on my experience as CARTA fellow (reviewed by the 4 other Makerere University PhD students in my cohort and one more from another cohort), I argue that all graduate students at Makerere University can benefit from the approaches used in CARTA – cohort supervision and thesis-by-publication format. The TBP format is attainable and improves the research skills of the doctoral students as they learn so many skillsets during training in a cohort or on the job.

I pointed out the challenges faced by students doing a TBP format PhD. The challenges in doctoral education at Makerere University include delays in the external examination process, the obstacles that part-time PhD studentships must overcome, lack of project management skills, and guidance in managing conflict between students and supervisors.

On the other hand, I advocated for more consistent and systemic implementation of best practices in doctoral supervision. These include the compulsory use of supervision contracts, continuous use of doctoral/thesis committees, promotion of a TBP format, timely written feedback by supervisors, and the continuous strengthening of research capacity through the training of doctoral students and supervisors through continuous professional development. I maintain that the implementation of these suggestions can enhance doctoral education at Makerere University in its quest to be a research-intensive university.

Acknowledgements

I acknowledge the funding from CARTA for my PhD studies. This research was supported by the Consortium for Advanced Research Training in Africa (CARTA). CARTA is jointly led by the African Population and Health Research Centre and the University of the Witwatersrand and funded by the Carnegie Corporation of New York (Grant No. G-21-58722), SIDA (Grant No:54100113), Uppsala Monitoring Centre, and Norwegian Agency for Development Cooperation (NORAD). The statements made and views expressed are solely the responsibility of the current fellow.

I also acknowledge the support from the DAAD and Stellenbosch University for funding the networking meeting in South Africa (2022). I am grateful for the financial support received from the Directorate of Research and Graduate Training (DRGT) at Makerere University. Finally, I acknowledge the peer reviews from the CARTA PhD fellows: Gabriel Tumwine, Scovia Mbalinda Nalugo, and Godwin Anywar.

References

Adams, T. E., & Herrmann, A. F. (2020). Expanding our autoethnographic future. *Journal of Autoethnography, 1*(1), 1-8.

Agné, H., & Mörkenstam, U. (2018). Should first-year doctoral students be supervised collectively or individually? Effects on thesis completion and time to completion. *Higher Education Research & Development, 37*(4), 669-682.

Aitchison, C., Catterall, J., Ross, P., & Burgin, S. (2012). 'Tough love and tears': Learning doctoral writing in the sciences. *Studies in Higher Education, 31*(4), 435-447.

Badley, G. (2009). Publish and be doctor-rated: The PhD by published work. *Teaching in Higher Education, 17*(4), 331-342.

CARTA. (2023). Our partners. *Consortium for Advanced Research Training in Africa (CARTA)*. https://cartafrica.org/our-partners-2/.

Carter, S., Kensington-Miller, B., & Courtney, M. (2017). Doctoral supervision practice: What's the problem and how can we help academics? *Journal of Perspectives in Applied Academic Practice, 5*(1), 1-11.

Choy, S., Delahaye, B. L., & Saggars, B. (2014). Developing learning cohorts for postgraduate research degrees. *The Australian Educational Researcher, 42*(1), 19-34.

Cornwall, J., Mayland, E. C., Van Der Meer, J., Spronken-Smith, R. A., Tustin, C., & Blyth, P. (2019). Stressors in early-stage doctoral students. *Studies in Continuing Education, 41*(3), 363-380.

Creswell, J. W. (2013). *Research design: Qualitative, quantitative, and mixed methods approaches* (4th ed.). SAGE.

Czigan, T. (2014). Combining coaching and temperament: Implications for middle management leadership development. *Journal of Leadership Development, 12*(2), 85-92.

Ezeh, A., Izugbara, C. O., Kabiru, C. W., Fonn, S., Kahn, K., Manderson, L., Undieh, A. S., Omigbodun, A., & Thorogood, M. (2010a). Building capacity for public and population health research in Africa: The Consortium for Advanced Research Training in Africa (CARTA) model. *Global Health Action, 3*, 1-12.

Ezeh, A. C., Izugbara, C. O., Kabiru, C. W., Fonn, S., Kahn, K., Manderson, L., Undieh, A. S., Omigbodun, A., & Thorogood, M. (2010b). Building capacity for public and population health research in Africa: The Consortium for Advanced Research Training in Africa (CARTA) model. *Global Health Action, 3*, 1-12.

Frick, L. (2019). PhD by publication – Panacea or paralysis? *Africa Education Review, 16*(1), 47-59.

Govender, K., & Dhunpath, R. (2011a). Student experiences of the PhD cohort model: Working within or outside communities of practice? *Perspectives in Education, 29*(1), 1-10.

Govender, K., & Dhunpath, R. (2011b). Student experiences of the PhD cohort model: Working within or outside communities of practice? *Perspectives in Education, 29*(2), 88-99.

Guerin, C., Kerr, H., & Green, I. (2015). Supervision pedagogies: Narratives from the field. *Higher Education Research & Development, 20*(2), 93-105.

Holloway, E. L., & Alexandre, L. (2012). Crossing boundaries in doctoral education: Relational learning, cohort communities, and dissertation committees. *New Directions for Teaching and Learning, 2012*(129), 85-97.

Hutchings, M. (2015). Improving doctoral support through group supervision: Analyzing face-to-face and technology-mediated strategies for nurturing and sustaining scholarship. *Studies in Higher Education, 42*(3), 533-550.

Hyatt, D. F. (2005). 'Yes, a very good point!': A critical genre analysis of a corpus of feedback commentaries on Master of Education assignments. *Assessment & Evaluation in Higher Education, 10*(4), 339-353.

Igumbor, J. O., Bosire, E. N., Karimi, F., Katahoire, A., Allison, J., Muula, A. S., Peixoto, A., Otwombe, K., Gitau, E., Bondjers, G., Fonn, S., & Ajuwon, A. (2022). Effective supervision of doctoral students in public and population health in Africa: CARTA supervisors' experiences, challenges, and perceived opportunities. *Global Public Health, 17*(3), 496-511.

Jacobs, L. (2020). Cohort supervision as an approach at postgraduate level: A conceptual framework for an open distance e-learning university. *Masters of Higher Education, Stellenbosch University*.

Kiley, M. (2009). 'You don't want a smart Alec': Selecting examiners to assess doctoral dissertations. *Studies in Higher Education, 34*(7), 889-903.

Kumar, V., & Stracke, E. (2007). An analysis of written feedback on a PhD thesis. *Studies in Higher Education, 12*(3), 461-470.

Lee, A. (2018). How can we develop supervisors for the modern doctorate? *Studies in Higher Education, 43*(5), 878-890.

Lee, A. M. (2007). Developing effective supervisors: Concepts of research supervision. *Research in Higher Education, 15*(2), 243-257.

Lindén, J., Ohlin, M., & Brodin, E. M. (2013). Mentorship, supervision, and learning experience in PhD education. *Higher Education Research & Development, 31*(2), 1-11.

Makerere University. (2016). *Doctoral supervision guidelines* (Kampala, Uganda).

Mason, S., & Merga, M. K. (2018a). A current view of the thesis by publication in the humanities and social sciences. *International Journal of Doctoral Studies, 13*, 139-154.

Mason, S., & Merga, M. K. (2018b). A PhD by publication is a great way to build your academic profile, but be mindful of its challenges. *Impact of Social Sciences Blog*. https://blogs.lse.ac.uk/impactofsocialsciences/

McAlpine, L., & McKinnon, M. (2013). Supervision – the most variable of variables: Student perspectives. *Studies in Continuing Education, 35*(3), 265-280.

Merga, M. K., Mason, S., & Morris, J. E. (2019). 'The constant rejections hurt': Skills and personal attributes needed to successfully complete a thesis by publication. *Learned Publishing, 32*(4), 271-281.

Mouton, J., & Valentine, A. (2017). The extent of South African authored articles in predatory journals. *South African Journal of Science, 113*(1-2), 1-9.

Niven, P., & Grant, C. (2012). PhDs by publications: An "easy way out"? *Teaching in Higher Education, 17*(1), 105-111.

Pańkowska, M. (2022). Autoethnography on researcher profile cultivation. *Information, 13*(2), 154.

Sun. (2023). Accredited journals. *Stellenbosch University (SUN)*. http://www.sun.ac.za/english/research-inno-vation/Research-Development/outputs-accredited-journals/accredited-journals#:~:text=%E2%80%8B%E2%80%8B%E2%80%8B%E2%80%8B%E2%80%8B%E2%80%8B%E2%80%8BClick%20here (Accessed May 10, 2023).

Teferra, D. (2015). Manufacturing - and exporting - excellence and 'mediocrity': Doctoral education in South Africa. *Higher Education, 29*(1), 8-19.

Titus, S. L., Ballou, J. M., & Ballou, M. T. (2014). Ensuring PhD development of responsible conduct of research behaviors: Who's responsible? *Journal of Research Ethics, 20*(3), 221-235.

Turner, G. (2015). Learning to supervise: Four journeys. *Studies in Higher Education, 52*(2), 86-98.

Uwizeye, D., Karimi, F., Otukpa, E., Ngware, M. W., Wao, H., Igumbor, J. O., & Fonn, S. (2020). Increasing collaborative research output between early-career health researchers in Africa: Lessons from the CARTA fellowship program. *Global Health Action, 13*, 1-12. https://doi.org/10.1080/16549716.2020.1732407

Verhoeven, J. C., & De Wit, K. (2022). How did Australian scholars perceive the Bologna Process? *Higher Education Research & Development, 41*, 132-145. https://doi.org/10.1080/07294360.2021.1939992

Wandera, S. O., Golaz, V., Kwagala, B., & Ntozi, J. (2015a). Factors associated with self-reported ill health among older Ugandans: A cross-sectional study. *Archives of Gerontology and Geriatrics, 61*, 231-239.

Wandera, S. O., Kwagala, B., & Ntozi, J. (2015b). Determinants of access to healthcare by older persons in Uganda: A cross-sectional study. *International Journal for Equity in Health, 14*, 26.

Wandera, S. O., Kwagala, B., & Ntozi, J. (2015c). Prevalence and risk factors for self-reported non-communicable diseases among older Ugandans: A cross-sectional study. *Global Health Action, 8*, 27923.

Wandera, S. O., Ntozi, J., & Kwagala, B. (2014). Prevalence and correlates of disability among older Ugandans: Evidence from the Uganda National Household Survey. *Global Health Action, 7*, 25686.

Welfare, L. E., & Sackett, C. R. (2011). The authorship determination process in student–faculty collaboration. *Teaching in Higher Education, 16*, 479-487. https://doi.org/10.1080/13562517.2011.569140

White, A. (2003). *How to get a PhD: A handbook for students and their supervisors* (2nd ed.). Open University Press.

Wilmot, K. (2021). 'Fail early and fail fast': The value of group supervision for doctoral candidates. *Higher Education Research & Development, 40*(5), 1-14. https://doi.org/10.1080/07294360.2021.1914644

Wrigley, C., Wolifson, P., & Matthews, J. (2020). Supervising cohorts of higher degree research students: Design catalysts for industry and innovation. *Higher Education, 81*, 1177-1196. https://doi.org/10.1007/s10734-020-00510-

Improving the quality of the PhD programme at the Center of Research and Valorization of Medicinal Plants in Guinea

Elhadj Saidou Baldé

Guinea has a population of 14.1 million. The country has 18 public universities. In 2021, a total of 128 doctoral students were enrolled at Guinean universities, 38 doctoral candidates graduated in 2021 and 2022.

The **University Gamal Abdel Nasser de Conakry** (UGANC) became a public university in 1989, tracing its origins to the Institut Polytechnique de Conakry (est. 1962) and the Institut Polytechnique Gamal Abdel Nasser de Conakry (est. 1970). UGANC has 650 academic staff members working in five faculties and two research centres, with a total student enrolment of 4 925 for the academic year 2022, which makes it one of the largest contact-education universities in Guinea. In 2022 UGANC had 56 doctoral candidates and awarded 10 doctoral degrees.

---

1. Background

For a long time, sub-Saharan countries in Africa have focused on primary and secondary education as the key to development and poverty alleviation (Beaudry et al., 2018; Halvorsen, 2016). Now there is a consensus that Africa needs many more doctorate holders to develop the robust knowledge needed to promote development (Bryman, 2012; Lewin & Stuart, 2003). Human resources for health are a critical element of having a functioning health system and providing universal access to quality healthcare. The doctoral qualification can be seen as a programme of research, scholarship and advanced study which enables candidates to make a significant contribution to knowledge and practice in their professional context (Maxwell & Kupczyk-Romanczuk, 2009). Thus, promoting the doctorate in health sciences could help sub-Saharan Africa countries to improve their human resources for health.

2. Context and aim

In Guinea, the quality of training in the medical and pharmaceutical sciences is insufficient, this is reflected, as elsewhere in Africa (Fonn et al., 2016), in the performance of health systems (Azevedo, 2017). Research with poorly evaluated capacity and low funding produces results of which very little is translated into decisions and practice (Curtis et al., 2017). As elsewhere in the world, the training for doctors, pharmacists and dentists in Guinea is provided by universities. The Guinean higher education system began its transformation from the classical French education system to the bachelor master doctorate (the *License Master Doctorat* or LMD) system in 2000. To facilitate the migration to the LMD system, in 2005 the authorities at University Gamal Abdel Nasser University of Conakry (UGANC) created an advanced postgraduate programme with two doctoral schools, the Doctoral School of Health, and the Doctoral School of Science and Natural Environment.

To date, the faculties of sciences, social sciences and economics and technical sciences have completed their migration. But the Faculty of Sciences and Techniques of Health has not made the migration to the LMD system.

In 2017, in the Faculty of Sciences and Techniques of Health of UGANC, which trains doctors, pharmacists and dentists, the ratio of all ranks of teaching staff to students was 1:11 (professor, associate professor, assistant professor and assistant), whereas for senior academic staff (professor and associate professor) the ratio was 1:40 (Ministère de l'enseignement supérieur et de la recherche scientifique, 2017). The research carried out within the faculty is done by academic staff for their academic promotion.

The analysis of data on the teaching staff of the Faculté de Medecine Pharmacie Odonto- Stomatologie clearly shows an aging of the teaching staff at the level of the teachers of Rank A and the insufficient succession planning in the field of Pharmacy. Guinea is a member of the African and Malagasy Council of Higher Education (CAMES) and a ministerial decree sets the criteria for recruitment and academic promotion.

According to the Ministry of High Education and Scientific Research decree (N ° 2013/063 / MESRS / CAB, February 1st, 2013) for medicine, pharmacy,

dentistry, veterinary medicine and animal productions candidates, it is necessary to hold a specialized qualification or a master's degree and to be 35 years
old at most on 1 January of the year of submission of the application for an
academic position. Once appointed, the promotion to the more senior academic
ranks (assistant master, lecturer, professor) happens based on the CAMES
criteria. In the case of the medical doctors, they can be promoted in terms of
the CAMES criteria to more senior academic levels based on the qualification
in medicine which they held when they first applied for the academic position.
However, for the pharmacists and dentists this is not the case. They must
obtain a PhD degree before the end of their period of assistantship to qualify
for promotion.

In the Faculty of Sciences and Techniques of Health, studies traditionally
last seven years (pharmacy) or eight years (medicine) before students graduate.
After the completing academic training, the student must complete at least two
years (pharmacy) or four years (medicine) before obtaining a diploma allowing them to be appointed as an assistant at the Faculty of Health Sciences and
Techniques of UGANC. For pharmacists, after their appointment as an assistant they must obtain a doctoral degree if they wish to continue their academic
career. PhD opportunities for pharmacists are very low in Guinea and only the
Center for Research and Development of Medicinal Plants (CRVPM) at UGANC
offers such opportunity.

The Center of Research and Valorization of Medicinal Plants (CRVPM) is a
public research center based in Dubreka, 50km from UGANC. The CRVPM is
a public scientific institution under the supervision of the Minister of Higher
Education and Scientific Research. Its financial resources come mainly from the
national development budget.

Currently, the centre itself does not have a specific doctoral programme but
accepts PhD students enrolled at UGANC and other partner universities into
its research programme. Since its creation in March 2001, more than ten PhD
candidates have received PhD degrees from the UGANC based on the research
that they have done at the CRVPM. The objective of this chapter is to critically
analyse the CRVPM doctoral programme and to make recommendations to
improve its quality.

3. Evaluation of PhDs completed at the CRVPM

Since 2005, the CRVPM has co-supervised 7 doctoral students enrolled in
an international scholarship programme with Belgium universities and the
University of Gamal Abdel Nasser of Conakry, and 8 doctoral students enrolled

in doctoral programmes of Guinean higher education institutions. Of these 15 PhD students, 6 are currently pharmacists with positions in the Pharmacy Department of the FSTS. Three pharmacists have obtained their PhDs. The average duration for graduation varies from one candidate to another and can range from 5 to 7 years. During my time as a PhD student at ULB Belgium (2005–2010), I observed that two PhD students dropped out, leaving 10 active students by 2010.

We evaluate the CRVPM programme according to Cross and Backhouse's model for evaluation of doctoral programmes in Africa which takes into account six elements, namely: the interest of the candidate, the context of the candidate, the prerequisites of the candidate, the structuring of the programme, the human, material and financial resources, and finally institutional partnerships (Cross & Backhouse, 2014).

3.1 The interest of the candidates

In focus group discussions with the PhD students (conducted specifically to gather data for this study), it emerged that the candidates' interests were not always aligned with that of their institutions of origin. Some candidates were enrolled for PhDs because they wanted to pursue an academic career, and they were aware that the PhD is essential for an academic career. Other candidates registered for the PhD primarily based on their research interests and because the PhD qualification attests to their status as researchers and links them more to the category teacher-researcher.

Based on its rector's leadership, an institution will either provide support to their academic staff enrolled in a PhD programme or not. If they view staff members' enrolment in a PhD program as an opportunity to enhance the quality of academic staff and prepare for the rejuvenation of their faculty, they provide support to the candidates. On the other hand, due to poor availability of resources for research, some institutions in Guinea do not support the PhD candidates.

Whether or not their institution of origin had an interest in their staff obtaining a PhD, most doctoral students remain motivated to complete their PhD studies, as is indicated by the low dropout rate (2/15) of this programme.

However, it appears that the candidates do not have a broader view of all the opportunities offered by a PhD for an academic career. Consequently, neither their institutions nor their disciplines, and still less their profession, fully benefit from the advanced research skills and knowledge they gain when they graduate.

3.2 The context of the candidate

PhD students hosted at the CRVPM are usually already employed by a higher education institution. They usually have at least a first degree either from the Faculty of Science of Julius Nyerere University of Kankan (UJNK) in Guinea or from the Department of Pharmacy in the Faculty of Science and Techniques of Health of UGANC. Regardless of their first degree, all the PhD candidates hosted by the CRVPM hold a Diplome d'Etude Approfondie in phytotherapy and medicinal plants. This is a diploma offered in terms of a collaboration agreement between the CRVPM, the FSTS of the UGANC and the Faculty of Sciences of the UJNK. With some exceptions at the time of their enrolment for the doctorate, the candidates are at least 35 years old and already have a family life. One of the challenges faced by the PhD candidates is that their educational institution is not in the same city as the CRVPM, the institution that hosts them for their PhD. They are therefore obliged in many cases to interrupt their research activities at the CRVPM for a period of 3 to 6 months every year to meet their teaching obligations at their home university. This situation has an impact on the progress of their doctoral work and is often a source of stress for doctoral students who feel they are not progressing with the recurring question: 'When will I be able to do my research and complete my thesis?'

3.3 Candidate's prerequisites

When they enroll, PhD students already have a basic knowledge of the study of medicinal plants, and they are familiar with the CRVPM's research programmes and strategies. But the students accepted for the PhD programme do not have a research topic when they enroll.

Order No. 2007/3474 / MENRS / CAB regulating advanced studies (2nd and 3rd Cycle) in Guinea in September 2007 requires the submission of a research project to the Admission and Evaluation Subcommittee, and knowledge of the English language validated by a certificate. This administrative requirement does not seem to be respected in practice if we consider that doctoral students hosted at the CRVPM participate in the programmes of the CRVPM.

3.4 The structuring of the programme

The decree N ° 2007/3474 / MENRS / CAB regulating advanced studies (2nd and 3rd Cycle) in Guinea of September 2007 sets the total value of PhD credits at 180. Participation in a seminar or conference counts for a minimum of 18 credits, while examination a doctoral degree is worth at least 12 credits. The thesis counts for a minimum value of 120 credits. The authority hosting PhD candidates has the responsibility to decide on the definition and the distribution of the 180 credits constituting the doctorate.

From my focus group discussions with the PhD students, it became clear that, in the case of the CRVPM, no detail is communicated by the responsible authorities to the PhD candidates about the credit structure and the requirements for the examination of the thesis. It is therefore possible that candidates can receive permission to defend their thesis as soon as the first scientific article is published. However, for some candidates, the defence of their thesis was permitted only after the publication of the third scientific article.

At the CRVPM the thesis is supervised by a thesis director only and there is no supervision committee. Consequently, the university of origin does not follow the progress of the doctoral student, and the doctoral student is not subjected to an annual evaluation. The uniqueness of the CRVPM's programmes is that they are all focused on medicinal plants. The big problem for PhD students integrating these programmes is that not all of them are able to do their PhD research in the field in which they have completed their first degree. The presence of a supervising committee would have allowed each candidate to be a specialist in natural substances but in their specific field. The current situation has the consequence that the CRVPM and the home university do not take full advantage of their doctoral candidates.

3.5 Human, material, and financial resources

The scientific staff of the CRPVM consists of 31 researchers (25 men and 6 women): 10 PhD holders including one CAMES professor and two CAMES associate professors, 9 master's degree holders, and 22 university degree holders. The scientific staff include pharmacists, biologists, medical doctors, chemists, botanists, agronomists, zootechnicians, veterinarians, and soil scientists. All the PhD students hosted at the CRVPM are supervised by a professor. The CRVPM has 4 laboratories specifically equipped for the extraction, separation, and isolation of natural substances of plant origin. The equipment includes items such as grinders, scales, Soxhlet extractors, rotary evaporators, microscopes, chromatography equipment and accessories, an oven, and a capsule-making machine. Biological activities are carried out by partner laboratories.

3.6 *Institutional partnerships*

The CRVPM is located at national level which allows the development of partnerships with institutions of higher education (UGANC, UJNK), with the pharmaceutical industry (AMB Pharma), and with an NGO (Foundation for the fight against diabetes and non-communicable diseases) of traditional healers.

Internationally, the CRVPM has partnerships with the University of Bamako (Mali), the National Institute of Public Health of Bamako (Mali), the University of Antwerp (Belgium), the Institute of Tropical Medicine (Antwerp, Belgium), Université Libre de Bruxelles (Belgium), University of Liège (Belgium), University of Angers (France), University of Toulouse (France), and the Michel Iderne group of Strasbourg (France).

PhD students hosted at the CRVPM benefit greatly from the CRVPM's international partnerships. The biological analyses of the plants studied are carried out in the laboratories of these institutions, which also host PhD students, either for internships or as part of co- supervision scholarship programmes.

The dissertation is the final product required for the PhD in the CRVPM programme. But the award quality is not internally uniform within, and it is urgent to establish clear guidelines to improve this programme. Also, considering the state of the global economy, there is a need to facilitate the integration of the PhD holder not only in academia, but PhD students also have to acquire more transferable 'soft skills', like courses in computing, management, presentation techniques (Maybee et al., 2019).

4. Recommendations to improve the quality of PhD programme at CRVPM

PhD curricula structure: The CRVPM PhD programme is a PhD by publication and according to the LMD system in Guinea, the PhD programme consists of one hundred eighty credits (180 ECTs). To standardise the criteria for the PhD, it is important to define how each doctoral student achieves the 180 credits. The research activities of the CRVPM are all related to a student participating in compulsory workshops (with certificates) on the following topics:

1. Training workshop in documentary research
2. Training workshop in research methodology
3. Training workshop in scientific redaction
4. Training workshop in grant application
5. Training workshop in leadership and communication
6. Training workshop in management

Given the importance of English as international academic language, it is also recommended that PhD candidates obtain an intermediate-level English certificate by the end of their second year of enrolment. These six certificates, along with the English certification, should collectively account for sixty credits (60 ECTS). In the modern international job market, holding a PhD is valuable not only for academic roles but also for a variety of positions and careers beyond academia (Ortega & Kent, 2018)

Like in many other countries where ability to publish is a major criterion for doctoral level studies (Badley, 2009), it is recommended that PhD candidates hosted by the CRVPM must be required to publish their own research before they present their dissertation. I propose that the PhD thesis should contain two or more peer-reviewed academic papers, published or accepted for publication. Each article published in a peer-reviewed journal can amount to 20 credits (20 ECTs), written and presented dissertation also earn twenty credits (20 ECTs), Thus, the two original scientific articles and dissertation presentation justify sixty credits (60 ECTs).

To facilitate PhD student progression, a doctoral research committee must be constituted for each candidate. This committee should have the responsibility of guiding the student through the dissertation process and to conduct the final oral defence. The research committee must comprise of at least four members. Two must be from the university of the student and among these one should be a specialist in the field under study to direct the dissertation. The two other members should be CRVPM staff, among which one should be the dissertation director. Adhering to these recommendations will better align current practices of the CRVPM with international best practices for examining PhD theses, emphasizing the importance of data quality and methodology as key criteria for thesis evaluation (Joyner, 2003; Holbrook et al., 2004; Tewari, 2012; Bourke & Holbrook, 2013). Each year of the programme, the PhD students should present a report of their activity to their doctoral research committee. Depending on the PhD programme duration, a student must present at least three reports to their committee by the end of programme. These three reports would net the PhD student forty-five credits (45 ECTs). To begin the construction of the identity of researcher, during their training, the doctoral students would have to present their work at an international congress of their specialties. This presentation would earn them fifteen credits (15 ECTs), thus completing the 180 ECTs required to obtain the PhD.

Table 1: Mandatory PhD programme activities

No.	Mandatory activities	Quantity	Credits
1	Workshops	6	60
2	Annually report	3	45
3	Participation to international congress	1	15
4	Articles published or accepted	2	40
5	Redaction and dissertation presentation	1	20
	Total		180

This structured programme could help the CRVPM and the candidates to better define the objectives of research learning, develop learning activities and evaluate the gains from this learning. However, it is recommended that two other weaknesses observed during the evaluation of the programme also be attended to:

- *Mobility and research identity*: Indeed, the process of introducing PhD candidates at the CRVMP into a community of scientists in his field is currently not optimal. As mobility is an element for the acquisition and qualification of skills, the programme must grant the doctoral student at least one semester to spend in other institutions outside Guinea for their research. Here, the adage *Chercheurs qui cherchent, on en trouve. Chercheurs qui trouvent, on en cherche* rings true (it can be loosely translated as, *"Researchers who are searching, we find them. Researchers who are finding, we are searching for them"*). It reflects the importance of the visibility of a researcher. And this visibility is facilitated largely through scientific publications and communication. The specification of a research theme and the researcher's regular publications on this research theme will enhance the visibility of the researcher. It is therefore important in the interest of the doctoral candidate to be integrated into the community of scientists in their field. To facilitate the mobility of PhD students, the CRVPM will have to strengthen its institutional partnerships.
- *Institutional partnerships:* The institutional partnerships of the CRVPM with (UGANC, UJNK), the pharmaceutical industry (AMB Pharma), and the Foundation for the fight against diabetes and non-communicable diseases of traditional healers mainly offer collaborations in the context of refilling activities but do not promote the transfer of skills. Except those who are in a sandwich fellowship programme, PhD students typically ship their work material to the partner and wait for the results. Not staying at the partnership institutions themselves, they do not acquire practical skills and do not benefit from any transfer of skills and technology. The

universities of origin of its doctoral students will have to offer study travel grants for the mobility of doctoral students and the transfer of skills.

5. Conclusion

For a training of trainers qualification in the health sciences, the doctorate is of obvious interest. The CRVPM, which hosts doctoral students in the health field must, however, better structure its PhD programme to ensure a certain level of quality for the students. But in the absence of funding and not very encouraging prospects in this regard, fewer candidates for certain basic disciplines come forward. The will of the authorities and the availability of funding are two essential conditions to improve the training of doctorates in our institutions.

References

Azevedo, M. J. (2017). *Historical perspectives on the state of health and health systems in Africa, Volume II: The modern era.* Cham: Springer.

Badley, G. (2009). Publish and be doctor-rated: The PhD by published work. *Quality Assurance in Education, 17*(4), 331–342.

Beaudry, C., Mouton, J., & Prozesky, H. (2018). *The next generation of scientists in Africa.* African Minds.

Bourke, S., & Holbrook, A. P. (2013). Examining PhD and research masters theses. *Assessment & Evaluation in Higher Education, 38*(4), 407–416.

Bryman, A. (2012). *Social research methods* (4th ed.). Oxford; New York: Oxford University Press.

Cross, M., & Backhouse, J. (2014). Evaluating doctoral programmes in Africa: Context and practices. *Higher Education Policy, 27*(2), 155–174.

Curtis, K., Fry, M., Shaban, R. Z., & Considine, J. (2017). Translating research findings to clinical nursing practice. *Journal of Clinical Nursing, 26*(5–6), 862–872.

Tewari, D. D. (2012). Examination of doctoral theses/dissertations: Models, practices, and guidelines. *African Journal of Business Management, 6*(9).

Fonn, S., Egesah, O., Cole, D., Griffiths, F., Manderson, L., Kabiru, C. W., ... & Ezeh, A. (2016). Building the capacity to solve complex health challenges in sub-Saharan Africa: CARTA's multidisciplinary PhD training. *Canadian Journal of Public Health, 107*(4–5), e381–e386.

Halvorsen, T. (2016). Higher education in developing countries: Peril and promise, a decade and a half later: Development lost? *International Journal of African Higher Education, 3*(1).

Holbrook, A., Bourke, S., Fairbairn, H., & Lovat, T. (2004). Investigating PhD thesis examination reports. *International Journal of Educational Research, 41*(2), 98–120.

Joyner, R. W. (2003). The selection of external examiners for research degrees. *Quality Assurance in Education, 11*(2), 123–127.

Lewin, K. M., & Stuart, J. M. (2003). Insights into the policy and practice of teacher education in low-income countries: The multi-site teacher education research project. *British Educational Research Journal, 29*(5), 691–707.

Maxwell, T. W., & Kupczyk-Romanczuk, G. (2009). Producing the professional doctorate: The portfolio as a legitimate alternative to the dissertation. *Innovations in Education and Teaching International, 46*(2), 135–145. https://doi.org/10.xxxxx

Maybee, C., Bruce, C., Lupton, M., & Rebmann, K. (2019). Informed learning design: Teaching and learning through engagement with information. *Higher Education Research & Development, 38*(3), 579–593

Ministère de l'enseignement supérieur et de la recherche scientifique. (2017). *Étude sur la réforme de l'enseignement et de la recherche en santé.*

Ortega, S. T., & Kent, J. D. (2018). What is a PhD? Reverse-engineering our degree programs in the age of evidence-based change. *Change: The Magazine of Higher Learning, 50*(1), 30–36.

CHAPTER 16

How are supervision skills developed? Perceptions of doctoral supervisors in selected universities in Kenya

Selline Atieno Oketch

The **Republic of Kenya** is on the eastern coast of Africa. With a population of about 50 million, it is the 27th most populous country in the world, and 7th in Africa. There are 61 fully chartered universities in Kenya. Of these, 36 are public and 25 private institutions. There are also five public and three private university constituent colleges in the country and eight degree-awarding institutions operating with letters of interim authority.

The **Catholic University of Eastern Africa** (CUEA) is in Lang'ata, on the outskirts of Nairobi. The CUEA received its charter in 1992 and currently it is one of the private universities in Kenya with students from across the Eastern African region. CUEA has 5 faculties, 2 schools, 2 institutes, and 1 centre, offering 11 doctoral programmes.

---

1. Introduction

The study reported in this chapter explored the state of doctoral supervision in Kenyan universities with an emphasis on the development of doctoral supervision skills. The discussion was based on doctoral supervisors' experiences with developing supervision skills in selected universities in Kenya. Supervision forms a critical component of the doctoral process. Supervision is fundamental because throughout the PhD journey, students encounter many challenges (Ndayambaje, 2018) and the supervisor, being a key person in the student's life throughout this period (Ali et al., 2016), is expected to offer the necessary support and guidance. To this extent, doctoral supervision entails guiding students in aspects such as identifying and critically interpreting relevant literature, developing research protocol and gaining skills in appropriate methods of conducting original research, managing and analysing the data as well as writing up their research (Manderson et al., 2017; Mouton et al., 2015). Doctoral supervisors should therefore be role models who pass on relevant skills to their students (Lugulu, 2022; Manderson et al., 2017).

Doctoral supervision comprises a tripartite relationship between the supervisor, the student and the institution. The doctoral supervisor supports the production of a quality thesis that will meet the expectations of the examination process and the entry of the doctoral student into the broader scholarly community (Amundsen & McAlpine, 2009). Doctoral students come from diverse backgrounds and have varied needs during their studies. The doctoral student expects an effective supervisor to be friendly, approachable, and aware of the standard of work expected from a student (Ali et al., 2006). Such a supervisor mentors a student to develop into an independent researcher (Manathunga, 2006). Problems related to supervision are the leading cause of untimely completion of PhD studies (Ndayambaje, 2018). Limiting itself to the supervisor's role, this study investigated how doctoral supervisors develop skills that ensure efficiency and quality in supervision. It was imperative to explore supervisors' perspectives on their own development of supervision skills.

2. Literature review

Doctoral education is increasingly becoming a critical area of research worldwide, with various institutions establishing frameworks and guidelines to ensure efficiency and quality in the various facets of doctoral education. Recognising and resolving the hurdles candidates face is critical and requires the attention of supervisors (Trafford & Lesham, 2009). Globally, questions are being asked about the quality of postgraduate studies and the supervision process (Spiller et al., 2013). There is increased emphasis on formal training, monitoring and accountability of doctoral supervisors, maintaining high standards as well as achieving higher and timely completion rates (Spiller et al., 2013; Halse, 2011). To enhance the quality of doctoral training, some universities have moved towards making supervisor training compulsory (Manderson et al., 2017). For example, several institutions in Europe have set up mandatory educational development programmes for research supervisors (Manthangu, 2006). A case in point is the Bologna seminar in Salzburg that brought together member universities of the European University Association (EUA) and other associations of higher education and research to deliberate on reforms in doctoral education leading to a consensus on ten basic principles (Botha et al., 2020; Manderson et al., 2017). Of these principles, the fifth one underscored the crucial role of supervision and assessment and emphasised the need for a contractual framework of shared responsibilities between doctoral candidates, supervisors and the institution (Botha et al., 2020; EUA, 2005, 2010). Research conducted in a UK university on supervisors' experiences of supervising PhD students identified five approaches which were then used to develop a framework for concepts of research supervision in tandem with the changes in the doctoral pedagogy (Lee, 2008).

Mouton et al., (2015) carried out a survey of doctoral supervisors in South Africa the focus of which was PhD supervisory approaches and styles as well as monitoring and feedback in the supervisor–student relationship. The study highlights Garfield's (2005) four-quadrant model of supervisory styles namely, laissez-faire, pastoral, directorial and contractual that a supervisor can adapt and vary at different stages of the student's doctoral research process; with the contractual style being the most preferred by supervisors. The study found that doctoral supervisors at South African universities faced many challenges such as the burden of large numbers of doctoral students to supervise, supervising outside one's area of expertise, poor quality and unpreparedness of many of the doctoral students, and the huge pressure to complete the doctoral study process due to competition for doctoral students. The concern for quality doctoral education in Africa resulted in the development of a comprehensive regional quality assurance framework by the Inter- University Council for East Africa (IUCEA) and the establishment of the Higher Education Qualifications Sub-Framework (HEQSF). Doctoral supervision is among the areas addressed in these frameworks (Botha et al., 2020).

The literature shows that earlier approaches to the development of supervisors focused on the individual supervisory relationships of a student learning from an expert supervisor with mutual roles and responsibilities of supervisors and students (Manathunga, 2006; Spiller et al., 2013). This model was supported by doctoral supervision development programmes such as the one-off workshop formula that sought to impart to the supervisors technical supervisory skills in the areas of roles and responsibilities of supervisors and students, project management, interpersonal relationships and communication (Manathunga, 2006). Largely, supervisors learned about supervision through their experiences of being supervised and received minimal educational development (Manathunga, 2006).

In more recent years, the literature demonstrates an emphasis on more innovative supervisor education programmes such as engaging small groups of supervisors in reflective practices about supervision (Spiller et al., 2013; Manathunga 2006; Amundsen & McAlpine, 2009). One example of such a programme is the Postgraduate Supervisors' Conversations set up in 2009 at the University of Waikato, New Zealand (Spiller et al., 2013), This programme utilises a conversational model whereby supervisors form a community to regularly exchange and explore narratives drawn from their own supervision experiences. The other examples are the Learning Circle on Postgraduate Supervision series and Compassionate Rigour: Effective Supervision programme established in 2002 (Manathunga, 2006). The former adopts methods that provide a context for supervisors to reflect on their own practice and share thoughts on their supervision strategies through informal presentations and reflection on postgraduate supervision experiences through activities such as role-plays, videos, dramatic performances and case studies. In the latter programme, supervisors are trained to strike a balance between having compassion for students and providing rigorous feedback on student performance.

In the African context, the literature shows that poor quality supervision is one of the innumerable challenges doctoral programmes faces (Ndayambaje 2018; Lugulu, 2022; Mohamedbhai, 2020; Rong'uno et al., 2016). Mbogo et al. (2020) cited the challenge of supervision as the main reason for delays in the completion of PhD studies in Kenyan universities, calling it an ethical matter that requires redress. The literature reviewed in their study reveals other factors associated with supervision such as a shortage of qualified supervisors, where some supervisors have insufficient knowledge of the students' research topics and hence are unable to provide constructive guidance. This latter view was confirmed by participant students in the findings of the same study while supervisors cited heavy workloads and non-enforcement of supervisory regulations as some of the supervision challenges they experienced. It is, therefore, imperative for supervisors to take cognisance of the triangular nature of the supervision process consisting of the student, the supervisor and their relationship where each has a significant role to play. This relationship needs to create a 'fit' which leads to the student's satisfaction with their supervision (Pyhältö et al., 2015).

This issue of 'fit' is pertinent because it is what can make or break a doctoral; and researchers elaborate on it in different ways (Lee, 2008; Keefer, 2015; Bastalich, 2017). Timely completion of doctoral studies can be enhanced if monitoring and structured systems such as deadlines and standard supervision guidelines are established (Rong'uno et al., 2016). This is akin to drawing up a memorandum of understanding (MoU) between the supervisor and the student that specifies meeting schedules as well as each party's responsibilities.

In Kenya, the Ministry of Education and the Commission for University Education (CUE) require universities to examine and improve higher degree training and supervision (Manderson et al., 2017). In 2019, there was a public outcry in Kenya when a public university awarded PhD degrees to an unusually high number of students. The CUE's report on the investigation highlighted, among other findings, inadequate supervision and heavy workload for some supervisors' way beyond the threshold of three PhDs and five master's in an academic year as provided under CUE's Universities' Standards and Guidelines (Ligami, 2019; Ndiege, 2019, Mohamedbhai, 2020). Training programmes for PhD supervisors have been cited as one of the steps towards solution of these challenges. This study joins these calls and extends the scholarly conversation on the significance of improving the quality of doctoral supervision by focusing attention on how supervisors develop their supervision skills.

3. Objectives

3.1 General

- To explore how doctoral supervisors develop supervision skills.

3.2 Specific

- To determine supervisors' opinions on whether they develop supervision skills within the guidelines for doctoral supervision in Kenyan universities.
- To assess the perceptions of doctoral supervisors on the specific indicators of how they developed supervision skills.
- To describe the challenges that new doctoral supervisors experience in the process of learning how to supervise.
- To recommend any practices that could enhance the supervisors' skills and improve doctoral supervision in Kenyan universities.

4. Methodology

The study was conducted in Kenya between October and November 2020. The study utilised qualitative research methodology where expert purposive sampling was used to identify eight doctoral supervisors drawn from five disciplines across six different universities in Kenya, five public and one private. The sample consisted of two supervisors with over ten years of doctoral supervision experience, four with over five years of doctoral supervision and two in their initial year of doctoral supervision. Discipline-wise, two supervisors specialized in literature, two in linguistics, two in education, one in business and one in women studies. In addition, one interviewee was at the level of professor; six were senior lecturers and only one was at the level of lecturer. Telephone calls and WhatsApp, and social media platforms were used to contact participants and explain to them the nature of the study. The respondents were sampled because they are doctoral supervisors and would provide information based on their knowledge and experience. An online questionnaire and phone interviews were used as the most appropriate data collection methods because they allowed the participants the flexibility of elaborating on their opinions on how they developed doctoral supervision skills, as the study sought from them. The link for the questionnaire was sent to the participants through emails. Data were downloaded and summarised according to the participants' responses to each item on the questionnaire. A qualitative descriptive methodology was used to describe and interpret the data collected. The participants were asked fifteen questions, and their responses were analysed and grouped into themes that formed the four main categories reflected by the objectives of this study.

5. Results and discussion

5.1 Views about guidelines for doctoral supervision in Kenyan universities

The Commission for University Education (CUE) (2014) stipulates that an academic staff member must be assigned to supervise a thesis considering their teaching load, administration duties, and supervision experience. Further, an academic staff member may supervise a maximum of five master's and three doctoral students in any given academic year. The regulatory body also requires each university to provide clear guidelines on various operations, including the conduct of studies and supervision (CHE, 2008).

The respondents were asked questions concerning eligibility for doctoral supervision, the number of years between PhD attainment and the assignment of first supervision as well as the maximum number of doctoral students that they supervise per year. On eligibility for supervision, all eight respondents cited the attainment of a doctorate and expertise in the student's area of research as key eligibility criteria for doctoral supervision. One respondent expressed reservations on the interpretation of 'expertise':

Expertise is sometimes taken to be so broad which is still likely to pose a challenge to a supervisor because within a discipline like Literature, for example, different specializations require specific expertise. A lecturer in say Genre Analysis and interpretation may not have the expertise to supervise in the area of performing arts or film studies. The same applies to linguistics and many other disciplines. (Senior lecturer, literature)

Concerning the number of doctoral students per supervisor, all respondents, except one, had a maximum of three doctoral supervisees in line with the Commission for University Education's regulation that each supervisor should not supervise more than three doctoral students per year. The one respondent shared that he had four doctoral students due to a shortage of supervisors. Studies show that additional numbers of students to supervise is increasingly becoming one of the challenges of doctoral supervision (Mouton et al., 2015).

On the period between the doctorate and first supervision, the responses show that the participants' institutions follow the guidelines set by their departments, that one was eligible for supervision three years after the doctorate. Only one began to supervise soon after attaining a PhD due to lack of doctoral supervisors in his field to match the number of students enrolled. A similar situation was reflected in a survey of doctoral supervisors in South Africa, with the researchers strongly recommending that novice supervisors do not initially accept more than one or two students to supervise or, preferably, to do so under an experienced supervisor (Mouton et al., 2015).

5.2 How the supervisors developed supervision skills, the core areas of the students' research that they examined and the students' main challenges in research

The main purpose of this survey was to determine from the participants how they developed their supervision skills. All the respondents expressed that they learned from their own experiences as postgraduate students and transferred their own supervisors' best practices first to supervision at the master's level which they then refined for the doctoral level. Additionally, one respondent stated that he learned supervision skills from a doctoral supervision course offered to supervisors across Africa, while two others highlighted self-learning on the job and reading manuals on requirements for supervision as well as consultations. This response corroborates the finding that supervisors learn self-protective strategies while supervising their students (Halse, 2011). In contrast, the study by Halse also found that supervisors learn disciplined supervision that entailed discarding their supervisors' mode of supervision during their own doctorate and shaping new identities. One respondent expressed the following opinion:

> *Ideally, you should learn through mentorship but in our institutions, mentors at the level of professors and associate professors are sometimes shuttled off into administration so they lose academic grounding with the field and leave supervision to young researchers. We need to understand our context and challenges and regularize scholarly communities.* (Senior lecturer, applied linguistics)

As an indicator of their doctoral supervision skills, the respondents were further asked to specify the core areas of the students' research that they examine. The recurrent areas in their responses include the research problem, literature review, methodology, application of theory and the ability to write the thesis. These areas would all fit in the category of the functional approach to supervision. Lee (2008) developed a framework for research supervision concepts that also includes enculturation, critical thinking, emancipation and relationship development. Lee notes that whereas pragmatic issues such as time and workload may create the option of a functional approach, the last two approaches help students to work towards independence.

The participants were also asked to mention the areas that doctoral students find most challenging during the research. They cited clear identification and explanation of research gaps, conceptualising the research problem, as well as identifying and applying a relevant theory. Other areas included the analysis and reporting of different categories of data, sampling and reluctance to read widely. Some of these challenges are like those identified in a study in Kenyan universities by Mbogo et al. (2020), which showed that students lacked sufficient writing skills, research skills and the competence to adequately read the literature on the research topic. Other literature relate doctoral students' challenges to the diverse nature of the postgraduate student population in terms of culture, gender, language and background experience (Mouton et al., 2015; Spiller et al., 2013; Halse, 2011; Amundsen & McAlpine, 2009).

Related questions within this objective asked how often the supervisor met the supervisee and their responsibilities in relation to those of the co-supervisor. From the responses, four met the students as often as possible and when the need arose, three met them once a month while one met them once a week. The respondents were further asked to specify their responsibilities in relation to those of the co-supervisors. From their responses, it was construed that all except two are first supervisors. Two respondents expressed that both supervisors are collectively and independently responsible for guiding the student and they exchange feedback. One stated that the first supervisor should mentor the co-supervisor, but this is not always the case. One other response was as follows:

> We expect teamwork although you find other members doing so little in terms of giving feedback to students. It becomes lopsided since there is no clear indication of who does what apart from that the first supervisor does a lot of correspondence between the student and the Graduate school. (Senior lecturer, women studies)

Another respondent had this to say:

> Our policies are not well-structured, especially on the role of the co-supervisor. From my own experience as a doctoral student in the West, my second supervisor provided a methodological angle to my study and acted as the critical eye. (Senior lecturer, linguistics)

Generally, what emerges from these responses is that although universities may have regulations governing doctoral supervision, it is important for supervisors to adopt best practices from other contexts such as drawing up a memorandum of understanding (MoU) between the supervisor and the student that spells out expectations and timelines so that even students begin to take charge of their own responsibilities. A written agreement of this kind enhances the working relationship and can highly minimize the challenges of supervision. Other practices include adopting a combination of "compassion" and "rigour" (Manthangu, 2006:17) in the supervision process and learning to be flexible to address students' needs at different stages of the doctorate (Halse, 2011).

5.3 The challenges that the supervisors experienced in the course of their first doctoral supervision

As indicated above, three years after attaining the doctorate, one is eligible for doctoral supervision. It is a transitional state from the supervised to being the supervisor. This study considered how universities facilitate that transition and sought to find out from the participants their own experiences of how they became supervisors. The respondents felt that they should have been formally inducted into supervision through some departmental or faculty training programmes. Seven respondents indicated that three years after attaining the

PhD, they were assigned students to supervise without any formal structure to train them as new doctoral supervisors, so they received no training on doctoral supervision. They relied on how they were supervised as doctoral students. One respondent indicated that she trained in her post-doctoral programme before she began to supervise.

It was evident that the respondents were conscious that doctoral study in itself does not train one to become a supervisor and there is a need for specialized training that focuses on doctoral supervision. One respondent indicated that he attends regular workshops and seminars organised by his departments on a wide range of academic areas. One other respondent had attended a course for training postgraduate supervisors before he began to supervise. One respondent pointed out the feeling of inexperience and fear associated with supervising outside his subject area even if slightly related. Another found herself arranging several meetings with students to discuss minor issues that students could work out independently.

A seminar organised by CUE and other partners in 2016 recognised the training of supervisors as a priority area (Botha et al., 2020). While workshops may be the initial starting points to train doctoral supervisors, the available literature indicates that the one-off workshop formula may not be adequate and there is a need to adopt more innovative practices such as bringing the doctoral supervisors together to reflect and have conversations on their own experiences (Manthangu, 2006; Spiller et al., 2013).

5.4   Suggestions on areas of improvement to ensure that the supervisors' skills yield quality doctoral supervision

All the respondents suggested that their departments should put in place training programmes to induct doctoral supervisors. They also expressed that exposure to more research opportunities for growth and diversification would greatly enhance their supervision skills. Other suggestions for improvement that the respondents made were regular submission of supervision reports, equitable distribution of supervision tasks and the need to put in place mechanisms to ensure that students admitted into the doctoral programme have the capacity to undertake research, and collaborations with other institutions as a way of addressing the problem of supervisory capacity as well as sharing the best supervision practices.

These suggestions show that doctoral supervision is a broad area that requires diverse research. They are also consistent with findings in previous literature that there is a need to invest in supervisor educational development for doctoral supervisors to reflect on their pedagogical understandings of their own supervision strategies (Manathunga, 2006; Spiller et al., 2013; Halse, 2011; Amundsen & McAlpine, 2009).

The data generated in this study, despite emanating from a small sample, is critical to understanding the current state of doctoral supervision and doctoral study completion rates in both private and public Kenyan universities. It corroborates findings in other studies (Rong'uno et al., 2016; Mbogo et al., 2022; Lugulu, 2022).

6. Limitations of the study

The study sample of eight doctoral supervisors was very small given that the eight were drawn from six universities in Kenya. The limited time for this study necessitated the researcher's use of expert purposive sampling methodology to identify doctoral supervisors who were already known and accessible through WhatsApp, email and telephone to provide the data. Furthermore, the study did not include doctoral students to assess their own perceptions of the quality of the supervision they received from supervisors hence the study only relied on the perceptions of the supervisors to assess how doctoral supervisors developed supervision skills.

7. Recommendations

Based on the findings, the study recommends that Kenyan universities enhance induction training for new supervisors in the form of workshops, seminars and conferences, both at the faculty and institutional levels. In addition, new supervisors should begin supervision as co-supervisors where the first supervisor should be an expert in the supervision field and thus provide mentorship. The universities should introduce the contract method where supervisors and students draw up a memorandum of understanding (MoU) to regulate their meetings, areas of the research to focus on, each party's responsibilities and clear timelines for the completion of the project. Doctoral supervisors should also be exposed to regular training with a focus on exposing them to diverse supervision styles and models. Specifically, the supervisors should be exposed to models such as Garfield's (2005) model elaborately discussed in (Mouton et al., 2015). The model identifies two dimensions of supervision namely, structure and support, and spells out the relevant supervision styles that supervisors can adopt in the various stages of supervision. There is a need to benchmark with more established universities to keep abreast with the current global doctoral supervision practices that may be transferable to their contexts. The study has already referred to the reflective practices of supervision (Manathunga, 2006) and the conversational approach of the case study at Waikato University, New Zealand (Spiller et al., 2013). Doctoral supervisors in Kenyan universities could initiate their own conversations to share and exchange ideas and thoughts about their supervision skills and strategies. Finally, there is a need to investigate the findings of this study further with a larger sample drawn from one university and later extend it to a few universities in Kenya.

8. Conclusion

The study sought to assess how doctoral supervisors developed their supervision skills. The data examined were based on the perceptions of eight supervisors drawn from six universities in Kenya. Questions on supervision guidelines and challenges encountered during supervision as well as the capacity-building measures taken by departments or faculties in the respective universities aimed at demonstrating the significance of supervisory skills to the whole doctoral study process. The study identified a few indicators to show that supervisors continue to develop supervision skills. However, it also identified challenges that supervisors experienced as new doctoral supervisors and those that persist as well as some strategies for improving the quality of doctoral supervision. These conclusions can be summarised as follows:

Doctoral supervisors in universities in Kenya generally follow standards and regulations on supervision set up by the Commission for University Education.

Mentorship in doctoral supervision is weak such that new doctoral supervisors who mostly begin to supervise three years after their doctorate receive minimal induction into supervision as many departments have not established such training programmes.

The initial skills that they bring into the supervision process are those that they gained from observing from their supervisors during their own doctoral studies.

However, doctoral supervisors are keen to develop their supervision skills, and they use every opportunity that avails itself in the process of supervision.

They systematically develop skills through experience, self-learning, reading manuals, consultations and attending workshops and seminars on doctoral supervision

References

Ali, P. A., Watson, R., & Dhingra, K. (2016). Postgraduate research students and their supervisors' attitudes towards supervision. *International Journal of Doctoral Studies, 11*, 227–221. https://eprints.leedsbeckett. ac.uk/id/eprint/2895/

Amundsen, C., & McAlpine, L. (2009). Learning supervision: Trial by fire. *Innovations in Education and Teaching International, 46*(3), 331–342. https://doi.org/10.1080/14703290903068805

Bastalich, W. (2017). Content and context in knowledge production: A critical review of doctoral supervision literature. *Studies in Higher Education, 42*(7), 1145–1157. https://doi.org/10.1080/03075079.2015. 1079702

Bitzer, E. (2016). Research into doctoral education: A survey of institutional research projects in South Africa. In J. Botha & N. Miller (Eds.), *Institutional Research in South Africa Higher Education.* pp. 277-297. Stellenbosch: SUN Press.

Botha, J., Kuria, M., Ozgoren, M., & Wilde, M. (2020). Quality doctoral education in Africa: A question of setting the right standards. In Rule, P., Bitzer, E., & Frick, L. (Eds.) *The Global Scholar: Implications for Postgraduate Studies and Supervision.* pp. 149-174. SUN Media.

Commission for University Education. (2014). *University standards and guidelines.* https://www.jooust.ac.ke/ downloads/insefood/CUE_UNIVERSITIES_STANDARDS_AND_GUIDELINES_June_2014.pdf

Commission for Higher Education. (2008). *Handbook on processes for quality assurance in higher education in Kenya.* https://www.cue.or.ke/index. php?option=com_phocadownload&view=category&download=67:handbook-on-processes-for-quali- ty-assurance-in-higher-education-in-kenya&id=12:general&Itemid=392

Dietz, T., Jansen, J., & Wadee, A. (2006). *South Africa–Netherlands research programmes in alternatives in devel- opment (SANPAD); Effective PhD supervision and mentorship: A workbook based on experiences from South Africa and the Netherlands.* Pretoria: UNISA Press.

Halse, C. (2011). Becoming a supervisor: The impact of doctoral supervision on supervisors' learning. *Studies in Higher Education, 36*(5), 557–570. https://doi.org/10.1080/03075079.2011.594593

Keefer, J. (2015). Experiencing doctoral liminality as a conceptual threshold and how supervisors can use it. *Innovations in Education and Teaching International, 52*(1), 17–28. https://doi.org/10.1080/14703297.20 14.981839

Lee, A. (2008). How are doctoral students supervised? Concepts of doctoral research supervision. *Studies in Higher Education, 33*(3), 267–381.

Ligami, C. (2020). Over 100 PhDs face review in single university. *University World News.* https://www.uni- versityworldnews.com/post.php?story=2019080207255286

Lugulu, J. (2022). Students' perception of factors that influence completion rates of doctoral studies in public universities in Kenya. *International Journal of Education, Humanities and Social Science.* https://doi. org/10/1054922/IJEHSS.2022.0366

Manderson, L., Bondjers, G., Izugbara, C., Cole, D. C., Egesa, O., Ezeh, A., & Fonn, S. (2017). Enhancing doc- toral supervision practices in Africa. *Journal of Higher Education in Africa, 15*(2), 23–40. https://www. jstor.org/stable/10.2307/26640369

Manathunga, C. (2006). The development of research supervision: "Turning the light on a private space." *International Journal for Academic Development, 10*(1), 17–30. https://doi. org/10.1080/13601440500099977

Mbogo, R. W., Ndiao, E., Wambua, J. M., Ireri, N. W., & Ngala, F. W. (2020). Supervision challenges and delays in completion of PhD programmes in public and private universities: Experiences of supervisors and graduate students in Kenya. *European Journal of Education, 6*(11), 261–278. https://www.oapub.org/edu

Mouton, J., Boshoff, N., & James, M. (2015). A survey of doctoral supervision in South Africa. *South African Journal of Higher Education, 29*(2), 1–22. https://doi.org/10.20853/29-2-467

Mohamedbhai, G. (2020). Quality assurance of doctoral education is now urgent. *University World News Africa Edition.* https://www.universityworldnews.com/post.php?story=20200609091837168

Ndayambaje, I. (2018). Effects of supervision on timely completion of PhD programme. *Rwandan Journal,* 4(2), 57–70. https://www.ajol.info/index.php/rje/article/view/175133

Ndiege, J. R. (2019). Kenyan varsities need training programmes for PhD supervisors. *Business Daily.* https://www.businessdailyafrica.com/analysis/ideas/Kenyan-universities-should-train-PhD-supervisors/4259414-5125406-11fwuus/index.html

Pyhältö, K., Vekalia, J., & Koeskinen, J. (2015). Fit matters in the supervisory relationship: Doctoral students and supervisors' perceptions about the supervisory activities. *Innovations in Education and Teaching International, 52*(1). https://doi.org/10.1080/14703297.2014.981836

Rong'uno, S. K., Okoth, U., & Akala, W. (2016). Supervision-related factors influencing doctoral studies completion rates in education at public universities in Kenya. *International Journal of Innovative Research and Development, 5*(10), 462–477. https://www.ijird.com

Spiller, D., Byrnes, G., & Ferguson, P. B. (2013). Enhancing postgraduate supervision through a process of conversational inquiry. *Higher Education Research & Development, 32*(5), 833–845. https://doi.org/10.1080/07294360.2013.776519

Trafford, V., & Lesham, S. (2009). Doctorateness as a threshold concept. *Innovations in Education and Teaching International, 46*(3), 305–316. https://doi.org/10.1080/14703290903069027

Appendix

Link to Google form questionnaire:
https://docs.google.com/forms/d/1GEnim_mu7h3SeZo-jHlkYkhVwki3IhHGx-VWLojHuH-g/edit

TOWARDS BECOMING A DOCTORAL SUPERVISOR

I am conducting a survey as part of a course on the Supervision of Doctoral studies in African Universities. Kindly fill out the survey below which is a brief exploration of the training of doctoral supervisors. Your voluntary participation is highly appreciated and no personal details will be shared in the write-up of the data. Thank you in advance for your responses.

Your email address

_____

Question 1- Demographics-Age
☐ 30-40
☐ 41-50
☐ 51-60
☐ 61 and above

Question 2- Qualification
☐ Master's Degree
☐ Doctorate

Question 3- Your discipline of study
Your answer

_____

Question 4- Number of PhD candidates currently under your supervision
☐ 1-3
☐ 4-6
☐ 0
☐ Other

Question 5- The years between your own PhD and your first doctoral supervision
☐ 1-3
☐ 4-6
☐ Other

Question 6-What three reasons motivate you to supervise doctoral students?
Your answer

_____

Question 7- Explain the policy of your institution or faculty governing the eligibility for doctoral supervision and the maximum number of supervisions.
Your answer

_____

Question 8- How did you acquire supervision skills? Did you require any form of training before you began to supervise doctoral students? Briefly explain.
Your answer

_____

Question 9- How often do you meet your supervisees?
☐ Once a week
☐ Once a month
☐ Other, specify

_____

Question 10-Which four core areas of the student's dissertation/thesis do you focus on in your supervision?
Your answer

_____

Question 11- Kindly share your experience on the area that doctoral students find most challenging during their research process.
Your answer

_____

Question 12- Kindly explain your responsibilities in relation to those for your co-supervisor.
Your answer

_____

Question 13- Kindly share the challenges that you may have experienced when you began your doctoral supervision.
Your answer

_____

Question 14- Does your Department have a programme of inducting young scholars into doctoral supervision? If yes, kindly explain.
Your answer

_____

Question 15- Kindly share your suggestions on the areas that your Department needs to improve on to ensure quality doctoral supervision.
Your answer

_____

CHAPTER 17

Remote supervision of doctoral research using WhatsApp in universities in Benin

Tognon Clotilde Guidi

Benin Republic is in West Africa. It has a population of 13 million. There are four public universities in Benin. The University of Abomey-Calavi (UAC), the University of Parakou (UP), the Agricultural University at Ketou (UK) and the National University of Sciences, Technologies, Engineering and Mathematics of Benin (UNSTIM). In 2022 more than 711 candidates were registered in seven doctoral schools in the country. The doctoral programme offers further education that can help a student become an expert in his or her field. A doctoral programme typically takes three to five years to complete and involves independent study and research in a focused area of interest. Doctoral programmes in Benin include course work and research that culminate in a final dissertation.

1. Introduction

This study focused on the use of WhatsApp as a tool to enhance doctoral supervision in the Benin Republic. Over the past twenty years or so, there has been a growing interest in doctoral education in the country, resulting in a rise in postgraduate enrolments. Regrettably, however, this increase in enrolments has not always led to successful completions. A significant factor contributing to this situation is the limited number of supervisors, many of whom are burdened with heavy supervision loads.

There have been studies on the use of social media technologies in education in recent years in many African countries. These include Pimmer (2016), who suggests the use of Facebook as a research education tool in disadvantaged areas, Rambe and Mkono (2019) who advocate for appropriating WhatsApp-mediated postgraduate supervision to negotiate "relational authenticity" in resource-constrained environments and Ngakane et al. (2022) who focus on effectiveness and policy implications of using WhatsApp to supervise research projects in open distance learning teacher training institutions. There has also been extensive research into the potential role of electronic and mobile learning. But no research exists on WhatsApp interventions in doctoral supervision in Benin Republic so far.

This study assesses the potential of WhatsApp-based supervision in supporting doctoral training in Benin Republic. As the largest messaging platform, WhatsApp has become the most used and useful application for mobile communication all around the world (Motteram, 2019). Groups of people only need an internet connection (wi-fi or cellular network) and smart phones to instantly share unlimited text messages, voice notes, voice calls, group calls, and files. WhatsApp came into being in 2009 and was reported to have 1.5 billion users in over 180 countries in 2019 (Motteram, 2019). It has become one of the most downloaded Android apps focused on mobile usage in developing countries (Porter et al., 2016). WhatsApp seems, therefore, a good starting point as an alternative method of facilitating communication with the potential of improving doctoral supervision.

This study, which assesses the level of practice and experiences in using WhatsApp to support doctoral supervision in Benin Republic, is structured around five points: literature review; study objectives; the case study; results/discussion; and the conclusion.

2. Literature review

Doctoral supervision deserves special attention for it is easy for doctoral candidates to become isolated, with busy supervisors who fail to interact with their supervisees. Jones (2013) indicates that most supervisors today lack adequate supervisory capabilities and time and largely tend to overlook their fundamental role as mentors. Using the social media space can lower learners' thresholds to accessing educational resources (Pimmer, 2015). WhatsApp can be an excellent tool for cooperation between supervisors and doctoral candidates. Authentic supervision can be constructed through supervisor–supervisees' negotiation of academic hierarchies, supervisees' self-expression and self-disclosure. Supervisors need to manage the significant yet unrecognised "nervous moments" in technology-mediated supervision environments, where compression of hierarchy may be conflated with negation of the supervisor's authority (Rambe & Mkono, 2019:702).

High-tech tools like video conferencing applications are attractive; however, they need higher bandwidth than media tools like WhatsApp (Motteram, 2019). If WhatsApp is well controlled and managed, it could be beneficial for education (Motteram et al., 2020). WhatsApp and similar multimodal devices — such as WeChat, Viber or Telegram — are able to handle text, pictures, sound files and video as well as voice calls. In low-resource and fragile contexts, teachers are often the most valuable resources available to students. Motteram (2020) identifies the potential for WhatsApp groups to contribute to learning in various ways: sharing of resources and materials and discussion on different aspects of learning. WhatsApp is an effective platform in research project supervision. However, the use of WhatsApp poses challenges to students who come from poor socio-economic backgrounds since they cannot always manage to buy compatible gadgets and data bundles. It also poses some challenges to those students who come from communities with poor or no internet connectivity (Ngakane et al., 2022).

3. Study objectives

This study aims to explore at what modalities low-tech, low-cost, readily available forms of technology might contribute to doctoral supervision in challenging contexts. The investigation sought supervisors and students' experiences and challenges relating to the use of WhatsApp for doctoral supervision in Benin Republic. To achieve its aim, we used the following research questions:

1. What forms of supervision practice emerge from the use of WhatsApp in the context under investigation?
2. What are the challenges in using WhatsApp for doctoral supervision?

4. The study

4.1 Context of the study

The majority of doctoral candidates in the context under investigation work outside of the university and reconciling study and work is a challenge. Some of those doctoral students have difficulties in making appointments and meetings with supervisors. Supervisors are too often faced with work overload. It is not uncommon to see supervisors teaching here and there, and supervising as well.

This leaves little to no time for 'free' supervision of students. Combining heavy teaching and research responsibilities with consultancy results in the fact that there is no time left for good supervision.

The mobile phone is the most accessible and commonly owned technology for participants in the context under investigation. Mobile data represented the most frequent way of connecting to the internet. Connecting to wi-fi at home is the least common method.

4.2 Participants and instruments

Twenty-two participants in science-related disciplines took part in the study, among which seventeen were supervisors (two females and fifteen males) and five doctoral candidates (one female and four males). The study focused on five doctoral students because only five respondent supervisors were able to provide doctoral candidates from whom to collect data for the study. A questionnaire was designed to collect background information from the seventeen supervisors and five doctoral candidates. This procedure was adopted primarily to understand more about the participants themselves (supervision experience and their employment situation). Then, I aimed at understanding the types of technology available to them personally, the way they connect to the internet and the reliability of that connection. I wanted to gauge their interest in online supervision and to discover the sorts of areas they would like to explore. I designed an interview schedule for the five supervisors and the five doctoral students suggested for the study.

The researcher met participants to explanation the project. This allowed them to give the researcher permission to be part of the research study in a format they could comfortably access. Another very important ethical consideration was the protection of the participants' identity and dignity. Therefore, to ensure anonymity, the researcher provided participants with pseudonyms which do not expose their identities.

5. Results

This section provides the outcomes of the study. It displays the answers to the questionnaire as well as the interview. The answers were analysed using descriptive statistics and thematic analysis.

5.1 Respondents' characteristics in the context under investigation

One of the aims of the study was to understand the sort of access participants had to the internet, how they accessed it and the equipment they had.

Table 1: Participants' personal access to technology

Population	Participants	Mobile phone	Laptop	Tablet	Desktop
Supervisors	17	17	17	11	13
Doctoral students	5	5	2	0	1

Table 1 shows the mobile phone as the most accessible and frequently owned technology for participants in the context under investigation. Mobile data represented the most frequent way of connecting to the internet (22 out of 22 in the study), while connecting through wi-fi at home was the least common method. Data connection was deemed reliable by fifty-two per cent (52%) of the respondents, with thirty-one per cent (31%) saying that it was not reliable.

5.2 Forms of practice and doctoral supervision by means of WhatsApp chats

WhatsApp activities were developed for supervision in the context under investigation. These groups primarily seek to share resources and information via WhatsApp. Attending meetings, sharing presentations and talking about candidates' difficulties are other forms of practice.

One of the student respondents said: *"My supervisor uses WhatsApp to announce events and scholarship opportunities and share administrative information and documents with me."*

For some supervisor respondents, WhatsApp constitutes a fantastic learning tool. Some asserted that WhatsApp could be used to work collaboratively. In that connection, another respondent added: *"It is awesome and fantastic to share our experiences to build relationships, and it is also good to improve our supervision practices in different ways."*

Learning happened around specific aspects of supervision; for example, the respondents spent a lot of time discussing the content of some chapters.

WhatsApp is crucial in offering psychological support and sharing information with doctoral students. Data collected from supervisors showed that time spent on WhatsApp positively affected doctoral student psychological wellbeing. This supportive relationship has helped sustain students' sense of wellbeing and commitment to their research work. It also recognises a collective responsibility to each other as supervisors and doctoral candidates collaborate in trust and respect for each other.

5.3 Challenges in using WhatsApp for doctoral supervision in the context under investigation

Even though WhatsApp could be used for supervision activities, it could also be challenging for teachers, whose difficulties with the application and context of its use included technical and technological, economic, political, data protection and time-related concerns.

Technological and technical challenges

Even though WhatsApp does not require sophisticated technical skills, the ability to install and use the application constitutes an issue. Participants in the context under investigation were not sufficiently prepared to meet the required technical standard skills for WhatsApp chats. The difficulty lay with supervisors who struggled to gain technological fluency. Many identified barriers continued to prevail in the study, not for lack of participants' trying but because of the overwhelming nature of technology. The study also shows that many supervisor respondents were often resistant to technology because they did not see it as part of their content responsibilities. Time allotted for mobile phones and computers means learning how to use a function with little or no concrete connection to supervision activities. Some of the respondents were reluctant to use WhatsApp and others were against social media entirely and did not want to join any WhatsApp group. Of those who were computer literate, some did not want to join any WhatsApp group because of an unfortunate event they experienced related to social media in the past.

> "I had downloaded a software as WhatsApp desktop application one day and the installation distributed malware that compromised my computer," Fedi complained.

Reliable connectivity remains another technical challenge. While city residents have access to better internet connection, rural area residents are poorly served. In any case and regardless of one's place of residence, connection is costly for the doctoral candidate with their meagre income. Many candidates who had smartphones could not afford the cost of mobile data. Furthermore, the network saturation and bandwidth in urban areas and the non-coverage of some remote villages made the use of WhatsApp very challenging for many informants.

Economic and political challenges

Communication has been identified as one of the 21st-century skills necessary for meeting many of the development imperatives expressed in the UN's Sustainable Development Goals for Africa. Information and communication technologies (ICTs) hold the potential to drive development and transform education. However, ICT policies and systems that may promote this growth are not in line with participants' economic realities. There are regions lacking electricity, a crucial component in ICT access. In Benin Republic, the use of technology-mediated learning that allows for improved learning and additional access to higher education is limited. In the extant literature, it is recognised that the diffusion and adoption of technologies uphold, or even further amplify, educational inequality. An example being the differences between those who can access and make use of digital knowledge sources and those who do not have such means at their disposal (Pimmer, 2016).

Time

Another major challenge was the time factor. Some participants saw WhatsApp as a time-consuming activity. One of the informants, declared the following: "*I prefer face-to-face collaboration with my doctoral candidates than wasting my time by punching fingers over a glass screen that takes the non-verbal aspect of communication away and replaces emotions with phony emoticons where a person types ten smileys even though they might be frowning.*" Furthermore, another challenge was agreeing on a time to engage with doctoral candidates through WhatsApp. Time zone differences makes it very hard for local students to learn from and share with international supervisors.

Data protection

During the study, many scholar respondents reported concerns about data protection issues. Respondents live in a data-driven world. Almost every transaction and interaction one has involves data sharing. Every time social media is used data is shared. Respondents value the use of one's data only in ways one would reasonably expect, and that it stays safe. Most of the participants were cautious regarding the use of WhatsApp in supervision because they thought students' projects may be exposed to data protection issues.

6. Discussion

The use of WhatsApp could strengthen the relationships between supervisors and candidates, moving the students from isolation to a supported community by fostering in them a sense of belonging in the context under investigation. Sharing resources and spreading information are significant activities. The feeling of belonging to a community tearing down the barriers that used to isolate the supervisor and the student. The WhatsApp platform could succeed in bringing the two parties together through a relatively universally accessible medium.

However, some challenges need to be considered as well: some doctoral candidates live in rural areas deprived of electricity and thus have very limited internet access. One candidate made the following comment: "*I am not lucky. I don't have electricity although I can afford to use my personal computer.*" The implication seems to be that not all candidates have the luxury of electricity. What is clear is that there is great variety in terms of access to electricity among the student respondents and therefore the state should provide electricity for the specific local, as well as national, context. Furthermore, the study revealed that WhatsApp cannot replace the face-to-face aspect of communication in the supervisory relationship; not everything can or should be done through social media.

Several previous studies have found that specific structural, programme-level characteristics are essential to the creation of a successful educational WhatsApp group. This study suggests that WhatsApp could play a vital role in doctoral supervision in challenging contexts.

7. Suggestions

Doctoral schools and laboratories should provide internet connection to both supervisors and doctoral candidates. For doctoral candidates in remote and rural communities, where access to the internet access is more sporadic, it may be necessary to purchase mobile data. That could increase their access to the internet. This might encourage continued uptake. More adapted software should also be designed. Providing dedicated time and space for reflection is essential for doctoral candidates, enabling supervisors to engage more deeply with the substance of their supervision.

8. Conclusion

This study investigated the possible role of WhatsApp in doctoral supervision in Benin Republic. The combination of the literature review and the implementation of the questionnaire and interview have shown how technological innovations have opened up supervisors' options for networking and improving their supervision practices. WhatsApp can be an excellent tool for compensating for the packed schedule of supervisors. It can be used to provide feedback and support to doctoral candidates. In today's knowledge economy, innovation and technological change are recognised as the primary drivers of progress. Creating a space and time for reflection is necessary for doctoral students. If WhatsApp is well controlled and managed, it can be beneficial for doctoral education. However, it needs to be set up and managed in a context of good connectivity.

References

Katz, R. (2016). Challenges in doctoral research project management: A comparative study. *International Journal of Doctoral Studies, 11*, 105–125. Retrieved from http://ijds.org/Volume11/IJDSv11p105-125Katz2054.pdf

Motteram, G., & Dawson, S. (2020). Resilience and language teacher development in challenging contexts: Supporting teachers through social media. British Council.

Motteram, G. (2019). Videoconferencing tools as mediating artefacts in English language teacher development in challenging contexts. *The Journal of Educators Online, 16*(1). https://doi.org/10.9743/jeo.2019.16.1.10

Ngakane, B., & Madlela, B. (2022). Effectiveness and policy implications of using WhatsApp to supervise research projects in open distance learning teacher training institutions in Swaziland. *Indiana Journal of Humanities and Social Sciences, 3*(3), 1–10.

Pimmer, C., & Tulenko, K. (2015). The convergence of mobile and social media: Affordances and constraints of mobile networked communication for health workers in low- and middle-income countries. *Mobile Media & Communication.* https://doi.org/10.1177/2050157915622657

Pimmer, C., Chipps, J., Brysiewicz, P., Walters, F., Linxen, S., & Gröhbiel, U. (2016). Supervision on social media: Use and perception of Facebook as a research education tool in disadvantaged areas. *British Journal of Educational Technology, 43*(5), 726–738.

Porter, G., Hampshire, K., Milner, J., Munthali, A., Robson, E., de Lannoy, A., Bango, A., Gunguluza, N., Mashiri, M., Tanle, A., & Abane, A. (2016). Mobile phones and education in Sub-Saharan Africa: From youth practice to public policy. *Journal of International Development, 28*, 22–39. https://doi.org/10.1002/jid.3116

Rambe, P., & Mkono, A. (2019). Appropriating WhatsApp-mediated postgraduate supervision to negotiate "relational authenticity" in resource-constrained environments. *British Journal of Educational Technology, 50*(2), 702–734. https://doi.org/10.1111/bjet.12688

CHAPTER 18

Supervisee to supervisor: 'Trial and Error'?

Caroline Kinuu Kimathi

The **Republic of Kenya** is on the eastern coast of Africa. With a population of about 50 million, it is the 27th most populous country in the world and 7th in Africa. There are 61 universities in Kenya, 36 public and 25 privates.

The **United States International University-Africa** (USIU-Africa) is in Nairobi, Kenya. It is the most diverse university in East and Central Africa with about 6 000 students from over 60 nations. USIU- Africa is the only university in sub-Saharan Africa whose degree programmes are accredited by both the Kenya Government and the American Government. USIU-African has six schools and 140 faculty members. In 2020 USIU-Africa had 161 doctoral enrolments and 26 doctoral degrees were awarded.

1. Introduction

Completion rate and satisfaction of doctoral candidates is partly dependent on the quality of the supervision the doctoral candidates get from their research supervisors (Bitzer, 2011). The supervisor's role is therefore crucial in that the supervisor is expected to meet the candidate's needs and expectations; the expectations of the university and the quality demands of a doctoral degree (Bøgelund, 2015). Wichmann-Hansen et al. (2012) observe that a good supervisor should create a conducive environment which enables personal and academic growth in a PhD candidate. Therefore, doctoral supervision, which is regarded as one of the highest levels of scholarly activity within the academic profession, puts high demands and expectations on the supervisor (Fillery-Travis et al., 2017).

Vilkinas (2002) views doctoral supervisors as managers of the PhD process of their students but is also keen to conclude that the role of a supervisor as compared to that of a business manager is more complex, because of the autonomy and (often) little experience of the student, thus an additional role of an integrator is expected of the supervisor. The supervisor is required to integrate all these roles to ensure the PhD process is successful. In addition to the various roles a supervisor has, Lee (2008) argues that the power of a supervisor lies in their own experiences as a doctoral student. These experiences could have positive or negative implications on the approach they take in their supervisory styles. Gatfield (2005) intimates that supervisory management styles change according to the different stages of the supervisory period and process. Consequently, the supervisor must keep abreast of the changing dynamics within the supervisory process.

Teferra (2015) further indicates that the quality of the PhD defines the quality of a country's research standards. Countries, especially those in Africa, are thus seeking to improve the quality and standards of their PhD programmes to match those of the universities in countries of the Global North, through investigating contextually appropriate doctoral supervision models (Cross & Backhouse, 2014). These models are dependent on universities' capacities to provide adequate and knowledgeable supervisors to students.

As part of this drive towards quality assurance in doctorate programmes, universities have put measures in place such as how many postgraduate students a supervisor can take on at a time. The Kenyan Commission for University Education (CUE) guidelines indicates that "the maximum number of students an academic staff shall supervise in any academic year shall be 5 masters and 3 doctorates" (CUE, 2014, p. 63). However, these regulations have not been strictly followed as is evident in the recent case of Jomo Kenyatta University of Agriculture and Technology where it was discovered that some supervisors had more than 15 doctoral students to supervise in an academic year (Kihu, 2019). Many of these students do not progress through the system quickly. Alneah (2018) explains why some doctoral students in Kenyan universities were registered for a decade and frustrations by supervisors was cited as one of the major reasons as to why the doctoral completion rate in Kenya was so low. Heavy supervisor workloads, different supervisor orientations, and poor communication between supervisors and their students were reported as leading to high student dropout rates (Omunga, 2017).

In addition to this guideline, in 2014 CUE directed all universities to hire only PhD holders as teaching staff from then onwards. Those who were already teaching without doctoral degrees were given a grace period with a deadline of October 2019 (CUE, October 2014). However, this goal is yet to be achieved.

Amid all these directives, guidelines and challenges, this chapter seeks to understand the place of the supervisor in ensuring that quality of the PhD degree is upheld. How do doctoral supervisors get inducted into doctoral supervision? Are they aware of their roles and responsibilities? If they are, how did they learn of their roles and responsibilities? Amundsen and McAlpine (2009) describe learning how to supervise as trial by fire, to indicate the challenges the novice supervisors encounter and to also communicate that much needs to be done to ensure supervision quality.

Novice doctoral supervisors in Kenya are often confronted with having to supervise with little experience, and no mentors or formal training programmes to guide them (Ayiro & Sang, 2011; Mbogo et al., 2020), despite international trends showing increased formal training, monitoring and accountability of doctoral supervisors elsewhere (Halse, 2011; Emilsson & Johnsson, 2007).

This chapter therefore investigates how supervisors learn to supervise and the challenges they face at the beginning of their careers as supervisors. The study reported here also sought to understand where and how the supervisors in selected Kenyan universities learned how to supervise.

2. Background to the study

There is a growing body of literature on the importance of supervision to doctoral success and on the development of doctoral supervision capacity. Wichmann-Hansen et al. (2012) postulate that for a PhD process to be successful, there must be reciprocity between the key players. Their paper gives insights on how supervisors and their students can work together to ensure a successful supervision process and ensure quality of the dissertation. Kumar and Stracke (2007) noted that feedback given to PhD candidates impacted on the relationship of the supervisor and the candidate depending on the type of feedback used in the supervision process. Bitzer (2016) explained the contextual, administrative and academic as factors that influenced doctoral provision and education; and supervision of the candidates was intertwined in these three factors, thus emphasising its importance. Pyhältö et al. (2015, 2012) highlighted challenges that both the supervisor and doctoral student face, and their perceptions of the doctoral supervision process. These studies all indicate the importance of the supervisor as a key player in doctoral education and supervision.

Lee (2008) investigated how doctoral students were supervised, and what influenced the methods, and styles of supervision. Amundsen and McAlpine's

(2009) study on learning supervision provides insights on the perceptions of new academicians and the challenges they face when they begin their roles as doctoral supervisors. Similarly, Turner (2015) explored the experiences of new academics as they begin their careers as doctoral supervisors, the challenges they face as they develop their expertise and experiences in doctoral supervision. Turner's paper was especially insightful for the current chapter in its exploration of how more needs to be done to induct new academics. Gatfield (2005) highlighted the different supervisory management styles that ensured high quality supervision and the changes within the supervisory period.

However, many proposed models of doctoral supervision might not always fit African contexts well. The models and programmes, according to Szanton and Manyika (2002) as seen in their review of PhD programmes in sub-Saharan Africa, are models that heavily depend on the guidance, knowledge and input of the supervisor. Cross and Backhouse (2014) noted that the various doctoral education models that were available did not seem to meet the needs and demands of African universities. They proposed a framework to evaluate the suitability of doctoral educational models within African contexts; one of the key elements in the framework being resources and funding as a way of ensuring quality supervision.

Szanton and Manyika (2002) are of the opinion that this framework might not be economically viable depending on the number of enrolled candidates. They noted that an individual supervision model made it possible for institutions that were struggling financially to offer doctoral programmes. This places the role of the supervisor on the African continent as one that is crucial in the doctoral programme.

This chapter used the modified competing values framework (Vilkinas & Cartan, 2001) which was a modification of the management framework by Quinn et al. (1996). This framework was modified to incorporate the role of the supervisor, who is viewed as a manager, as well as an integrator – the balance required to operate successfully (Vilkinas, 2002, p. 132). This model is used as a representation of the expectations and roles of a supervisor.

Although models of supervision from the Global North may not always be suitable for Global South contexts, this framework outlines the roles that supervisors take on, particularly that of an innovator and broker, to ensure effective supervision by adapting to diverse settings and environments.

Figure 1: Modified competing values framework (CVF) (adapted from Vilkinas & Cartan, 2001, p. 178)

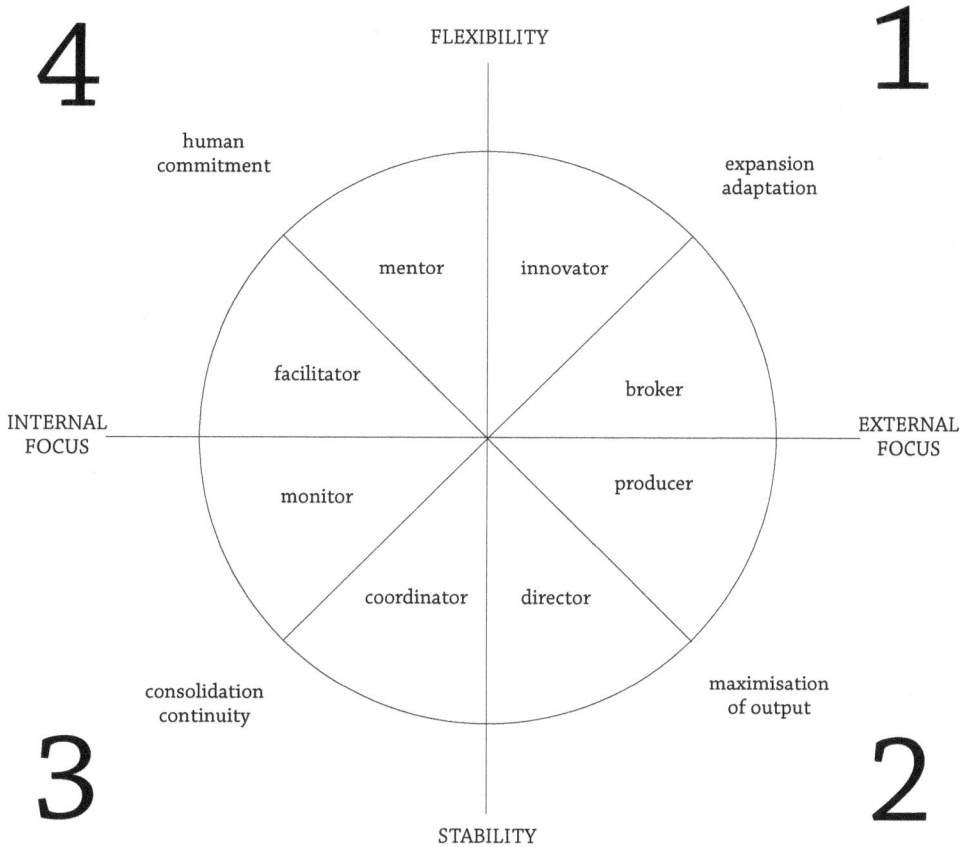

3. Methodology

This study reports on semi-structured interviews that were conducted with eight participants. The interview questions were partly influenced by the theoretical framework, especially on whether the supervisors were aware of their roles in the PhD process. The eight purposively sampled participants were drawn from various universities in Kenya namely: The Catholic University of Eastern Africa, Machakos University, Kenyatta University, Mount Kenya University, Laikipia University and Daystar University.

The participants were supervisors who had supervised at least one doctoral candidate to completion or were currently supervising a doctoral candidate.

The participants had completed their doctoral degrees in different years, therefore having varied supervision experience. They had also acquired their doctoral degrees from different universities in the world. In addition, they were also from different disciplinary backgrounds. These variations were targeted to ensure diversity in the issues under investigation and to also find out whether novice supervisors from different academic disciplines and regions in the world went through the same challenges and experiences when not adequately or formally inducted.

4. Results and discussion

As a background to making sense of the data, Table 1 provides an overview of the eight participants from various universities in Kenya included in the study.

Table 1: Overview of study participants

Participant	Gender	Year PhD attained	Master's supervised to completion	PhD candidates supervised to completion	PhD candidates currently supervising
Participant 1	Male	2014	5	3	4
Participant 2	Male	2013	2	0	1
Participant 3	Female	2017	3	0	1
Participant 4	Female	2014	7	1	2
Participant 5	Male	2003	31	12	6
Participant 6	Female	2013	12	1	3
Participant 7	Male	2010	25	9	6
Participant 8	Male	2012	8	0	1

Participants' perceptions of their roles as supervisors were discussed to ascertain knowledge of their roles and supervisory practices. Results indicated that the participants were aware of their roles, but more needed to be done to improve awareness of their importance in the supervision process. Lee (2008) indicates that a supervisor plays a definite role in students' success. The supervisor must be aware of their roles to qualify to supervise a doctoral candidate. One of the participants (Participant 6) indicated that their university normally took them through their responsibilities as supervisors and this helped her a great deal especially as a novice supervisor.

According to Vilkinas (2002), the supervisor is a manager and plays various roles to ensure that the supervision process runs smoothly and that by the end of the process the PhD candidate produces a dissertation of quality and within the time stipulated. In their interviews, all participants stated that their role was to help the candidate formulate the topic, give instruction on methodology, and generally guide the candidate in all areas of the dissertation writing as described here by Participant 6:

> *I ensure that the thesis is put together; I give direction, but I can't do work for them; ensure we meet often albeit challenges and prepare them to defend their proposals and dissertations.*

Participant 2 touched on supervisors being mentors and said their major role was to encourage the doctoral student, as many students dropped out because of feeling discouraged by their supervisors, while others felt that the PhD was too tough for them. This response gave insight to the concept of liminality in the doctoral student experience (Maistry, 2015; McKenna, 2017). This phase calls for the supervisor to be there for the student, to ensure that their candidate can find their way out of this liminal phase and complete their degree successfully and within the minimum period. Pearson and Kayrooz (2004) argue that there is more to supervision such as progressing the candidature, mentoring, coaching the research project, and encouraging student participation in academic practice.

The participants were asked how they learned to supervise. From the participants' perspectives, a new supervisor with no mentorship and guidance from experienced supervisors would struggle which could affect the completion rate of PhD candidates being supervised by novice supervisors. It is therefore the responsibility of the university to ensure that new supervisors are adequately informed of their role. Participant 3 noted a lack of clear guidelines to assist in supervision:

> *Immediately I joined the university, I was given a doctoral candidate to supervise and I had no mentor as I am actually the first supervisor. Mine is trial and error, asking colleagues and reading a few books here and there. My co-supervisor is not a full-time staff member in my university, meaning that we have limited time to discuss the candidate's work. The candidate has not graduated.*

Amundsen and McAlpine (2009) note that most supervisors learned how to supervise through experience. Participants in this study had many challenges at the beginning, but eventually figured out how to supervise through trial and error. Most participants asserted that they learnt how to supervise through experience. They said that each candidate came with their varied personalities and the way a supervisor handled one candidate would not be the same way they handled another. They argued that since they were endowed differently as individuals, different styles of supervision were necessary for each candidate. According to Pearson and Brew (2002), there is a need for effective supervision through training and supervision development to deal with such differences.

This assertion was confirmed by Participant 2 who has supervised two master's students to completion and is currently supervising one doctoral student:

> I pity my first student that I supervised because I did it just the way my supervisor had done it with me. This I realized later was subconscious. At the time I thought this was the best way. I was more of an editor than a supervisor and the student had to follow my ideas and everything I wanted. However, I left for South Africa (post doc) and did training on supervision and I was shocked at how wrongly I had done supervision. When I came back, I was different. The training opened my eyes.

This participant highlighted that supervisors also learn how to supervise from the experiences they had as students themselves. These sentiments were also echoed by other participants. This view is confirmed by Lee (2007), who asserts that novice supervisors may copy their doctoral supervisors in the way that they were supervised. This is an indicator of the need for some form of formal training to induct novice supervisors to contextually relevant supervision. Participant 3 articulated this aspect as follows:

> I learnt more of my supervision from my master's first supervisor than my PhD supervisors. My master's first supervisor was German. She was a very good listener, kind, and well informed in her area. You simply had to keep time. I use those skills from her.

Participants also indicated that some universities had unstructured mentorship programmes whereby new supervisors worked under the supervision of seasoned supervisors until they were ready to supervise on their own. However, sometimes the seasoned supervisor would be so busy that the novice ended up supervising the doctoral candidate alone. The progress report expected of the mentor could take a year or more. The importance of mentorship in research supervision cannot be overemphasised. Robertson (2017) views mentorship as an important role in doctoral supervision, with collaboration as a key ingredient in the mentoring of novice supervisors by experienced supervisors and in team supervisions.

Finally, participants indicated that they learnt how to supervise through asking and inquiring from their colleagues. This is in line with the findings of Amundsen and McAlpine (2009), who postulated that new supervisors relied heavily on their colleagues for guidance, input and advice on how to supervise. Participant 8 noted:

> *Anytime I felt stuck I would quietly approach a colleague whom I knew would not embarrass me for not knowing. Sometimes it would be one not in my field of study. To begin with I found it a bit embarrassing, but I realized everyone was at one point asking someone.*

The participants all accepted that one learns on the job and that the input and suggestions of other colleagues have kept their supervision alive. They also agreed that discussing with colleagues on the challenges they were facing always provided relief and assistance on how to deal with the challenges. Eraut (2007) suggests that most people gain experience and informal training in their workplaces through the assistance of colleagues and others around them in their workplace.

Participants were asked what challenges they faced when they first began supervising master's or doctoral candidates. All the supervisors noted that ensuring that the candidates completed in time as a challenge. This aspect of supervision was characterized by a myriad of issues such as lack of doctoral student funding and huge supervisor workload, among others.

Participants further indicated that the lack of funding was a major concern to them and their students. Most doctoral candidates personally finance their studies, and the doctoral programmes are relatively expensive. There is little funding allocated to doctoral studies in Kenya as compared to other universities in Global South countries like South Africa. Lack of funding forces doctoral candidates to drop out or take too long to complete. For a new supervisor, who is still not familiar with the challenges, this could be discouraging and disillusioning. Participant 8 commented on this challenge:

> *I was allocated one PhD candidate to supervise (first supervisor) five years ago yet this student has never graduated. He keeps dropping out and coming back which is now really discouraging. The worst is when you cannot be given another because you have not seen the only one given to you to completion and the university doesn't want to understand. I am stuck with my student.*

The funding problem is also highlighted by Szanton and Manyika (2002) as they acknowledge that universities are poorly funded, thus the model that seems to work for most sub-Saharan African universities is one of individual research under the guidance of one supervisor. While this is often the go-to model within these universities, it is debatable whether this model is necessarily the best suited. A distinction needs to be made between financial considerations, and quality teaching and learning at the doctoral level. Due to this lack of funding, most doctoral candidates must work to fund their studies, forcing them to be part-time students. This leaves them with little time to meet with their supervisors as required, which slows the completion process.

Participants also found it difficult to juggle supervising many students (master's students included), their teaching workload, and other administrative duties. This workload seems to be the norm for universities in Kenya, especially the recently chartered universities where there are reports of under-staffing (Mukhwana & Koskei, 2017). This issue should be seen within the wider context of growing numbers of doctoral candidates and other degree programmes at universities all over the world. Participant 7 explained the situation as follows:

> *Immediately after I completed my doctoral studies, I left for South Africa for a post-doctoral programme which lasted six months. I then came back to Kenya, got a job at the university and was immediately appointed head of department. I felt overwhelmed, but we still have very few PhD holders in our university. The work is too much.*

Most of the participants found themselves in a similar predicament and had to also struggle with multiple responsibilities as they learned how to supervise. The participants furthermore received relatively low remuneration by the government, with poor working conditions and infrastructure, which has caused a brain drain of Kenyan PhD holders to countries that provide better pay and working conditions (Mukhwana & Koskei, 2017).

Working with co-supervisors (mentors) that are insensitive to the novice supervisors' needs and the needs of the candidates being supervised was also cited by some of the participants as a concern. Some participants said that their mentors behaved like small gods; they ordered them around since they held senior offices. This situation eventually created a destructive relationship between them and the supervisee.

Participant 4 noted that she looked for someone to mentor her in her department, but no one was willing to do so as the experienced supervisors were already overwhelmed with their own workloads. She had to 'sink or swim'. She finally managed to supervise one doctoral candidate to completion, but she felt that she had struggled too much.

Finally, most participants talked of having low self-esteem at the beginning because they were venturing into the unknown and so much was expected of them despite their limited knowledge. There were no clear guidelines to assist them. They were also always anxious when giving feedback to students. Participant 8 explained:

> *I had to learn to trust my guts! As a doctoral student I had a terrible supervisor, whom I dreaded so much, so I didn't even know how to behave with my student. All I knew is that I did not want to be like my most dreaded supervisor to my student.*

Participants also had to deal with their own relationships with the candidates and enforce work ethics. Some described some of their students as 'cheeky and lazy'. This made working with them somewhat stressful, especially learning to create that balance in the relationship between cordial and being firm on the quality of their work.

5. Conclusion

The transition from being a doctoral candidate to becoming a doctoral supervisor is a pertinent issue that has not been given much weight in Kenyan universities. With the increasing demand for quality doctoral degrees, supervision must be urgently addressed.

This study established that there were no definitive methods or programmes set for inducting novice supervisors into the doctoral supervision process in most Kenyan universities. A few universities have a set of guidelines on the responsibilities and roles of postgraduate supervisors, while others have vague mentorship programmes. The findings also suggest that many supervisors did not fully understand the diverse roles of a doctoral supervisor, which hindered the progress of the supervision process. The few novice supervisors who understood their roles either learnt through their past experiences as doctoral students with their supervisors or 'trial and error' with their first postgraduate students. This situation has caused frustration to both the novice supervisors and the students, causing many students to drop out of their PhD programmes or relocate to other universities abroad. The completion rate has also been affected, with some students taking as many as ten years to complete the doctoral programme.

What is still not well established is whether the experienced doctoral supervisors are aware of their roles and responsibilities as supervisors. Further research should be done on the experiences of doctoral students who have been supervised by novice supervisors in African universities. A comparative study should also be carried out to investigate the quality of doctoral supervision done by a novice doctoral supervisor who has gone through a formal induction programme and an experienced supervisor who did not go through any induction programme as is the case of most seasoned doctoral supervisors in Kenyan universities.

In conclusion, for Kenyan universities to ensure doctoral degree quality that is recognized worldwide, the vital role supervisors play must be recognised. Workshops targeting supervision, courses ensuring development for supervisors and induction courses and workshops for novice supervisors with strong mentorship programmes must be put in place. Clear guidelines on the doctoral supervision process must also be drafted by the faculties and followed to minimize uncertainty of both the supervisors and the doctoral candidates.

References

Alnea, A. 2018. Why PhD students spend a decade in school. Standard Digital: Retrieved from https://www. standardmedia.co.ke/article/2001304484/why-phd-students- spendhttps://www.standardmedia.co.ke/article/2001304484/why-phd-students-spend-a- decade-in-schoola-decade-in-school

Amundsen, C. & McAlpine, L. 2009. 'Learning supervision': trial by fire. *Innovations in Education and Teaching International*, 46(3), 331-342

Ayiro, L. P. & Sang, J. K. 2011. The award of the PhD degree in Kenyan universities: a quality assurance perspective. *Quality in Higher Education*, 17(2), 163-178.

Bitzer, E. 2016. Research into doctoral education: A survey of institutional research project in southern Africa. Botha, J. and Muller, N. (eds). *Institutional Research in South African Higher Education*. pp.277-279. Stellenbosch: SUN PRESS

Bitzer, E. M. 2011. Doctoral success as ongoing quality business: A possible conceptual framework. *South African Journal of Higher Education*, 25(3), 425-443.

Bøgelund. P. 2015. How supervisors perceive PhD supervision – And how they practice it. *International Journal of Doctoral Studies*, 10, 39-55.

Commission for University Education. 2014. *Universities standards and guidelines*: Kenya. Retrieved from www.cue.or.ke/index.php/university-standards-guidelines-1

Cross, M., & Backhouse, J. 2014. Evaluating doctoral programmes in Africa: Context and practices. *Higher Education Policy*, 27, 155–174

Emilsson, M. & Johnsson, E. 2007. Supervision of supervisors: on developing supervision in postgraduate education. *High Education Research & Development*, 26 (2), 163-179

Eraut, M. 2007. Early career learning at work and its implications for universities. In N. Entwistle & P. Tomlinson (Eds.), *Student learning and university teaching* (Psychological Aspects of Education – Current Trends, Monograph Series, No. 4; pp. 113–133). Leicester, UK: British Psychological Society.

Fillery-Travis, A., Maguire, K., Pizzolatti, N., Robinson, L., Andrew Lowley, A., Stel, Lee, A. 2017. *Insights from Practice: A Handbook for Supervisors of Modern Doctorate Candidates.* https://eurodoc.net/sites/default/files/news/2017/09/11/attachments/train-the-trainers-handbook.pdf

Gatfield, T. 2005. An Investigation into PhD Supervisory Management Styles: Development of a dynamic conceptual model and its managerial implications. *Journal of Higher Education Policy and Management,* 27(3), 311.

Halse, C. 2011. 'Becoming a supervisor': The impact of doctoral supervision on the learning of supervisors. *Studies in Higher Education,* 36(5), 1-13

Kihu, M. 2019. Spare JKUAT PhDs and address real issues in varsities. *The Standard.*

Kumar, V. & Stracke, E. 2007. An analysis of written feedback on a PhD thesis. *Teaching in Higher Education,* 12(4), 461-470

Lee, A. 2007. Developing effective supervisors: Concepts of research supervision. *South African Journal of Higher Education,* 21(4), 680-693

Lee, A. 2008. How are doctoral students supervised? Concepts of doctoral research supervision. *Studies in Higher Education,* 33(3), 267–281.

Maistry, S. 2015. Crossing over to education for Ph.D. study: Liminality and threshold crossing. *Alternation Special Edition,* 17, 209-225

Mbogo, R. W., Ndiao, E., Wambua, J. M., Ireri, N. W., & Ngala, F. W. 2020. Supervision challenges and delays in completion of PhD programmes in public and private universities: Experiences of supervisors and graduate students in selected universities in Nairobi, Kenya. *European Journal of Education Studies* 6, 261-278.

McKenna, S. 2017. Crossing conceptual thresholds in doctoral communities. *Innovations in Education and Teaching International,* 54(5), 458-466

Mukhwana, E., & Koskei, L. 2017. Tackling the challenge of staffing young upcoming public universities in Kenya. *RUFORUM Working Document Series (ISSN 1607-9345),* 15, 63-74.

Omunga, D. 2017. *Why Kenya ranks so low in doctoral studies among peers in the region. The Standard.*

Pearson, M., & Brew, A. 2002. Research training and supervision development. *Studies in Higher Education,* 27(2), 135–50.

Pearson, M., & Kayrooz, C. 2004. Enabling critical reflection on research supervisory practice. *International Journal for Academic Development,* 9(1), 99–116.

Pyhältö, K., Vekkaila, J., & Keskinen, J. 2012. Exploring the fit between doctoral students' and supervisors' perceptions of resources and challenges 'vis a vis' the doctoral journey. *International Journal of Doctoral Studies,* 7, 395–414.

Pyhältö, K., Vekkaila, J., & Keskinen, J. 2015. Fit matters in the supervisory relationship: doctoral students and supervisors' perceptions about the supervisory activities. *Innovations in Education and Teaching International,* 52(1), 4-16

Quinn, R., Faerman, S., Thompson, M. & McGrath, M. 1996. *Becoming a Master Manager.* (2nd ed.) Wiley, New York.

Robertson, M. 2017. Aspects of mentorship in team supervision of doctoral students in Australia. *The Australian Education Researcher,* 44(4-5), 409-424

Szanton, D.L. & Manyika, S. 2002. *PhD Programs in African Universities: Current Status and Future Prospects.* Berkeley: The Institute of International Studies and Center for African Studies, University of California, Berkeley.

Teferra, D. 2015. Manufacturing – and exporting – excellence and 'mediocrity'. *South African Journal of Higher Education,* 29(5), 8–19.

Turner, G. 2015. Learning to supervise: four journeys. *Innovations in Education and Teaching International,* 52(1), 86-98.

Vilkinas, T., & Cartan, G. 2001. The behavioural control room for managers: the integrator role. *Leadership and Organization Development Journal,* 22(4), 175-185.

Vilkinas, T. 2002. The PhD Process: The Supervisor as Manager. *Education + Training.* 44(3), 129-37.

Wichmann-Hansen, G., Bach, L., Eika, B., & Mulvany, M. 2012. Successful PhD supervision: A two-way process. *The Researching, Teaching, and Learning Triangle, Mentoring in Academia and Industry,* 10, 55-64

CHAPTER 19

Enhancing feedback for effective supervision in the doctoral journey

Fraj Chemak

Tunisia has a population of 12 million. The country has 13 public universities with a total enrolment of 256 564 students (http://www.mes.tn/page.php?code_menu=13). Doctoral enrolments in Tunisia reached 9 478 in 2022 (MERST). Doctoral graduates increased from 726 in 2008 to 1 114 in 2016, with a total number of 7 130 graduates for the same period (Beït al- Hikma, 2019).

The **University of Carthage** (UCAR) was created in 1988. UCAR has 3 191 academic staff members working in 33 faculties and institutes, with a total student enrolment of 32 458 in 2022. UCAR has eight doctoral schools, 56 research laboratories and 18 research units. The national agricultural research system relies on more than 50 research structures (laboratories and units) hosting more than 500 PhD and master students (http://iresa.agrinet.tn/index.php/fr/companies/statistiques).

---

1. Introduction

In 2016, a master's graduate decided to enroll in a doctoral programme and she wanted to keep working with me as her supervisor. I was glad to have her as a PhD student. It was my first experience supervising a PhD and I felt responsible for providing her with conditions favourable for successful completion of her postgraduate programme. While I regard her success as mine, too, the experience should nevertheless be assessed because I think that supervising a PhD student goes beyond obtaining the graduation mainly for two reasons. First, as supervisors we are responsible for building students' capacity to potentially join the academic community, to teach students and to do research. Second, the doctoral journey is also a two-way commitment that takes more than three years,[1] where the supervisor-student relationship could be the main factor for enhancing or hampering the student's conduct in their future social and professional environment. The mission of supervision extends beyond the academic realm, potentially concealing fundamental aspects of diversity in behaviour, including variations in values, beliefs, and practices (Grant, 2005).

In the absence of any local training in the doctoral supervision process and professional insight into what the key elements of achieving this mission are, I attended the DIES/CREST short course for novice doctoral supervisors. Attending this course constituted an opportunity to learn about the doctoral supervision process, to get a clear idea on the different stages thereof and to recognise the substantial responsibility of this mission. Specifically, this course gave me approaches and tools to reflect critically on my supervisory experience for future improvement. Therefore, as this was my first experience supervising a PhD, the main question driving me was 'Am I on the right track?'

Doctoral studies are the most important level of postgraduate education to improve scientific knowledge and to make effective advancement of research. Student and supervisor are the two main actors in this process and their joint commitment is crucial for success in the journey, sometimes under constrained and restrictive regulation, material and moral conditions. Globally, the supervisor–student relationship is mutually influential, with the quantity and quality of feedback playing a critical role in determining the success or failure of the doctoral journey. Jackson et al. (2021, p. 1) define feedback as, "information from a provider, intended to inform a receiver about the quality of his/her work in order to be able to see where improvements might occur and to signpost issues to be carried into future work". Feedback may be given orally and/or in written form to convey a message that should be considered by the receiver. In doctoral education feedback is a relevant mechanism for supporting doctoral students from the proposal design to the thesis defence and to facilitate them becoming self-regulating (Xu, 2017; Basturkmen et al., 2014). Supervisors, as the main feedback providers, are expected to improve students' performance and to assist them in the transition from being knowledge consumers to knowledge producers. Therefore, the quality and the quantity of feedback may shape the supervisor–student relationship. The supervisor fulfils not only an academic mission, but also a social role (Kleijn et al., 2014).

---

1 In Tunisia the legal period for finalising the doctorate is 3 years, but students might request an exemption of 2 years. In the case of the National Engineers School of Tunis the average number for the period 1996-2017 reached 5.5 years (Beït al-Hikma, 2019).

Ensuring the quality of feedback is a particularly important issue within the context of African universities where the funds set aside for research and the development of supervisory skills are limited. Hence, supervisors should play a double role in helping their students overcome scientific difficulties, as well as logistic constraints and sometimes personal issues. Feedback serves as a vital mechanism for clarifying roles and fostering strong supervisor–student relationships, grounded in a shared understanding between both parties.

Regarding my first experience, I am tried to meet all the needs of my student. I provided feedback on research advancement (e.g. methodology, research field, result analysis, chapter organisation, writing and submitting papers), as well as all the other activities (e.g. attending trainings, workshops and conferences). My feedback focused mainly on how to proceed in any stage of the PhD journey and to overcome eventual difficulties. I thought that I was sustaining a good relationship with my student, but I wondered whether I was meeting her expectations.

Within this context, this chapter provides a reflective account of the suitable gateway to sustain clear and effective supervisory process towards developing a good and trusting relationship between the supervisor and the doctoral candidate. As feedback is one key element of this relationship, I will describe doctoral students' perceptions of their study experiences at the National Institute for Agricultural Research of Tunisia (INRAT) using the Feedback Expectation Tool (FET) (Appendix B). Hence, the remainder of this chapter unfolds in three sections. The first section presents a theoretical overview of supervisory feedback. The second section is devoted to methodology. I present and discuss the results in section three, whereafter I conclude with key recommendations to improve the supervisory process in my own context within Tunisia.

2. Theoretical perspectives on feedback

Supervision remains the main pillar of the doctoral process. It is a key determinant of time-to-candidacy and the decision of undertaking a doctorate. Moreover, supervision may also determine the quality of acquired skills and the degree of student satisfaction during the doctoral journey (Pyhältö et al., 2015). Supervision quality has also been identified as a determinant in enhancing knowledge, boosting skills and guiding students' careers (Lee, 2018; Mainhard et al., 2009; Lee, 2008; Vilkinas, 2002), and traits of the supervisor–student relationship (Jenkins, 2018; Yeatman, 1995; Wadesango & Machingambi, 2011). In the United Kingdom, the Quality Assurance Agency (QAA) stipulates that supervisors should possess recognised subject expertise and have the necessary skills and experience to monitor, support and direct research student work (Wadesango & Machingambi, 2011). The supervisor assumes defined roles that should fit student expectations, which is not always the case and thus leads to problems.

Being a key factor in the doctoral journey, the supervisor–student relationship might foster progress in the PhD project and enable student satisfaction (Golde, 2000; Kam, 1997; Marsh et al., 2002; McAlpine & Norton, 2006). But it may also reveal problems that leave candidates struggling in achieving their goals (Mainhard et al., 2009). This relationship presents in various styles and may reveal tensions within the relationship (Wadesango & Machingambi, 2011; Lee, 2008). In the absence of a memorandum of understanding (MoU) to provide transparency within the relationship for both parties, differences in expectations may cause problems and may lead to disappointment (Jenkins, 2018). These differences in expectations might also become more complicated due to the students' origin (domestic, international) and to the disciplines (Egan et al., 2009; Pyhältö et al., 2015). Disagreement in this relationship might hamper the student's progress. Moreover, such disagreements in expectations might result in the institution's reputation and credibility being damaged (Jenkins, 2018). A two-way commitment and joint understanding about the supervisory relationship may provide the opportunity to develop proactive strategies, avoiding eventual conflicts and enabling doctoral candidates to succeed in their thesis journeys with enthusiasm and resilience (Pyhältö et al., 2015)

Feedback from supervisors is critical to building the supervisor–student relationship (Wadesango & Machingambi, 2011) and plays an important role in assisting students' development throughout the academic research journey (Wang & Li, 2011). The quantity and the quality of the feedback provided by the supervisor are determinants in guiding the advancement of doctoral research. By interviewing 40 postgraduate students, Wadesango and Machingambi (2011, p. 31), revealed that 75% of respondents were not satisfied with their supervisors' feedback in relation to their research work. Students estimated that they were not getting enough time with their supervisors, observing how some supervisors are overworked and/or have an outdated approach (Wadesango & Machingambi, 2011, p. 36). Perception of feedback depends on the perceived supervisor–student relationship. Kleijn et al. (2014, p. 346) found that, from students' perspectives, interpersonal affiliation is most important to perceive learning and to feel supported and motivated by their supervisors; but the role of feedback perception is most important in situations in which such a relationship could not be established.

Kumar and Stracke (2007) developed a model for analysing feedback based on three fundamental functions of speech (referential, directive and expressive). In the referential feedback function, supervisors address editorial, organisational and content concerns; while directive feedback includes suggestions, questions, and instructions. The expressive function of feedback comprises of praise, criticism and supervisors' opinions. Based on this model, the authors found that expressive feedback benefitted supervisees the most, and the interaction between both parties played an important role for the induction of the student into the academic community. By investigating the supervisory process of international doctoral students, Wang and Li (2011) identified two tendencies in students' feedback experiences: 'frustrated/uncertain', and 'inspired/confident'. The authors invited supervisors and international students to openly discuss their expectations of the supervisory relationship as well as approaches to academic writing and feedback strategies. Also, East et al. (2012, p. 3) posit that "What the student wants to receive by way of feedback may sometimes differ from what the supervisor gives, thereby creating potential tensions in the supervisor-student relationship and marring its effectiveness".

Feedback facilitates navigating the mission of supervision and enables a successful doctorate journey. Feedback could be more effective when supervisors also consider the feedback of the doctoral candidates themselves and their expectations about the supervision process. Listening to students' concerns about this process is crucial for improving it and reinforcing the supervisor–student relationship. In the rest of the chapter, I provide evidence of such a process.

3. Methodology

The Feedback Expectation Tool (FET) constitutes an important means for providing insight into the supervisory process and categorising the supervisor–student relationship. Developed and implemented by Stracke and Kumar (2020), the FET features 13 conflicting statements facilitating the dialogue between supervisors and doctoral students. Using the FET, I carried out face-to-face interviews with 13 PhD students and 3 post-docs, constituting a group of early-career researchers from different departments of the National Institute for Agricultural Research of Tunisia (INRAT). The objective is to gather their views about feedback and their perspectives on their relationships with their supervisors. Based on their own experiences, I asked the participants to identify key issues they faced with feedback through indicating their position from A=1 to B=6. I asked my student to provide her point of view as well using the FET.

In order to analyse the results, I restricted the responses of the participants to 3 positions only: (i) 'A', if the response was 1 or 2, (ii) 'Between', if the response was 3 or 4, and (iii) 'B', if the response was 5 or 6. Through comparing my student's point of view to those of the other participants, I sought to investigate the quality of our supervisory relationship. Being a first-time doctoral supervisor, I approached the results with the understanding that they could guide me to strengthen my professional relationship with my student and provide quality feedback on the work done.

4. Results and discussion

I first analysed the results of the other participants before looking at my own student's responses. Table 1 below provides an overview of the results obtained from the group of early-career researchers, as well as that of my student. The green components of Table 1 highlight where the view of my student is the same as that of the majority of participants' responses. Yellow aspects are indicative of concordance between my student's view and the second majority of participants' responses, while the red parts show significant difference between my student's response and the view of the majority of participants.

Table 1: **The perception of PhD students and post-docs on feedback using the FET**

Statements	My student	Group of ECRs	Split of the responses received		
			A	B	Between
The supervisor should give feedback on any aspect of the thesis (for instance, content and language). The supervisor should give feedback only on aspects the candidate asks about.	Between	Between	5	2	9
Feedback is an instruction to revise. Feedback is an invitation to revise.	Between	Between	6	0	10
The feedback must tell the candidate what they did well and what they did not do well. The feedback must give a clear direction for the candidate's future work.	Between	Between	3	6	7
The supervisor is responsible for handling issues about language. The candidate is responsible for handling issues about language.	B	Between	0	7	9
Handwritten and electronic feedback is the best way to give and to receive feedback. Oral feedback is the best way to give and receive feedback.	A	Between	5	2	9

Statements	My student	Group of ECRs	Split of the responses received		
			A	B	Between
The supervisor should give, and the candidate can ask for, feedback about sections and chapters that are not finished. The supervisor should give, and the candidate should only ask for, feedback on sections or chapters that are finished.	Between	Between	3	2	11
The candidate should regularly ask for feedback from the primary supervisor. The candidate should regularly ask for feedback from all their supervisors.	Between	Between	1	6	9
The supervisor and candidate can ask other people (for instance, peers, other academics) to give feedback. The supervisor and candidate can only ask the supervisor team to give feedback.	Between	Between	3	4	10
The candidate should handle conflicting feedback from the supervisory team and decide the right direction to take. The main supervisor should structure conflicting feedback from the supervisory team in a way so they can give the candidate clear direction.	Between	Between	2	1	13
Feedback is effective when it highlights the strengths of the candidate's work. Feedback is effective when it highlights the weaknesses of the candidate's work.	B	Between	0	0	16
The candidate should expect to get feedback quickly. The candidate should not expect to get feedback quickly.	B	Between	3	1	12
The supervisor and the candidate should consider emotions when giving and receiving feedback. The supervisor and the candidate should not consider emotions when giving and receiving feedback.	A	Between	5	2	9
The candidate should think about the supervisor's culture when receiving feedback from them. Supervisors should provide feedback that is culturally appropriate to the candidate.	Between	Between	1	2	13

The results displayed in Table 1 showed that the majority of the student participants did not exactly agree with both statements (A or B), with most responses falling somewhere in between. The perceptions of my student were similar for eight statements (see Table 1 rows in green). Regarding the statements that showed differences, it is important to highlight that the perceptions of my student align with that of the second majority of the remainder of students for three statements (Table 1 rows in yellow). Hence, the perceptions of my student differ with the others only for the two statements (statements 10 and 11, see Table 1 rows red). Regarding statement 10, my student considered feedback to be effective when it highlights the strengths of the candidate's work. This result aligns with my own practice because I usually highlight what she has done well to encourage her and to build her confidence. Regarding statement 11, my student expected that the candidate should not expect to get feedback quickly. I do not agree with her on this point. I think that supervisors should provide feedback quickly, which is what I am trying to do with her. There might be confusion about the word 'quickly', because my student is dynamic and she wants to progress her work at her own pace, as expressed in her observation:

> "for the PhD student the time is determinant, unfortunately the majority of people does not know that for a PhD student,1 year =1 day = Student disappointed".

Some early-career researchers seized this opportunity to talk to me about their doctoral journey. Some of the students expressed their satisfaction as follows:

> My supervisor monitors my research progress perfectly and usually encourages me to be able to supervise graduate student and to write scientific articles.

> I am Post Doc. The doctorate journey is very good. My supervisor helped me at the different stages of my journey and sometimes helped me to overcome some personnel issues.

> My supervisor is my friend, we discuss about all issues, always he encourages me, he supports me, and he advances me to wait for an academic post as researcher.

Others were less satisfied, as the following responses indicate:

> My supervisor did not encourage me, she did not allow me to attend conferences, and she wants to present my results.

> PhD is good but supervisors speculate and look only for their own interests.

> Doctorate journey is a lot of stress, sometimes I feel ill, there is no human relationship and there is no employment perspective.

Examining these insights and varying expectations through the FET highlighted a strong interest in deeper reflection on the supervisory process. Central to this reflection is the enhancement of feedback, which plays a crucial role in identifying the strengths and weaknesses of both students and supervisors.

5. Conclusion

Tunisian universities presently do not provide any training programme towards for improving supervision skills and enhancing the pedagogy of feedback. Focusing on feedback is a relevant approach to bring together students, supervisors and the institution around suitable strategies to improve the supervisory process. The FET has surprised my colleagues, as well as the participating early-career researchers, as a novel and interesting approach to investigate the supervisor–student relationship. The findings of this study highlight the importance of gathering student feedback about the supervisory process. The FET is useful for ascertaining the expectations of both students and supervisors in developing productive student–supervisor relationships and learning about possible systemic gaps in need of address. Despite it having been a small-scale study that, therefore, does not allow us to generalize beyond the scope of the actual investigation, an important lesson from this study is being mindful of the student–supervisor relationship as a key factor for a successful doctorate journey.

In Tunisia, research on doctoral studies remains limited. More research around the determinants of the high level of doctoral attrition rates in Tunisia is necessary (see Appendix A and Beït al-Hikma (2019)). Such studies might provide more insights about the relevant knowledge and skills that Tunisian supervisors need.

References

Basturkmen, H., East, M., & Bitchener, J. (2014). Supervisors' on-script feedback comments on drafts of dissertations: Socialising students into the academic discourse community. *Teaching in Higher Education, 19*(4), 432–445. https://doi.org/10.1080/13562517.2012.752728

Beït al-Hikma. (2019). *Etude sur le système national de doctorat: Rapport final du groupe de travail sous la direction de Mustapha Besbes.* Academy of Sciences, Letters and Arts "Beït al-Hikma.".

East, M., Bitchener, J., & Basturkmen, H. (2012). What constitutes effective feedback to postgraduate research students? The students' perspective. *Journal of University Teaching & Learning Practice, 9*(2). http://ro.uow.edu.au/jutlp/vol9/iss2/7

Egan, R., Stockley, D., Brouwer, B., Tripp, D., & Stechyson, N. (2009). Relationships between area of academic concentration, supervisory style, student needs, and best practices. *Studies in Higher Education, 34*(3), 337–345. https://doi.org/10.1080/03075070802597143

Golde, C. M. (2000). Should I stay or should I go? Student descriptions of the doctoral attrition process. *The Review of Higher Education, 23*(2), 199–227. https://doi.org/10.1353/rhe.2000.0004

Grant, B. M. (2005). *The pedagogy of graduate supervision: Figuring the relations between supervisor and student* (Doctoral dissertation). University of Auckland. http://hdl.handle.net/2292/295.

Jackson, D., Power, T., & Usher, K. (2021). Feedback as a balancing act: Qualitative insights from an experienced multi-cultural sample of doctoral supervisors in nursing. *Nurse Education in Practice, 54.* https://doi.org/10.1016/j.nepr.2021.103125

Jenkins, M. P. (2018). Mind the gap: Developing the roles, expectations, and boundaries in the doctoral supervisor–supervisee relationship. *Studies in Higher Education, 43*(1), 57–71. https://doi.org/10.1080/03075079.2016.1153622

Kam, B. H. (1997). Style and quality in research supervision: The supervisor dependency factor. *Higher Education, 34*(1), 81–103. https://doi.org/10.1023/A:1002946922952

Kleijn, R. A. M., Meijer, P. C., Pilot, A., & Brekelmans, M. (2014). The relation between feedback perceptions and the supervisor-student relationship in master's thesis projects. *Teaching in Higher Education, 19*(4), 336–349. https://doi.org/10.1080/13562517.2013.860109

Kumar, V., & Stracke, E. (2007). An analysis of written feedback on a PhD thesis. *Teaching in Higher Education, 12*(4), 461–470. https://doi.org/10.1080/13562510701415433

Lee, A. (2008). How are doctoral students supervised? Concepts of doctoral research supervision. *Studies in Higher Education, 33*(3), 267–281. https://doi.org/10.1080/03075070802049202

Lee, A. (2018). How can we develop supervisors for the modern doctorate? *Studies in Higher Education, 43*(5), 878–890. https://doi.org/10.1080/03075079.2018.1438116

Mainhard, T., van der Rijst, R., van Tartwijk, J., & Wubbels, T. (2009). A model for the supervisor–doctoral student relationship. *Higher Education, 58*(3), 359–373. https://doi.org/10.1007/s10734-009-9199-8

Marsh, H. W., Rowe, K. J., & Martin, A. (2002). PhD students' evaluations of research supervision: Issues, complexities, and challenges in a nationwide Australian experiment in benchmarking universities. *The Journal of Higher Education, 73*(3), 313–348. https://doi.org/10.1353/jhe.2002.0028

McAlpine, L., & Norton, J. (2006). Reframing our approach to doctoral programs: An integrative framework for action and research. *Higher Education Research & Development, 25*(1), 3–17. https://doi.org/10.1080/07294360500453012

Pyhältö, K., Vekkaila, J., & Keskinen, J. (2015). Fit matters in the supervisory relationship: Doctoral students' and supervisors' perceptions about supervisory activities. *Innovations in Education and Teaching International, 52*(1), 4–16. https://doi.org/10.1080/14703297.2014.981836

Stracke, E., & Kumar, V. (2020). Encouraging dialogue in doctoral supervision: The development of the feedback expectation tool. *International Journal of Doctoral Studies, 15*, 265–284. https://doi.org/10.28945/4568

Vilkinas, T. (2002). The PhD process: The supervisor as manager. *Education + Training, 44*(3), 129–137. https://doi.org/10.1108/00400910210424337

Wadesango, N., & Machingambi, S. (2011). Postgraduate students' experiences with research supervisors. *Journal of Sociology and Social Anthropology, 2*(1), 31–37. https://doi.org/10.1080/09766634.2011.11885545

Wang, T., & Li, L. Y. (2011). 'Tell me what to do' vs. 'guide me through it': Feedback experiences of international doctoral students. *Active Learning in Higher Education, 12*(2), 101–112. https://doi.org/10.1177/1469787411402438

Xu, L. (2017). Written feedback in intercultural doctoral supervision: A case study. *Teaching in Higher Education, 22*(2), 239–255. https://doi.org/10.1080/13562517.2016.1237483

Yeatman, A. (1995). Making supervision relationships accountable: Graduate student logs. *Australian Universities' Review, 37*(2), 9–11. https://eric.ed.gov/?id=EJ523102

Appendix A

Brief overview of the national doctoral system of Tunisia

In Tunisia, doctoral studies were implemented ten years after the creation of the first Tunisian university at the end of the 1950s. These studies are mainly conducted under the supervision of the Ministry of higher education and scientific research and under double supervision in the case of specific domains like the sectors of agriculture and health. The budget allocated to support scientific research in 2019 reached only 135 million TND, which represents around 0.6% of national GDP. This budget is expected to finance more than 600 research structures (laboratories and units) which host more than 11 629 PhD students, of which two thirds are female (Figure 1) and 36 290 master's students. Despite this potential, the report of the Tunisian Academy of Sciences, Letters and Arts, *Beït al-Hikma*, pointed out a higher attrition rate of doctoral students which accounted for two thirds, up to 73%, in 2013 (Beït al-Hikma, 2019).

Figure 1: Evolution of enrolled number of doctoral students

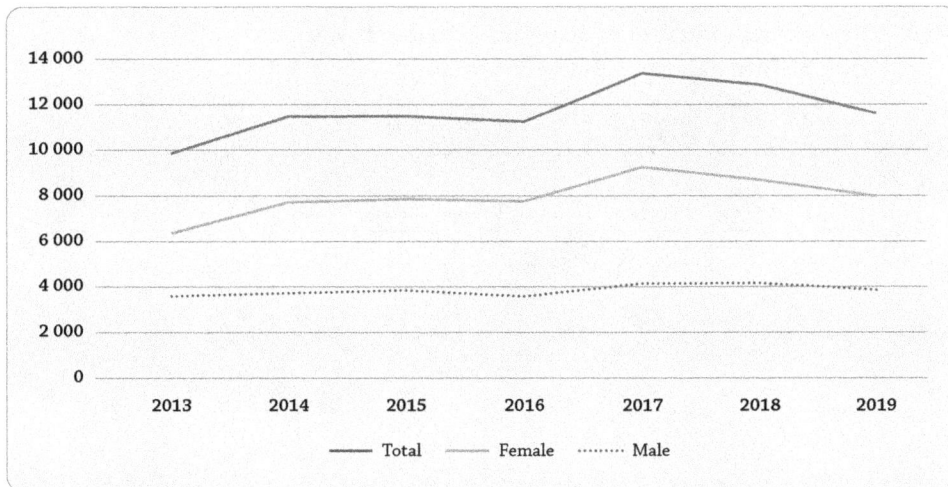

Source: UNESCO Statistics

In 2020, the budget reserved for the national agricultural research system, which is dedicated to funding 51 research structures involving 342 PhD students and 376 master's students, did not exceed 12%. Statistics (Table 2) show that the number of doctoral students halved between 2016 and 2023. The two main factors explaining this regression are the lack of funding and the low number of supervisors. Indeed, it should be noted that if the research structure should ensure all the logistics and operating costs for carrying out research work, it does not offer a research allowance to the doctoral student who receives a government grant (TND 250/ month) for three years only. This lack of funding and the weak perspective in the academic sector do not encourage students to embark on this doctoral adventure. Therefore, facing the challenge of a doctoral journey in such conditions relies only on student willingness and the responsibility of the supervisor who will often establish problematic relationship and remains decisive for the progress and the success of the research work.

In Tunisia, the supervisor–student relationship begins when the student selects a supervisor upon enrolling for a PhD, often without a clear understanding of the key dynamics and expectations of the relationship. In fact, before submitting their application, the student has to get the prior agreement of a supervisor. The doctoral committee cannot oppose this choice unless they judge the supervisor's expertise as ill-suited to the requested scientific profile. Hence, this relationship may be filled with conflict and tension, leading sometimes to student attrition which in some way explains the decreasing number of enrolled PhD students between 2016 and 2023 (Table 2).

Table 2: Evolution of number of students enrolled in agricultural higher education in Tunisia

	2014	2015	2016	2017	2018	2019	2020	2021	2022	2023
PhD	721	699	786	605	576	342	342	333	237	241
Master	376	336	456	352	311	376	263	259	284	291
Total	1097	1035	1242	957	887	718	605	592	521	532

Source: Institute of Agricultural Research and Higher Education

Appendix B

Feedback Expectation Tool (Stracke & Kumar, 2020, p. 283)

Feedback is at the heart of any learning and teaching process. Giving and receiving written feedback during a doctoral candidature is a complex task that covers many issues. This *Feedback Expectation Tool (FET)* lists some important issues that the supervisor and candidate may face when giving and receiving feedback. The *FET* helps each to state their beliefs and expectations clearly and transparently. The *FET* aims to encourage discussion. Its objective is to establish a working relationship that is respectful during the research degree.

Each supervisor and candidate should complete the *FET* separately. They should discuss their responses at a supervision meeting. Both can use the *FET* at any time during the candidature, and as often as agreed. Both can add statements to the *FET* if these statements suit the supervisor's practice and the candidate's needs.

Use the statements below to provide your views about feedback. The statements are on a spectrum.
Circle the dot point on the far left if you strongly agree with the statement on the left.
Circle the dot point on the far right if you strongly agree with the statement on the right.
Circle one of the other dots along the spectrum if your view is somewhere in between.

1	The supervisor should give feedback on any aspect of the thesis (for instance, content and language).	●—●—●—●—●	The supervisor should give feedback only on aspects the candidate asks about.
2	Feedback is an instruction to revise.	●—●—●—●—●	Feedback is an invitation to revise.
3	The feedback must tell the candidate what they did well and what they did not do well.	●—●—●—●—●	The feedback must give clear direction for the candidate's future work.
4	The supervisor is responsible for handling issues about language.	●—●—●—●—●	The candidate is responsible for handling issues about language.
5	Handwritten and electronic feedback is the best way to give and receive feedback.	●—●—●—●—●	Oral feedback is the best way to give and receive feedback.
6	The supervisor should give, and the candidate can ask for, feedback about sections and chapters that are not finished.	●—●—●—●—●	The supervisor should give, and the candidate should only ask for, feedback on sections or chapters that are finished.
7	The candidate should regularly ask for feedback from the primary supervisor.	●—●—●—●—●	The candidate should regularly ask for feedback from all their supervisors.
8	The supervisor and candidate can ask other people (for instance, peers, other academics) to give feedback.	●—●—●—●—●	The supervisor and candidate can only ask the supervisory team to give feedback.
9	The candidate should handle conflicting feedback from the supervisory team and decide the right direction to take.	●—●—●—●—●	The main supervisor should structure conflicting feedback from the supervisory team in a way so they can give the candidate clear direction.
10	Feedback is effective when it highlights the strengths of the candidate's work.	●—●—●—●—●	Feedback is effective when it highlights the weaknesses of the candidate's work.
11	The candidate should expect to get feedback quickly.	●—●—●—●—●	The candidate should not expect to get feedback quickly.
12	The supervisor and the candidate should consider emotions when giving and receiving feedback.	●—●—●—●—●	The supervisor and candidate should not consider emotions when giving and receiving feedback.
13	The candidate should think about the supervisor's culture when receiving feedback from them.	●—●—●—●—●	Supervisors should provide feedback that is culturally appropriate to the candidate.

CHAPTER 20

The role of feedback in supervision and thesis writing

Selma Tuemumunu Karuaihe

South Africa has a population of 59.4 million. The country has 26 public universities with a total enrolment of 1.1 million students. Doctoral enrolments in South Africa have increased from 9 994 in 2008 to 23 588 in 2020 (CHE *Vitalstats*). Between 2000 and 2018, a total of 32 025 doctoral students graduated at South African universities. Doctoral graduates increased from 972 in 2000 to 3 339 in 2019 (SciSTIP Tracer Study).

The **University of Pretoria** (UP) became an independent university in 1930, tracing its origins to the Normal College (est. 1902) and the Transvaal Technical Institute (est. 1904) which merged to form the Transvaal University College (1908). UP has 2 217 academic staff members working in nine faculties and a business school, with a total student enrolment of 53 900, which makes it one of the largest contact-education universities in Africa. In 2021 UP had 2 537 doctoral enrolments.

Namibia is located in south-western Africa, and had a population of 2.53 million in 2021. The country has three public and 13 private higher education institutions. In 2020, a total population of 66 656 students were enrolled in higher education programmes, including 768 doctoral enrolments, and 75 doctoral degrees were awarded (NCHE).

The **University of Namibia** (UNAM) was established as an independent university in 1992, after combining the three entities of the Academy of Tertiary Education in Windhoek (a colonial apartheid institution, established in 1980). UNAM has approximately 2 500 staff spread across 12 campuses and 11 regional centres. UNAM has six faculties, five schools and a centre for Post Graduate Studies. UNAM offers 15 doctoral programmes.

1. Introduction

This chapter looks at the role of feedback in supervision and thesis writing, and why it is important for effective graduate supervision. Feedback is a critical element, and one of the most important aspects of ensuring success in graduate student supervision. Students use feedback to improve their writing, while supervisors use feedback to ensure quality of the final product (Bastola & Hu, 2021). It helps the candidates reflect on areas for improvement and get guidance that they can refer to during their studies. Similarly, supervisors can use the feedback as an assessment tool, but also as a way of monitoring and guiding future work (Bastola & Hu, 2021; Stracke & Kumar, 2020; Baydarova et al., 2021; Guerin & Green, 2015; Silva & Marcuccio, 2019). However, the success of feedback depends on whether it addresses the student needs (Bastola & Hu, 2021), such that feedback does not lead to confusion or to supervisors being seen as 'the bosses' (Guerin & Green, 2015). That is why Stracke and Kumar (2020, p. 266) emphasise the importance of expectations and the need for negotiation from both parties, as echoed below, "expectations play a crucial role in a supervisory relationship".

The provision of is the primary strategy by which students learned to write. While acknowledging the challenge of writing as a student, submitting a written section to my supervisor was the most effective way of 'communicating' where I was, and what I needed guidance on. Similarly, written feedback (sometimes oral feedback during meetings where I had to take notes) was very useful to me as I would always refer to the notes. The same approach has proven effective with my students, involving the use of 'Track Changes' to provide feedback and adding written comments in the margins as questions to seek clarification.

Hyatt (2005) describes different types of feedback, such as phatic, developmental, structural, stylistic, content-related, methodological and administrative comments. These comments all have different impacts and focus on different issues candidates need to pay attention to. Another issue raised in the feedback literature is the focus on language and editorial issues, instead of content, which tends to be more common (Hyatt, 2005; Bastola & Hu, 2021; Stracke & Kumar, 2020; Baydarova et al., 2021; Guerin & Green, 2015; Silva & Marcuccio, 2019). Such comments are both beneficial and can also be discouraging to students as as they overlook the more significant aspect of their efforts, the content (Bastola & Hu, 2021; Guerin & Green, 2015). Some of the comments are referred to as structural or stylistic (Hyatt, 2005), while others are referred to as referential, directive and expressive (Kumar & Stracke, 2007). For supervisors, it is important to go beyond grammar and sentence construction and focus on the important ideas students are trying to build for their research. Supervisors and candidates need to develop and maintain healthy relationships for success in their respective supervision and postgraduate journeys (Hyatt, 2005; Bastola & Hu, 2021; Stracke & Kumar, 2020; Baydarova et al., 2021).

In the end, a negotiated approach to feedback that allows students to provide their own feedback is more beneficial. Thus, getting the students' views on feedback is important for the supervisor as well. Therefore, this chapter reviews literature and evaluates the role of feedback in thesis writing from selected graduate students at the University of Pretoria as a case study. The next section of the chapter reviews the literature, section three looks at the methods and data; four presents the results, five covers the discussions and the conclusion and limitations are elaborated in six.

2. Literature review

2.1 Providing feedback

In evaluating the role of feedback to students it is important to note that there are different models of supervision, and each model provides its own benefits and associated challenges. The type of supervisory models include: the traditional single supervisor, the co-supervision of two supervisors, or the committee or team supervision models (Guerin & Green, 2015; Harrison & Grant, 2015). Each model has its own benefits and disadvantages, but the traditional model of single supervision is becoming less popular in the developed world, with teamwork seen as more beneficial for multidisciplinary feedback to the candidates. Caution should be exercised as such feedback could cause confusion for students if such diverse opinions are communicated without being well coordinated (Guerin & Green, 2015).

The advantages of co-supervision and research committees are beneficial for emerging researchers and junior academics, who benefit from a team of experts as co-supervisors. Among the benefits of such models are the distribution of tasks through shared responsibility, quality improvement through shared ideas and the development of a community of practice through mutual benefits for students and supervisors (Frick, 2019; Guerin & Green, 2015; Bastola & Hu, 2021; Harrison & Grant, 2015). Co-supervision is also beneficial for sharing diverse knowledge with the student, while developing and maintaining a healthy student–supervisor relationship. A healthy relationship is seen as essential in ensuring student success and is beneficial to both the student and the supervisory team (Baydarova et al, 2021; Stracke & Kumar, 2020). Such a relationship lays a foundation for open and effective feedback from the supervisory team to the student.

According to Aitchison et al. (2012), there is little understanding of how doctoral candidates learn through research writing. Their study shed light on the academic realities (struggles and frustrations) that students and supervisors face in the supervision journey. The supervisors are expected to play a key role in ensuring that their students' findings are accurately communicated to local and global audiences through publications. As noted by Stracke and Kumar (2010), the main goal of doctoral education is to groom novice candidates into independent scholars and scientists. The challenge is for supervisors to endure the same journey as their students and discover their supervision qualities, which implies that supervision is a learning process for both. Stracke and Kumar's (2010) study provide a link between written feedback and the self-regulated learning (SRL) process between a supervisor and the doctoral candidate. In their study titled *tough love and tears*, Aitchison et al. (2012) built on the three aspects of *writerly identity* identified by Ivanic (1998) in the form of (i) the autobiographical self; (ii) the discoursal self; and (iii) the authorial self.

Furthermore, following the different types of feedback proposed in the literature (Hyatt, 2005; Stracke & Kumar, 2010) helped me to understand the impact of each comment I give my students during the review process. Using this approach, I appreciated to see how different types of comments different impacts on students' writing have, as I have applied some in my own journey of supervision. I found the phatic, developmental and structural comments more fascinating, as positive feedback can encourage even a weak student to do more next time, while negative comments can discourage even a good student. This kind of feedback also reminds supervisors to see their role as facilitators of learning (Guerin and Green, 2015).

Kumar and Stracke (2007) developed a model for analysis of feedback based on the three fundamental functions of speech classified as referential, directive, and expressive. For example, the expressive statements have a long-lasting effect when a student recalls what a supervisor said verbally or even expressed in writing. From my own experience, I try to remember that when giving comments.

2.2 *The Feedback Expectation Tool (FET)*

The Feedback Expectation Tool (FET) was developed by Stracke and Kumar (2020). The main goal of the FET is to encourage dialogue, allow negotiation around expectations between supervisors and candidates. Such dialogue allows for the setting of boundaries for mutual benefit and ensures effective feedback through negotiation for learning facilitation. The FET's main objective is to strengthen a working relationship that considers the views and expectations of both parties (Stracke & Kumar, 2020). This supports the building of relationships for long-term success (Baydarova et al., 2021).

The FET is open and applicable to all graduate supervision, with the aim of providing feedback. The tool (see Table 2 under the methodology section) uses the 1-5 Likert rating scale of three sections with 13 statements that cover different aspects (Stracke & Kumar, 2020). The FET lists important issues that the supervisor and candidate should consider and may face when giving and receiving feedback.

To implement the FET, both supervisor and candidate should complete it separately. Once completed, they can discuss their responses at their meeting and exchange views on how best to benefit from their relationship. This innovative pedagogical tool is flexible and can be adapted to different situations along the supervision journey (Stracke & Kumar, 2020). It is against this background that this chapter used the FET to get some views from graduate students at the University of Pretoria.

3. Methods and data

3.1 Methods

The study applied the Stracke and Kumar's (2020) FET to analyse feedback from graduate students in the environmental economics programme at the University of Pretoria (UP). The FET is modified to unpack written feedback from graduate students on their expectations about supervision feedback. The survey was conducted in October 2020.

The study used a questionnaire (see Appendix) to conduct a survey with selected environmental economics graduate students in the Department of Agricultural Economics, Extension and Rural Development at the University of Pretoria. The questionnaire was administered online by sending it to the respondents and asking them to complete and return it. Analysis was done using Microsoft Excel. Most of these students were under my supervision, some with co-supervisors, and a few who were supervised by my colleagues. The study used convenience sampling to select students from one programme, under different supervision models, such as two supervisors, or teams of three or four supervisors. The questionnaire was sent to 18 students, but the results presented in this study came from 15 students (see Table 1), representing an 83% response rate.

3.2 Data

The data were collected in 2020 from 15 students in total, consisting of three female and twelve male students. Of the females, two were doing their PhD, and one a master's. Among the whole group, I was main supervisor of four PhD and eight master's students, under a co-supervision model. All the students were registered with UP and at different stages of their studies, except one former student who had completed his master's degree in 2019. The rest of the students were supervised by environmental economics colleagues. Table 1 presents the respondents by demographics and level of study.

Table 1: Representation of Participants – Type of Students

	Program	Gender	Age	County/ Nationality	Supervision Model	Year of Study
1	PhD	F	36-40	Kenya	Co-supervision	First
2	PhD	F	40 plus	Mozambique	Co-supervision	Second
3	PhD	M	40 plus	Zambia	Committee	Third
4	PhD	M	30-35	Eswatini	Co-supervision	Fourth
5	PhD	M	30-35	Ghana	Co-supervision	First
6	PhD	M	30-35	Lesotho	Co-supervision	Third
7	MSc	M	26-30	South Africa	Co-supervision	Second
8	MSc	F	30-35	Eswatini	Single supervision	Second
9	MSc	M	26-30	Eswatini	Single supervision	Second
10	MSc	M	26-30	Zambia	Single supervision	Completed
11	MSc	M	26-30	Zambia	Single supervision	Second
12	MSc	M	30-35	Malawi	Single supervision	Third
13	MPhil	M	26-30	Sudan	Single supervision	Second
14	MSc	M	26-30	Zambia	Co-supervision	Completed
15	MSc	M	20-25	South Africa	Single supervision	First

Source: Student demographics

4. Findings

4.1 Feedback expectation tool (FET) responses

The findings of the study are based on the students' responses using the FET by Stracke and Kumar (2020). The responses are provided in Table 2. Since all the students were supervised by at least more than one supervisor, it implies that their responses are not only referring to the feedback from one supervisor, but from more than one. The diverse opinions on the students' work by their respective supervisors are seen as a challenge for students (Guerin & Green, 2015), especially if such feedback is not well coordinated by the main supervisor (Kumar & Stracke, 2007; Stracke & Kumar, 2020). However, the extent to which feedback from supervisors can be beneficial to students (Guerin & Green, 2015), depends on whether it can address students' needs and challenges adequately (Bastola & Hu, 2021). Some of the benefits of effective feedback are guiding the study and ensuring that the research standard is maintained throughout the study period.

Table 2: Feedback expectation tool (FET) responses[1]

Statements	Strongly disagree (1)	Disagree (2)	Neither agree nor disagree (3)	Agree (4)	Strongly Agree (5)	Total Respondents
1. The supervisor should give feedback on any aspect of the thesis (for instance, content and language).				6	9	15
2. The supervisor should give feedback only on aspects the candidate asks about.	5	6	1	3		15
3. Feedback is an invitation to revise.		1		11	3	15
4. The feedback must tell the candidate what they did well and what they did not do well.				5	9	14
5. The supervisor is responsible for handling issues about language.	1	7	3	1	1	13
6. The candidate is responsible for handling issues about language.			3	8	4	15
7. Handwritten and electronic feedback is the best way to give and receive feedback.			3	7	5	15

---

1 The total column reflects responses as given. Some respondents did not answer some questions and that is why the total does not add up to 15 for some responses.

Statements	Strongly disagree (1)	Disagree (2)	Neither agree nor disagree (3)	Agree (4)	Strongly Agree (5)	Total Respondents
8. Oral feedback is the best way to give and receive feedback.	1	5	3	5	1	15
9. The supervisor should give, and the candidate can ask for, feedback about sections and chapters that are not finished.	1	1	4	7	2	15
10. The candidate should regularly ask for feedback from the primary supervisor.			2	7	5	14
11. The candidate should regularly ask for feedback from all their supervisors.			2	7	4	13
12. The supervisor and candidate can ask other people (for instance, peers, other academics) to give feedback.	1		4	6	4	15
13. The supervisor and candidate can only ask the supervisory team to give feedback.	1	5	1	4	4	15
14. The candidate should handle conflicting feedback from the supervisory team and decide the right direction to take.	1	3	4	7		15
15. The main supervisor should structure conflicting feedback from the supervisory team in a way so they can give the candidate clear direction.			2	8	5	15
16. Feedback is effective when it highlights the strengths of the candidate's work.			3	8	4	15
17. Feedback is effective when it highlights the weaknesses of the candidate's work.		1	1	9	3	14
18. The candidate should expect to get feedback quickly.			2	9	3	

Statements	Strongly disagree (1)	Disagree (2)	Neither agree nor disagree (3)	Agree (4)	Strongly Agree (5)	Total Respondents
19. The candidate should not expect to get feed-back quickly.	2	6	5		1	14
20. The supervisor and the candidate should consider emotions when giving and receiving feedback.	1	1	4	7	1	14
21. The supervisor and candidate should not consider emotions when giving and receiving feedback.	1	6	3	3	1	14
22. The candidate should think about the super-visor's culture when receiving feedback from them.	1	2	6	6		15
23. Supervisors should provide feedback that is culturally appropri-ate to the candidate.	1	3	4	6	1	15

Source: Modified from Stracke & Kumar (2020)

Data from student surveys, October 2020.

4.2 Analysis of findings[2]

About 53% (8 out of 15) of students strongly agree that the supervisor should give feedback on any aspect of the thesis (for instance, content and language), while 47% agree. The majority (87%) of students disagreed that the supervisor should give feedback only on aspects the candidate asks about, while most students (86%) agreed that feedback is an invitation to revise their work. All the respondents indicated that the feedback should tell them what they did well and what they did not do well.

With regards to handling issues about language, 63% (10) of students disagreed that it should be the responsibility of the supervisor. This makes sense since language should not be the main issue for the supervisor. However, most academics spend time on the language, and this is one of the aspects of writing that takes a lot of time and can, in fact, waste productive time in giving feedback. It is important to note that writing is a process (Inouye & McAlpine, 2019)

---

2 The 'agree' and 'strongly agree' statements are put together in the analysis to save space and remain within the set page limits. The same applies to the 'disagree' and 'strongly disagree' statements.

where grammar is a minor concern, and one should focus on the scholarly ideas pertinent to the thesis instead. 75% (12) of students agreed that the candidate is responsible for handling issues about language, while 4 were neutral.

Over 90% (15) of students agreed that handwritten and electronic feedback is the best way to give and receive feedback. Respondent views towards oral feedback as the best way to give and receive feedback was spread among the options.

About 63% of students agreed that the supervisor should give, and the candidate can ask for, feedback about sections and chapters that are not finished, and 19% were neutral, while 13% disagreed. 88% of students agreed that the candidate should regularly ask for feedback from the primary supervisor and 12% were neutral. Relating this response to my own view and experience, I agree that the main supervisor should be 'the go-to person' for regular feedback, while the co-supervisor or committee members should be consulted on specific components of the thesis. As a PhD student in the US, I had three PhD Committee members with my main supervisor as the Committee Chair. I would regularly consult the main supervisor and arrange meetings (sometimes he suggested) with other members for them to share their views, especially on the methodology and the statistical quality of the models during the data analysis sections. It is against this background that I try to apply the team supervision method to my students at UP, which has proven to be beneficial to the students, not only in terms of sharing knowledge, but also reducing the burden of having to read the thesis and commenting alone, where we now take turns to read and save time, while focusing on our core areas.

Like the question on consultation with the main supervisor, 86% (12/14) of the respondents agreed that the candidate should regularly ask for feedback from all their supervisors. Relating this to our current practice with my co-supervisors at UP, we usually meet at the start during topic identification. Thereafter, as the main supervisor, I refer the master's students to the co-supervisor after we have covered some groundwork, like the first three chapters. However, with the PhD students, we arrange to meet the student with the co-supervisor from the start, which I found beneficial as I do my part in terms of project management and other skills, while the co-supervisor does theirs. The early and regular meetings with PhD students help them get clarity on the objectives and the methods they plan to use.

Eleven (69%) respondents felt that the supervisor and candidate can ask other people (for instance, peers, other academics) to give feedback, compared to 5 (31%) who agreed that the supervisor and candidate can only ask the supervisory team to give feedback. With regards to the candidate handling conflicting feedback from the supervisory team and deciding on the right direction to take, responses were spread among the various categories, with 20% (3/15) disagreeing. On the contrary, 88% (14/16) of students indicated that the main supervisor should structure conflicting feedback from the supervisory team so they can give the candidate clear direction. From my own experience, having a meeting with the supervising team is always beneficial, as it provides an opportunity for exchange of views in the presence of the candidate. Of course, this can be disadvantageous (or lead to conflict) if the supervisory team are not on the same page.

73% (11/15) students agreed that feedback is effective when it highlights strengths and 80% (12/15) agreed on highlighting weaknesses in the candidate's work. Comparing the two questions on how long the candidate should wait to receive feedback, the responses were interesting, with 63% students agreeing with quick feedback and 38% disagreeing with not getting quick feedback.

On whether the supervisor and the candidate should consider emotions or not when giving and receiving feedback, the responses are spread across the different options. To me, considering emotions is necessary as some comments (feedback) can 'destroy the emotions' of the students and they are likely to remember those negative remarks more than the rest of the comments. On the last questions about cultural considerations, the responses were spread on the issues of whether the candidate should think about the supervisor's culture when receiving feedback from them.

5. Discussion

The findings from the selected environmental economics students at the University of Pretoria, using the FET, reflected the diversity among respondents in terms of their demographics and stage or level of studies. Most of the students were aged between 26-30 and 31-35. The stage of their studies was diverse, with four PhDs, two in their first year, one in their second year, two in their third year, and one who was doing his fourth year of studies. Their responses are helpful since they are all at different stages of their studies and had different experiences of feedback along the supervision journey.

Another important observation is that while the responses come from students supervised by teams and/or co-supervisors, there seems to be consistency on what they agree and disagree on. For example, most students agreed on (see the questions 1-11 on the FET) issues concerning feedback on content, type of feedback, frequency and from whom. When it came to building and managing relationships (questions 12-15 on the FET), the students' views were spread between those who agreed and those who didn't. Worth noting are issues on how to handle conflicting feedback, where the candidate is expected to handle that (question 14) or the main supervisor to handle conflicting feedback (question 15). These findings suggest that on the one hand, most students agree that they should be the ones to handle conflicting feedback from teams, while others felt that the main supervisor should handle the conflicting feedback. These findings shed light on what was highlighted as an important issue of team supervision models, which is that of building relationships and managing conflicting feedback to students. On the issue of timing and how soon feedback should be provided (questions 17 and 18), respondents were consistent. For the last section, that deals with considering other elements like emotional and cultural issues, the findings were spread between those who agreed and those who do not exist.

6. Conclusions

The study used the feedback expectation tool by Stracke and Kumar (2020) to analyse the expectations of graduate students completing degrees in environmental economics at the University of Pretoria. The findings are relevant to emerging and seasoned scholars of PhD supervision. It is advisable for academics to compare the feedback from students with their own expectations by completing the FET and use it during future consultations with their students. The diversity in student demographics provides useful insight on their expectations, since they were at different stages of their studies, especially the PhD candidates.

7. Limitations

This study is limited in scope, focusing only on selected graduate students doing environmental economics at the University of Pretoria. For a detailed analysis of feedback, it is recommended that future studies cover a larger sample that is representative of most PhD programmes and diverse in nature by focusing on different programmes. Another limitation is that the FET was only applied to students, and not to the supervisors or the supervision teams, which is recommended for future studies.

References

Aitchison, C., Guenther, J., & O'Neill, P. (2012). "Tough love and tears": Learning doctoral writing in the sciences. *Higher Education Research & Development, 31*(4), 435-447. https://doi.org/10.1080/07294360.2012.684637

Bastola, M. N., & Hu, G. (2021). Supervisory feedback across disciplines: Does it meet students' expectations? *Assessment & Evaluation in Higher Education, 46*(3), 407-423. https://doi.org/10.1080/02602938.2020.1780562

Baydarova, I., Collins, H. E., & Ait Saadi, I. (2021). Alignment of doctoral student and supervisor expectations in Malaysia. *International Journal of Doctoral Studies, 16*, 1-29. https://doi.org/10.28945/4682

Boughey, C., & McKenna, S. (2019). Roles and responsibilities of the supervisor and student. In *Course material of Module 3 of the DIES/CREST Training Course for Supervisors of Doctoral Candidates at African Universities*. Stellenbosch University.

Guerin, C., & Green, I. (2015). "They're the bosses": Feedback in team supervision. *Journal of Further and Higher Education, 39*(3), 320-335. https://doi.org/10.1080/0309877X.2013.831039

Hyatt, D. F. (2005). "Yes, a very good point!" A critical genre analysis of a corpus of feedback commentaries on Master of Education assignments. *Teaching in Higher Education, 10*(3), 339-353. https://doi.org/10.1080/13562510500120760

Inouye, K., & McAlpine, L. (2019). Developing academic identity: A review of the literature on doctoral writing and feedback. *International Journal of Doctoral Studies, 14*, 1-31. https://doi.org/10.28945/4168

Ivanic, R. (1998). *Writing and identity: The discoursal construction of identity in academic writing*. John Benjamins.

Kumar, V., & Stracke, E. (2007). An analysis of written feedback on a PhD thesis. *Teaching in Higher Education, 12*(4), 461-470. https://doi.org/10.1080/13562510701338347

Silva, L., & Marcuccio, M. (2019). Advisor's feedback as assessment practices in doctoral programs: A scoping review of empirical research. *Form@re - Open Journal per la formazione in rete, 19*(3), 26-47. https://doi.org/10.13128/form-7701

Stracke, E., & Kumar, V. (2010). Feedback and self-regulated learning: Insights from supervisors' and PhD examiners' reports. *Reflective Practice, 11*(1), 19-32. https://doi.org/10.1080/14623940903526670

Stracke, E., & Kumar, V. (2020). Encouraging dialogue in doctoral supervision: The development of the feedback expectation tool. *International Journal of Doctoral Studies, 15*, 265-284. https://doi.org/10.28945/4568

Witt, R. E., & Cunningham, W. C. (1984). Doctoral students and supervisors: A professional partnership. *Marketing News, 18*(15), 19.

Appendix: Questionnaire

Introduction

Hello, my name is Selma Karuaihe, from the University of Pretoria, South Africa. The main purpose of this study is to evaluate the role of feedback in thesis writing. The survey will be conducted with graduate students in the Environmental Economics Program at the University of Pretoria (UP).

This study is meant to be anonymous and the information provided will be treated as confidential. Your information will be kept confidential and only used by me as the main and only researcher for this project. You are requested to give your honest and most possible responses to the questions. Your responses will be used to guide my supervision work in future and findings can be used for publications in books or journal articles.

1. Identification

Name (student number)	
Degree	
Faculty	
Student status (full time or part-time):	
Year of enrolment	
Year of completion	
Nationality	
Current occupation	

2. Gender of respondent

Male	1
Female	2

3. Age group of respondent

	Tick one	List your answer here
20-25		
26-30		
30-35		
36-40		
40 plus		

4. Level of study. At what stage are you in your graduate/thesis work?

	Tick one	List your answer here
Beginning (1st year – course work)		
Half-way (proposal writing)		
Advanced stage (data analysis)		
Final stage (write-up)		
Thesis submitted		
Studies completed/ graduated		

5. How many supervisors do (did) you have?

	Tick one	List your answer here
One		
Two		
More than two		

6. Was it easy to find a supervisor?

	Tick one	List your answer here
Yes		
No		

7. Were you allocated a supervisor, or did you choose (spoke to) a supervisor?

	Tick one	List your answer here
Self-chosen/ approached		
Allocated		

8. Type of funding for your studies

	Tick one	List your answer here
Self/parents		
Scholarship		
Part-time job		
Tuition waiver		
Teaching Assistantship		
Research Assistantship		
Other: Specify		

Application of the Feedback Expectation Tool (FET)

Feedback is at the heart of any learning and teaching process. Giving and receiving written feedback during a doctoral candidature is a complex task that covers many issues. This *Feedback Expectation Tool (FET)* lists some important issues that the supervisor and candidate may face when giving and receiving feedback. The *FET* helps each to state their beliefs and expectations clearly and transparently. The *FET* aims to encourage discussion. Its objective is to establish a working relationship that is respectful during the research degree.

9. Use the statements below to provide your views about feedback. Use the five-point Likert scale to select the answer that you best agree with.

	Strongly disagree (1)	Disagree (2)	Neither agree nor disagree (3)	Agree (4)	Strongly Agree (5)
1. The supervisor should give feedback on any aspect of the thesis (for instance, content and language).					
2. The supervisor should give feedback only on aspects the candidate asks about.					
3. Feedback is an invitation to revise.					
4. The feedback must tell the candidate what they did well and what they did not do well.					
5. The supervisor is responsible for handling issues about language.					
6. The candidate is responsible for handling issues about language.					
7. Handwritten and electronic feedback is the best way to give and receive feedback.					
8. Oral feedback is the best way to give and receive feedback.					
9. The supervisor should give, and the candidate can ask for, feedback about sections and chapters that are not finished.					
10. The candidate should regularly ask for feedback from the primary supervisor.					
11. The candidate should regularly ask for feedback from all their supervisors.					
12. The supervisor and candidate can ask other people (for instance, peers, other academics) to give feedback.					

	Strongly disagree (1)	Disagree (2)	Neither agree nor disagree (3)	Agree (4)	Strongly Agree (5)
13. The supervisor and candidate can only ask the supervisory team to give feedback.					
14. The candidate should handle conflicting feedback from the supervisory team and decide the right direction to take.					
15. The main supervisor should structure conflicting feedback from the supervisory team in a way so they can give the candidate clear direction.					
16. Feedback is effective when it highlights the strengths of the candidate's work.					
17. Feedback is effective when it highlights the weaknesses of the candidate's work.					
18. The candidate should expect to get feedback quickly.					
19. The candidate should not expect to get feedback quickly.					
20. The supervisor and the candidate should consider emotions when giving and receiving feedback.					
21. The supervisor and candidate should not consider emotions when giving and receiving feedback.					
22. The candidate should think about the supervisor's culture when receiving feedback from them.					
23. Supervisors should provide feedback that is culturally appropriate to the candidate.					

Modified from Stracke & Kumar (2020)

CHAPTER 21

Supervisor–student relationship as a determinant of PhD thesis quality at the University of Buea, Cameroon

Sophie Ekume Etomes

Cameroon, in West Africa, has a population of approximately 28.5 million. The country has 11 public universities and 244 accredited private higher education institutions under the mentorship of state universities (Ministry of Higher Education, 2017). Only two private higher education institutions have accreditation to run doctoral programmes, while all state universities offer doctoral programmes.

The **University of Buea** is the first Anglo-Saxon university in Cameroon, established in 1993 with 768 students in four units (three faculties and one school). In 2022, it had grown to a student population of 19 331 with 672 academic staff members hosted in 11 units (eight faculties, two colleges and one school). Between 2020-2022, the University of Buea produced 211 doctoral graduates across six faculties and in 2023 it had enrolment of 154 doctoral candidates.

1. Introduction

Higher education institutions in Cameroon began with the creation of the first state university in 1962, the Federal University of Cameroon, following presidential decree 62DF/289 of July 1962. Thirty-one years later, the 1993 reforms on higher education created six state universities. Today, Cameroon has eleven state universities with three newly created ones with respect to Presidential Decree No. 2022/003 of 5 January 2022 and a host of private higher education institutions. Currently, 10 higher education institutions produce PhDs in Cameroon, eight state universities and two accredited private higher education institutions in varied disciplines. With the creation of more higher education institutions, there is a need to train many more PhDs to strengthen the capacity of these institutions. But training alone is not enough, the PhD graduates are expected to be of high quality. To that end, this study considers supervisory relationship as a major factor. Effective supervisory processes will reduce attrition rate, provide students with in-depth knowledge in a particular field of study and research, and lay a solid foundation for continuity as today's graduates are tomorrow's supervisors.

In executing any project involving more than one person, the quality of the relationship and collaboration between parties have an impact on the project outcome. This is not different in the case of doctoral supervision, and perhaps even more so, since supervision is considered one of the most influential factors in the doctoral experience (Sverdlik et al., 2018). The student–supervisor relationship is a key issue in doctoral education, as identified by Jones (2013) after examining 1 995 papers written over 40 years (1971-2012) on doctoral studies. He emphasised that the supervisory relationship is likely have a significant impact on the doctoral candidature regardless of any other element that may support it. This interaction not only determines how students acquire knowledge and research skills, but also influences doctoral student completion and attrition rates (Doloriert et al., 2012). Therefore, while the educational institution plays a notable role in shaping the doctoral student into a future academic or practitioner (McAlpine & Amundsen, 2012), it is the doctoral supervisor who is fundamental to this transition and in refining the future roles that these future expert researchers will play in society and academia.

The study reported in this chapter investigated the relationship between a supervisor and student and its effects on the quality of the doctoral thesis. The study was guided by the following three research objectives: examine the effects of (1) policy regarding choice of supervision, determine how (2) supervisor–student contact hours and (3) feedback affect the quality of a PhD thesis. An exploratory survey research design of quantitative approach was adopted for the study. Open-ended questionnaires were used to collect data from 56 participants: 32 PhD students and 24 PhD supervisors from varied disciplines in the University of Buea. The findings indicated that the allocation process for pairing students with supervisors, the frequency of student-supervisor contact, and the quality of feedback are key components of the supervisor-student relationship that significantly influence the quality of PhD theses produced. Effective supervisory processes may reduce attrition rates, provide students with in-depth knowledge in a particular field of study and research, and lay a solid foundation for continuity of graduates as future supervisors.

2. Background to the study

The Doctor of Philosophy (PhD) qualification is acknowledged as the engine of knowledge production of economies across the world (Confait, 2018), but the quality and tempo of knowledge created therein remain concerns. Many economies, including Cameroon, have put in major efforts to increase the production of PhDs. In the case of Cameroon, this effort is aimed at attaining its vision to become a middle-income country by 2035. As such, over the past six years, there has been an increase in the enrolment and production of PhDs in Cameroon. An example is the case of the University of Buea, as seen in Table 1.

Table 1: Trends in the Production of PhDs at the University of Buea (2010-2019)

Year	2010	2012	2014	2015	2017	2019
No. of PhDs	5	10	7	21	40	24

It is evident on Table 1 above that the production of PhDs has been increasing considerably every year. This growth has raised concerns for the production of quality theses, which of course requires quality supervision. The supervisory process is the most relevant aspect of a PhD journey and the quality of relationship between the supervisor and the PhD student determines the quality of supervision, the end product (thesis), and the potential of the student as an emerging researcher.

The relationship between the doctoral supervisor and the student is a complex one. When this relationship is neither effective nor efficient, it will yield negative consequences: a delay in completion of the doctoral programme, student dropout and a breakdown in interpersonal relationships between supervisor(s) and supervisee are common outcomes (Diamandis, 2017). Katz (2016) added that a poor supervisor–supervisee relationship can ruin a doctoral project regardless of other elements that may support it. In this relationship, the supervisor(s) has more institutional and knowledge power than the student, especially in making decisions. Quality research and skills of doctoral students are assets to universities for continuity, and to communities for societal development and improvement. In addition, the quality of an institution and society is determined by the quality of its graduates. It is accepted that an effective supervisor–supervisee relationship is more likely to produce a PhD of acceptable quality. However, we observe in the Cameroonian context that many students take long to complete, many more drop out, while others end up producing theses of questionable quality. These problems necessitate an investigation for which the following specific research objectives were set:

1. To examine the effect of policy regarding choice of supervisor on the quality of theses.
2. To determine how supervisor-student contact hours affect the quality of theses.
3. To find out the effect of feedback on the quality of theses.

3. Literature review

While a significant volume of literature exists conceptualising and theorising supervision, empirical research on determinants of supervisors, the process of supervision, its challenges and outcomes remain limited, particularly in the broader African context. Pyhältö et al. (2015) suggest that the fit between the students' and supervisors' perceptions of supervisory activities was related to students' satisfaction with their studies and the supervisory relationship. Similarly, Ives and Rowley's (2005) longitudinal study on the patterns evident in the relationships PhD students and supervisors developed highlighted the allocation of supervisors to students and continuity of supervision in relation to student progress and satisfaction with supervision as key to student success. Results revealed that students who felt involved in supervisor selection, whose topics were matched with their supervisor's expertise, and who developed good interpersonal working relationships with supervisors were more likely to make progress in their studies and be satisfied with the supervisory process. In a related study, Van Rooij et al. (2019) studied factors that influenced PhD candidate success and found that the quality of the student–supervisor relationship depended on the doctoral student's sense of belonging, the amount of freedom in the project, and working on a project closely related to the supervisor's research area were positively related to satisfaction and negatively correlated with dropout intentions.

Recently, Omona (2020) examined cordial relationships (pleasant, genial affective, warm, jovial and amiable characterized by respect, trust, freedom and friendship), conflictual relationships (no harmony between parties which may emanate from gender, power dynamics, age differences, content knowledge, lack of emotional awareness, unethical behaviour, disrespect, lack of motivation and cultural issues) and mixed relationships (prone to both cordiality and confliction caused by mood swings, behavioural change and attitude of either the supervisor or supervisee) as indicators of supervisor–student relationships that can possibly affect doctoral students' completion rates. Findings revealed that all three types of relationships determine students' completion rates. Masek (2017) highlighted deliberative, sceptical and trustworthy relationships as determinants of quality of supervision. I believe that trust is built when both the student and the supervisor fulfil their respective roles effectively.

The studied literature revealed that the field is underexplored in the African context and the studies surveyed did not look at the three objectives mentioned above, and particularly not from both student and supervisor perspectives. No study of this nature known to the researcher has been conducted in the Cameroonian context. While this presents a problem, it also justifies research into this field in Cameroon.

4. Methodology

An exploratory survey research design of quantitative approach was adopted for the study. Open-ended questions were used to collect data for the study. Relationships are complex. As such, in-depth information was required to understand, qualify and clarify these complex issues between supervisor and supervisee. The sample population comprised 32 PhD students (out of 54) and 24 PhD supervisors (12 senior lecturers, 8 associate professors and 4 professors, out of a population of 34) drawn from various disciplines (arts, education, sciences, and management sciences) at the University of Buea, Cameroon. Proportionate, purposive and snowball techniques were used to this end. Only PhD supervisors with at least two years of experience and only PhD students who had started research work in 2019 were selected for the study considering that these students must have worked with their supervisors for at least one year following the university curriculum. Data for the study were collected in August 2020. Policy documents on supervision from the Cameroonian Ministry of Higher Education, which is applicable to the University of Buea, and other empirical study findings were used to corroborate data obtained from questionnaires. Quantitative content analysis was used to analyse the data. This includes themes and frequencies or groundings. Themes are umbrella words which capture the main idea of the participants' statements with respect to the research questions, while frequency represents the number of times that a particular theme/concept surfaces from the direct statements of the participants. Ethical approval was given by the University of Buea research unit.

5. Findings and discussion

5.1 Policy on choice of supervisor and quality of supervision

In this section, the study sought to find out whether (1) students choose their supervisor(s); (2) the allocation process takes into consideration the supervisor's area of specialty; and (3) the number of supervisors allocated to a student. Policy documents on supervision were analysed alongside results from the data collected.

In Cameroonian universities, the selection of candidates for supervision is defined by the Ministerial Order No. 18/00617/MINESUP/SG/DAJ of 2018 that spells out the modalities for the allocation of PhD and master's students to supervisor(s). Section 2 article 3 of this policy document states that supervision is designated by the head of the university following a proposal from the dean or director of the faculty or school respectively, after the student has successfully completed their course work. Section 2 article 4 of the document stresses that supervision should respect the area of specialty and the ethical/ moral attributes of the supervisor, while article 9 of section 3 holds that students can choose their supervisors, as long as their choice is mindful of the number of students per supervisor. It further encourages co-supervision across disciplines depending on the student's area of interest. The number of students allocated to a lecturer is entirely dependent on the number of teachers in the disciplines, number of theses to be supervised, mobility of the lecturer, and workload. Nevertheless, lecturers cannot supervise more than ten theses at any point in time (according to article 11(1), section 3). In terms of the policy document, students are therefore expected to select their supervisors based on their research interests, while the final allocation is done by the academic department taking into consideration the workload and expertise of the supervisor.

While the policy document clearly addresses the above three questions on selection, specialty of supervisor and the number of supervisors allocated to a student, the extent of application may vary and may determine the outcome of the supervisory process and the quality of the thesis produced, which is detailed below.

5.2 Choice and specialty of the supervisor

This section examines whether students choose their supervisors, if the supervisor's specialty is in line with that of the student, and its effects on the production of quality thesis. Table 2 presents the views of students on the choice and specialty of the supervisor.

Table 2: Students' views on the choice and specialty of supervisors

Themes	Frequency	Sample quotations
Supervisors assigned to students by area of interest/choice	24	"Students are assigned to supervisors according to their area of interest." "Students are allocated to supervisors of their choice. This is so because students will work with those they best understand, making the process less stressful to supervisees." "Students are allocated to supervisors with explicit knowledge of their topic." "Well, I am comfortable with my supervisor because he is an expert on my research area." "I think the procedure used by the faculty is appropriate but it is advisable to listen to a student who in the course of working with the supervisor encounters difficulties which are beyond their control." "The policy is good because it links the student to the supervisor who has mastery of the student topic."
Proposed supervisors not respected	8	"The policy is not the best because most at times, the supervisors proposed are not the ones given to the students." "Some students are allocated to supervisors who were not amongst the ones chosen to work with." "Students' opinion needs to be taken into consideration but this is hardly done as students are at times assigned to supervisors which they did not choose."
Supervisors assigned to students not based on specialty/outside their faculty	6	"According to me, students and supervisors should be based on the field or domain of studies. A student carrying out research on a particular field should be assigned to a competent supervisor within the field but this is not the case as students are forced to work with supervisors out of their faculty." "Students should be allocated following the area of research."
Students' choice based on personal relationship	5	"Allocation of supervisors should not be based on students' choice because some may choose supervisors with whom they are emotionally or socially related and this will affect the quality of research work." "When allowed to make a choice, most students choose their supervisors based on personal interest and do not bother about the quality of the thesis."

Table 2 above shows that while some students (n=24) reported that supervisors are assigned to students based on students' choice and area of study, others (n=8) indicated that students are assigned to supervisors that they did not propose/choose as reported by some of them. Some of the students (n=6) also reported that supervisors are allocated to students who are not from the students' department/field of study. When asked if they would prefer a situation where students are allowed to choose supervisors, five students (n=5) were of the opinion that students should not be given the right to choose supervisors because some might choose supervisors based on affinity.

The students' findings are in line with that of the supervisors (n=24), who agreed that while students are allowed to propose supervisors, the final allocation is done by the department taking into consideration the specialty of the supervisor, workload of proposed supervisor and availability of staff. When all these factors are put together, some students end up with supervisors they proposed, while others are allocated to other qualified staff members. Some supervisors (n=6) also revealed that some students' selection of a particular supervisor is not often motivated by specialty but based on other subjective variables such as social relationships/personal attachments and other affiliations, and the supervisor's achievements in graduating students. Nine supervisors (n=9) also acknowledged that students are sometimes supervised by supervisors outside their area of specialty, but that this decision is often based on what some of them termed 'the situation on ground' which included limited staff, the fact that those proposed by students may be overloaded, and that the topic may not be of interest to any supervisor in the academic department. In such situations, colleagues in associated fields are co-opted as supervisors. There is also the fact that the number of doctoral students successfully supervised by an associate professor determines his/her promotion to the rank of professor, which has also determined the allocation of students to various supervisors.

Given that Ives and Rowley (2005) found that students who felt involved in supervisor selection, whose topics were matched with their supervisor's expertise, and who developed good interpersonal working relationships with supervisors were more likely to make good progress and be satisfied, the practice of involving students in the selection process should constitute best practice. Nevertheless, students who select their supervisors on the basis of personal reasons could run the risk of being supervised by academic staff members who have little expertise in their area of research (Gube et al., 2017). It is therefore the duty of the university administration to ensure that policy is implemented for the production of quality theses.

The findings indicated that the policy is being implemented. However, it was largely accepted by respondents that aspects such as limited staff and co-opting supervisors from associate disciplines may negatively impact the supervisory process. The respondents also agreed that supervisors in the associate professor rank put in more effort in terms of quality and duration of supervision than supervisors who had already attained professorship. That notwithstanding, it was revealed that some theses defended within the timeframe prescribed were of poor quality because the supervisors were eager to use the candidates' successful completion of studies for promotion to the rank of professor. A similar situation is presented by Davis (2019), where newly graduated PhDs were quite bitter that supervisors were more interested in the students' work for the purpose of adding publications to their curriculum vitae rather than focusing on the students' progress.

5.3 The number of supervisors allocated per student

The policy on the selection and allocation of PhD students to a supervisor recommends a maximum of ten PhD students per supervisor and encourages co-supervision (section 3, article 11(1)). I think 10 PhD students per supervisor is too much for quality assurance. Considering that most supervisors also have other master's students to supervise and administrative duties, this may be too many to handle which may affect the time spent with students, ability of in-depth review of students' work, and building a working relationship with students. This study supports the work of Gube et al. (2017), which viewed supervisor expertise as key to the development of 'insider' knowledge of doctoral research and for doctoral students to develop expertise in a particular field of study. Apart from research direction, some discipline-expert supervisors were able to give students content-related feedback. Although the alignment between the research interests of doctoral students and supervisors is desirable (Moxham et al., 2013), matching the research expertise between supervisors and doctoral students can be challenging partly due to the rising number and diversity of students enrolled in postgraduate research programmes (McCallin & Nayar, 2012).

When asked about the number of supervisors assigned to each student, a majority of the students (n=28) indicated that they were supervised by more than one supervisor. This finding is in line with section 3 article 10(1) of the policy document. Nevertheless, four of the students (n=4; 13%) were each allocated a single full professor supervisor. It is usually said 'two heads are better than one'. In research supervision, allocating more than one supervisor per student has the tendency of improving the quality of the thesis, especially in research work that is multidisciplinary. But the specialty of the supervisors and extent to which they agree and disagree on the thesis process also determines the quality of a thesis produced under co-supervision. Wisker and Robinson (2013) see co-supervisors as relevant to make up for colleagues who may be on leave, sick or busy with other administrative responsibilities, thus avoiding abandonment of the student. Co-supervision in addition provides an opportunity for experienced colleagues to train junior academics and early-career researchers (Guerin, 2021). Table 3 depicts supervisors' views on the number of supervisors assigned to a student and the justifications thereof.

Table 3: Number of doctoral students assigned to supervisor(s)

Number of doctoral students assigned to supervisor(s)	Frequency	Reasons	
		Themes	Sample quotations
Two	18	Mentoring of lecturers	"Two supervisors for a junior colleague to be mentored by a senior colleague." "Usually, two supervisors mentor the lecturer." "Two because we practise mentorship of younger colleagues in supervision as well." For mentoring in the case of PhD."
		To improve on work quality	"Usually, two to improve on the quality of the work."
Three	12	Few numbers of candidates	"Three depending on the number of candidates." "Depending on the number of students available."

With respect to the number of supervisors allocated per student, eighteen supervisors (n=18) reported that the number of supervisors assigned to doctoral students is two which is in line with findings from students. One of the major objectives of co-supervision is to encourage mentorship of less experienced colleagues by the experienced and also to improve on the quality of the thesis. This is in line with the study of Guerin (2021) that mentorship is relevant in the supervisory process. Also, some of the doctoral supervisors (n=12) indicated that three supervisors are sometimes assigned to students, which largely depended on the number of students available. That is, the fewer the number of students, the more the number of supervisors per student. This is to ensure that all those eligible for supervision have a student from each batch of admission.

5.4 Student–supervisor contact and quality of thesis

Student contact with supervisor is relevant for guidance, follow-up and intellectual input to their research. During such meetings, the students can discuss their challenges in the research process which stimulates critical thinking. The frequency and purpose of the meeting may determine the quality and duration of completion of the research project. Table 4 depicts students' views on the frequency and substance of their meetings with their supervisors.

Table 4: Students' views on the frequency and substance of supervisory meetings

Frequency of meeting	Frequency	Purpose of meeting with supervisor(s)		
		Themes	Frequency	Sample quotations
Once a month	24	To get directives and correction of work	24	"For corrections and to collect instruction on more exercises". "To discuss corrections of the work done so far". "To provide feedback on corrections". "Corrections and guidance". "Directions and corrections". "To discuss and correct the work".
Twice a month	14	Discuss work progress	10	"Discussion on the progress of the thesis". "To know how far the research has gone". "To discuss the progress of the work". "To discuss research and other teaching and learning issues". "To find out the students' progress with the assigned task".
Very often	8	Clarification of doubts	8	"Clarification of doubts". "To ask questions to enhance understanding".
Twice a week	6	Discussion of supervisors' feedback	6	"To discuss feedback made by the supervisor". "To discuss the comments he made on my work and to guide the structure". "Meetings are to discuss the correction and the way forward".
Not very often	2	To address difficulties	2	"To address the difficulties encountered". "To ask for a way forward when I get stock".
Once a week	2			
Twice in four months	2			

Table 4 suggests that most of the students do not have a scheduled time of meeting with their supervisor(s). Of the total sample, 24 students have meetings with their supervisor once a month, while 10 students reported that they have meetings with their supervisor(s) twice per month, and 6 students discussed their work with their supervisors up to twice per week. The rest of the student respondents either have weekly meetings (n=2), or only twice in four months (n=2). Based on the purpose of the meeting, there was a general consensus that meeting with the supervisor enabled students to get valuable feedback and to discuss the progress of their work. Clarifications of doubts, discussion of supervisor feedback, and addressing difficulties faced were other reasons for student–supervisor meetings. This implies that, on average, the majority of the students have contact with their supervisors once every two months, but that there is quite a variation in the frequency of supervisory meetings across the sample. This result is in line with Heath's (2002) research, who argues that the success of the PhD student heavily depends on the supervisors, who must provide the time, expertise and support to foster the students' research skills and attitudes, and to ensure the production of a thesis of acceptable standard. Importantly, he concludes that although the frequency of meetings between supervisors and students is essential, the quality of these meetings is even more so (cf. Li & Seale, 2007). Table 5 depicts students' views on the factors that affect students' contact with their supervisors.

Table 5: Students views on factors that affect students' meeting with supervisors

Themes	Frequency	Sample quotations
Unavailability of supervisor(s)	24	"His busy schedule and long distance make him unavailable all the time". "At times, he is not available". "Most often, they get busy when we need them". "He is too busy, hence as we move along, the frequency reduces". "My supervisor is very busy with other duties and hardly finds time to read the work. So, delay the process".
Imposing attitude from supervisor	8	"At times, he imposes his ideas on me" "He does not take the student's perspective into consideration".
Lack mastery of supervisee work	4	"My supervisor is not from my faculty and she does not really have a mastery of my research area". The fact that he is an administrator and I am a special education student made us have some challenges".
Unclear corrections	4	"He does not take time to explain corrections to be effected in a particular task. His corrections are sometimes not clear enough". "Lack of understanding of correction makes you stay in the same spot for a long period of time".
Supervisor not from supervisee department	2	"We are not from the same department". "Differences in opinion because our research interests differ which usually spurs conflict and tension between my supervisor and I.
Resistance of supervisor to new knowledge	2	"Supervisor is not flexible and resistant to update knowledge on new approaches while forcing students to stick to old principles".
Supervisors do not critique	2	"The supervisor corrects very little on the work and does not challenge me with questions".

When asked about the factors that affect students' contact with their supervisors, unavailability of supervisors was the most frequently mentioned challenge (n=24). This finding supported the study of Pearce et al. (2006) on throughput rates at one South African university, which found that only one out of 15 students interviewed had easy supervisor access, with 12 claiming inadequate contact. Frequency of contact can impact student motivation, build a cordial supervisor–student relationship, and create opportunities for better understanding of feedback. It is also an opportunity for students to contribute productively to the research process for quality output. But irregular contact may lead to what Wisker and Robinson (2013) called 'doctoral orphans', which demotivates supervisees and delays their completion.

Eight (n=8) students reported that some supervisors impose their own ideas on students without taking into consideration students' own ideas. Research is a learning process for both the student and the supervisor. Students' contribution in a research project is relevant to stimulate their intuition, motivation and critical thinking which encourages the development of their scholarship. Student contribution is also relevant for the production of quality theses and to enable students to become independent researchers. The acknowledgement by both the supervisor and the supervisee that they are learners and therefore bringers and givers of knowledge could help support this process (Omona, 2020, p. 23).

Other factors mentioned included a lack of mastery of the supervisor's work (n=4), unclear corrections (n=4), resistance to new knowledge (n=2), and inadequate critical review of the work by supervisor (n=2). Unclear corrections and inadequate critique depend on the type of feedback that students receive from their supervisors. Students are expected to have discussions with their supervisors after corrections to enable proper understanding and for the student to properly effect corrections. Discussion of thesis corrections with the supervisor also enables the supervisor to better understand the student's work.

While students have their challenges, supervisors also expressed factors that affect their contact with students. Table 6 presents supervisors' views on the factors that affect their contact with students.

Table 6: Supervisors' views on factors that affect meeting with their students

Themes	Frequency	Sample quotations
Long duration to effect correction	8	"Some students take too long to make corrections". "Their inability to respect deadlines". "They usually delay in responding to feedback" "Time consciousness and meeting up with deadlines is a major problem".
Non-respect of deadline	6	"Some students do not respect deadlines". "They find it difficult to respect deadlines and schedules". "Meeting deadlines is a major challenge".
Non-respect of correction	6	"Some students do not follow corrections". "Rejection of new ideas and resistance to change".
Poor mastery of topic	3	"Some students have a poor mastery of their topic".
Laziness by supervisee	2	"Laziness on the part of some supervisees
Inconsistency	2	"Inconsistency in research".

From the results presented in Table 6, eight supervisors (n=8) reported that students take longer to effect corrections, while some students do not respect deadlines and corrections (n=6), lack adequate mastery of the topic (n=3), have inconsistencies in their work (n=2), or are deemed lazy (n=2). Such attitudes towards the research project also have a tendency of affecting the supervisor's attitude. Supervision requires input from the supervisor and the student, each has to fulfil their responsibilities and play their roles for effective outcome of the project.

5.5 Feedback and quality of supervision

Feedback is an important aspect in the supervisor–student relationship. It is through feedback that the student can understand that writing is a form of learning, as revising drafts after feedback can lead to a process of discovery, an integral part of PhD education. Feedback also allows the supervisee to engage in critical thinking and writing; thus, communicating ideas (Kumar & Stracke, 2007). In the present study, three aspects of feedback were examined: type of feedback, scheduled time for feedback, the regularity and duration of contact time on feedback, and discussion and challenges that the students encounter in the supervisory process. Table 7 presents the type of feedback that students receive from their supervisors as related by students and supervisors.

Table 7: Types of feedback students received from supervisor

	Feedback students received from supervisor		Discuss feedback with supervisor
	Types of feedback	Frequency	
Students' views	Verbal	2	
	Written Both	6 24	Yes (n=32)
	Total	32	
Supervisors' views	Verbal, Written and Discussion	To enhance understanding of correction/ follow up	"Verbal, written and discussion in case the student does not understand the written comment and has questions to ask". "Written and discussion for concrete and proper follow up". "I use all three methods to enhance the student's understanding as much as the quality of the work". "All of them to better cover loopholes".

The findings from Table 7 show that out of the 32 students sampled, 24 received both verbal and written feedback from their supervisors, while only 2 received exclusively verbal feedback, and 6 received exclusively written feedback. All the students (N=32) agreed that they have a discussion with their supervisors after receiving feedback. On the side of supervisors, they agreed that they used verbal, discussion and written feedback because they wanted to enhance students' understanding of corrections and follow up actions required. They all agreed that discussion facilitated understanding of written and verbal feedback and also encouraged critical thinking in students.

The ability of students to understand feedback also depends on the duration taken to effect corrections. If students take a longer period than expected to effect corrections, they may lose focus. However, the ability of students to effect corrections on time depends on the timeframe given by the supervisors which may vary depending on the stage in the research process. Table 8 presents supervisors' views on scheduled time for feedback.

Table 8: Supervisors views on timeframe for feedback

Scheduled time for feedback		Themes	Frequency	Sample quotations
No	16	Pace	10	"No, they should work at their pace and get material they are requested to get".
		Students perceived as workers	6	"No. Many of the students are workers and have other responsibilities".
Yes	8	To sustain quick response to correction	8	"One week so that they do not forget the subject and keep up the trend". "Yes, in general, respect of deadlines is the hallmark of a good researcher". "I set deadlines and time frames for each section of the work".

When asked if supervisors had a scheduled time for feedback, most supervisors (n=16) reported that they do not. They also revealed that not having a fixed schedule enabled students to work at their own pace. On the contrary, 8 supervisors argued that scheduled time for students to respond to feedback ensured quick response to corrections, so that they do not forget what was discussed, and learn good scholarly habits. Table 9 presents students' views on feedback received from their supervisors.

Table 9: Students' opinions on feedback received from supervisor

Themes	Frequency	Sample quotations
Good	31	"Very good and efficient". "The feedback I received from my supervisor is good and I have learnt from it". "The feedback is generally positive because it provides a platform for understanding and continuity". "Feedback is generally good as I learned so much from him". "Very good and supportive". "Good and enlightening". "Feedback from my supervisor makes me work harder".
Not good	7	"Supervisors should try as much as possible as they can to first understand the student's reason for choices so as to know how best to make them understand the feedback they give". "Much time should be taken by supervisors to make the student understand clearly the feedback being given, rather than assume that the student has been taught research or will read books and understand". "Poor supervisor-supervisee relationship".

Findings from Table 9 show that while some of the students (n=7) reported that the feedback received from their supervisors was not good because of a poor supervisor–supervisee relationship, supervisors did not take time to read the work, and feedback was usually not clear, a majority of student respondents (n=31) indicated that feedback from their supervisors was of a high quality. Table 10 presents challenges in understanding feedback as presented by students and supervisors.

Table 10: Challenges students encountered in understanding feedback from supervisors

	Themes	Frequency	Sample quotations
Students' views	Unclear feedback due to supervisor not being a specialist in the field of study	10	"The fact that I have a different background from my supervisor, e.g. Special Education and Educational Administration, it is very difficult for me to understand his feedback". "My greatest challenge is that she does not understand my research area because we are from different departments".
	Clarity	8	"His feedback sometimes is inexplicit". "I find it difficult to understand some principles because of the limited explanation or corrections he makes". "I usually received mostly written feedback which is usually not explicit. Therefore, I am forced to work with other lecturers for better understanding".
	Inadequate correction from supervisor	4	"The main supervisor does not always read the work to correct where necessary".
	Feedback relating to supervisors'	4	"Since my supervisor is not from my faculty, she tends to explain feedback on my variables relating

	Themes	Frequency	Sample quotations
	field of study		to her own area of study".
	Language barrier	2	"Language barrier since my supervisor has a
			French background. He finds it difficult to
			communicate the ideas he has on his mind".
	Imposing attitude	2	"Some supervisors refuse to exhibit flexibility and
	from some		do not consider opinions from students".
	supervisors		
Supervisors' views	Disregard for certain feedback	10	"Hard time accepting certain aspects of feedback that might be contrary to their opinion, etc." "Most students claim to have understood but repeat the same errors". "Assimilating new ideas and introducing new materials is a major challenge". "Some students do not take all corrections into consideration". "Misinterpretation of feedback". "They usually find it hard to understand the procedures".
	Misinterpretations	6	
	Unclear correction	4	"The comments or feedback may not be clear or may be different from what they know". "I have observed that written feedback without discussion makes students interpret feedback wrongly".
	Timeframe	4	"Some students take too long to make corrections. Sometimes the supervisor could not remember the details". "Some students take two months just to effect corrections which demotivates the supervisor, especially at the introductory chapter"

Some of the challenges faced by students in understanding feedback from supervisors include unclear feedback, misfit in the area of specialty/field of study, inadequate corrections, language barriers for supervisors of French background, imposing attitude from supervisors, and contradiction between supervisors for candidates that have more than one supervisor. On the part of the supervisors, the findings showed that non-respect of corrections, misinterpretation and unclear corrections were the most common challenges students face in supervisors' views. Supervisors also reported that many of their supervisors take long to effect corrections, do not respect deadlines for corrections, lack adequate mastery of their study topics, are inconsistent and seem to be lazy. Therefore, the attitude of the supervisee towards their work also affects the relationship with the supervisor.

A crucial element in becoming independent is effective feedback (Lantolf, 2000). In examining feedback for postgraduate students, East et al. (2012) explain that what students may wish to receive by way of feedback may differ from what supervisors give, thereby creating potential tension in the relationship and hindering effective learning. Effective commentary on students' work is a key characteristic of quality teaching (Ramsden, 2003), and supervisors' constructive and detailed feedback on written work has been identified as a key characteristic of good research supervision (Engebretson et al., 2008). One of the ways that students can easily understand feedback is to work in groups with other doctoral students. According to McKenna (2017), the traditional model of supervision in which the single scholar charts their individual research path is giving way to a more collaborative learning environment. She emphasised that doctoral programmes in which communities of scholars work together enable the conceptual depth expected at the doctoral level. This approach has the tendency to improve on the quality of theses produced. Table 11 presents students' views on research communities.

Table 11: Students working with other doctoral students in the research process

Work with other students	Themes	Sample quotations
Yes 20	Editing of work	"Yes, I do. When I write, give some of my mates to read for editing".
	To seek help	"Yes, I seek help when I get stuck". "They are students who are experienced in research and I often seek their advice when I am struck". "Since my supervisor was not from my area of study, I had to work with other students". "Yes, since nobody knows all, when I encounter difficulties, I work with my mates and even when I am right, we discuss it". "Yes, I do because I am going to get the right direction, some mistakes they see that my supervisor did not".
	Sharing of ideas	"I relate with some of my mates to share ideas".
No 12	Working on different research topics	"No, because we have different research topics".

Findings from Table 10 above show that a majority of the doctoral students (n=20) indicated that they work with other students for editing of their work, sharing of ideas and seeking help from other sources. Some of the students (n=12) reported that they cannot work in a group because they are working on different research topics.

The findings from the students are similar to that of supervisors. While the majority of the supervisors encouraged a research community for students, some did not see the need. The findings are depicted in Table 12.

Table 12: Supervisors' views on how their supervisees work

Supervisees work in team	Reasons	
	Themes	Sample quotations
Yes 15	To increase self-efficacy	"Yes, discussing their difficulties to increase self-efficacy and to enable them to move ahead'.
	To enhance collaboration	"To provide feedback to each other in a bid to avoid making the same errors and corrections". "They discuss their projects and share related materials". "I give them some little tasks to work as a group and to foster collaboration among them".
No 9	Differences in topic and methodologies	"They work individually as per their topic and their pace after receiving an orientation as a group". No, but most often advised to consult each other for peer supervision". "They preferred to work individually because they have different research topics, methodology and study area".

Findings from Table 12 show that while some supervisors (n=15) encouraged their supervisees to work as a team to increase their self-efficacy and to enhance collaboration among them, others (n=9) did not because their students worked on different topics and used different methodologies. Though students may be working in different projects and methodologies, sharing a project problem and methodological issues with other researchers gives students a sense of belonging, which Van Rooij et al. (2019) found to be positively related to satisfaction and negatively related to dropout intentions of students. Working in a team can help students to break through major challenges in the research process.

In addition to the research community, the kind of support that students receive from supervisors facilitates their understanding and reply to feedback. Table 13 depicts the kind of support students received from their supervisors.

Table 13: The kind of support students received from supervisors

	Themes	Frequency	Sample quotations
Students' views	Academic support	20	"Academic support". "Purely intellectual support". "Academic support like skills in scientific writing and publishing". "Mostly academic support (Sources of research materials)".
	Moral support	10	"Moral support". "Moral and academic support". "Encouragement".
	Guidance/directives	10	"Guiding me on how to go about with my research work". "Suggestions on how to tackle the research topic". "Advice on how to do research sometimes". "Professional support". "He advised me on how to go about everything in the research process".

	Themes	Frequency	Sample quotations
	Material support	6	"Sometimes he gives me some documents to use for my work". "Material support". "Supply of relevant books".
	Financial	2	"Financial and academic".
Supervisors' views	Material support	16	"I get resources for them". "Documentation from the Internet". "Assist with books and other materials". "Research materials". "Provide them with materials and information".
	Counselling	3	"I send them links to journals and online materials, documents, and books". "Counselling". "Advise how to handle personal issues while undertaking research".
	Encouragement	1	"Encouragement".

The findings on Table 13 show that, in terms of support, students received mostly academic, material, followed by moral support, directives, and lastly, financial support and encouragement. Supervision is much more than reading a student's work and providing feedback for corrections. Students need support from the supervisor to effectively respond to feedback as seen on Table 13. This supports the findings of Le et al. (2021), that the supervisor helping a PhD student is one of the factors that were positively associated with PhD students' satisfaction with the supervisor's supervisory style.

5.6 Challenges faced by students and supervisors in the supervisory process

Exploring the challenges faced by students and supervisors in the supervisory process informs current practice on how to improve on the supervisory process. Table 14 captures the views of supervisors and students on the challenges faced in the supervisory process.

Table 14: Challenges encountered in the process of supervision

	Themes	Frequency	Sample quotations
Students' views	Unavailability of supervisors	20	"Some supervisors are not accessible". "Not meeting him all the time when there is need". "Difficulty in meeting the supervisor". "The supervisor had too much on his plate, hence he is not always available when we had a meeting". "Most often, my supervisor is not available". "Sometimes, the supervisors are too busy to attend to students".

	Themes	Frequency	Sample quotations
	Lack of mastery of students' work by supervisors	3	"Some supervisors assigned to students do not really have a mastery of the students' area of interest or the student research topic". "The fact that my supervisor was not from my area of specialty makes it very difficult for him to understand my topic".
	Inadequate meetings with supervisors	2	"Short meetings with supervisors". "Inadequate face-to-face meetings with the supervisor as he is highly mobile. He is in the administrative rank of the faculty thus making him not available".
	Imposing attitude of supervisors	2	"Some supervisors do not take the student's perspective into account". "Some supervisors are at times too hard and not considerate to accept students' views".
	Conflict of views	2	"Conflicting views on concepts, methods and approaches between supervisors and supervisee". "At times, the two supervisors have conflicting ideas".
	No support documents from supervisors	1	"Problem of support documents from my supervisor".
	Lack of adequate follow-up of students by supervisors	1	"Students with remote supervisors have insufficient follow-up".
	No supervisor motivation	1	"Little motivation of supervisee by supervisors".
	Time constraints	1	"Time management".
	Supervisor not from supervisee department	1	"The challenge is that my supervisor is not from my department".
	Financial constraints	1	"Financial constraints".
Supervisors' views	Supervisors supervising students outside their specialty	9	"Sometimes, experts in a particular domain are few and they are overloaded with work, So, supervisors may end up supervising in areas where they are not experts". "Some students are allocated to supervisors in other disciplines which bring friction in the process and delay of completion". "The issues of compatibility". "Wrong student, wrong supervisor pairing'. "Some supervisors have low professional rank".
	Low rank of supervisors	1	
	Inequality for supervisors	1	"Some supervisors are given more preference than others".
	Supervisors assigned out of students' interest	3	'Allocation is done without considering the student area of interest". "The topic vis-à-vis the supervisor's research interest".
	Accessibility of supervisors	1	"The issue of accessibility of supervisors".

The findings show that unavailability of supervisors was the most mentioned challenge some students faced in the process of supervision. Lack of adequate knowledge on the students' research topic because a supervisor was not from the student's specialty was another challenge that some students are faced with during the supervision process. Furthermore, a lack of adequate meetings with supervisors, imposing attitudes by some supervisors, conflicting ideas between supervisors, lack of supporting documents from supervisors, lack of adequate student follow-up and motivation from supervisors, students' laziness and financial constraints were other challenges that students are faced with during the supervision process. A contrary finding was presented by Ungadi (2021) on challenges in doctoral supervision in South African universities. PhD supervisors had a challenge of limited time spent with supervisees due to too much workload with respect to teaching, learning and administrative responsibilities. Overenrolled PhDs was another factor because the society and university want to graduate many more PhDs which is affecting quality. PhD students also had the challenge of limited time of meeting with the supervisor which supports the present study.

6. Conclusion

The study concludes that policy on supervision, student–supervisor contact and feedback, as constructs of supervisor-student relationships, affect the quality of theses produced at the University of Buea. The study has demonstrated that there is a policy in place at the university which determines the allocation of students to supervisors, and which speaks to general practice in other institutions. The data suggest that the policy is being implemented. However, several local realities constrain the application of this policy and continue to hamper the quality of supervision.

Though a majority of the participants agreed that choice of supervisor aligns with their specialty, a mismatch can be detrimental to the educational system because it may lead to dropout or delay in completion. This reduces the productivity of the institution. Therefore, the choice of supervisor should consider the specialty of the supervisor for optimal output. Most students have more than one supervisor which is in line with the policy document. While this is expected to strengthen the supervisory process, disagreement between supervisors negatively influenced the supervisory process.

The study concludes that the frequency and quality of time students spend with their supervisor(s) improve on the quality of their work. Students can understand and respond to feedback on time. This also enables the supervisor and student to better understand each other for an effective working relationship. This improves the quality of the thesis. Based on feedback from supervisors, the study concludes that the type of feedback, scheduled time for feedback and the frequency at which the supervisee receives feedback improves on the quality of the thesis. In addition, the supervisor's attitude towards correction of feedback such as time taken to respond to feedback and the extent to which corrections are made determine the quality of the thesis.

While supervisors have their role in supervision, supervisees should also perform their responsibilities for a successful outcome. It is suggested that further research be carried out on doctoral studies especially in Cameroon and Africa to improve on the productivity of higher education. Further research on the same topic within private universities in Cameroon is essential for comparative analysis. Additionally, exploring other aspects of doctoral studies, such as the demand for PhDs in Africa, is necessary. This will have a multiplier effect on economic growth and development.

References

Confait, M. F. (2018). *Maximizing the contributions of PhD graduates to national development: The case of the Seychelles*. Retrieved from http://ro.ecu.edu.au/theses/2060

Davis, D. (2019). Students' perception of supervisory qualities: What do students want? What do they believe they receive? *International Journal of Doctoral Studies, 14*, 432–462.

Diamandis, E. (2017). A growing phobia. *Nature, 544*, 129.

Doloriert, C., Sambrook, S., & Stewart, J. (2012). Power and emotion in doctoral supervision: Implications for HRD. *European Journal of Training and Development, 36*(7), 732–750.

East, M., Bitchener, J., & Basturkmen, H. (2012). What constitutes effective feedback to postgraduate research students? The students' perspective. *Journal of University Teaching & Learning Practice, 9*(2), 1–16.

Engebretson, K., Smith, K., McLaughlin, D., Seibold, C., Teret, G., & Ryan, E. (2008). The changing reality of research education in Australia and implications for supervision: A review of the literature. *Teaching in Higher Education, 13*(1), 1–15.

Gube, J., Getenet, S., Satariyan, A., & Muhammad, Y. (2017). Towards "operating within" the field: Doctoral students' views of supervisors' discipline expertise. *International Journal of Doctoral Studies, 12*, 1–16.

Guerin, C. (2021). Co-supervision in doctoral education: Challenges and response. *United Kingdom Council for Graduate Education: Research Supervisors Network Blog.*

Heath, T. (2002). A quantitative analysis of PhD students' views of supervision. *Higher Education Research & Development, 21*(1), 41–53.

Ives, G., & Rowley, G. (2005). Supervisor selection or allocation and continuity of supervision: PhD students' progress and outcomes. *Studies in Higher Education, 30*(5), 535–555.

Jones, M. (2013). Issues in doctoral studies – forty years of journal discussion: Where have we been and where are we going? *International Journal of Doctoral Studies, 8*, 83–104.

Kam, B. H. (1997). Style and quality in research supervision: The supervisor dependency factor. *Higher Education, 34*, 81–103.

Katz, R. (2016). Challenges in doctoral research project management: A comparative study. *International Journal of Doctoral Studies, 11*, 105–125.

Kumar, V., & Stracke, E. (2007). An analysis of written feedback on a PhD thesis. *Teaching in Higher Education, 12*(4), 461–470.

Lantolf, J. (2000). *Sociocultural theory and second language learning.* Oxford University Press.

Le, M., Pham, L., Kim, K., & Bui, N. (2021). The impacts of supervisor–PhD student relationships on PhD students' satisfaction: A case study of Vietnamese universities. *Journal of University Teaching & Learning Practice, 18*(4).

Li, S., & Seale, C. (2007). Managing criticism in PhD supervision: A qualitative case study. *Studies in Higher Education, 32*(4), 511–526.

Masek, A. (2017). Establishing supervisor-student relationships through mutual expectations: A study from supervisors' point of view.

McAlpine, L., & Amundsen, C. (2012). Challenging the taken-for-granted: How research analysis might inform pedagogical practices and institutional policies related to doctoral education. *Studies in Higher Education, 37*(6), 683–694.

McCallin, A., & Nayar, S. (2012). Postgraduate research supervision: A critical review of current practice. *Teaching in Higher Education, 17*(1), 63–74.

McKenna, S. (2017). Crossing conceptual thresholds in doctoral communities. *Innovations in Education and Teaching International, 54*(5), 458–466.

Ministry of Higher Education. (2018). the modalities for the allocation of doctoral and masters students to supervisor(s) in Cameroon. Circular Letter No. 18/00617/MINESUP/SG/DAJ.

Moxham, L., Dwyer, T., & Reid-Searl, K. (2013). Articulating expectations for PhD candidature upon commencement: Ensuring supervisor/student 'best fit'. *Journal of Higher Education Policy and Management, 35*(4), 345–354.

Omona, A. D. (2020). To be or not to be? The effect of supervisor-supervisee relations on student completion of doctoral studies. *World Journal of Education, 10*(1), 23–29.

Pearce, C., Holtman, L., & Maurtin-Cairncross, A. (2006). Decreasing the time-to-degree and throughput rate for masters and doctoral students: Exploring the experiences of postgraduate students at UWC. *University of the Western Cape: Dynamics of Building a Better Society (DBBS) Programme.*

Pyhältö, K., Vekkaila, J., & Keskinen, J. (2015). Fit matters in the supervisory relationship: Doctoral students and supervisors' perceptions about the supervisory activities. *Innovations in Education and Teaching International, 52*(1), 4–16.

Ramsden, P. (2003). *Learning to teach in higher education* (2nd ed.). Routledge Falmer.

Sverdlik, A., Hall, N. C., McAlpine, L., & Hubbard, K. (2018). The PhD experience: A review of the factors influencing doctoral students' completion, achievement, and well-being. *International Journal of Doctoral Studies, 13*, 361–388.

Ungadi, B. A. (2021). Challenges in doctoral supervision in South African universities. *Open Science Journal, 6*(2).

Van Rensburg, G. H., Mayers, P., & Roets, L. (2016). Supervision of postgraduate students in higher education. *Trends in Nursing, 3*(1).

Van Rooij, R., Fokkens-Bruinsma, M., & Jansen, E. (2019). Factors that influence PhD candidates' success: The importance of PhD project characteristics. *Studies in Continuing Education 43(1),* 48–67.

Wisker, G., & Robinson, G. (2013). Doctoral 'orphans': Nurturing and supervising the success of postgraduates who have lost their supervisors. *Higher Education Research & Development, 32*(2), 300–313.

CHAPTER 22

Overcoming perpetual liminality among doctoral candidates in a Kenyan university

Tom Kwanya

The **Republic of Kenya** is on the eastern coast of Africa. With a population of about 50 million, it is the 27th most populous country in the world and 7th in Africa. There are 61 universities in Kenya, 36 public and 25 private.

The **Technical University of Kenya** (TU-K) is the first technical university in the history of independent Kenya. As the former Kenya Polytechnic University College, this university (established in 2007) is mandated to offer technology-based and vocational education and training programmes ranging from certificate to post-doctoral levels. The university has three faculties with 18 schools. In 2022 TU-K had 153 doctoral candidates and 48 doctoral degrees were awarded.

1. Introduction

The demand for doctoral degrees has grown globally due to the shifting dependence of economic productivity on knowledge (Cloete et al., 2015). Urbancova (2013) argued that talent, or knowledge, has lately become the primary source of competitive advantage for companies and nation states. This pivotal role played by knowledge in economic development has shone a spotlight on universities as sources of talent and the doctoral degree as the pinnacle of learning and talent development. According to Louw and Muller (2014), the interest in the doctorate degree, which surged from the 1990s, has increased in recent years. Consequently, there is an increase in the production of doctorates the world over. Cyranoski et al. (2011) argue that the world is producing far more doctorates than ever before. They reported that the number of science doctoral graduates rose by 40% annually between 1998 and 2008 in the member states of the Organisation for Economic Co-operation and Development (OECD). They predicted that this trend was unlikely to slow down because many countries, including non-members of the OECD, have recently put in place systems to enhance their capacity to produce even more doctoral graduates as a means of improving their socio-economic development. Nonetheless, Cloete et al. (2015) argue that the importance attached to the doctorate globally has increased disproportionately in relation to its share of the overall graduate output over the last decade. Friesenhahn (2014) argues that although the number of doctoral graduates in a country is likely to promote development, there are many other factors at play in promoting economic development in any given country at any given time.

Despite the increases in doctorate production, there is concern about high attrition rates among doctoral candidates globally. According to Cyranoski et al. (2011), more than a third of doctoral candidates in the United States do not graduate at all. They further report that more than half of doctoral students in engineering in Poland do not complete their studies. In South Africa, Mouton (2011) reported that 46% of the students enrolled in doctoral programmes across all disciplines in 2001 did not complete their studies at all, while about 13% of the doctoral candidates in South Africa took more than six years to complete their studies. In Uganda, Wamala et al. (2011) reported a graduation rate of 39.7% of doctoral candidates. Matheka et al. (2020) and Rong'uno (2016) report a graduation rate of below 50% among doctoral students enrolled in Kenyan universities. Rong'uno (2016) also reported that the average doctorate completion period in Kenya between 2001 and 2008 was nine years, instead of the ideal three. Mouton (2011) points out that the highest rate of attrition occurs within two years after enrolment. He reported that about 29% of the candidates who dropped out did so in the first two years of their enrolment.

In Kenya, like other countries in sub-Saharan Africa, enrolment in doctoral programmes has grown in the recent past. According to Matheka et al. (2020), the number of doctoral candidates in Kenyan universities grew by 34% in 2015 and 2016. With an increase in the number of universities from 32 in 2011 to 74 in 2017 (CUE, 2017), there was an acute need for doctoral graduates to take up administrative, teaching, research and outreach roles in the universities. Given the low completion rate, there is a deficit in the number of doctorates required by academic institutions, as well as the public and private sectors of the economy in Kenya. There is need to address how to improve not only the enrolment in doctoral programmes, but also the completion rate of doctoral candidates in Kenya.

Doctoral candidates encounter several hurdles on their way to graduation. Most of these hurdles are experienced in the liminal stage. This chapter examines the causes and experiences of perpetual liminality among doctoral students in Kenya. Primary data were collected from 14 doctoral candidates through online focus group discussions using the Zoom conferencing platform. All participating candidates acknowledged that they had experienced extended liminality, particularly while preparing and defending their research proposals. According to the students, the extended liminality experienced emanates from individual and institutional challenges. There was consensus, however, that the major causes of extended liminality are institutional or programmatic challenges revolving around inadequate supervision, insufficient institutional support, and lack of clarity on expectations. Improving the structure and depth of supervision, institutional support, as well as closer monitoring can reduce the prevalence and effects of extended liminality on high dropout and low completion rates among doctoral students in Kenya. Ethical clearance to use the data in this publication was granted by the Research Ethics Committee of Stellenbosch University (Project number 2273).

2. Doctoral liminality: Being neither here nor there

Doctoral candidates encounter several hurdles on their way to the doctorate. Keefer (2015) likens the doctoral journey to a rite of passage in which candidates acquire new skills and personalities qualifying them as new people, doctorates. According to Wisker et al. (2010), during this journey doctoral candidates acquire multidimensional skills encompassing ontological, epistemological, emotional and professional realms of development. Candidates who successfully make it through this journey experience a transformation akin to what initiates experience after a rite of passage. Through the transformation, initiates leave behind their previous (inferior, novice) selves to embrace new (superior, expert) selves exemplified in transformed ways of understanding, interpreting, viewing or comprehending of concepts in the relevant subject matter, landscape or worldview (Meyer & Land 2003). Kiley (2009) avers that this transformation is experienced at both personal and disciplinary learning levels. The transformation is so deep that Trafford (2008) opines that it remarkably changes the candidates' identity and perspectives. Keefer (2015) asserts that when these changes occur, doctoral candidates' identities change to the extent that they are no longer the same people who entered the programme.

Attaining a doctorate is, therefore, akin to crossing an identity-changing threshold which significantly transforms the candidates. Turner (2011) asserts that the identity-changing experience follows a transition period of uncertainty, confusion or doubt known as liminality. According to Keefer (2015), doctoral liminality is the period when candidates are not who they were when they enrolled in the programme but have not attained a full transformation into a doctorate. Therefore, liminality is a wavering between two worlds experienced after separation from the previous life but before getting incorporated into the new one. Jazvac-Martek (2009) posits that doctoral candidates in liminal periods oscillate between learner and academic identities enroute to scholarly expertise.

Trafford and Leshem (2009) explain that attaining a doctorate is intellectually challenging and presents doctoral candidates with myriad scholarly challenges in conducting research as well as writing and defending theses. These challenges, which are found at various stages of the doctoral journey, are likened to portals through which the candidates must pass to experience meaningful transformation. The period between the time the candidates enroll into the doctoral programmes and their graduation is characterized by scholarly struggles leading to confusion and uncertainty. According to Kiley and Wisker (2010), doctoral candidates in liminal periods experience an intellectual feeling of being stuck or going round in endless circles. Kiley (2009) argues that during doctoral liminality, candidates mimic the behaviour and language perceived as expected of one to fit into the learned community. This mimicry subsides as the candidates become confirmed as expert academics within a scholarly discipline or institution (Jazvac-Martek, 2009). During the liminal period, the candidates possess no rank, insignia or kinship position which distinguishes them from other researchers (Adorno et al., 2015). They are neither here nor there. They experience an identity crisis which makes them uneasy and unsettled.

Adorno et al. (2015) explain that just like in ethnographic rites of passage, candidates are guided out of liminality by experienced 'elders' in the form of supervisors in academic contexts. Moore (2016) opines that liminal periods are characterized by scholarly ambiguity and complexities which candidates attempt to navigate and discern. Turner (1969) argued that persons in liminal periods support each other out of the stage through mystical solidarity. Kralik et al. (2006) explain that the only route out of liminality is transition, which represents change enabling the doctoral candidates to cut links with their former selves and develop attributes that connect them to the scholarly community of doctorates. Clouder (2005) argues that the process and results of this transition are gradual but irreversible. Meyer and Land (2005) explain that this transition is preceded by a season of troubled knowledge when the candidates go through intellectual thresholds to get integrated into the academic environment and community. According to Szakolczai (2009), doctoral transition begins with rites of separation and ends with rites of re-aggregation. In between these two rites is a boundary which separates the two phases. Wisker (2018) opines that intellectual transitioning through doctoral liminality involves ontological and epistemological change leading to breakthroughs in terms of thinking, under-standing, researching and writing. Leshem (2020) also emphasises the role of supervisors ('elders') in helping doctoral candidates transition effectively through these stages into genuine scholars in their respective areas of specialty.

According to Wisker (2018), doctoral candidates adopt diverse mechanisms or strategies to facilitate breakthroughs during liminality. Some of these include taking time off from the thesis to 'let it settle' or re-shape. Experienced super-visors use these opportunities to support the candidates in concretising their thoughts by suggesting further readings or providing opportunities for them to share and validate their ideas. By providing these opportunities, the supervisors do not impose their own thinking onto their students. Conversely, they create opportunities for their students to share their own experiences in ways which enable them to question, develop their own insights, query others, and discern how breakthroughs took place or develop analogies from other contexts.

3. Context, rationale and methodology of study

This study is focused on candidates enrolled in a Doctor of Philosophy in infor-mation and knowledge management programme. It is a three-year doctoral programme executed through course work, thesis and examination. The course work is structured to be completed in the first year of study and consists of six taught units of which four are examined. Thereafter, the candidates are expected to venture into their research which is structured into semester-based milestones of research proposal development; data collection or fieldwork; thesis compilation; as well as thesis defence and submission.

Currently, there are 31 candidates enrolled in the programme. Of these, nine were enrolled in 2018; seven in 2019; nine in 2020; and six in 2021. The majority (25) of the doctoral candidates have completed their course work. Even though the 2018 cohort completed their course work in 2019 (according to the structure of the programme, they were supposed to have completed and defended their research proposals in the month of August in 2019), none of them had submitted a complete research proposal by July 2020 when data for this study were collected. The 2019 cohort was also expected to have developed their research concept papers, but these were still outstanding at the time of data collection. For the purposes of this chapter, the two groups were perceived to be stuck in an extended period of liminality. They all seemed to be stuck in a cycle of continuous drafts and corrections. Efforts by the school and department to support them in completing their proposals or concept notes, for instance through seminars and individual mentoring, had been unsuccessful. Unless appropriate interventions to reduce the period of doctoral liminality are designed and implemented by the school and department, many of these candidates are likely to take long to graduate or drop out of the programme. This study investigated the reasons for the evident long period of doctoral liminality as experienced by the sixteen candidates.

Data were collected from 14 candidates from the 2018 and 2019 cohorts through focus group discussions held during July 2020 using the Zoom conferencing platform. The author, who is also the academic coordinator of this doctoral programme, was the facilitator of the focus group discussion which lasted about two hours. As the academic coordinator of the programme, the author needed to understand why the candidates experienced a longer period of liminality to help them overcome it. Given the growing number of students getting enrolled in the programme, prompt completion is desired. The session began with a presentation by the author on the concept of doctoral liminality as a means of creating a common understanding among the candidates. This was followed by a guided discussion on the causes and symptoms of extended doctoral liminality among the students, as well as how to facilitate breakthroughs for the candidates.

4. Findings and discussion

All fourteen doctoral students who participated in the focus group discussions acknowledged that they were somehow stuck in a period of extended doctoral liminality and were not making the expected breakthroughs to get out of it.

4.1 Causes of extended doctoral liminality

From the findings of the study, there are three main categories of causes of extended periods of liminality among information and knowledge management doctoral students in Kenya. The first category relates to inadequacies in supervision and mentoring. The students explained that some supervisors did not take their roles seriously. This lack of commitment was manifested by an inability or unwillingness to set aside adequate time to attend to the students and their work promptly. Inadequate supervision resulted in insufficient guidance in terms of the content and methodological issues relating to doctoral work. One candidate explained this challenge as follows:

I know many students whose supervisors do not provide review comments promptly. The longer they take to review the drafts, the more they forget what the research is about thereby making it difficult for the students to make progress. (FGDR4)

There were also cases where the supervisors did not possess the expected level of competency in their students' areas of research. In such cases, the students were left in the dark to find their own way through trial and error. The verbatim response below demonstrates the frustrations students experience when dealing with inadequate supervisors:

Some supervisors are learning while also supervising at the same time. To provide credible guidance, supervisors are expected to know more than the students. Supervisors who lack the requisite competency in the area of research end up only correcting grammar or not providing comprehensive comments to the students. (FGDR7)

The students were also of the view that some supervisors treated them as lesser academic beings and not as budding scholarly colleagues seeking mentorship to attain the skills and attitudes of doctorateness. The verbatim response below captures the gist of this attitude:

Some of the supervisors treat us as schoolchildren who are expected to be generally passive in the learning process. This is inappropriate for this level. Are we not supposed to be treated as junior colleagues in academics? (FGDR3)

These findings underscore the role of supervision in facilitating successful transitions in the doctoral journey and generally concur with the views of several scholars (e.g. Backhouse, 2009; Langa, 2010; Cloete et al, 2011). According to Grant (2005), relationship difficulties between doctoral students and their supervisors emanate from power dynamics which can interfere with the quality of communication between them, leading to feelings of inferiority and marginsalisation among the students. Mcclure (2005) clarifies that in these circumstances students exercise situational adjustment to avoid confrontation with supervisors. Deuchar (2008) asserts that the relationship between doctoral candidates and their supervisors is pivotal to the successful completion of the doctorate. Deuchar adds that most students value supervisors who foster a sense of collegiality and who facilitate the interchange of ideas with other research students. The Academy of Science of South Africa (ASSAf) (2010, p. 93) state that effective supervisors apply multiple styles to support the students under their mentorship: they see themselves as "providing students with much more than research skills and an amount of subject knowledge; there is a strong emphasis on developing students as independent academics and peers". Pyhältö et al. (2012) assert that supervisors should apply student-centred approaches to facilitate and promote effective learning.

The second category of reasons for doctoral liminality relates to the students and their willingness and ability to work on the doctoral study. The respondents pointed out that all the doctoral candidates were working while also pursuing their studies. Being part-time students reduces the amount of time candidates can commit to their doctoral work as explained in the verbatim response below:

Many of us are working while also pursuing the PhD work. It is sometimes difficult to balance expectations of both roles. This leads to procrastination or general delay in completing revisions or drafts. (FGDR6)

While acknowledging the difficulty of balancing work and student roles, the respondents also stated that some students are lazy and are unable to commit the requisite amount of time or effort to make progress. Other challenges in this regard include failure to take doctoral studies seriously; poor time management and procrastination; inability to apply oneself maximally in terms of attending to comments or suggestions; lone-ranger syndrome, which sees students working in isolation; a culture of secrecy and negative competition; personalising comments and suggestions from supervisors and colleagues; as well as difficulty in understanding important elements of the thesis such as conceptual and theoretical frameworks. The respondents also pointed out that students became less motivated when they realised that they were not progressing as expected. The verbatim response below captures this opinion:

PhD work can be draining on students especially when one is made to believe that they are not making good progress. (FGDR8)

These findings generally concur with those of Liechty et al. (2009) that individual issues such as psychological factors and skill preparation influence dissertation completion period. D'Andrea (2002) argues that student characteristics such as procrastination, dependency, unrealistic thinking, and relationship stress hinder progress in doctoral studies. Kluever and Green (1998) argue that independence and responsibility are highly demanded for doctoral work and that there is greater risk of attrition among students who lack these attributes. Vekkaila et al. (2013) acknowledge that doctoral students experience periods of disengagement and negative emotions which affect their progress. The authors add that disengaged students generally withdraw and become passive to learning opportunities. In these periods, they can only make progress if they are able to draw encouragement from a support network of supervisors and peers. Ali and Kohun (2006), as well as Spaulding and Rockinson- Szapkiw (2012) suggests that support from a strong community of scholars can motivate, and challenge disengaged students to re-engage. This parallels the support offered among members of an age-group, fostering mutual growth and success in life. Therefore, students need to collaborate with supervisors and their peers to progress out of perpetual liminality. Green (1997) suggests the use of regular meetings to keep students on track.

The other cause of delay for doctoral students in the liminal period revolves around availability and adequacy of institutional support and resources as well as clarity about expectations. The doctoral journey is taken in an environment. Candidates perform better if the environment is conducive for learning. This environment is generally created through institutional support in terms of clear rules and regulations; provision of adequate reading and other learning materials; availability of conducive physical and social workspaces; and financial support for needy students. The provision of this support contributes to the creation of an environment in which students are confident, safe and comfortable to work. Vekkaila et al. (2013) argue that there is a need for a close student–environment fit if the students are to make good progress and avoid being stuck in doctoral liminality. Golde (2005) asserts that the ability of the candidates to be resilient in the face of challenges depends on how closely they fit in the learning environment. Therefore, a misfit would discourage and delay progress out of liminality. Golde further states that whereas some elements of institutional support may be offered from a corporate level, departments should strive to offer structural support to their doctoral candidates for optimal results.

4.2 Symptoms of being stuck in doctoral liminality

The participants explained that in their liminal period, they felt stuck, timid, diffident and confused. Their efforts to break free and make progress seemingly led nowhere. Consequently, they felt frustrated, humiliated, failed and defeated as indicated in the verbatim responses below.

> *For me, I just hang in there confused but hoping something happens to enable me to make progress. It is the most frustrating part of the PhD journey.* (FGDR7)

Because of the slow pace of progress, the affected students avoid contact with their colleagues, supervisors and administrative staff at the university. There are also instances when they avoid some family members or friends.

> *Sometimes people, including family members, can be real tormentors. This is so unfortunate because they ought to support you more but sometimes they join the rest of the world to crucify you. One feels so helpless and alone.* (FGDR10)

The participants also explained that in this state, they become irritable, defensive and even suicidal. They also reported that they experience physical, social and mental fatigue. Some, like the respondent below, feel utterly helpless.

> *Sometimes, I cry to let out the anger and frustration. I know other people who do the same. It is no joke.* (FGDR9)

Some candidates consider dropping out of the programme because they feel they do not have the adequate energy and skills to complete their studies. This feeling is reflected in the verbatim response below:

> *I feel the PhD is for the selected few; it is not for me; I am not good enough; I am just wasting time and money trying to do something I am not cut [out] for.* (FGDR11)

Additionally, the literature reveals that doctoral candidates stuck in long periods of liminality demonstrate low energy (burnout), reduced involvement and inefficacy. Other symptoms include fear and anxiety (Strachan et al., 2004); cognitions such as self-criticism and self-doubt (Gordon, 2003); being troubled and constricted (Greco & Stenner, 2017); uncertainty and precarity (Gill & Orgad, 2015); fluidity, feeling unsettled and unstable (Salvatore & Venuleo, 2017); as well as depression and self-pity (Tigranyan et al., 2020).

From the foregoing, it is evident that if not addressed, then the consequences of liminality can be felt in the physical, social and psychological realms of students' lives as well. Supervisors and host departments are encouraged to watch out for any of the symptoms above to be able to provide prompt and proactive support to students who are stuck in liminality. Whereas the symptoms may be varied and may at times be caused by issues outside their doctoral journey, basic support such as merely providing a listening ear can make a whole difference to candidates who are experiencing liminality.

4.3 Overcoming doctoral liminality

The question on how to break through doctoral liminality persists. According to Liechty et al. (2009), there is a need for interventions at individual, relational, and institutional/departmental levels if doctoral candidates are to be helped of extended liminal periods. The participants in this study suggested the following strategies:

- The institution should design and implement an appropriate incentive and reward system for doctoral supervisors which would encourage them to prioritize supervision.
- Use supervision committees as a means of addressing personality conflicts between students and individual supervisors. The committees may also help to harmonize the comments and suggestions given by the supervisors to the students.
- Establish and promote doctoral work groups to provide a mechanism for peer support and monitoring. Students, supervisors and the department should participate freely in the formation of these groups.
- All doctoral supervisors should be trained to enhance their skillsets and to execute their roles in the best interests of the student and the university. Such training should be regular and mandatory.
- Allocation of supervisors should be transparent (and consultative) and done with the goal of matching the research needs of the students with the research interests and competence of the supervisor. There should be mechanisms for changes where and when the need arises.
- The selection of doctoral students should be structured and elaborate to ensure admission only of students who demonstrate the interest and

capacity to pursue the programme successfully. Those who do not make good progress should be allowed to drop out.

- Supervisors should use a structured system to track and monitor students' progress periodically according to the milestones in the doctoral programme. The system should have provisions for and encourage interventions to sustain progress.
- Regular seminars and workshops on topical issues of interest both for students and the supervisors should be held. These can be used as platforms for the exchange of ideas, experiences, best practices and lessons learnt.
- Explore opportunities for offering financial support to students in the form of tuition fee waivers and stipends. This can be achieved through appropriate scholarships and student work programmes.
- Work closely with institutional student support services to escalate needs which supervisors or departments cannot directly provide. Of interest here are professional counselling and guidance services.

5. Conclusions

This study demonstrates that most doctoral students experience liminality which is caused by a mix of factors. Three categories of factors were identified in this study. The first related to inadequacies in supervision and mentoring. While some supervisors committed insufficient time for their students, some were either less interested or incompetent in the students' topics of research. Inadequate supervision left the students without the requisite guidance in terms of conceptual and methodological issues relating to their doctoral work. Therefore, they worked alone through trial and error thereby making little progress. The second category of factors relate to the personal willingness and ability of students to work on the doctoral study. It emerged that all the students were working while pursuing their studies part-time. Therefore, they struggled to balance their job and student roles. This affected their progress. Nonetheless, there were also students who did not take their studies seriously. Such students did not respond appropriately to their supervisors' comments and suggestions. The third category of factors causing perpetual liminality among doctoral students in Kenya emanated from inadequate institutional support and resources.

Doctoral students experiencing liminality were fatigued, timid, confused and diffident; frustrated, humiliated and defeated; as well as irritable, defensive and suicidal. Therefore, if not addressed, liminality can affect the physical, social and psychological realms of students' lives. The need to address doctoral liminality is exigent. This can be done through diverse strategies. Having an appropriate incentive and reward system for doctoral supervisors; addressing personality conflicts between students and individual supervisors through supervision committees; training all doctoral supervisors to execute their roles in the best interest of the student and the university; allocating supervisors through a transparent and consultative process which matches the research needs of students with those of supervisors; and closely monitoring the progress of doctoral students so as to identify and mitigate indicators of liminality promptly.

This chapter used data generated by doctoral students in one programme in one university in Kenya and can therefore not be generalized beyond this context. This is only one part of the liminality story. There is need for further research on doctoral liminality at the national level; experiences of students who have completed their doctoral journeys; and the perspectives of supervisors on the causes of and solutions to doctoral liminality. Despite these limitations, the chapter is anchored in the author's experience as a supervisor of completed doctoral studies elsewhere as well as scholarly literature.

This chapter concludes that perpetual doctoral liminality is prevalent and is caused by students' personal contexts as well as the adequacy of the supervisor and institutional support they receive. Extended doctoral liminality can be avoided by adequately nurturing students through effective supervision and facilitative institutional support.

References

Academy of Science of South Africa. (2010). *The PhD study: An evidence-based study on how to meet the demands for high-level skills in an emerging economy.* Retrieved August 3, 2020, from https://www.assaf.org.za/files/2010/11/40696-Boldesign-PHD-small.pdf

Adorno, G., Cronley, C., & Smith, K. S. (2015). A different kind of animal: Liminal experiences of social work doctoral students. *Innovations in Education and Teaching International, 52*(6), 632–641. https://doi.org/10.1080/14703297.2013.866051

Ali, A., & Kohun, F. (2006). Dealing with isolation feelings in IS doctoral programs. *International Journal of Doctoral Studies, 1*(1), 21–33. https://doi.org/10.28945/58

Backhouse, J. P. (2009). *Doctoral education in South Africa: Models, pedagogies, and student experiences* (Unpublished doctoral dissertation). University of the Witwatersrand, Johannesburg. Retrieved August 3, 2020, from https://www.academia.edu/download/4911125/backhouse_doctoral_education_in_south_africa.pdf

Cloete, N., Bailey, T., Pillay, P., Bunting, I., & Maassen, P. (2011). *Universities and economic development in Africa.* Cape Town, South Africa: African Minds.

Cloete, N., Mouton, J., & Sheppard, C. (2015). *Doctoral education in South Africa.* Cape Town, South Africa: African Minds.

Clouder, L. (2005). Caring as a 'threshold concept': Transforming students in higher education into health (care) professionals. *Teaching in Higher Education, 10*(4), 505–517. https://doi. org/10.1080/13562510500239141

Commission for University Education. (2014). *Universities standards and guidelines, 2014.* Retrieved August 1, 2020, from http://www.cue.or.ke/index.php/provision-of-securityservices/ category/16-standards-and-guidelines?download=101:universities-standards-and-guidelines-2014

Commission for University Education. (2017). *Universities authorized to operate in Kenya.* Nairobi, Kenya: CUE.

Cyranoski, D., Gilbert, N., Ledford, H., Nayar, A., & Yahia, M. (2011). Education: The PhD factory. Retrieved July 30, 2020, from http://tcct.amss.ac.cn/newsletter/201202/images/THE%20PHD%20FACTORY.pdf

D'Andrea, L. M. (2002). Obstacles to completion of the doctoral degree in colleges of education: The professors' perspective. *Educational Research Quarterly, 25*(3), 42.

Deuchar, R. (2008). Facilitator, director, or critical friend? Contradiction and congruence in doctoral supervision styles. *Teaching in Higher Education, 13*(4), 489–500. https://doi.org/10.1080/13562510802193905

Friesenhahn, I. (2014, June 25). Making higher education work for Africa: Facts and figures. *SciDevNet.*

Gill, R., & Orgad, S. (2015). The confidence cult (ure). *Australian Feminist Studies, 30*(86), 324–344. https:// doi.org/10.1080/08164649.2015.1011484

Golde, C. M. (2005). The role of the department and discipline in doctoral student attrition: Lessons from four departments. *The Journal of Higher Education, 76*(6), 669–700. https://doi.org/10.1353/ jhe.2005.0039

Gordon, P. J. (2003). Advising to avoid or to cope with dissertation hang-ups. *Academy of Management Learning & Education, 2*(2), 181–187. https://doi.org/10.5465/amle.2003.9901684

Grant, B. M. (2005). Fighting for space in supervision: Fantasies, fairytales, fictions and fallacies. *International Journal of Qualitative Studies in Education, 18*(3), 337–354. https://doi. org/10.1080/09518390500082483

Greco, M., & Stenner, P. (2017). From paradox to pattern shift: Conceptualising liminal hotspots and their affective dynamics. *Theory & Psychology, 27*(2), 147–166. https://doi.org/10.1177/0959354317693120

Green, K. E. (1997). Psychosocial factors affecting dissertation completion. *New Directions for Higher Education, 99*, 57–64. https://doi.org/10.1002/he.9904

Jazvac-Martek, M. (2009). Oscillating role identities: The academic experiences of education doctoral students. *Innovations in Education and Teaching International, 46*(3), 253–264. https://doi. org/10.1080/14703290903068862

Keefer, J. M. (2015). Experiencing doctoral liminality as a conceptual threshold and how supervisors can use it. *Innovations in Education and Teaching International, 52*(1), 17–28. https://doi.org/10.1080/14703297. 2014.981839

Kiley, M. (2009). Identifying threshold concepts and proposing strategies to support doctoral candidates. *Innovations in Education and Teaching International, 46*(3), 293–304. https://doi. org/10.1080/14703290903069001

Kiley, M., & Wisker, G. (2010). Liminal spaces and doctoral examining: Evidence of research learning. In M. Kiley (Ed.), *Quality in postgraduate research: Educating researchers for the 21st century* (pp. 219–223). CEDAM, The Australian National University.

Kluever, R. C., & Green, K. E. (1998). The responsibility scale: A research note on dissertation completion. *Educational and Psychological Measurement, 58*(3), 520–531. https://doi. org/10.1177/0013164498058003007

Kralik, D., Visentin, K., & Van Loon, A. (2006). Transition: A literature review. *Journal of Advanced Nursing, 55*(3), 320–329. https://doi.org/10.1111/j.1365-2648.2006.03899.x

Langa, P. V. (2010). *Disciplines and engagement in African universities: A study of the distribution of scientific capital and academic networking in social sciences* [Doctoral dissertation, University of Cape Town]. OpenUCT Repository. https://open.uct.ac.za/handle/11427/14621

Leshem, S. (2020). Identity formations of doctoral students on the route to achieving their doctorate. *Issues in Educational Research, 30*(1), 169–186.

Liechty, J. M., Liao, M., & Schull, C. P. (2009). Facilitating dissertation completion and success among doctoral students in social work. *Journal of Social Work Education, 45*(3), 481–497. https://doi.org/10.5175/JSWE.2009.200800068

Louw, J., & Muller, J. (2014). *A literature review on models of the PhD.* Cape Town: CHET. Retrieved December 9, 2020, from http://www.chet.org.za/papers/literature-review-models-phd

Matheka, H. M., Jansen, E. P., & Hofman, W. A. (2020). Kenyan doctoral students' success: Roles of motivation and self-efficacy. *Perspectives in Education, 38*(1), 115–129. https://doi.org/10.18820/2519593X/pie.v38.i1.9

McClure, J. W. (2005). Preparing a laboratory-based thesis: Chinese international research students' experiences of supervision. *Teaching in Higher Education, 10*(1), 3–16. https://doi.org/10.1080/1356251052000305536

Meyer, J. H., & Land, R. (2003). Threshold concepts and troublesome knowledge: Linkages to ways of thinking and practising within the disciplines. In *Improving student learning: Improving student learning theory and practice – Ten years on* (pp. 412–424). OCSLD, Oxford Brookes University.

Meyer, J. H., & Land, R. (2005). Threshold concepts and troublesome knowledge (2): Epistemological considerations and a conceptual framework for teaching and learning. *Higher Education, 49*(3), 373–388. https://doi.org/10.1007/s10734-004-6779-5

Moore, K. (2016). Living liminal: Reflexive epistemological positioning at the intersection of marginalized identities. *Qualitative Social Work* 15(5-6):715-726.

Mouton, J. (2011). Doctoral production in South Africa: Statistics, challenges and responses. *Perspectives in Education, 29*(1), 13–29.

Pyhältö, K., Toom, A., Stubb, J., & Lonka, K. (2012). Challenges of becoming a scholar: A study of doctoral students' problems and well-being. *ISRN Education, 2012*(934941), 1–12. https://doi.org/10.5402/2012/934941

Rong'uno, S. K. (2016). *Institutional and student-related factors and doctoral studies completion rates in education at selected public universities in Kenya* (Doctoral dissertation, University of Nairobi). University of Nairobi Repository.

Salvatore, S., & Venuleo, C. (2017). Liminal transitions in a semiotic key: The mutual in-feeding between present and past. *Theory & Psychology, 27*(2), 215–230. https://doi.org/10.1177/0959354317692772

Spaulding, L. S., & Rockinson-Szapkiw, A. J. (2012). Hearing their voices: Factors doctoral candidates attribute to their persistence. *International Journal of Doctoral Studies, 7*(1), 199–219. https://doi.org/10.28945/1589

Strachan, R., Murray, R., & Grierson, H. (2004). A web-based tool for dissertation writing. *British Journal of Educational Technology, 35*(3), 369–375. https://doi.org/10.1111/j.0007-1013.2004.00396.x

Szakolczai, A. (2009). Liminality and experience: Structuring transitory situations and transformative events. *International Political Anthropology, 2*(1), 141–172.

Tigranyan, S., Byington, D. R., Liupakorn, D., Hicks, A., Lombardi, S., Mathis, M., & Rodolfa, E. (2020). Factors related to the impostor phenomenon in psychology doctoral students. *Training and Education in Professional Psychology.* https://doi.org/10.1037/tep0000321

Trafford, V. (2008). Conceptual frameworks as a threshold concept in doctorateness. In *Threshold concepts within the disciplines* (pp. 273–288). Brill Sense.

Trafford, V., & Leshem, S. (2009). Doctorateness as a threshold concept. *Innovations in Education and Teaching International, 46*(3), 305–316. https://doi.org/10.1080/14703290903069027

Turner, V. (1969). *The ritual process: Structure and anti-structure.* Ithaca, NY: Cornell University Press.

Turner, V. (2011). *The ritual process: Structure and anti-structure.* New Brunswick, NJ: Aldine Transaction.

Urbancová, H. (2013). Competitive advantage achievement through innovation and knowledge. *Journal of Competitiveness, 5*(1), 82–96. https://doi.org/10.7441/joc.2013.01.06

Vekkaila, J., Pyhältö, K., & Lonka, K. (2013). Experiences of disengagement: A study of doctoral students in the behavioral sciences. *International Journal of Doctoral Studies, 8*(2013), 61–81. https://doi.org/10.28945/1871

Wamala, R., Oonyu, J., & Ocaya, B. (2011). Completion time dynamics of doctoral studies at Makerere University: A hazard model evaluation. *Journal of International Education Research (JIER, 7*(3), 49–58.

Wisker, G. (2018). Different journeys: Supervisor perspectives on disciplinary conceptual threshold crossings in doctoral learning. *Critical Studies in Teaching and Learning, 6*(2). https://doi.org/10.14426/cristal.v6i2.148

Wisker, G., Morris, C., Cheng, M., Masika, R., Warnes, M., Trafford, V., Robinson, G., & Lilly, J. (2010). *Doctoral learning journeys: Final report* (pp. 1–61). London: Higher Education Academy. Retrieved August 2, 2020, from https://www.advance-he.ac.uk/knowledge-hub/doctorallearning-journeys

CHAPTER 23

Career and professional development of the doctoral candidate

Tracy Kellermann

South Africa has a population of 62 million. The country has 26 public universities with a total enrolment of 1.1 million students. Doctoral enrolments in South Africa have increased from 9 994 in 2008 to 23 588 in 2020 (CHE, Vitalstats). During the period 2000-2018, a total of 32 025 doctoral students graduated at South African universities. Annual doctoral graduates increased from 972 in 2000 to 3 339 in 2019 (SciSTIP, Tracer Study).

Stellenbosch University became an independent university in 1918, tracing its origins to the Theological Seminary of the Dutch Reformed Church (est. 1859) and Stellenbosch College (est. 1880). The university has ten faculties located on four campuses (in Stellenbosch, Bellville Cape Town and Saldanha). In 2021 it had 1 400 academic staff members and 32 471 students, including 1 611 doctoral candidates, and 310 doctoral degrees were awarded. The first doctoral degree was awarded by Stellenbosch University in 1923, in physics.

---

1. Introduction

Since the 1990s, an emphasis has been placed on the influence of knowledge and information technology on economic growth (Bryan & Guccione, 2018; Hancock, 2019). Academic education is associated with wealth generation in the global move towards knowledge-based economies (Goneos-Malka, 2018). Consequently, the importance of higher education in the promotion of socio-economic development in the Africa region has become a political agenda (Friesenhahn, 2014). Human capital is seen as the capacity for innovation and subsequent productivity (Pederson, 2014) and the assumption exists that having a doctorate allows its bearer to have a choice of employment opportunities, either in academia or industry. A doctorate, internationally recognised, is seen as prerequisite preparation for a career in academia (Bazeley, 1999) and perhaps a PhD qualification, as a measure of quality, can be used as a screening tool by prospective employers (Pederson, 2014). The desire to undertake a PhD is dependent on the job market for such highly qualified individuals. Due to an increasingly competitive and evolving job market, decreases in governmental funding, commercialization and internationalization (Matas, 2012), the applicability of a PhD in its traditional format and its translation into the employability of its holder needs to be reconsidered.

With the increasing demand for PhD studies, attention needs to be given to the market needs for not only highly specialized knowledge, insights and skills, but also 'soft' skills (Young et al., 2020) and eventual employment opportunities of these highly qualified people, as relatively few candidates continue to do research within academia (Mulvaney, 2013; St Clair et al., 2019; Stringer et al., 2018; Sharmini & Spronken-Smith, 2020). The traditional apprenticeship model PhD format is perhaps not 'fit for purpose', as it prepares graduates for faculty research careers despite a large proportion eventually working in non-academic environments. How are current doctoral programmes and institutions guiding and preparing PhD candidates for employment opportunities outside of academia to fulfil their roles in the global knowledge-based economy?

This chapter aims to investigate career guidance and development opportunities for biomedical PhD students at Stellenbosch University, South Africa, as well as to evaluate the employment opportunities for biomedical PhD graduates. Furthermore, I shall draw on global research in this field to consider the challenges and opportunities in aligning doctoral studies with available academic and industry employment opportunities.

2. Literature review

Globally, there has been an increase in the number of PhDs generated annually (Cyranoski et al, 2011). However, the perceived demand for PhDs to boost economies by investment in human capital might not be as great as previously predicted and PhD graduates may struggle to find employment (Pederson, 2014; Cyranoski et al., 2011; Åkerlind, 2005; Barnacle & Dall'Alba, 2011; McAlpine & Emmioğlu, 2015; Palumbo & Cavallone, 2022), an observation that has also been made in the South African context (Blitzer, 2016; Goneos-Malka, 2018).

A *Nature* survey conducted by Woolsten (2017) showed that many PhD student respondents hoped to secure an academic job after graduation, despite a global decrease in available academic positions. Various authors investigated issues to related to the employment prospects of doctoral candidates (Bazely, 1999; Matas, 2012; Acker & Haque, 2017; Leathwood & Read, 2020; Kyvik & Olsen, 2012). After completing a PhD, researchers wanting to embark on an academic career enter into post- doctoral training, viewed as a transition-ary phase for growth and development in preparation for a research career (Åkerlind, 2005). However, they are increasingly frustrated by low pay and an inability to secure permanent academic jobs where they are kept in a cycle with no job security, no benefits and no guarantee of future employment (Åkerlind, 2005; Acker & Haque, 2017). This has led to a decrease in the number of post-docs, with potentially negative consequences for the quantity and quality of biomedical research (Garrison et al., 2016). Furthermore, after post-doctoral positions, there are limited employment opportunities for junior researchers (Bazely, 1999) and an increasing global trend of short-term contracts within academia, with women especially overrepresented in these precarious positions (Stringer et al., 2018). This, together with the alienation of academics from their profession by mass education and corporatized management structures, creates high levels of dissatisfaction, stress and insecurity (Åkerlind, 2005; McCarthy et al., 2017; Leathwood & Read, 2020; Vohlídalová, 2021; Stringer et al., 2018).

In South Africa, approximately half to two thirds of PhD graduates across all scholarly fields are employed in the higher education sector (ASSAf, 2010; Goneos-Malka, 2018; Mouton & Van Lill, 2022), with only 17% employed in business enterprise, 11% in government and 0.07% employed permanently by the top 200 companies of the Johannesburg Stock Exchange (Goneos-Malka, 2018). A recent study showed that only 2–3% of doctoral graduates in South Africa were not employed (Mouton & Van Lill, 2022). Therefore, in the South African context, PhD holders appear to be highly employable, but approximately 18% of graduates are not able to find employment in their area of expertise (Mouton & Van Lill, 2022).

STEM (science, technology, engineering and mathematics) education, knowledge and innovation are seen as essential drivers of economic growth (Hancock, 2019). In the early 2000s, policies aimed at increasing the number of PhDs in STEM fields were implemented with a view to create innovation and technological advancement (Pederson, 2014), but in recent times factors such as political agendas, Visa restrictions and the Covid-19 pandemic have all influenced the representation of minority groups globally in STEM fields (McGee et al., 2021; Kahn & MacGarvie, 2020). In a global STEM pipeline that urgently needs diversification, it is alarming that females are still underrepresented in research and more likely to leave the STEM workforce altogether compared with other groups (Turck-Bicakci et al., 2014), no doubt compounded by gender-associated remuneration gaps in the labour force, although previous inequalities are becoming more balanced (Shauman, 2017). In some parts of the world, the movement of female STEM doctorates into business and industry is now gender neutral, women are more likely to obtain tenured faculty positions and women are as likely as men to stay in the STEM field, although less likely to hold research-associated jobs (Shauman, 2017).

Policies need to be implemented at national, industry and institutional level to foster growth in STEM fields (TurkBicakci et al., 2014). It is possible to minimize attrition rates of underrepresented minorities (URM) in STEM higher education using interventions targeting recruitment (recruitment drives in historically underrepresented communities, removal of socio-economic barriers), admissions (thorough management of admissions review), inclusion and retention (academic and social support groups), and faculty demographics (mentor diversity to mimic demographics of URM students) (Wilson et al., 2018). In South African higher education, policies have been implemented to increase the number of female PhD graduates, particularly African women, in the historically white male dominated STEM fields. These policies have not, however, considered how underlying subtle prejudices and assumptions about identity influence inclusion and sense of belonging, which influences participation, retention and advancement in an academic environment (Idahosa & Mkhize, 2021).

A *Nature* survey of 5 700 PhD candidates conducted by Woolsten (2017) indicated that worry and uncertainty are rife, with 12% of all respondents having sought help for mental health issues related to their PhDs. Most worry about their futures and whether their efforts will pay off in the form of a well-compensated job (Woolsten, 2017; Mata, 2012). Where supply outstrips market demand, the possibility of an over-skilled labour force arises, where a PhD degree is not necessary for the position held. This could have implications for the PhD graduates' motivation and subsequent career trajectories (Pederson, 2014; Bazeley, 1999) and leave individuals feeling as though their studies were a waste of time (Bazeley, 1999). Where an individual's path to a PhD is purely incidental, they may not have such strong feelings, but there have been reports of higher levels of burnout in these individuals than other groups (Bazeley, 1999).

Only 31% of the *Nature* survey respondents stated that their PhD programme was preparing them well for a fulfilling career. 18% responded that they did not have useful career-related discussions with their supervisor, particularly about careers that are non-academic (Woolsten, 2017), a widely confirmed observation (McAlpine & Emmioğlu, 2015; Turk-Bicakci et al., 2014; Gibbs & Griffin, 2013; St Clair et al., 2017; Matas, 2012; Bazeley, 1999). Furthermore, supervisors are often reported as being disparaging of careers outside of academia (Woolsten, 2017; Åkerlind, 2005). Career guidance in the doctoral environment is typically not structured and largely ad hoc and most graduates feel that career guidance at the post-doctoral stage is too late and should be provided before embarking on a PhD (Åkerlind, 2005).

3. Methodology

Open access publications or those available through Stellenbosch University library subscriptions were obtained by means of Google Scholar searches using the following key words, phrases and combinations thereof: 'PhD employment/ employability'; 'PhD skills'; 'biomedical science PhD'; 'biomedical PhD South Africa'; 'social cognitive career theory'; 'doctoral degree biomedical South Africa'. Information from the DIES/CREST Training Course for Supervisors of Doctoral Candidates at African Universities was also utilised. In addition, the Stellenbosch University Career Services and Faculty of Medicine and Health Sciences Doctoral Office were contacted. Both groups were asked the following questions:

- Do you provide any career counselling services for PhD candidates?
- Do you ever receive requests for career guidance from PhD candidates?
- Can you recommend a department/group that could be contacted in this regard?

A South African recruitment agency, SciStaff, which specializes in matching science-based jobs with prospective employees, was contacted and the following questions regarding PhD employment were posed:

- How often do you have requests from prospective employers for jobs requiring a PhD in a biomedical field? Often (5+ requests per month), occasionally (5 requests every 3 months) or seldom (5 requests every 6 months).
- As a percentage of these requests, how many are for jobs in academia and how many are for industry?
- For these jobs, what would the salary range offered be?
- How much value do prospective employers place on prior work experience?

- Are industry jobs for management positions, R&D, delivery of a service, or other?
- Other than the PhD qualifications, what other skills do prospective employees list as being a requirement for these jobs?
- Have you noticed areas in which the PhD graduates are lacking in their job applications which results in them not being considered for the positions?
- Do you think that short courses or workshops on project management, writing skills, teaching courses etc. would make any difference to a candidate's CV?
- Any other comments/observations?

4. Results

Career guidance is provided to undergraduate students by Stellenbosch University Career Service, and they do not receive requests for, or offer to provide, career counselling to PhD students. The Doctoral Office at the Faculty of Medicine and Health Sciences indicated that they do not provide career counselling to doctoral students and were not aware of any group that offers this on a formal basis within the faculty. These institutional findings are concurrent with literature findings of a lack of formal career guidance, particularly for non-academic career trajectories (McAlpine & Emmioğlu, 2015; Turk-Bicakci et al., 2014; Woolsten, 2017; Åkerlind, 2005; St Clair et al., 2017), as well as the author's experience of postgraduate studies at three different South African universities in the field of biomedical sciences.

The SciStaff recruitment agency responded that they seldom (5 requests every 6 months) receive job opportunities for PhD graduates and that any requests were typically for industry positions, predominantly for research and development and for sales and application specialist positions. Apart from technical skills such as laboratory methodology techniques (e.g. ELISA, flow cytometry), method development and validation, prospective employers also required report writing skills and the ability to work in a team. Additional course certificates or workshop attendance in ISO17025/15189, good laboratory practice, good clinical practice and statistics could benefit a candidate in a research position. Employers place an enormous amount of weight on prior work experience. The respondent emphasised that students should realise that most employers do not regard PhD research as work experience. It was suggested that PhD candidates get more exposure to industry, either by doing a project in collaboration with industry partners or by doing temporary vacation work in industry.

5. Discussion

A broad range of literature pertaining to the employment and employability of PhD graduates globally has been incorporated into this chapter and will be discussed further in the context of the findings of the study. These findings are like previous observations that PhDs are not financially rewarded for having their degree. One explanation for this trend is that while PhDs are completing their studies, individuals with master's degrees are gaining work experience, allowing them to become attached to the industry, giving employers a means of gauging their skill level (Pederson, 2016). It is possible that certain industries only require master's graduates, and that there is an oversupply of PhDs who are over-skilled for the work description and have insufficient experience in the soft skills required within a cooperative environment (Goneos-Malka, 2018; Bazeley, 1999). PhDs are therefore not able to fulfil their training to advance knowledge and industry is not able to exploit their human capital. (Bazeley, 1999; Bryan & Guccione, 2018). Those who are employed outside of academia are often moved into management positions, becoming further removed from hands-on research (Bazeley, 1999). Several authors also comment that previous work experience, whether paid or through integrated work experiences, has a positive effect on permanent job attainment (Jackson & Michelson, 2015; Pederson, 2014), which concurs with the present author's own work experience between industry and academia. The success of any employment application was always based on the experience and skills obtained in industry. When recruited for an academic job, industry experience and a sought-after, rare skillset was valuable, but an insufficient number of publications was a disadvantage. As an academic, a publication track record is essential for obtaining early-career seed funding with which to initiate research.

Industries in certain countries may not be sufficiently developed to convert PhD skills into a financial asset, which is possibly the case in South Africa too. Alternatively, there is a lack of understanding in South African (and other countries') industry of the value PhD graduates can contribute, or inadequate marketing (Goneos-Malka, 2018; Bryan & Guccione, 2018). Employers have the impression that PhD graduates are overqualified, too expensive and may not remain in a company for a prolonged period, views that are exacerbated by openly discriminatory stances of human resource departments, effectively the gatekeepers of hiring (Goneos-Malka, 2018).

There is a clear gap between employers' needs and what is currently being generated through conventional doctoral programmes (Young et al., 2020; Acker & Haque, 2017). Market forces define the needs as not only highly specialized knowledge, insights and skills that go beyond the commercialization and application to industry, but also soft skills (Young et al., 2020). If one measures the success of doctoral education as high employment rates in a satisfying and stimulating workplace and graduates who are equipped for global citizenship, then doctoral programmes in their current apprenticeship format are failing (Spronken-Smith, 2018). PhD programmes that are enriched with practice-directed learning activities help with graduate employment, suggesting that interventions aimed at supplementing the quality of learning experiences are successful (Pulambo & Cavallone, 2022). Development should not stop after graduation, but early-career researchers must continually be supported and developed professionally to secure permanent positions (Robbins & LePeau, 2018).

5.1 Strategies to consider for improving PhD graduate employment outcomes

Traditional PhD programme structures favour academic career paths, despite a paucity of positions and a growing number of graduates employed in industry. Solutions to improving doctoral employability should involve better alignment of the needs of the student, institution and industry (Young et al., 2020; Sharmini & Spronken-Smith, 2020). These strategies need to consider the formative process of developing a doctoral professional identity, the environmental and social characteristics that drive career choices, development of skills required in industry and the introduction of career guidance and professional development into doctoral curricula.

Development of professional identity

Reforms should be implemented during doctoral studies to aid with professional identity development and exposure to a research career intended to boost the resilience of these highly skilled individuals to ensure their valued social, cultural and economic contributions (Hancock & Walsh, 2016; Roberts, 2018), while taking the individual nature of a PhD into consideration and enabling communities of practice (Hancock, 2019). This includes the creation of interdisciplinary research spaces in which STEM doctoral students can interact across fields to share their doctoral experiences, such as the doctoral group monthly engagement in the Faculty of Medicine and Health Sciences at Stellenbosch University, hosted by an experienced health sciences education researcher. These discussions include social, economic and ethical issues with a view towards identity formation which allows adaptability within the dynamic environment of scientific research (Spronken-Smith, 2018; Hancock & Walsh, 2016), but also promotes development of global citizens and informed leaders with critical awareness of themselves and their actions (Spronken-Smith, 2018). Any measures introduced to improve the employability of PhD graduates should not detract from the academic rigour as a respected outcome of a PhD, or the professional identity associated with completing a doctorate (Roberts, 2018).

Social cognitive career theory

The social cognitive career theory (SCCT) proposes that individual interests influence a training path which requires actions and self-belief to achieve those envisioned goals while also considering how personal characteristics, learning experiences and support/obstacles can influence this process (Gibbs & Griffin, 2013). A modified SCCT model can be applied where an individual adapts their career choices and development according to the resources and challenges experienced (St Clair et al., 2017), such as having to work while completing their PhD (Bekova, 2021; Mouton & Van Lill, 2022). Academic and demographic characteristics affect strategy to secure preferred futures, with the PhD viewed as a time for calculated risk-taking (Hancock, 2019).

The importance of social interactions and networking at the level of engagement in the career development process cannot be understated (St Clair et al., 2017; Vekkaila et al., 2016). Advisors and faculty can form social capital resources or barriers to candidates pursuing and seeking career progression resources (St Clair et al., 2017; St Clair et al., 2019). High levels of supervisor support are associated with a lower likelihood of pursuing career development resources, while low support levels from departments, supervisors and peers leads to a lower likelihood of seeking any type of career development resource. Individuals with low self-efficacy or interest in a broader range of career opportunities are most interested in structured career development opportunities (St Clair et al., 2019; St Clair et al., 2017).

Race, ethnicity and belonging to an underrepresented demographic can have significant influence on agency in pursuit of career paths within doctoral programmes (Jaeger et al., 2017; Gibbs & Griffin, 2013). Being one of few students (or employees) of colour or being an international candidate within a department can create feelings of isolation (Jaeger et al., 2017; St Clair et al., 2017; Idahosa & Mkhize, 2021) and for longevity requires an individual to brush off negative experiences related to their social identity (Gibbs & Griffin,

2013). Faculties promoting diversity and inclusion should provide opportunities to engage and connect students and staff, creating a support structure to develop agency in their doctoral career progression and beyond (Jaeger et al., 2017; Idahosa & Mkhize, 2021).

Career coaching model

Traditionally, doctoral students rely on the mentorship of advisors and faculty members to acquire formal research skills and informal life coaching, provided the mentors have the skills and time to impart this knowledge (Thakore et al., 2014; Wilson et al., 2018). However, perhaps mentoring as a construct is flawed due to mentor workload, time constraints, subjectivity of the mentor and challenges with integration of individuals from different backgrounds (Thakore et al., 2014). Faculty demographics must mirror student demographics to be effective, particularly for formerly underrepresented groups such as women (Wilson et al., 2018). Programmes have been implemented for training of mentors, as can be seen with the DIES/CREST Training Course for Supervisors of Doctoral Candidates at African Universities. A formal group coaching approach can be used to overcome these obstacles while considering the development of professional identity. This concept incorporates the communities of practice principle which states that individuals with a common interest and goal work together to achieve their goal (Thakore et al., 2014). This could be particularly beneficial with minority students who have a relative lack of social and cultural capital. Individual development plans and self-assessment exercises should be undertaken for the process of career development (Thakore et al., 2014; Sharmini & Spronken-Smith, 2020; Williams et al., 2016).

Critical skills development

Despite country-specific variations in approaches to PhD programmes (Williams et al., 2019), doctoral studies largely equip students to design, conduct and communicate research. Some programmes involve the formalized acquisition of broader applied skills and knowledge base, such as the professional or 'new route/modern' doctorates where the student serves as the project manager with access to a network of expert assistance of colleagues and technicians (Mulvaney, 2013; Mulvaney & Lackovic, 2012; Botha, 2019; Matas, 2012; Spronken-Smith, 2018). PhD graduates often lack the know-how to adapt their academic knowledge and skills to an industry-related environment (Pederson, 2016; Bazeley, 1999; Young et al., 2020). To overcome this obstacle, transferable skills development and career guidance should be implemented as a structured part of a PhD curriculum, or even at an earlier stage (Åkerlind, 2005; Bazeley, 1999; Gibbs & Griffin, 2013; Spronken-Smith et al., 2018; Young et al., 2020; Spronken-Smith, 2018; Sharmini & Spronken-Smith, 2020; Mulvaney, 2013).

PhD graduates are often found lacking in the generic and technical skills required for their positions (ASSAf, 2010). The soft skills most sought-after by potential industry employers of PhD graduates include technical skills, communication, capacity to learn new skills, adaptability, critical and systematic thinking, statistics, teamwork, data analysis, project and finance/business management, leadership, commercial awareness and application of skills, work experience, personal motivation, resilience, commitment, perseverance and ability to network (Bazeley, 1999; Matas, 2012; Jackson & Michelson, 2015; Pederson, 2014; Kyvik & Olsen, 2012; ASSAf, 2010; Spronken-Smith, 2018). Traits reportedly required for academic careers include theoretical knowledge within the scholarly field, computer proficiency, decision-making and problem-solving skills, publication rate and presentations at conferences (Bazeley, 1999; Åkerlind, 2005). Furthermore, the concept of 'who you know' is becoming increasingly more important than 'what you know', emphasising the importance of networking opportunities for postgraduate students (Jackson & Michelson, 2015). Initiatives must be implemented to create a holistic set of skills within doctoral programmes (Spronken-Smith, 2018), while taking care against reducing doctoral studies to a set of activities to acquire generic skills at the expense of respected academic rigour and professional identity (Roberts, 2018).

Inclusion of career guidance and development in the PhD curriculum

Often PhD candidates have few opportunities to learn about career possibilities and the skills associated with jobs, particularly outside of their knowledge field (Bazeley, 1999; Gibbs & Griffin, 2013; Spronken-Smith, 2018; McAlpine & Emmioğlu, 2015; St Clair et al., 2017). Supervisors or faculty form the primary source of career guidance for doctoral students, mostly on an informal basis and often with a bias towards academic career paths (Gibbs & Griffin, 2013; Sauermann & Roach, 2012) and reticence to guide outside of their chosen career paths (Hancock, 2019) due to lack of exposure, particularly to industry (Gibbs & Griffin, 2013). Doctoral students are often not realistic about their preferences for faculty careers considering the low availability of academic positions and relative oversupply of PhD graduates (Sauermann & Roach, 2012; McAlpine & Emmioğlu, 2015). There is a need to more clearly define career paths (Pederson, 2014; McAlpine & Emmioğlu, 2015; Spronken-Smith et al., 2018).

Given the lack of influence of the supervisor on graduate employment, career development and exposure should be implemented and promoted within institutions for academic and non-academic careers paths (McAlpine & Emmioğlu, 2015; Williams et al., 2019). Institutions could organise career workshops in which PhD graduates describe their career paths, including the influences of personal circumstances (McAlpine & Emmioğlu, 2015). Effective integration of career planning into a PhD curriculum should be implemented to understand short- and long-term career trajectories (Jackson & Michelson, 2015; Pederson 2014; Sauermann & Roach, 2012; Spronken-Smith, 2018; Sinche et al., 2017; Williams et al., 2019), while taking personal values into consideration (Gibbs & Griffin, 2013). Such a career-conscious model should help trainees recognise their existing skills, and address shortfalls according to employee ratings of importance (Sinche et al., 2017). Doctoral students could also benefit from an institutional career development service (Jackson & Michelson, 2015), but students should also be encouraged to make use of such services and start thinking about potential career pathways earlier in their studies too (McAlpine & Emmioğlu, 2015).

Universities should enable work experience during the PhD process, either by integrating work experiences into the course design, or by encouraging or facilitating part-time employment in academia or a related industry (Hancock & Walsh, 2016; Young et al., 2020; Mulvaney, 2013; Roberts, 2018). A team approach to supervision could provide exposure to a broad range of academic and non- academic networks with an increased possibility of access to integrated career experience (Scaffidi & Berman, 2012; Pyhältö et al, 2015). These opportunities can serve to break down the perceived strict boundaries between industry and academia and to broaden horizons (Hancock, 2019). Programmes can even include personal professional development plans with formative portfolios (Sharmini & Spronken-Smith, 2020) and perhaps PhD training should be tailor-made to fulfil the needs of PhD holders and various employment sectors (Kyvik & Olsen, 2012; Pederson, 2014; ASSAf, 2010; Spronken-Smith, 2018; Palumbo & Cavallone, 2022; Sharmini & Spronken-Smith, 2020; Roberts, 2018).

6. Conclusion

Globally, it has been acknowledged that pedagogical changes need to be implemented to improve the employability of doctoral students. Solutions to improving doctoral employability should involve better alignment and defining of the needs of the student, institution and industry (Young et al., 2020).

Spronken-Smith (2018) proposes that a reformation is required in global doctoral education where rates of employment, satisfaction with the types of employment and graduates who are global citizens equipped with the hard and soft skills to thrive, should be the indicators of success. Aligning doctoral education with desired career paths can introduce an apprenticeship model tailored to create graduate attributes in individuals. This can be achieved by additional training in generic and transferable skills to all doctoral candidates, possibly even at an earlier stage of postgraduate studies. This training can be provided as formal group or individual sessions, as well as an online tool geared towards a non- academic training matrix. Furthermore, the role of the individual supervisor in providing or facilitating such training should be explored with the aim of creating awareness of the importance of improving the preparedness of doctoral students for academic and non-academic career paths.

Career planning and professional development are essential to achieving these goals in quality- controlled PhD programmes (Spronken-Smith, 2018; Palumbo & Cavallone, 2022; Sharmini & Spronken-Smith, 2020; Sinche et al., 2017; Mulvaney, 2013). Institutions, supervisors and mentors should be clear to students about the value, purpose and essence of a doctorate and its contribution to the knowledge economy (Hancock, 2019; Mulvaney, 2013). Awareness of the value of employing doctoral graduates must be raised among industry employers to promote an understanding of the varied and unique benefits that doctoral graduates can provide to an employer, and this mutual appreciation by both the employer and the graduate could bridge the gap between supply and demand of doctoral graduates (Bryan & Guccione, 2018). Similar to reforms that have been implemented in other parts of the world, South African higher education institutions need to provide career development opportunities and engage with industry partners to create collaborations that could provide applied integrated work experience. Such partnerships can harness the creativity and innovation that PhD graduates contribute to solving industry-focused problems, while respecting the academic rigour and unique professional identity formed during a PhD (Roberts, 2018).

References

Academy of Science of South Africa (ASSAf). (2010). *The PhD study: An evidence-based study on how to meet the demands for high-level skills in an emerging economy.* https://doi.org/10.17159/assaf.2016/0026

Acker, S., & Haque, E. (2017). Left out in the academic field: Doctoral graduates deal with a decade of disappearing jobs. *Canadian Journal of Higher Education / Revue canadienne d'enseignement supérieur, 47*(3), 101–119. https://doi.org/10.7202/1043240ar

Åkerlind, G. S. (2005). Postdoctoral researchers: Roles, functions and career prospects. *Higher Education Research and Development, 24*(1), 21–40. https://doi.org/10.1080/0729436052000318550

Barnacle, R., & Dall'Alba, G. (2011). Research degrees as professional education? *Studies in Higher Education, 36*(4), 459–470. https://doi.org/10.1080/03075071003698607

Bazeley, P. (1999). Continuing research by PhD graduates. *Higher Education Quarterly, 53*(4), 333–352. https://doi.org/10.1111/1468-2273.00135

Bekova, S. (2021). Does employment during doctoral training reduce the PhD completion rate? *Studies in Higher Education, 46*(6), 1068–1080. https://doi.org/10.1080/03075079.2019.1672648

Blitzer, E. (2016). Research into doctoral education: A survey of institutional research projects in Southern Africa. In J. Botha & N. Muller (Eds.), *Institutional research in South African higher education* (pp. 277-279). Stellenbosch: SUN PRESS.

Botha, J. (2019). *The nature, purpose, standard and format of the doctoral degree.* Course material for Module 2 of the DIES/CREST Training Course for Supervisors of Doctoral Candidates at African Universities, Stellenbosch University.

Bryan, B., & Guccione, K. (2018). Was it worth it? A qualitative exploration into graduate perceptions of doctoral value. *Higher Education Research & Development, 37*(6), 1124–1140. https://doi.org/10.1080/07294360.2018.1479378

Cyranoski, D., Gilbert, N., Ledford, H., Nayar, A., & Yahia, M. (2011). The PhD factory: The world is producing more PhDs than ever—Is it time to stop? *Nature, 472,* 276–279. https://doi.org/10.1038/472276a

Frick, L. (2019). *Supervisory models and styles.* Course material for Module 4 of the DIES/CREST Training Course for Supervisors of Doctoral Candidates at African Universities, Stellenbosch University.

Friesenhahn, I. (2014). Making higher education work for Africa: Facts and figures. *SciDev.Net.* https://www.scidev.net/global/features/higher-education-africa-facts-figures/

Garrison, H. H., Justement, L. B., & Gerbi, S. A. (2016). Biomedical science postdocs: An end to the era of expansion. *FASEB Journal, 30*(1), 41–44.

Gibbs, K. D., Jr., & Griffin, K. A. (2013). What do I want to be with my PhD? The roles of personal values and structural dynamics in shaping the career interests of recent biomedical science PhD graduates. *CBE—Life Sciences Education, 12*(4), 711–723. https://doi.org/10.1187/cbe.13-02-0021

Goneos-Malka, A. (2018). PhD employability in corporate South Africa. In E. Blitzer, L. Frick, M. Fourie-Malherbe, & K. Pyhältö (Eds.), *Spaces, journeys and new horizons for postgraduate supervision.* Stellenbosch: SunPress. https://doi.org/10.18820/9781928357810

Hancock, S. (2019). A future in the knowledge economy? Analysing the career strategies of doctoral scientists through the principles of game theory. *Higher Education, 78*(1), 33–49. https://doi.org/10.1007/s10734-018-0329-z

Hancock, S., & Walsh, E. (2016). Beyond knowledge and skills: Rethinking the development of professional identity during the STEM doctorate. *Studies in Higher Education, 41*(1), 37–50. https://doi.org/10.1080/03075079.2014.915301

Idahosa, G. E., & Mkhize, Z. (2021). Intersectional experiences of Black South African female doctoral students in STEM: Participation, success and retention. *Agenda, 35*(2), 110–122. https://doi.org/10.1080/10130950.2021.1919533

Jackson, D., & Michelson, G. (2015). Factors influencing the employment of Australian PhD graduates. *Studies in Higher Education, 40*(9), 1660–1678. https://doi.org/10.1080/03075079.2014.899344

Jaeger, A. J., Mitchall, A., Grantham, A., Zhang, J., O'Meara, K. A., Eliason, J., & Cowdery, K. (2017). Push and pull: The influence of race/ethnicity on agency in doctoral student career advancement. *Journal of Diversity in Higher Education, 10*(3), 232–252. https://doi.org/10.1037/dhe0000018

Kahn, S., & MacGarvie, M. (2020). The impact of permanent residency delays for STEM PhDs: Who leaves and why. *Research Policy, 49,* 103879. https://doi.org/10.1016/j.respol.2019.103879

Kyvik, S., & Olsen, T. B. (2012). The relevance of doctoral training in different labour markets. *Journal of Education and Work, 25*(2), 205–224. https://doi.org/10.1080/13639080.2010.538376

Leathwood, C., & Read, B. (2020). Short-term, short-changed? A temporal perspective on the implications of academic casualisation for teaching in higher education. *Teaching in Higher Education.* https://doi.org/10.1080/13562517.2020.1742681

Matas, C. P. (2012). Doctoral education and skills development: An international perspective. *Revista de Docencia Universitaria, 10*(2), 163–191.

McAlpine, L., & Emmioğlu, E. (2015). Navigating careers: Perceptions of sciences doctoral students, post-PhD researchers and pre-tenure academics. *Studies in Higher Education, 40*(10), 1770–1785. https://doi.org/1 0.1080/03075079.2014.914908

McAlpine, L., Pyhältö, K., & Castelló, M. (2018). Building a more robust conception of early career researcher experience: What might we be overlooking? *Studies in Continuing Education, 40*(2), 149–165. https://doi. org/10.1080/0158037X.2017.1408582

McCarthy, G., Song, X., & Jayasuriya, K. (2017). The proletarianisation of academic labour in Australia. *Higher Education Research & Development, 36*(5), 1017–1030. https://doi.org/10.1080/07294360.2016. 1263936

McGee, E., Fang, Y., Ni, Y., & Monroe-White, T. (2021). How an antiscience president and the COVID-19 pandemic altered the career trajectories of STEM PhD students of color. *AERA Open, 7*(1), 1–15. https:// doi.org/10.1177/23328584211039217

Mouton, J., & Frick, L. (2019). The need for the doctorate and the state of doctoral studies in Africa. *Course Material of Module 1 of the DIES/CREST Training Course for Supervisors of Doctoral Candidates at African Universities*. Stellenbosch University.

Mouton, J., & Van Lill, M. (2022). How employable are South Africa's doctoral graduates? *SciByte@SciSTIP, 5*. DSI-NRF Centre of Excellence in Scientometrics and STI Policy, Stellenbosch University. Retrieved from https://www0.sun.ac.za/scistip/publications/scibytes/

Mulvaney, M. J. (2013). Biomedical PhD education – An international perspective. *Basic & Clinical Pharmacology & Toxicology, 112*(4), 289–295. https://doi.org/10.1111/bcpt.12063

Mulvaney, M., & Lackovic, Z. (2012). PhDs fit for industry and commerce, too. *Nature, 488*, 591. https://doi. org/10.1038/488591c

Palumbo, R., & Cavallone, M. (2022). Unravelling the implications of learning experiences on doctoral degree holders' employment: Empirical insights and avenues for further developments. *European Journal of Higher Education*. https://doi.org/10.1080/21568235.2022.2049838

Pedersen, H. S. (2014). New doctoral graduates in the knowledge economy: Trends and key issues. *Journal of Higher Education Policy and Management, 36*(6), 632–645. https://doi.org/10.1080/136008 0X.2014.957891

Pedersen, H. S. (2016). Are PhDs winners or losers? Wage premiums for doctoral degrees in private sector employment. *Higher Education, 71*, 269–287. https://doi.org/10.1007/s10734-015-9901-y

Pyhältö, K., Vekkaila, J., & Keskinen, J. (2015). Fit matters in the supervisory relationship: Doctoral students' and supervisors' perceptions about the supervisory activities. *Innovations in Education and Teaching International, 52*(1), 4–16. https://doi.org/10.1080/14703297.2014.981836

Robbins, C. K., & LaPeau, L. A. (2018). Seeking "better ways": Early career faculty researcher development. *Studies in Graduate and Postdoctoral Education, 9*(2), 113–126. https://doi.org/10.1108/ SGPE-D-17-00029

Roberts, A. G. (2018). Industry and PhD engagement programs: Inspiring collaboration and driving knowledge exchange. *Perspectives: Policy and Practice in Higher Education, 22*(4), 115–123. https://doi.org/10.1 080/13603108.2018.1456492

Sauermann, H., & Roach, M. (2012). Science PhD career preferences: Levels, changes, and advisor encouragement. *PLoS ONE, 7*(5), e36307. https://doi.org/10.1371/journal.pone.0036307

Scaffidi, A. K., & Berman, J. E. (2011). A positive postdoctoral experience is related to quality supervision and career mentoring, collaborations, networking, and a nurturing research environment. *Higher Education, 62*, 685–698. https://doi.org/10.1007/s10734-011-9407-1

Sharmini, S., & Spronken-Smith, R. (2020). The PhD – Is it out of alignment? *Higher Education Research & Development, 39*(4), 821–833. https://doi.org/10.1080/07294360.2019.1693514

Shauman, K. A. (2017). Gender differences in the early employment outcomes of STEM doctorates. *Social Sciences, 6*(24), 1–26. https://doi.org/10.3390/socsci6010024

Sinche, M., Layton, R. L., Brandt, P. D., O'Connell, A. B., Hall, J. D., Freeman, A. M., et al. (2017). An evidence-based evaluation of transferrable skills and job satisfaction for science PhDs. *PLoS ONE, 12*(9), e0185023. https://doi.org/10.1371/journal.pone.0185023

Spronken-Smith, R. (2018). Reforming doctoral education: There is a better way. *Research & Occasional Paper Series: CSHE.9.18.* University of Otago. https://escholarship.org/uc/item/4s08b4jx

Spronken-Smith, R., Brown, K., & Mirosa, R. (2018). Employability and graduate attributes of doctoral graduates. In E. Blitzer, L. Frick, M. Fourie-Malherbe, & K. Pyhältö (Eds.), *Spaces, Journeys and New Horizons for Postgraduate Supervision.* SunPress. https://doi.org/10.18820/9781928357810

St. Clair, R., Hutto, T., MacBeth, C., Newstetter, W., McCarty, N. A., & Melkers, J. (2017). The new normal: Adapting doctoral trainee career preparation for broad career paths in science. *PLoS ONE, 12*(5), e0177035. https://doi.org/10.1371/journal.pone.0177035

St. Clair, R., Mellkers, J., Rojewski, J. W., Ford, J. K., Dahl, T., McCarty, N. A., & Chatterjee, D. (2019). Doctoral trainee preferences for career development resources: The influence of peer and other supportive social capital. *International Journal of Doctoral Studies, 14,* 675–702. https://doi.org/10.28945/4436

Stringer, R., Smith, D., Spronken-Smith, R., & Wilson, C. (2018). "My entire career has been fixed term": Gender and precarious academic employment at a New Zealand university. *New Zealand Sociology, 33*(2), 169–201.

Thakore, B. K., Naffziger-Hirsch, M. E., Richardson, J. L., Williams, S. N., & McGee, R. (2014). The Academy for Future Science Faculty: Randomized controlled trial of theory-driven coaching to shape development and diversity of early-career scientists. *BMC Medical Education, 14*(160), 1–11. https://doi.org/10.1186/1472-6920-14-160

Turk-Bicakci, L., Berger, A., & Haxten, C. (2014). The non-academic careers of STEM PhD holders. *American Institutes for Research.* https://www.air.org/sites/default/files/downloads/report/STEM%20nonacademic%20careers%20April14.pdf

Vekkaila, J., Virtanen, V., Taina, J., & Pyhältö, K. (2018). The function of social support in engaging and disengaging experiences among post-PhD researchers in STEM disciplines. *Studies in Higher Education, 43*(8), 1439–1453. https://doi.org/10.1080/03075079.2016.1259307

Vohlídalová, M. (2021). The segmentation of the academic labour market and gender, field, and institutional inequalities. *Social Inclusion, 9*(3), 163–174. https://doi.org/10.17645/si.v9i3.4190

Williams, A., Jones, M. G., Jonsson, R., Harris, R. A., & Mulvany, M. J. (2019). A comparison of doctoral training in biomedicine and medicine for some UK and Scandinavian graduate programmes: Learning from each other. *FEBS Open Bio, 9,* 830–839. https://doi.org/10.1002/2211-5463.12629

Williams, S. N., Thakore, B. K., & McGee, R. (2016). Career coaches as a source of vicarious learning for racial and ethnic minority PhD students in the biomedical sciences: A qualitative study. *PLoS ONE, 11*(7), e0160038. https://doi.org/10.1371/journal.pone.0160038

Wilson, M. A., DePass, A. L., & Bean, A. J. (2018). Institutional interventions that remove barriers to recruit and retain diverse biomedical PhD students. *CBE Life Sciences Education, 17*(2), ar27. https://doi.org/10.1187/cbe.17-09-0210

Woolsten, C. (2017). Graduate survey: A love-hate relationship. *Nature, 550,* 549–552. https://doi.org/10.1038/nj7677-549a

Young, S., Kelder, J.-A., & Crawford, J. (2020). Doctoral employability: A systematic literature review and research agenda. *Journal of Applied Learning & Teaching, 3*(Special Issue 1), 1–11. https://journals.sfu.ca/jalt/index.php/jalt/index

CHAPTER 24

Doctoral education in context: Perspectives from scholars in Africa

Kirsi Pyhältö

Doctoral supervision is one of the most studied areas of research on doctoral education. Yet *Doctoral Eduation in context. Perspectives from African contexts* manages to make an interesting contribution to the body of literature on doctoral supervision. This is mainly for two reasons: first, the book is written by doctoral education practitioners, which includes a mix of novice and experienced doctoral supervisors from various fields who took part in an online course for supervisors. Hence the book provides an interesting example of promoting research-based doctoral education, more specifically with regards to doctoral supervision. Second, the book offers empirically grounded contextualized insights on doctoral education and doctoral supervision across the African continent, a topic that has lacked adequate evidence and scholarship.

The development of doctoral education across the globe is largely driven by policies that aim to enhance social and economic competitiveness and societal health (Anders et al., 2015). Respectively, doctoral supervision and supervisory development still heavily rely on supervisors' own experiences as supervisees, and learning from the experience, occasionally observing and discussing topics with their colleagues, being examiners, and on 'how to' literature (Wisker & Kiley, 2014). Accordingly, the role of formal training for supervisors in many contexts is still of minor importance in cultivating supervisor competence, as compared to informal learning (Pyhältö et al., 2022; Lee, 2018).

Considering the importance of doctoral supervision for doctoral education outcomes and development (Hanesova & Saari, 2019; Denis et al. 2019), only somewhat recently have more extensive and systematic measures to improve the quality of doctoral supervision been called for and implemented at many universities (e.g. Olson & Clark, 2009; Löfström et al. in press). Such measures have involved the development of supervisors through courses, workshops, mentoring and awards, though providing these activities is a relatively new area of staff development in universities (Taylor & McCulloch, 2017). A recent survey study involving 311 universities from 32 European countries showed that compulsory specialized supervisory training for PhD supervisors was required in only 17% of responding institutions, either in the majority or in all their doctoral programmes (Hasgall et al., 2019). Courses for PhD supervisors were offered by 43% of universities, either in the majority or in all their doctoral programmes (Hasgall et al., 2019). The findings imply that universities are seeking more systematic and effective ways to engage and support doctoral supervisors as part of supervisors' professional development. While we do not have comparable data from across African regions, we do know that a similar need exists (see e.g. Jowi, 2021; Sooryamoorthy & Scherer, 2022). This book presents such an endeavour at a continental scale.

Building a solid grounding for systematically developing doctoral education, supervision included, provides commitment to research-based doctoral education and models to implement it (Pyhältö, in press). This means that in addition to research policies, socio-economic demands, or the experiences of those involved in doctoral education, the practices of doctoral education and its development should be informed by research evidence on doctoral education and researchers' careers. The book provides an interesting example of a model for engaging supervisors in research-based development of doctoral education.

The chapters that comprise this volume originate from capstone assignments in the online DIES/CREST Training Course for Supervisors of Doctoral Candidates at Universities in Africa (organised in collaboration with the Centre for Higher Education Research, Teaching and Learning (CHERTL) at Rhodes University, and the Centre for Higher and Adult Education (CHAE) at Stellenbosch University) (Botha et al., 2019). The course was launched to cultivate supervisory development on the African continent and has been offered to doctoral supervisors across African higher education contexts since 2018.

Between 2018 and 2023, more than 500 doctoral supervisors affiliated to universities across 34 African countries completed the course. Through writing this book, the authors themselves engaged in research-based supervisory development, while simultaneously addressing topical issues with regards to doctoral education in their country, institutional or disciplinary contexts and so contributing to the existing body of knowledge within these areas.

The contributions to the book were selected by the editors, considering the quality of the assignments, as well as a diversity of countries and regions, languages, gender, fields of study, topic, and approaches on doctoral supervision. The invited authors refined and developed their capstone assignments into book chapters based on the editors' feedback. Altogether, supervisors from 16 African countries, including Angola, Benin, Burkina Faso, Cameroon, Egypt, Guinea, Kenya, Mauritius, Namibia, Nigeria, Rwanda, South Africa, Sudan, Tunisia, Uganda and Zambia contributed to this book. As a result, the book gathers doctoral supervisor perspectives from a region in the Global South that are often overlooked in the literature on doctoral education.

All authors are doctoral supervisors themselves and experienced scholars in their own disciplinary fields, though not specialists in research on doctoral education. Accordingly, the book focuses on practitioner perspectives on doctoral education, with some having a particular focus on doctoral supervision. The chapter topics are grounded in the authors' experiences both as supervisors and supervisees (during their own doctoral studies), their identification of a relevant topic (in most cases related to the author's own context in Africa), and the development of useful and interesting ideas, findings and/or recommendations for the theory and practice of doctoral supervision in their own contexts. As such the topics of the chapters largely arise from the authors' experiences within their specific doctoral education context that are further framed, scaled up, and addressed via research literature on the topic. As such, the book provides an interesting example of applying a bottom-up approach, ingraining supervisory experience in scholarly literature on doctoral supervision and in promoting epistemic agency with regards to doctoral education among scholars across disciplines.

The book has three loosely coupled themes: doctoral research and the doctoral qualification in Africa, doctoral pedagogy, and the supervisor–candidate relationship. Accordingly, the primary focus of the book is on doctoral supervision since two out of three sections address this theme. The choice is well justified since most research-based doctoral education boils down to supervisory practices. The reason for this is that the quality and quantity of supervision is a primary predictor of a positive doctoral experience and degree completion (Corner et al., 2017; Anttila et al., 2023), hence supervisors and supervision play a key role in the development of doctoral education. At their best, chapters build insightful bridges between supervisory practice and theory. Hence, the approach adopted in the book has ensured that the questions/issues addressed in the chapters are relevant and well-grounded in the everyday practices/problems of doctoral supervision in these contexts. This adds to the usability of the book within varied African contexts.

Also, more generally speaking, the well-grounded problem identification can be considered as a precondition for any doctoral education development initiative to take a root, to be effective and sustainable over time. In other words, supervisory development support should be well ingrained in and aligned with the needs and everyday practices of a supervisor's work. Unfortunately, this is not always the case in institutional actions taken to promote supervisory development. Another precondition for doctoral education development work to be sustainable is that its implementation is systemic (see the seminal work in this regard by Bronfenbrenner, 1977; Navarro & Tudge, 2022). This means that the development efforts and activities at the different levels of doctoral education, ranging from national, to institutional and all the way to micro levels of supervisory relationship, are aligned (Pyhältö, 2022). In addition to the theme-based organisation of the book, orchestrating chapters based on whether they address doctoral education issues primarily related to macro, meso and/or micro levels may have further contributed to a systemic understanding of doctoral education development needs in Global South context(s).

The approach adopted in the book also gives rise to some limitations. First, there is considerable variation regarding chapter quality. This may partly stem from the fact that the chapters are authored by doctoral education practitioners. These are doctoral supervisors from various disciplines, rather than researchers specialized in research on doctoral education. On the other hand, the book also offers some interesting cross-disciplinary titbits such as in Chapter 1 by Oosthuizen, 'Presenting Bibliometric Analysis of Doctoral Supervision Literature using Topic Modelling'. Second, the bottom-up approach used in comprising the book has resulted to some degree in a lack of alignment between the chapters. Accordingly, the book offers selection of topics, methods, and perspectives, some of which are highly contemporary and/or original, instead of a systematic examination of the themes.

To sum up, the book provides significant added value by introducing a model for promoting research-based supervisory development that is inherent to the bottom-up approach applied by engaging practising doctoral supervisors in conducting research on doctoral education as part of their own supervisory development. So far there has been a very limited number of empirical studies on doctoral supervision from a range of African countries and across disciplines. The book contributes to bridging this gap. It provides glances at the diversity in systems, policies and enactment of doctoral education and supervision within a variety of contexts on the African continent.

References

Andres, L., Bengtsen, S. S. E., Gallego Castaño, L. D. P., Crossouard, B., Keefer, J. & Pyhältö, K., (2015). Drivers and interpretations of doctoral education today: National comparisons, *Frontline Learning Research*, 3(3), 1–18. https://doi.org/10.14786/flr.v3i3.177

Anttila, H., Pyhältö, K., & Tikkanen, L. (2023). Doctoral supervisors' and supervisees' perceptions on supervisory support and frequency of supervision: Do they match? *Innovations in Education and Teaching International*. https://doi.org/10.1080/14703297.2023.2238673

Botha, J., De Klerk M. & Vilyte, G. (2019, November 15). Digital training can help supervisors lift PhD output. *The Conversation*. https://theconversation.com/digital- trainingcan-help-supervisors-lift-phd-output-126391

Bronfenbrenner, U. (1977). Toward an experimental ecology of human development. *American psychologist*, 32(7), 513–531. https://doi.org/10.1037/0003-066X.32.7.513

Corner, S., Löfström, E., & Pyhältö, K. (2017). The relationship between doctoral students' perceptions of supervision and burnout. *International Journal of Doctoral Studies*, 12, 91–106. https://helda.helsinki.fi/server/api/core/bitstreams/856f6c2d-a4f2-45cd-9589-98cc93a4b923/content

Denis, C., Colet, N. R., & Lison, C. (2019). Doctoral supervision in North America: Perception and challenges of supervisor and supervisee. *Higher Education Studies*, 9(1), 30–39. https://www.ccsenet.org/journal/index.php/hes/article/view/0/37661

Hanesova, D., & Saari, S. (2019). International comparative perspectives of the trends in development of PhD supervisors. In *ICERI 2019: 12th international conference of education, research and innovation proceedings* (pp. 1764–1773). International Association of Technology, Education and Development (IATED).

Hasgall A., Saenen, B. & Borell-Damian, L. (2019). *Doctoral education in Europe today: Approaches and institutional structures* (Survey). European University Association. https://eua.eu/downloads/publications/online%20eua%20cde%20survey%2016.01.2019.pdf

Hopwood, N., & Frick, L. (2023). Research supervision as praxis: A need to speak back in dangerous ways?. *Journal of Praxis in Higher Education*, 5(2), 140–166. https://doi.org/10.47989/kpdc411

Jowi, J. O. (2021). Doctoral training in African universities: recent trends, developments and issues. *Journal of the British Academy*, 9(1), 159–181.

Lee, A. (2018). How can we develop supervisors for the modern doctorate? *Studies in Higher Education*, 43(5), 878-890. https://www.tandfonline.com/doi/full/10.1080/03075079.2018.1438116

Navarro, J. L., & Tudge, J. R. (2022). Technologizing Bronfenbrenner: neo-ecological theory. *Current Psychology*, 1–17. https://doi.org/10.1007/s12144-022-02738-3

Olson, K., & Clark, C. (2009). A signature pedagogy in doctoral education: The leaderscholar community. *Educational Researcher*, 38(3), 216–21. https://journals.sagepub.com/doi/abs/10.3102/0013189X09334207?journalCode=edra

Pyhältö, K., Tikkanen, L., & Anttila, H. (2023). The more the merrier? PhD supervisors' perspectives in engaging in co-supervision. *Innovations in Education and Teaching International*. https://doi.org/10.1080/14703297.2023.2258853

Pyhältö, K., Tikkanen, L., & Anttila, H. (2022). Relationship between doctoral supervisors' competencies, engagement in supervisory development and experienced support from research community. *Innovations in Education and Teaching International (Print)*. https://doi.org/10.1080/14703297.2022.2160369

Sooryamoorthy, R., & Scherer, C. (2022). Doctoral training in Africa: Taking stock. In *Doctoral training and higher education in Africa* (pp. 1–17). Routledge.

Taylor, S. & McCulloch, A. (2017). Mapping the landscape of awards for research supervision: A comparison of Australia and the UK. *Innovations in Education and Teaching International*, 54(6), 1–14. https://www.tandfonline.com/doi/full/10.1080/14703297.2017.1371058

Taylor, S. (2023). The changing landscape of doctoral education: A framework for analysis and introduction to the special issue. *Innovations in Education and Teaching International, 60*(5), 606–622. DOI: 10.1080/14703297.2023.2237962

Wisker, G. and M. Kiley. (2014). Professional learning: Lessons for supervision from doctoral examining. *The International Journal for Academic Development* 19. DOI: 10.1080/1360144X.2012.727762.

Contributors

Ahmed Elsayed is a professor in the Department of Surgery in the Faculty of Medicine at Alzaiem Alazhari University and director of the Alazhari Health Research Center in Sudan. He holds an MBChB from the University of Khartoum and was awarded a master's in Medical Education by the University of Gazira. Google Scholar: https://scholar.google.com/citations?user=f6Z79wgAAAAJ&hl=en

Ané Orchard is a senior lecturer in the Faculty of Health Sciences, School of Therapeutic Sciences, Department of Pharmacy and Pharmacology at the University of the Witwatersrand in South Africa. She has authored several articles in antimicrobial activity of natural products. She holds a PhD from the University of the Witwatersrand, and her research interests include anti-microbial research, non-communicable diseases, and higher education. She has received several teaching awards and is a National Research Foundation Thuthuka grant recipient. She was selected as an African Academy of Sciences affiliate member for 2022-2026.
ORCID: https://orcid.org/0000-0001-6767-7110.

Bernard Ugochukwu Nwosu is a senior researcher at the Institute for Development Studies, University of Nigeria, Enugu Campus, He also holds a teaching position in the Department of Political Science. He obtained a PhD at the University of Waikato, New Zealand. His research interest is in the area of governance, democratization, conflicts and sociology of knowledge. Ben's book, *Civil society and democracy in Nigeria* (Routledge 2022), explores the contrasting engagement of social forces in the struggle of democracy. He is a regular contributor to the weekly policy briefs on security and development of Nextier SPD (a security and development consulting firm).
ORCID: https://orcid.org/0000-0001-5871-2738.

Caroline Kagwiria Kinuu Kimathi is an assistant professor in the Department of Languages and Literature of United States International University-Africa (USIU-A) in Nairobi, Kenya. She holds a PhD in Applied Linguistics from Laikipia University, an MA in Linguistics from the University of Nairobi, and a bachelor's degree in education (English and Literature) from Kenyatta University. She is a member of the Language Association of Eastern Africa (LAEA) and

— —

the International Sociological Association (ISA). Her research interests include language planning and policies, second language learning and teaching, pragmatics and postgraduate studies in Africa.
ORCID: https://orcid.org/0000-0002-4780-9128

Elhadj Saidou Baldé a pharmacist and holds a PhD in Pharmaceutical Sciences (Université Libre de Bruxelles, Belgium). He is a full professor in the Institute for Research and Development of Medicinal and Food Plants of Guinea (IRDPMAG) at the Université Gamal Abdel Nasser de Conakry, Guinea. His research focuses on ethnomedical, ethnobotanical and ethnopharmacological investigations related to Guinean pharmacopoeia and traditional medicine.
ORCID: https://orcid.org/0000-0001-7029-8680.

Estelle Seyivé Bancole-Minaflinou is a researcher and professor in the Department of English at the University of Abomey-Calavi in Porto Noveo, Benin.
ORCID: https://orcid.org/0000-0001-8856-3323

Fraj Chemak is a senior lecturer at the Department of Rural Economics of the National Institute of Agricultural Research of Tunisia (INRAT), University of Carthage. He holds a PhD from the University of Montpellier I (France). In 1997, he received the prize for best research master thesis of the International Center for Advanced Mediterranean Agronomic Studies (CIHEAM-IAMM). Since 2014 he has been an editorial board member of the *Annales de l'INRAT*. His research is focused on farming system analysis and decision-making processes in the economic and institutional environments. His analysis approaches are based particularly on farm modelling (multi-agents, mathematical programming, data envelopment analysis, bio-economic model, etc.) which allows simulating strategic decision and policy measurements with the perspectives of optimal resource uses as well as income enhancement and farmer wellbeing improvement.
ORCID: https://orcid.org/0000-0002-5164-5410

Isabel Meyer is an operations researcher and veterinarian with experience in modelling, research, and analysis of complex systems. Isabel's research and consulting portfolio includes modelling and analysis of business and organisational systems, development initiatives, and supply networks. A specific interest of hers is the design of rural economic development initiatives and associated organisational and project structures such that sustained benefit is delivered within communities. Isabel holds PhD (Information Systems), MSc (Industrial Systems), MBA, and BVSc degrees. She works with CSIR's Smart Mobility Cluster in Pretoria as principal researcher and has associate roles at the Universities of Cape Town (statistical sciences) and Stellenbosch (industrial engineering). She is a board member of the Society for Animals in Distress and a member of the Animal Ethics and Welfare committee of the South African Veterinary Association.

ORCID: https://orcid.org/0000-0003-3338-754X

Jan Botha is an emeritus professor at the Centre for Research on Evaluation, Science and Technology (CREST) at Stellenbosch University, South Africa. Previously, he held the position of Senior Director for Institutional Research and Planning at the same institution. During his career, he contributed to national policy-making efforts, serving on task teams of the Council for Higher Education (CHE) responsible for the *National Programme Accreditation Framework and Criteria* (2004) and the *South African Doctoral Qualification Standard* (2018–2019) as well as the task team of the Department of Higher Education and Training (DHET) that developed the *National Policy Framework for Higher Education Internationalisation in South Africa* (2020). He is a previous president of the Southern African Association for Institutional Research (SAAIR).

ORCID: https://orcid.org/0000-0002-9765-0506

Kirsi Pyhältö is professor of educational sciences in the Faculty of Educational Sciences, at the University of Oulu, research director in the Centre for University Teaching and Learning, at the University of Helsinki and Extra Ordinary Professor, at the University of Stellenbosch. Her research interests include doctoral education and post PhD careers, school development, teachers' professional agency, and student and teacher well-being.

ORCID: https://orcid.org/0000-0002-8766-0559

Kokouvi Edem N'Tsoukpoe is associate professor of solar thermal engineering at the International Institute for Water and Environmental Engineering (2iE), an engineering school founded 50 years ago in Burkina Faso by 14 French-speaking African States. After completing his PhD in Energy and Process Engineering at Université de Grenoble (France), he spent 2 years in Germany as research associate at the Innovations Incubator of Leuphana Universität Lüneburg, prior to returning to 2iE in 2013. Edem is currently the centre leader of the College of Engineering 2iE, an Africa Center of Excellence of the World

Bank. He is in charge of training and capacity building of PhD students at the 2iE doctoral school. Edem has led various EU and AU funded research projects as well as capacity building programmes.

ORCID: https://orcid.org/0000-0002-4013-6370

Liezel Frick is professor in the Department of Curriculum Studies at Stellenbosch University within the Centre for Higher and Adult Education. She currently serves the Faculty of Education as Vice-dean for Research and Postgraduate Studies. She is a research fellow at the DSI/NRF Centre of Excellence in Scientometrics and Science, Technology and Innovation Policy (SciSTIP). She is a member of the International Doctoral Education Research Network (IDERN) and the Special Interest Group of the European Association for Research on Learning and Instruction (EARLI). She uses her research as the basis for supervisor and early career researcher capacity development and has been invited to facilitate workshops and short courses in a variety of African and European countries.

ORCID: https://orcid.org/0000-0002-4797-3323

Meera Manraj is Associate Professor in the Department of Medicine, Faculty of Medicine and Health Sciences of the University of Mauritius. She holds a PhD from the University of Mauritius. Her research focuses on the genetics of premature coronary heart disease, interactions between microbiota and NAFLD/metabolic syndrome, and the efficacy of lifestyle interventions in delaying dementia. She supervised her first PhD candidate to completion in 2019, and the second one in 2023. Since 2011 she has been involved in the setting up of an undergraduate medical programme of six-year duration, adapted from the curriculum offered by the University of Geneva (UNIGE), Switzerland. Meera was the link coordinator in the collaboration set up for this purpose between the University of Mauritius, the University of Geneva and the Ministry of Health and Wellness in Mauritius.

ORCID: https://orcid.org/0000-0001-5563-3348

Mohamed Khalil is an Egyptian architect, and associate professor of architecture at the Department of Architectural Engineering in the Faculty of Engineering at Mansoura University, Egypt. He has headed the Department of Architecture and Interior Design in the Scientific College of Design, Muscat in the Sultanate of Oman since 2022. He holds a PhD in Architecture from Palermo University, Italy. Mohamed carries out research activities in the field of urban

conservation, rehabilitation of historic cities, and environmental assessment of heritage buildings.
ORCID: https://orcid.org/0000-0001-9690-5442

Nompilo Tshuma is a senior lecturer in the Centre for Higher and Adult Education (CHAE) in the Faculty of Education at Stellenbosch University, South Africa. She coordinates the Postgraduate Diploma in Higher Education and the MPhil in Higher Education. She also supervises Masters and Doctoral students in Higher Education Studies. Her research focuses on a critical and nuanced study of educational technology integration for research, teaching and learning. Nompilo is passionate about developing researchers and has been involved in designing and facilitating short courses for the professional development of academic staff both within South Africa and in several African countries.
ORCID: https://orcid.org/0000-0002-7842-5426

Paulo Conceição João Faria is the chair of the Culture, Religion, Media, Youth and Sport Committee in the National Assembly of the Republic of Angola. Since September 2022 he is a Member of Parliament for the main opposition party, the Union for the Total Independence of Angola (UNITA). Until 2021 he was a professor in political science at Agostinho Neto University. He is a research associate in the South Africa-UK Bilateral Chair in Political Theory at the University of the Witwatersrand, co-founder of the Angolan Political Science Association and founder of the think tank, *Ambuila – Pesquisa e Produção Científica*. He holds a PhD in Politics and Government from the University of Kent and has taught BA, MA, and PhD courses in Angola. His research interests include state reform, security studies, and foreign policy.
ORCID: https://orcid.org/0000-0002-8178-1536

Rudolph Oosthuizen is an associate professor in the Graduate School of Technology Management at the University of Pretoria. Formerly he was a senior systems engineer at the Counsel for Scientific and Industrial Research in the Command, Control, and Integrated Systems impact area. He holds a PhD in Engineering Management from the University of Pretoria, where he now teaches and supervises postgraduate students in systems engineering and systems thinking, focusing on modelling complex sociotechnical systems. Rudolph has 25 years of industry experience in systems engineering. He is registered as a professional engineer with ECSA and a certified systems engineering professional with INCOSE.
ORCID: https://orcid.org/0000-0002-2333-6995

Samuel Mutarindwa is a senior lecturer in the School of Business, College of Business & Economics at the University of Rwanda. He obtained his PhD in Business Administration from Jönköping University in Sweden. Samuel also holds an MPhil in Science and Technology Studies from Stellenbosch University, South Africa. His research interests include sustainable finance and growth, focusing on topics such as credit risk rating and pricing of green bonds for sustainable development. Samuel's research has been published in top economics and finance journals including the *Journal of Institutional Economics, Emerging Markets Review, Journal of Financial Stability, the Journal of International Financial Markets, Institutions, and Money,* and the *South African Journal of Higher Education.* He is an associate editor of the *Rwanda Journal of Social Sciences, Humanities and Business.*
ORCID: https://orcid.org/0000-0002-2662-2479

Selline Atieno Oketch is a senior lecturer of literature in the Department of Languages, Literature and Communication in the Faculty of Arts and Social Sciences at the Catholic University of Eastern Africa, Nairobi, Kenya. She holds a doctorate (D.Litt.) in Literature from Nelson Mandela University in South Africa and Master of Arts degree in Literature from the University of Nairobi. Her research interests include African literature and gender, doctoral supervision, and ethics in higher education. Her publications are in the areas of literature and gender, literature and ethics, and teaching English and literature in Kenya's secondary school curriculum. She also holds the British Academy Certificate in International Writing Workshop: Emerging Initiatives and Socially Just Research Leadership in the Global South (2023).
ORCID: https://orcid.org/0009-0000-2023-2384

Selma Tuemumunu Karuaihe is a senior lecturer and acting head of the Department of Agricultural Economics, Extension and Rural Development at the University of Pretoria in South Africa. She is originally from Namibia. In 2005, Selma obtained a PhD in Environment and Natural Resource Sciences with a focus on Environmental and Resource Economics from Washington State University in the USA. She was the first female scholar from Namibia to obtain a PhD in Economics, which caught the attention of newspapers in 2006. She is an environmental economist with teaching, research and consultancy experience, performed at different institutions and in different capacities. Her research interest is in development and issues arising from utilisation of natural and environmental resources for sustainable development.
ORCID: https://orcid.org/0000-0003-1453-7979

Sophie Ekume Etomes is a senior lecturer in the Department of Educational Foundations and Administration, Faculty of Education, University of Buea, Cameroon. She also serves as the head of Service for Teaching Staff in the same University. She holds a PhD in Educational Foundations and Administration from the University of Buea. She has authored articles and book chapters focused on the economics of education, leadership and management of higher education. She holds a certificate in science leadership from the University of Pretoria. She is currently a fellow with the Carnegie Corporation coordinated by Future Africa, University of Pretoria, South Africa.
ORCID: https://orcid.org/0000-0003-4337-8129

Stephen Ojiambo Wandera is a gerontologist and population scientist. He is a lecturer (2006 – present) in the Department of Population Studies, Makerere University, Kampala, Uganda. He holds a PhD in Population Studies. His CARTA-funded PhD research (2012-2016) focused on 'Disparities in health and access to healthcare among older persons in Uganda'. His research interests include violence against women and children, inequalities in dementia, ageism, HIV, inequalities in health, and access to healthcare among older persons in Uganda. He is a member of the WHO Ethics Research Committee and the TASO Research and Ethics Committee. He is an associate editor of *BMC Public Health* and the *International Journal of Public Health*.
ORCID: https://orcid.org/0000-0002-5617-0274

Susan Williams completed her undergraduate medical training at the University of the Witwatersrand before continuing her specialist training in ophthalmology at Wits and receiving her Fellowship in Ophthalmology from the Colleges of Medicine and Surgery of South Africa. She has a Master of Medicine in Ophthalmology and completed her doctoral studies in ophthalmology and genetics in 2013. She runs the glaucoma unit at Charlotte Maxeke Johannesburg Academic Hospital. Her areas of interest include glaucoma surgery, exfoliation syndrome, glaucoma genetics and ophthalmic genetics.
Researchgate: https://www.researchgate.net/profile/Susan-Williams-20

Tognon Clotilde Guidi is a professor in Mechanical Engineering at the National University of Sciences, Technologies, Engineering and Mathematics (UNSTIM) in Goho Abomey, Benin.
ORCID: https://orcid.org/0000-0002-8288-9274

Tom Kwanya is a professor in the Department of Information and Knowledge Management of the Technical University of Kenya. He is currently also serving as director of the School of Information and Communication Studies. Prior to joining academia full-time in 2013, he worked as a consultant in public information and knowledge management. He is the author of several peer-reviewed journal articles and book chapters, two scholarly books, several conference papers, and four edited books. He has also supervised and examined several postgraduate dissertations and theses. He has served as an external examiner of information science and knowledge management in several universities in Kenya and abroad. He sits on the Information Science Services Technical Committee of the Kenya Bureau of Standards (KEBS).
ORCID: https://orcid.org/0000-0002-6306-2669

Tracy Kellermann is a senior lecturer and the Analytical Pharmacology Lead in the Division of Clinical Pharmacology in the Department of Medicine at Stellenbosch University, South Africa. She holds a PhD in Pharmacology from the University of Cape Town. She currently coordinates the BSc Honours and structured MSc courses in the Division of Clinical Pharmacology at Stellenbosch University and supervises postgraduate research projects. Her research interests involve analytical pharmacology, bioanalysis and pharmacokinetics pertaining to clinical trials, as well as toxicology.
ORCID: https://orcid.org/0000-0003-1542-4976

Wilma Sithabiso Sichombo Nchito is senior lecturer in the Department of Geography and Environmental Studies and director of Research and Postgraduate Studies at the University of Zambia. She has an MSc in Geography from the London School of Economics and Political Sciences and a PhD in Urban Geography from the University of Zambia. Her areas of research include urban geography, urban services provision, water and solid waste management, urban informality and renewal, small town development, border town dynamics, tourism, African Diaspora in African towns, interdisciplinary research, knowledge co-production, urban transport, cities and climate change.
ORCID: https://orcid.org/0000-0001-7089-9777

www.ingramcontent.com/pod-product-compliance
Lightning Source LLC
Chambersburg PA
CBHW080353030426
42334CB00024B/2860